Planets, Ages, and Empires

By

William Schulting

AuthorHouse™
1663 Liberty Drive
Bloomington, IN 47403
www.authorhouse.com
Phone: 1-800-839-8640

No part of this book may be reproduced, stored in a retrieval system, or transmitted by any means, electronic, mechanical, photocopying, recording, or otherwise, without written permission from the author.

© 2009 William Schulting. All rights reserved.

No part of this book may be reproduced, stored in a retrieval system, or transmitted by any means without the written permission of the author.

First published by AuthorHouse 3/31/2009

ISBN: 978-1-4184-6766-1 (sc)
ISBN: 978-1-4184-7127-9 (e)

Printed in the United States of America
Bloomington, Indiana

This book is printed on acid-free paper.

Scriptures taken from the HOLY BIBLE NEW INTERNATIONAL VERSION®. NIV. Copyright © 1973, 1978, 1984 by International Bible Society. Used by permission of Zondervan. The "NIV" and "New International Version" trademark are registered in the United States Patent and Trademark Office by International Bible Society. Pictures of the split rock near Mt Horeb courtesy Jim and Penny Caldwell www.splitrockresearch.com

Dedication

Dedicated to Joyce
who all those years put up with a distracted husband.

The LORD answered Moses, "Walk on ahead of the people. Take with you some of the elders of Israel and take in your hand the staff with which you struck the Nile, and go. I will stand there before you by the rock of Horeb. Strike the rock, and water will come out of it for the people to drink." So Moses did this in the sight of the elders of Israel.

                                          Exodus 17:5, 6

Contents

Thesis	vi
Israel and Egypt	1
Venus	107
The Thutmose Dynasty	140
The Ramessides	183
The Assyrian and the Passover	231
The Covenant	339
References	458
Bibliography	467

Thesis

This book elaborates on a theory that I believe to be fundamentally correct. This theory maintains that well meaning historians place their trust in a scheme of history that is simply dead wrong. The reason is basic and profound. Egyptology, the measuring stick of ancient history, is based on defective assumptions. Pharaohs, dynasties and even kingdoms were mistakenly assigned their places in history before the Egyptian language was even deciphered!

It is easy to see how this could happen. When European explorers discovered the records and monuments of ancient Egypt, they found murals of battles fought by powerful kings. Without the benefit of any historical standard there was no way to know when these pharaohs lived, so the explorers guessed. The inevitable happened, they guessed wrong. Later scholars relied on the so-called Sothis dating to establish the time of certain dynasties. This is not at all sure, and based on an erroneous interpretation of the Canopus decree. Besides, the length of the Sothis period is the object of serious debate.

The reconstructed version of history places the pharaohs where they belong, at a much later time, with surprising results. It will be seen that many of these kings are known to us by different names, in different dynasties. Merely by relocating the exodus from the beginning of New Kingdom to that of the Second Intermediate Period, we arrive at very different conclusions. It enables us to find the pharaoh who welcomed Joseph, the dynasty that suppressed Israel, and even the identity of the pharaoh who died in the Sea of Passage. It testifies to the historical accuracy of the Old Testament. For contrary to what is generally believed, there are Egyptian records that describe the events, associated with the exodus. In other words, the exodus account is not at all a fictional story, it really happened. This creates a problem all its own. Skeptics have a legitimate question: "What caused these disasters?" There is a provocative explanation that is worthy of our consideration; it involved a cosmic catastrophe.

It is only natural to assume that history unfolded rather uneventfully, and that global disasters never happened, at least not in recent times. Yet the Bible and historical records allude to recent, worldwide catastrophes. They speak of a global flood, of a catastrophe at the time of the exodus and of strange events that happened as recently as the times of the Hebrew prophets, during the 8th Century B.C. and shortly thereafter.

There are a number of puzzling events that happened in those days. What made the shadow of King Ahaz' sundial move back? What was the cause of the instantaneous death of Sennacherib's army, and what did Isaiah mean when he said that God would devastate the earth and scatter humanity? This book seeks to find an explanation, and its thesis is this: planet Earth in recent, historical times has been repeatedly shaken by catastrophes. As a result history developed very different than is generally believed. This is particularly true of the exodus, which witnessed the collapse of the 13th Dynasty and the invasion of the Hyksos.

It will be shown beyond a doubt that several dynasties have been duplicated, in some cases even kingdoms. Ramses II and the Hittites fought their battles at a much later time, and are mentioned in the scriptures by other names. Ramses III never battled the so-called "Sea People," he was a pharaoh who lived in Persian times. As a result later dynasties that are mentioned in the scriptures and by Greek authors exist in a historical void. Virtual nothing is known about them from Egyptian sources. It affects all of near-eastern history, with strange results. The so-called Dark Age of Greece, a sort of black hole in history, is wholly imaginary. It was confused with later catastrophic events. Around 700 B.C., world-wide destructions resulted in great migrations; the foundations were laid for western civilization.

Through it all the Spirit of God was at work. The prophets foretold the disaster that overcame Sennacherib, the future of Israel and Judah and the coming of the Messiah and his kingdom. The prophecies of Isaiah are of great importance, and they are quoted at length. The problem of "Deutero" or Second Isaiah (an unknown prophet who labored during the Babylonian captivity) is addressed as well.

Although intended for the general reader, this book attempts to evaluate the theories of Immanuel Velikovsky. This Russian-born psychiatrist wrote a number of books dealing with catastrophic events which he believed to be cosmic in nature. In many ways critical, (disassociated memories transformed into disassociated facts), I nonetheless appreciate his insight and daring; it is often the unconventional that in the long run has real impact. He contributed greatly to science and historical research. Like any pioneer he made his share of mistakes. It is quite understandable that established historians and scientists would deny his theories and those of his disciples, who by the way are frequently disenchanted and in disagreement with him. Unfortunately some resort to name calling and tactics that can only be called regrettable. Let's keep an open mind. Reject what is foolish; investigate what might open doors to new vistas.

The theory of cosmic catastrophism that underlies the reconstruction of history as described in this book is controversial. Did it happen that way? All I can say is, perhaps. Nonetheless, I am convinced the historical reconstruction is correct. It is of considerable interest that several scientists have come to the conclusion that planetary catastrophes did happen. As a result a new theory was developed that deserves our attention. What runs the universe is not gravity, but electricity. An electromagnetic force produces and maintains galaxies and suns. It explains the behavior of the solar system and comets, and even why Venus is so very different from all the other planets.

I do not pretend to be a specialist in any field. I am merely interested in history, and how that affects our appreciation of the Bible. As to odd ball theories that are well known, I believe the Bermuda triangle is a hoax, von Daniken a fraud and Zachariah Sitchin a bad joke, and the only aliens I have seen were illegal aliens. To avoid possible misunderstandings, it is assumed that the Genesis record of early history is essentially correct, that there was a global flood which happened around 3000 B.C., and that human history dates from that time. That is unconventional, but the reasons will become clear.

Finally, as an elder of the Presbyterian Church in America (PCA), I would be remiss if I did not expound on the message of salvation that rings throughout the scriptures. As a Christian it is a delight to explain why Jesus is the only way. As a Calvinist it is a high duty and privilege to say things people hate to hear. But I will say it anyway. It is my prayer that the blessing of Almighty God rests upon that message.

If the controversy surrounding the historical reconstruction bothers some, who knows, it may just stir a lively debate. The historical theory, after all, provides a possible background, but it is in no way essential to the Christian faith. We can take it or leave it. The events happened; whatever caused it we can only theorize.

Chapter One

Israel and Egypt

Jerusalem, 687 B.C.

It was the night of the Passover. The Assyrian army was sound asleep, guarded by sentries. The guards were ill at ease. They could hear distant strains of music; the Judeans were singing "hallels," songs of praise, to their deity. How strange. How could the people of Jerusalem in the face of imminent attack, sing to a god who would not or could not be represented by idols? Maybe the Hebrews did not realize how precarious their position really was. They should be terrified. Come dawn, Sennacherib, king of the Assyrians, was personally going to lead the assault on Jerusalem. Earlier that day he viewed the fortress from Nob, on the Mount of Olives. He was astounded at the small size of the temple city. Tomorrow they were going to take the place by storm. Tomorrow.

Out of nowhere, a blinding wall of fire engulfed the Assyrian camp. An enormous lightning bolt reached far into the heavens. Man and animal alike perished in the stupendous arc. It was but a momentary discharge, then air rushed into the huge vacuum with a tremendous roar. Hurricane force winds obliterated everything in its path. An earthquake struck, mountains quaked, tidal waves irrupted. The Assyrian army lay where they slept, dead.

The next day, after the expected assault failed to materialize, a Hebrew scouting party arrived. They were stunned at the sight of the destruction. A hundred-eighty-five-thousand Assyrians had died in a single moment. Yes, but how? The Hebrews were at a loss to explain the strange phenomenon they witnessed. The nearest description they could find was, "Their souls were burnt, though their garments remained intact." The army had been fried: electrocuted, asphyxiated and their lungs scorched.

Sennacherib himself survived, seriously wounded. He had been badly burned. He returned to Nineveh, the Capitol city, and stayed there. He never fought another battle. A few years later, two of his sons killed the crippled king in an abortive coup. A power struggle followed and Essarhadon, a younger son, became king.

In the history of Israel this was not the first time an enemy had been miraculously annihilated. Maybe Hezekiah, king of Judah, was reminded of the first Passover, centuries earlier, when Israel left Egypt. Then, too, they had been wonderfully delivered from a foreign oppressor. The Passover, the center piece of the Hebrew religion, was initiated when Israel left Egypt to escape slavery and return to the Promised Land. That happened in the middle of the Second Millennium before Christ, nearly eight centuries before the army of Sennacherib was wiped out at the gates of Jerusalem. But is there any historical evidence that the exodus actually happened?

Egypt, 1446 B.C.

The first Passover and the exodus that followed can be dated with certainty. It happened 480 years before the year in which King Solomon began to build his temple (I Kings 6:1). That was the year 966 B.C. It follows that the exodus happened 1446 B.C., give or take a year or so.

Now we would assume of course, that the histories of Egypt and Israel agree rather in detail. Israel was virtually born in Egypt. The kings of Judah and Israel (the ten tribes) were to large extent vassals of the pharaohs, and frequently were involved in conflicting alliances. There was a strong pro-Egyptian faction in the royal courts, much to the dismay of the prophets, and as a result Egypt is often mentioned in both the historical and the prophetic books.

It is very strange indeed that there is virtually no Egyptian reference at all to Israel and Judah. The Old Testament creates the distinct impression that Egypt was a power to be reckoned with. If we are to believe historians however, the exact opposite is true. The Nineteenth and Twentieth Dynasties were those of the Ramessides; it was a golden age, during the last two centuries of the judges. It ended shortly before the reigns of Saul and David, the first kings of Israel. After that, Egypt was supposedly ruled by a priestly caste, weak and done with.

How can we possibly reconcile these totally different accounts? They cannot be reconciled. The differences are too great. Then who is at fault? There can only be one answer: either the Bible is wrong or very learned historians have their dates and dynasties all mixed up. Ramses II marched his army through Palestine and Syria, where he fought a battle with the Hittites, a battle he lost. Why does the book of Judges fail to record this? How could the Hebrews be unaware of a prolonged war between these two adversaries, a war fought on their soil that lasted nearly two decades? Why is there no mention of Egypt at all until the reign of King Saul? Something is very wrong. This affects more than just the scriptures, for Egyptology is the standard for ancient history.

Origins

Anyone who has read the book of Genesis is familiar with the story of Abraham and his relatives. They left Ur of the Chaldeans for Canaan. That sounds like an anachronism, as if it was the Chaldean Empire of Nebuchadnezzar 600 B.C. But Chaldean tribes existed in the days of Abraham. They were marauding robbers, probably descendants of Arphaxad son of Shem, who hailed from the Urartu-

Ararat area. They worshiped the Khaldis, a collective of some eighty gods. Eventually they became known as followers of Khaldis, or Khaldeans. "Ur of the Chaldis" involved a religion, not a people.

When clans and tribes left Mesopotamia following the confusion of tongues, they occupied different territories. Archaeological evidence indicates that this happened during the Early Bronze I, and it involved migrations on an enormous scale. The settlers of the Euphrates valley were Hamites, as were the Egyptians. "Ur of the Chaldeans" could have hardly been the Ur in Iraq. Abraham the Hebrew was of Semitic stock. The descendants of Shem lived in the plains that stretch from present-day Iran to Turkey, south of the mountain range of Ararat. Ur was located in present day Turkey.

It appears that Terah, father of Abraham, came from Turkey/Armenia, rather than Iraq. He and his clan were altogether different from the Hamites. It makes little sense for Terah to leave Ur in Iraq, travel due west and suddenly veer to the north to Haran. It does make sense that he would travel due south and settle in Haran in western Mesopotamia. His son Abraham, in obedience to the call of God, afterwards traveled on to Canaan or Palestine. All indications are that Terah was still alive when Abraham left, and lived another seventy years. Canaan was the land of promise; although Abraham was old and had no children, God would make him a great nation in this pagan land. The whole world would be blessed through him.

According to the Genesis account, "the Canaanites were then in the land." (12:6) It could be argued that this must be an editorial comment, since Moses would have obviously never said that. However, the famous Rabbi Rashi insisted that the Canaanites at that time *entered* to conquer the land that by right belonged to the Semitic people. Archaeological finds indicate that Abraham's departure was part of an Amorite migration. Rashi reasoned that Israel afterwards merely captured their inheritance when they returned to the Promised Land.[1] That may have been an excuse to justify the Hebrew settlement of Palestine, but it does explain the presence of believers in Syria-Palestine, such as Isaac's relatives, Melchizedek the priest-king of Salem and even Balaam the clairvoyant. It also explains the strange association with Canaan, the grandson of Noah: he was considered cursed, fit only for servitude.

Canaan

Genesis nine relates that Noah became intoxicated. He lay naked in his tent, a fact noted and trumpeted by his son Ham. Shem and Japheth on the other hand covered their father with a garment, taking care not to look at him. When Noah learned of this, he said,

> Cursed be Canaan!
> The lowest of slaves
> will he be to his brothers.
> He also said,
> blessed be the Lord, the God of Shem!
> May Canaan be the slave of Shem.
> May God extend the territory of Japheth
> may Japheth live in the tents of Shem,
> and may Canaan be his slave.
> Genesis 9:24-27

Now why would Noah single out Canaan? Canaan is not even mentioned in the story. It is a result of eastern values. If Noah had cursed Ham, he would have cursed himself as well. To curse a son was to curse his father. Canaan may have been involved, but the most probable reason is that Ham was Noah's youngest son. Noah in turn placed a curse on Ham's youngest son. That affronted Ham as much as it did Canaan. There is something prophetic about it, for the land of Canaan has always been associated with appalling sex perversions.

The blessing upon Japheth and Shem from the earliest times has been considered to be prophetic. It points at a special relationship between their descendants. Japheth was the ancestor of European nations. The inheritance of Shem was not that of mighty nations, but of the great promise. It was through the line of Shem that the world would be blessed. Abraham's arrival in Canaan was another step in that direction.

Canaan became God's country, the land of promise. It cannot be said that the line of Ham was cursed. The Mesopotamians and Egyptians were Hamites. The Indo-Iranian people were descendants of Ham, and there are reasons to believe the Oriental nations belong in the same category. The table of nations of Genesis 10 deals largely with the Semitic nations, because they were the ones who kept the genealogical records.

Egypt soon became a dominant force. After the pre-dynastic period, several kingdoms arose. The Old Kingdom included six dynasties. Then came an interregnum, a time of chaos, the First Intermediate Period, dynasties 7-10. With the establishment of the Middle Kingdom, which included dynasties eleven and twelve, order was restored. Another time of chaos erupted during the 13th Dynasty. This was the Second Intermediate Period, dynasties 13 thru 17, of which 15 and 16 were the Hyksos and 17 the southern princes who more or less remained independent. They existed side by side, and after several centuries were superseded by the 18th, the Thutmose Dynasty. Our story concerns these dynasties.

Israel in Egypt

The Judeo-Christian religion is a historical religion, meaning that it is rooted in historical fact, rather than fanciful and perhaps well intended tales. These people were for real. We are not, as certain scholars would have us believe, dealing with pseudo history. How important that is we will see when we study the history of Israel and its nursery, Egypt. The two were closely associated.

Abraham's son Isaac had two sons, twins, Esau and Jacob. Jacob cheated his older brother out of his birthright, and having fled the wrath of Esau was swindled into marrying two wives; the deal included two concubines. From this fractured family twelve sons were born, of whom Joseph was Jacob's favorite. His older brothers, no angels, sold Joseph into slavery to Egypt where, following a strange set of circumstances, he became second in command. Joseph eventually was reunited with his father and brothers, and to escape a famine, the Hebrews migrated to Egypt.

The Egyptians were very forthcoming. They allowed the Hebrews to settle in Goshen, about 1685 B.C. Over the centuries the children of Israel grew into a large nation. They never mixed with the Egyptians because they were shepherds, something abhorrent to the Egyptians. That is how they kept their ethnic identity. Then a new dynasty arose, one that had no use for Joseph. These kings enslaved the growing Hebrew population in huge building projects, which must have been in the eastern delta, where the Hebrews lived. What was worse, one of these pharaohs resorted to the brutal policy of killing male babies.

One Hebrew couple managed to hide a baby boy. When they could keep him no longer they put him in a basket and let him float down the Nile River. A princess found him; her motherly instincts took over, and she adopted the infant. She called him Moses, meaning "drawn from the water."

All we know from the Scriptures is that Moses became a prince. Josephus claims that he was not merely an heir to the throne, but a successful General as well. He ran into trouble when he killed an Egyptian guard. To escape the wrath of the pharaoh he fled to Midian, today's northeastern Saudi Arabia, where he took refuge with Jethro, a local chief related to Abraham. He married Jethro's daughter and became a shepherd; somewhat humiliating, no doubt. For forty years he had been a ruler, the next forty he tended sheep, the dumbest animals on the planet.

Does any of this fit the accepted chronology of Egypt? No! If we are to believe Scripture, Moses lived around 1500 B.C., that is in the days of the New Kingdom, the era of the Thutmose and Ramses Dynasties. Nothing of the kind happened in the days of these kings. There are no records of an enslaved people, no literary documents that speak of a natural disaster.

But what if the dates of the Egyptian kingdoms and dynasties are wrong? What if these pharaohs were mistakenly misplaced and they lived at different times? What if Israel entered Egypt during the

Middle Kingdom, in the middle of the Second Millennium B.C., and the New Kingdom existed at a much later time? All of a sudden there is an abundance of evidence, beginning with the 11th Dynasty, which records the mysterious appearance of a powerful vizier, a virtual genius with the powers of a king. The 12th Dynasty saw the rise of a brutal regime that enslaved an Asiatic (Palestinian) people and the fall and return of a popular pharaoh. The 13th Dynasty (Second Intermediate Period) suffered a catastrophe that decimated Egypt, and was eliminated by invading foreign rulers. All this fits the first book of the Bible, Genesis.

Toledoth

How true is the book of Genesis? There is a distinct difference in style between the story of Joseph and everything that precedes it. There are good reasons. The structure of Genesis is unlike any other in the Bible; it employs a "toledoth," meaning "these are the generations" format. Now it is well known that the so-called Higher Critics, literary butchers, theorize Genesis is a patchwork of traditions, put together (fabricated) by several pious editors, some 400 years before Christ. Archaeology proved them wrong. It was found that the earliest civilizations for lack of paper wrote on clay tablets. When at last scholars were able to read these ancient documents, they were in for an unexpected surprise: these records, like Genesis, followed the "toledoth" format. Particularly historical tablets, which were very important, would record family histories which were signed off by the authors with "these are the generations of so-and-so." This "toledoth" phrase was a customary way of identifying the author. It was his official stamp of approval, a sign-off.

The oft-repeated phrase, "these are the generations "or, "this is the historical record" therefore appears, not at the beginning of the story, but at the end. There is near-universal agreement that the creation account does just that. It follows that the story of the creation was recorded by the only eyewitness present: the Creator. Consistency demands that subsequent records are the personal memoirs of Adam (5:1), Noah (6:9), Noah's sons (10:1), Shem (11:10), Terah

(11:27), Isaac (25:19), and Jacob (37:2). Two sub-records provide the accounts of Ishmael through Isaac, and Esau through Jacob. Later editors attached genealogical records to both. The flood record incorporates the personal accounts of three authors: Shem, Ham and Japheth.

It was customary to date these records by identifying the whereabouts of the author and relate dates to kings or events. Tablets being limited, phrases were repeated to connect a tablet with the next. Such duplicated phrases and locators appear frequently in Genesis – up to the story of Joseph. It is significant that following the phrase "these are the generations of Jacob," very little is said of Jacob. It is all about Joseph. Joseph did not write his story on clay tablets. The Egyptians used papyrus, which enabled them to develop a novel style, freed from the limitations of tablets. The story of Joseph is written in the literary style of the Middle Kingdom. The final editor of Genesis had before him Joseph's account and records that incorporated the toledoth accounts of numerous ancestors. He evidently knew a great deal about Egypt, but next to nothing about Canaan, which makes Moses the prime candidate.

The Hebrews

There are, of course, those who argue that the story of Joseph who saved his family is a wonderful tale, but no more. What good is the use of a fictional event? We have good reasons to believe the account is factual. The Middle Kingdom is rich in literature, and Joseph's account is written in the style of that time. If indeed Joseph was a powerful vizier, we should be able to find his Egyptian counterpart in that era. Josephus says that Joseph, following the death of the pharaoh, became a virtual king who ruled over Upper and Lower Egypt. In the light of this we should be able to identify Joseph and the pharaoh who welcomed him. For this we must establish exactly how long Israel resided in Egypt. It goes back to God's covenant with Abraham, shortly before the destruction of Sodom and Gomorrah. (Gen 15)

It involved an ancient ritual, employed when two parties entered into a solemn agreement. To seal the covenant they agreed upon, they would each take an animal, slaughter it and cut it up, and place the parts parallel to each other. As the blood of the animals ran down a runnel, both parties would walk down the bloody stream. The meaning was akin to the otherwise inane oaths of the freemasons: if I break the terms of the covenant, my body will be cut up just like the slaughtered animals. That is what happened here with a difference: God's presence alone passed through the parts. Abraham did not, the reason being that he and his descendants were unable to keep the terms of the covenant, "sealed in blood." God bound himself in a solemn oath and said this about the future.

> Know for certain that your descendants will be strangers in a country not their own, and they will be enslaved and mistreated four hundred years. But I will punish the nation they serve as slaves, and afterward they will come out with great possessions.
> Gen 15:13, 14

Four hundred years is a round number, equivalent to four centuries. The exact number according to the exodus account was 430 years. (Ex 12:40) The question is, when do we begin to count these 430 years? When Israel entered Egypt, a superficial reading suggests. But Rashi made a valid point. He insisted that this time span began, not with Israel's arrival in Egypt, but with the birth of Abraham's son Isaac. It was not merely the nation of Israel, but all of Abraham's descendants, including Isaac, who would live as strangers in a foreign country. They would *sojourn as strangers* (the two Hebrew words are related) in a land not their own. The translators of the Septuagint amplified the text to read, "And the habitation of the children of Israel when they dwelt in Egypt *and other lands* was four hundred and thirty years." It is so stated in foot notes to this text.

Since Isaac was 60 years old when his son Jacob was born, and Jacob was 130 when he entered Egypt, it follows that 190 years elapsed since the birth of Isaac. This leaves a total of 240 years for the actual presence of Israel in Egypt. It fits the genealogy of the sons of Jacob as recorded in Exodus 6. The line of Levi through Moses is the only one to include any ages. Levi lived to be 137 years old. His son Kohath came with him to settle in Egypt, and he lived to the ripe old age of 133. Kohath's son Amram, the father of Moses, died at the age of 137, and Moses left Egypt when he was 80 years old. Their years obviously overlapped, which leaves by far not enough time to account for 430 years, but it does fit 240 years. Two and a half centuries are enough for thirteen families to grow into a nation of a million people. They also kept their ethnic identity intact.

There are good reasons to believe Israel entered Egypt at the beginning of the Middle Kingdom, during the reign of the 11th Dynasty kings. It follows that they were oppressed during the brutal reign of the 12th Dynasty rulers who enslaved an Asiatic people. Many of these kings are well known, and we can be fairly certain about their place in the scriptural account. The problem is largely with the Old Kingdom, for all fact and purpose a phantom kingdom.

The Enigma of Egypt's Kingdoms

It is generally believed that the Exodus occurred during the hey days of Egypt's New Kingdom. This is a mistaken assumption. All the evidence points at the Middle Kingdom as the era, mentioned in Genesis and Exodus. However, there are serious complications, largely the result of the very incomplete records of Egypt's history. Well meaning scholars were forced to speculate, with unhappy results. There are real difficulties with the various dynasties of the Old Kingdom. The problem is that the same events are ascribed to the Old and Middle Kingdoms with equally good evidence, for good reasons. The dynastic succession of the New Kingdom is well established. However, there is a definite relationship between the Old- and Middle Kingdoms, they are more or less the same.

The Middle Kingdom consists of but two dynasties, eleven and twelve. The Old Kingdom (dynasties 3-6) has two dynasties (3 and 4) that closely resemble the Middle Kingdom. Based upon archaelogical and literary evidence there are good reasons to believe the

First Dynasty was contemporary with the third. The 5th Dynasty is generally believed to be a continuation of the 4th, but the 6thDynasty has much in common with the 4th, and for that matter the 12th. The dynasties of the First Intermediate Period (7-10) are very similar to those of the Second (13-17). The reasons for this confused state of affairs are apparent. The early records of Egypt are scanty to say the least. Huge gaps in history must be filled with speculation. It is only natural to assume that kings (who often go by different names) ruled sequentially rather than simultaneously.

It had to be that way. Surely the history of Egypt must be very old. The very notion of gradual evolution demands that. It follows that ancient Egyptians must have evolved over thousands of years. The facts however belie this seemingly logical assumption. Surprisingly, civilization did not produce kingdoms until about 2000 B.C., or perhaps a few centuries later. Presumably the confusion of tongues produced different languages, isolation and consequent nationalism. And Upper and Lower Egypt were not united until the rise of the powerful Vizier Mentuhotep, who had the powers of a king, the biblical Joseph.

Now we enter into a confused web of duplicated dynasties and kings, a web we can only entangle with caution and trepidation. It amounts to this. Dynasties 1 and 3 of the Old Kingdom were contemporaneous with dynasty 11, which generously welcomed the Hebrews. The Old Kingdom dynasties 4 and 6 were the same as dynasty 12, whose father/son pharaohs enslaved the greatly increased Hebrew population. These kings were brutal and hated. There was however another, popular pharaoh, who was known to be gentle and just, Senuhe, or Moses. Granted the names and identity of these pharaohs are bound to be confusing, but it does involve fascinating detective work.

The Vizier Joseph

The pharaohs of the Third Dynasty were the first really outstanding rulers. They were the pyramid builders. Little is known about the first king, named Sanakhte, but his successor, perhaps his brother, was the famous Djoser (Zoser). It was Djoser who built the step pyramid at Saqqara. His architect was a virtual genius, the Vizier Imhotep. Imhotep's title read: "The treasurer of the King of Lower Egypt, the first after the King of upper Egypt, Administrator of the great palace, Hereditary Lord, the High Priest of Heliopolis, Imhotep the builder, the sculptor, the maker of stone vases."

In view of numerous similarities between the First and Third Dynasties it is interesting to discover a pharaoh in the First Dynasty called Uenephes, in whose days a famine struck. He was succeeded by a ruler named Usaphais. The first part of this name, "Usaph," closely resembles the Hebrew "Yusef," or Joseph.

According to an inscription dating from Ptolemaic times, Djoser asked Imhotep for wise counsel regarding a severe famine, lasting seven years. By that time Imhotep was deified, and worshiped as a god of architecture and medicine. It is known that he lived to a very high age. Genesis records that the pharaoh, warned of a severe famine, made Joseph second in command and gave him as wife Asenath, the daughter of Potiphera, the priest of On. The biblical On was Heliopolis, associated with Imhotep.

The Egyptian Imhotep and the biblical Joseph are so similar that historians were forced to take note. Of course, they could never admit that Imhotep was Joseph. After all, according to conventional dating the two lived a thousand years apart. The story of Joseph as recorded in Genesis therefore must be pseudo history. Well, yes, if indeed the official version of ancient history is correct, and it is not.

The Old Kingdom being part and parcel of the Middle Kingdom, it follows that the Old Kingdom Third Dynasty was more or less the same as the Middle Kingdom Eleventh. There are valid reasons to question the Intef kings who are reported to have rescued Egypt from foreign oppression, but there can be no doubt about Mentuhotep, the king-like vizier who united both Upper and Lower Egypt. Imhotep and Mentuhotep, it turns out, were remarkably alike. Mentuhotep was connected with the priesthood and had all the powers of a king. Great personages bowed down before him at the royal palace. His titles read, "Vizier, Chief Judge, Overseer of the Double

Granary, Chief Treasurer, Governor of the Royal Castle, Wearer of the Royal Seal, Chief of all the works of the King, Hereditary Prince, Pilot of the People, Giver of Good-Sustaining Alive the People, Count, Sole Companion, Favorite of the King."

The Genesis account of Joseph, it turns out, was hardly a fable. If anything, he was far more powerful than we would think. Josephus informs us that Joseph, following the death of the pharaoh, became the sole ruler of Egypt. Since he was 30 years of age when he came to power and lived to be 110, he must indeed have ruled a very long time. There was but one Mentuhotep and not four, as is believed. Joseph was the Mentuhotep I who unified Egypt, Mentuhotep II who ruled 51 years, and Mentuhotep III and IV, associated with a famine. The Turin code mentions "Seven empty years," connected with Mentuhotep IV.

Obviously both Imhotep and Mentuhotep have the element "hotep" in common. Both were closely associated with the god Ptah. Well now, Psalm 105:16-23 recounts the mighty deeds of the Lord, how he dealt with Israel and Egypt.

> He called down a famine on the land
> And destroyed all their supplies of food;
> And he sent a man before them-
> Joseph, sold as a slave.
> They bruised his feet with shackles,
> His neck was put in irons,
> Till what he foretold came to pass,
> Till the word of the Lord proved him true.
> The king sent and released him,
> The ruler of peoples set him free.
> He made him master of his household,
> Ruler over all he possessed,
> To instruct his princes as he pleased
> And teach his elders wisdom.

Israel and Egypt

All of a sudden we find details, omitted in the Genesis account. His stay in prison was hardly a happy one. There was however an upside. Joseph was a Hebrew, but being young, he easily learned how to speak Egyptian, something essential when he suddenly was called before the king. What concerns us is a curious note, Joseph was not merely a ruler, he also instructed the Egyptians in wisdom.

There exists in Egyptian wisdom literature a set of instructions, considered to be a master piece, the "Maxims of Ptahhotep." It is dated to perhaps the 5th Dynasty. The Vizier Ptahhotep informs us that he reached the age of 110, the very age of Joseph. He left instructions for etiquette and a successful life, based upon personal experiences. Scholars noted with wonder that the author refers to one God, not many, as one would expect of an Egyptian. In a number of cases the author relates to problems, such as experienced by Joseph, like his unfortunate run-in with Potiphar's wife. If it is true, as some claim, that Potiphar was a eunuch, it becomes understandable why his wife would be attracted to a handsome guy like Joseph. She tried to seduce him, but he refused, until frustrated she accused him of attempted rape, and an innocent Joseph ended up in jail. Ptahhotep warns his hearers of the lady of the house.

> If you desire that friendship should endure
> In a house which you enter
> As a lord, as a brother, or as / a friend:
> In any place which you enter,
> Avoid approaching the women,
> For there is nothing good in any situation where such is done.
> It is never prudent to become overly familiar with them,
> For countless men have thus been diverted /
> from their own best interests.
> One may be deceived by an exquisite body,
> But then it suddenly turns to misery. [2]

The theophoric names Ptah, Im and Mentu could have easily been attached to "hotep," according to the deities of various cities such as Memphis, Thebes, Heliopolis, and so on. In any event, all these names point at one man, the biblical Joseph. Now scripture says that Joseph was handsome, and Josephus adds that he looked like his mother Rachel, a beauty. Another reason why he was his father Jacob's favorite. A statue of Mentuhotep survives. It reveals a very handsome man with surprising features. His eyes have an Asiatic slant, meaning he was not a native Egyptian.

Mentuhotep – Joseph

Joseph's unfortunate experience with Potiphar's wife may have very well been the inspiration for another story, "The Tale of the Two Brothers," an interesting fairy tale. Anubis was the older brother, and Bata the younger. One day Anubis asked Bata to get seed from the village. The younger brother found Aniubis' wife plaiting her hair. She seized him and asked him to sleep with her, but he refused furiously. Anubis' wife then told her husband his younger brother had tried to seduce her. Anubis in a rage tried to kill Bata, but he escaped, after which the story turns to myth and folklore. Nonetheless, the similarities with the Genesis account are striking.

Fascinating evidence of Joseph's contributions to Egypt survive to this day in an irrigation project. A creek, connected with the Nile, was canalized to divert its water to a natural depression called the Fayoum. This channel, called "Bahr Yasuf," the Joseph Canal, dates from the 11th and 12th Dynasties. The Fayoum still exists. It is a vast oasis that supplies Egypt with fruit, vegetables, tomatoes and so on.

Pharaoh Moses

If Joseph was a vice king in the Third Dynasty, then the Fourth Dynasty must have had a prince of Hebrew descent, Moses. As it turns out Moses was not merely a prince, he was a pharaoh.

The first pharaoh of the Fourth Dynasty was Snefru. He was of an altogether different line. He probably received his royal title by marrying Hetep-heres, daughter of Huni, the last pharaoh of the Third Dynasty. She was the mother of Khufu, whom the Greek called Cheops. He married his half sister Meresankh, the mother of the famous Kaphre or Chephren.

His reputation is mixed. Khufu built the great pyramid of Giza. However, he is said to have been a cruel task master who imposed forced labor in building his grandiose project. His successor was the short-lived Djedefre, the first to call himself "Son of Re," or Ramesse. After his death came Kaphre (Chephren), the builder of the second pyramid of Giza. He was fascinated by sphinxes. The Great Sphinx bears his face. He was just as harsh as his father.

In sharp contrast to these despotic rulers, Pharaoh Menkaure or Mycerinus (the Greco-Roman version) was beloved. He was modest, gentle and just. However, it seems he ran into dynastic trouble. The gods were unhappy about his benign rule, and his short lived kingship came to sad end. Now it is certain that Menkaure was not a native Egyptian. A splendid statue of the king, flanked by the goddess Hathor who resembles his wife, reveals a friendly face and eyes that, like those of Joseph, have a distinctly Asiatic slant. The Egyptians by and large looked Caucasian.

The rulers of the Fourth Dynasty conducted massive building projects, including the pyramids. Josephus states flatly that the pharaohs who succeeded Joseph used Hebrew forced labor to build the pyramids. Khufu (Cheops) and Kaphre (Chephren) were the pharaohs mentioned in Exodus, and Menkaure, Kaphre's adopted son was Moses. Mycerinus has the elements Mu-Se-Ra. Eliminate Ra, the sun god, and we have Mu-Se or Moses. Scripture says that Moses was a humble man, and he certainly was just. Although not a native Egyptian he was adopted into the royal family, which was common practice.

Menkaure (Mycerinus) - Moses

Within the Old Kingdom, the 5th Dynasty as we have seen, in all likelihood was a continuation of the 4th, although the last fifty years probably paralleled the 6th. Dynasties 4 and 6 were the same. For all his achievements, almost nothing is known about the 4th Dynasty Khufu (Cheops); a three-inch statue of this king survives. It is revealing to compare this with the face of Teti, the founder of the 6th Dynasty. They look like identical twins. Khufu/Teti married the daughter of the obscure 3rd Dynasty king Huni, establishing his claim to royalty. Teti's son Pepi (or Piops) married two daughters of Khui, a wealthy prince from the south. For some odd reason they had the same name, Akhnesmerire. Both had a son. As in the 4th Dynasty, the reign of the first king (Menenre) was brief. He was succeeded by his half brother Pepi II, who ruled a very long time.

If we compare the 4th and 6th Dynasties with the 12th, numerous similarities are apparent. Its founder, the grim faced Amenemes, is believed to have been a commoner from southern Egypt. He called himself Mehet-Meswt, "He who repeats births," meaning he began an altogether different order. Amenemes and his equally brutal son

Sestrosis were involved in huge building projects, including palaces and pyramids. They shared this fascination with the 4th Dynasty pharaohs Khufu (Cheops) and Kaphre (Chephren). Excellent statues of Chephren and Sestrosis reveal the same man. It is nearly impossible to tell them apart. On top of that, both were equally obsessed with sphinxes. Chephren's real name was Ka-kheper-re; Sestrosis or Senusret had the nearly identical name Kheper-ka-re. [3]

Scholars noted a curious coincidence; Teti and Amenemes share several features. They had the same throne name, Sehetibre, the same Horus name, Sehetep-Tawy, "He who pacifies the two lands," and both are reported to have been assassinated. In addition, Khufu and Kaphre, like Amenemes and Sestrosis, had a reputation for being harsh and cruel. They enslaved an Asiatic people that evidently had become very numerous, and forced them to work on their grandiose building projects. Flinters Petrie discovered gruesome evidence of infanticide. Underneath the floors of many homes in the Illahun he found wooden boxes filled with the remains of babies, which was contrary to Egyptian custom. Two third of the burials in the Delta dating from that time were children less than eighteen months old.

The similarities between the Old and Middle Kingdoms are evident in Egyptian literature. The tale of "King Cheops and the Magicians" is set in the 4th Dynasty. Yet scholars unanimously agree that the story was written at the time of the 12th Dynasty. This is strange indeed. These dynasties are separated by some six hundred years, yet they give a vivid contemporary account of ruling kings. Is it just possible that the 4th and 12th Dynasties were the same?

From the time of the 12th Dynasty dates a tale of great interest, the "Story of Senuhe." Senuhe definitely was a man of high rank. He is called "Hereditary noble and commander, warden and district officer of the estates of the sovereign in the lands of the Asiatics, - truly beloved royal acquaintance." The translator explains that "Asiatics" means the peoples of Palestine. He was associated with Queen Nofru, daughter of Amenemes, and wife of Senusret. Upon the assassination of Pharaoh Amenemhet, Senuhe found himself in serious trouble. When Senusret was told of his father's death, he hastened back from a raid in Africa. He evidently feared Senuhe and tried to kill him. But Senuhe escaped to Asia (Palestine), where he met a chieftain who, impressed with the fugitive, asked him to stay, and gave him his oldest daughter in marriage. While in exile Senuhe had a family and several adventures (one of which resembles the David/Goliath battle), until many years later he was called back to Egypt an old man, where he was restored in good graces.

Exodus relates the story of Moses who was saved from certain death when the daughter of the pharaoh, in defiance of her father's decree, adopted him. That was Meresankh, wife and half sister of Sestrosis (Senusret), the Merris of tradition. Moses is reported to have risen to high rank. Josephus claims that the pharaoh made Moses a General, and that Moses defeated the Ethiopians. The 12th Dynasty did in fact occupy Ethiopia. But Moses beat a hasty retreat when the pharaoh tried to arrest him for killing an Egyptian foreman. As we have seen, he fled for Midian, where he was welcomed by Jethro, a distant relative and a believer in the one God. He married Jethro's daughter and remained forty years in his service.

The name Senuhe closely relates to the Greco/Roman Mycerinus, the pharaoh of the 4th Dynasty who ran into dynastic difficulties. The Egyptian Mu-se-ra is nearly identical with Senuhe. The elements Se and Nu (or Mu) could easily be reversed to Mu-se-he, which was quite common in ancient Egypt, "he" being Hathor, also associated with Mycerinus. If indeed Moses was the beloved Senuhe or Mycerinus who returned to Egypt an old man, it explains why he was so highly regarded not only by the Hebrews, but by the Egyptians as well, which would seem rather strange. (Ex 11:3)

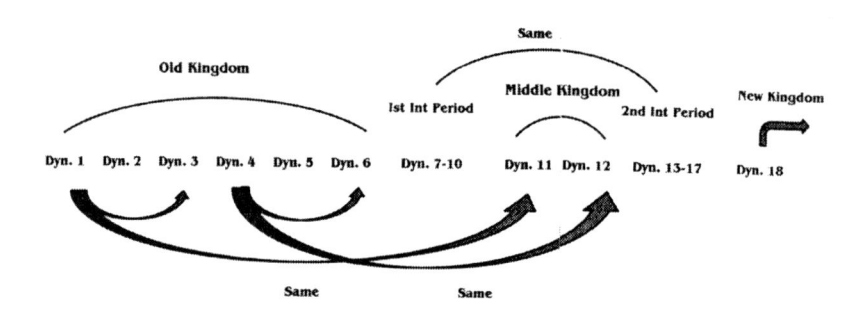

Israel and Egypt

Mount Horeb

When Moses fled to escape the wrath of the pharaoh, there was but one way to go. He could not flee west or south because that was all part of Greater Egypt. Nor could he enter the Sinai Peninsula because that, too, was Egyptian territory. There was a sizable Egyptian military force to protect turquoise and copper mines. Canaan was under Egyptian dominion as well, so the only place left was Midian, east of the Gulf of Aqaba, in what is now Saudi Arabia. It is still known as Madyan.[4] According to local tradition, his father-in-law Jethro lived in caves near Elim, an oasis with twelve springs and palm trees. The Arabs insist that the prophet Musha lived there. It is now called Al Bad. A current map positively identifies this location as the place where Moses lived. Just north of Al Bad, on the crossing of two highways, is a place called *Jethro*.[5]

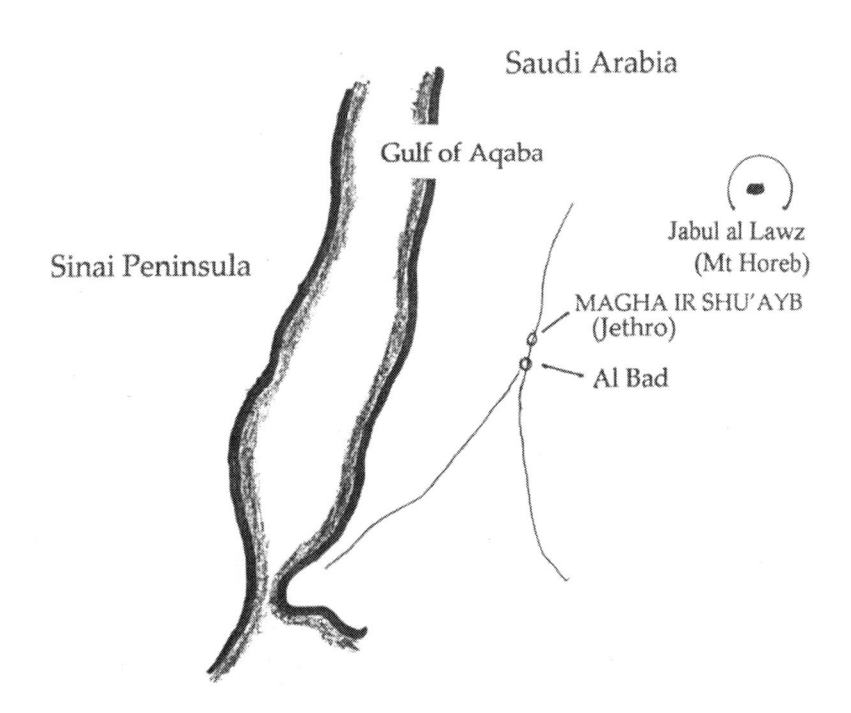

Saudi Arabia

Gulf of Aqaba

Sinai Peninsula

Jabul al Lawz
(Mt Horeb)

MAGHA IR SHU'AYB
(Jethro)

Al Bad

The all-important question facing us is this: exactly where was Horeb, the mountain of God? It could never be in the Sinai Peninsula, the traditional site. Jethro lived in Midian, east of the Gulf of Aqaba, and the scriptures repeatedly say that Horeb was in Arabia. That can only mean Moses was outside Egyptian jurisdiction. He would never guide his flock hundreds of miles around the Gulf of Aqaba through the waste desert of the Sinai Peninsula, occupied by people who were out to get him. When his wife Zipporah bore him a son, he called him Gershom, meaning *an alien there* for, he said, "I have become an alien in a foreign land." (Ex 2:21). All those years he considered himself banished, a stranger in a harsh country.

Mount Horeb could hardly be in the Sinai Peninsula, far from Jethro's base. The territory obviously was familiar to Moses. He had been there many times before, since it was a grazing ground for his sheep. There is one mountain that satisfies all requirements, and that is Jabul al Lawz (Mount of Almond Trees). It rises 8,465 feet above sea level, and it fits the description of Mount Horeb exactly. It is important to establish this, because it determines where the Israelites crossed the Red Sea. It has major implications for our study. To first move into the Sinai Peninsula and then enter Midian, they must have crossed the southern tip of the Gulf of Aqaba, which is exactly what happened. The Strait of Tiran was the Sea of Passage. It connects the Red Sea with the Gulf of Aqaba, and provided ready-made access.

The Story of Senuhe relates how the hero fled Egypt following the assassination of Amenemes, to return an old man. According to Acts 7, Moses was forty years old when he fled for Midian. That happened during the reign of Sestrosis. Since Sestrosis lived another thirty-four years, it allows for perhaps a decade following his death before Moses was called back to lead God's people out of Egypt. We do not think about it that way, but it was the return of a king. Was this king able to rule a nation of slaves? Pharaohs after all were not inclined to be patient, something needed in abundance in leading a slave people through harsh conditions.

Moses had a terrible temper, which frequently got the best of him. How could he lead a people at all? God takes all the time we need. Moses knew all about statesmanship (his diplomatic training is evident), in Midian he learned about patience. All those years he led sheep, the dumbest animals around, always astray and always in need of care. So it was that the guided his flock along the edge of the desert toward Mount Horeb. There he saw something very strange. A bush was burning without being consumed. He walked up to this strange sight and suddenly heard a voice. God spoke to him.

The Plagues of Egypt

When Moses approached the curious sight of the burning bush, the Lord called him by name. He told Moses to lead Israel out of Egypt, something the reluctant leader was not at all eager to do. Forty years of isolation and tending sheep had tempered him. He was no more the prince, the self-appointed leader who took the law in his own hand. Besides, the prospect of confronting the pharaoh in his splendid court must have frightened him. The encounter is highly significant because God revealed something about himself that was altogether new. It is all in the context of a covenant promise. God heard the cries of his oppressed people, and he sent Moses to face the pharaoh and guide Israel out of Egypt. They would meet at this very mountain. Moses was not convinced. He considered himself unqualified and besides, all those years he had been out of touch, and he was not at all sure that the Hebrews even knew God.

> Moses said to God, "Suppose I go to the Israelites and say to them, 'the God of your fathers has sent me to you,' and they ask me, 'What is his name?' Then what shall I tell them?"
> God said to Moses, "I am who I am. This is what you are to say to the Israelites: 'I AM has sent me to you.'"
>
> Exodus 3:21

Quite likely Moses afterwards in compiling ancient records replaced "El Shaddai," (God Almighty) the meaning of which over the years had been corrupted, with "Yahweh." Yahweh speaks of the self-determining nature of the God who "works out everything in conformity with the purpose of his will."(Eph. 1:11) The name Yahweh is always used in connection with God's covenant people, and is considered sacred by the Jews; so much so that they refuse to utter it. Instead they say "Adonai." (Lord)

Still, Moses hesitated. He came with every possible excuse, even after God gave him several miraculous signs. He was not a public speaker. Fine. His brother Aaron would speak for him. When he still remonstrated, the Lord finally became angry and ordered him to go. So he returned to Egypt, was reunited with his relatives, and faced the pharaoh. He demanded that Israel be allowed to leave, but was laughed at. In fact, the Egyptians increased the burden of slavery. However, Moses was on a divine errant, and he warned the pharaoh of disasters to come.

What follows defies belief. Water changed into blood, frogs crawled everywhere, gnats and flies swarmed all over, cattle died of a plague, festering sores broke out over man and animals. Hail mixed with fire killed men and cattle alike, stripped every tree and flattened everything that grew. What was left was devoured by swarms of locusts, so great that the ground looked black. Then came a pitch-black darkness that lasted three days. It was so intense that the Egyptians could not move from their place.

Meanwhile the Israelites were preparing to leave. Moses gave them distinct instructions, received from God, to initiate a Passover meal. God would pour out his wrath over Egypt, but "pass over" the homes of those who covered their door post with the blood of a lamb. The Israelites made sure they did just that.

That night Egypt was destroyed. The dead were everywhere. The Egyptians begged the Israelites to leave. Upon request they gave them gold, silver and clothing. Israel was finally paid for centuries of slave labor. They left hurriedly. A mass of humanity ran for freedom. Then the pharaoh came to his senses. Why let a pool of cheap labor run away? And with all that loot! He gathered his army to pursue the runaway slaves.

They trapped the fleeing slaves near a place called Pi-ha-Khiroth, by the Gulf of Aqaba, but darkness kept them away. Then the impossible happened. The waters of the sea parted and the Israelites escaped across a road through the sea. The Egyptians followed in hot pursuit, but their chariots bogged down; the waters returned and the army perished. Israel had been wondrously delivered. It was an experience the nation never forgot. To this day, the exodus is remembered in the Passover.

Egyptology

Where does all this fit into the history of Egypt? That's easy, nowhere. According to conventional dating there were two kingdoms lasting from 3,000 B.C. to about 1,800 B.C. As we have seen, there was but one kingdom that began around 2,000 B.C. and ended about 1450 B.C. It perished after an invasion of Arab hordes. Egypt was oppressed by foreigners, known as Hyksos or king-shepherds, who ruled more than four centuries. They were expelled by Pharaoh Ahmose, supposedly 1575 B.C., but actually around 1,000 B.C. This was the beginning of the New Kingdom.

Ahmose was the first pharaoh of the Thutmose Dynasty. Among these rulers was Queen Hapshetsut, who sent an expedition to a mysterious country called Punt. Her stepson, Thutmose III, was bent on conquest. He raided Palestine and captured Kadesh, an important city, without a fight. One of the pharaohs was Amenhotep IV or Akhnaton, the great heretic. His son was the famous Tut-ankh-amon, well known, not because of his achievements, (little is known), but because of the great riches of his tomb. This dynasty supposedly lasted until about 1300 B.C.

The Nineteenth Dynasty was that of Ramses I, Seti the Great, Ramses II and Merneptah. Ramses II marched through Palestine 1285 B.C. to fight a battle against the Hittites, a battle he ingloriously lost. Hostilities that lasted two decades continued on Palestinian soil, then friendly relations were established. Merneptah is the only pharaoh to mention Israel by name.

The Twentieth Dynasty was that of Ramses III, 1182 - 1151 B.C., regarded to have been the last great pharaoh. Hordes of armed troops, known as "Sea People," came from the north. They were called "Pereset," and are believed to have been the Philistines of biblical times. They devastated nations in their path, but were stopped at the border of Egypt by Ramses. All of this is said to have happened in the period of the Judges, about 1400 - 1000 B.C. This supposedly was the Late Bronze Age, (New Kingdom) although the world of early Israel was that of the end of the Early Bronze Age.

It does not take a genius to see that this version of history nowhere resembles that of the scriptures. Which raises the question, is Egyptology based upon irrefutable facts that are beyond dispute? Well, not exactly. We have had ample opportunity to question the accuracy of conventional history. No less an authority than Sir Alan Gardiner left this appraisal regarding Manetho, an Egyptian priest and historian, whom he regarded as reliable.

> Manetho undertook a chronicle of the Egyptian kings of which, apart from some much edited extracts preserved by the Jewish historian Josephus (A.D. 70), there remains only a garbled abridgment in the works of the Christian chronographers Sextus Julius Africanus (early 3rd century A.D.), and Eusebius (early 4th century A.D.), a much later compiler named George the Monk, known as Syntellicus (ca A.D. 800), contributed greatly to the transmission. In Manetho's work the entire history of Egypt, after the reigns of the gods and demi gods, was divided up into thirty-one dynasties of royal families beginning with Menes and ending with Alexander the Great's conquest in 332 B.C. In spite of all defects this division into dynasties has taken so firm a root in the literature of Egyptology that there is but little chance of its ever being abandoned.
>
> In the forms in which the book has reached us there are inaccuracies of the most glaring kind, these find their climax in Dyn. XVIII, where the names and true sequences are now known from indisputable monumental sources. Africanus and Eusebius often do not agree; for example Africanus assigns nine kings to Dyn. XXII while Eusebius has only three. Sometimes all that is vouchsafed for to us is the number of kings in a dynasty (so in Dyns. VII-X, XX) and their city of origin.

The royal names are apt to be incredibly distorted, that of Senwosre of Dyn. XII, for instance, being assimilated in the form of Sesonchosis to that of Soshenk of a thousand years later. The lengths of reigns frequently differ in the two versions, as well as often showing wide departures from the definitely ascertained figure. When textual and other critics have done their best or worst, the reconstructed Manetho remains full of imperfections. [6]

The Titanic

That should ring alarm bells. It has happened before that supposedly infallible creations of man's hand turned out to be flawed. That was the case with the Titanic, the ship that "God himself could not sink." Nothing, it was believed, could sink the Titanic. The construction of watertight compartments in steel ships would not allow that. Captain Smith was so sure that he raced his ship through the ice infested waters of the North Atlantic. Then the lookout to his horror saw an iceberg dead ahead. The Titanic collided on the starboard (right) side. The first six watertight compartments flooded; the ship went down by the bow and sank. A board of inquiry theorized that the iceberg ripped a hole in the hull which seemed reasonable enough, and that has since been proclaimed as fact.

Then the Titanic was found on the bottom of the Atlantic. There was no hole; rather it turned out the hull crackled and the rivets popped along the seams. The Titanic had a fatal flaw; the steel was not good enough. Metallurgy had not yet caught up with technology. The steel contained too much phosphorus, which rendered it brittle. The water of the North Atlantic was below the freezing point, and as a result the shell plating and the rivets froze and crystallized. The area of impact was not all that large, but the brittle steel was not able to absorb the stress, and the shell plating tore at the seams. The unsinkable ship, it turned out, was a floating death trap. The experts were badly mistaken.

It appears that Egyptology is another Titanic. The one sure source that provided a yardstick for ancient history, the Bible, was hardly considered. To some extent that may have been religious prejudice, but the real reason was the strange story of the plagues of Egypt and the exodus. It is understandable enough; who would believe it?

A little boy visited Sunday school and told his mother what he had learned. "The Israelis left Egypt, and when they came to the Red Sea, Moses called the Corps of Engineers. They build a pontoon bridge and all the Israelis escaped. The Egyptians followed them across the bridge, but when they were halfway, Moses called the Israeli Air Force. They bombed the bridge and all the Egyptians were killed."

"But Johnny," his mother asked, "are you sure that is what happened?"

"No, mom," Johnny admitted, "but if I told you what they said, you would never believe it."

That is the problem with the story of the exodus, it is difficult to believe. Yet the impact of the exodus on the Judeo-Christian religion and history is so profound that historians are forced to admit there must be a core of historical fact. That is all the more remarkable because biblical scholars so far have failed to find any record that even hints at an exodus. Not until recently.

The Velikovsky Case

Over the centuries the history of Egypt has frequently been questioned by reputable scholars, Newton among them. In modern times the great heretic was Immanuel Velikovsky, a Russian-born psychiatrist who, after fleeing Lenin's regime, left first for Israel but settled in the United States. He was one of those rare all-around scholars who was educated in many disciplines, including natural sciences, history, biology, law and psychoanalysis. Since he studied under a student of Siegmund Freud, he became interested in the Oedipus legend, the Greek story of the king who married his own mother and suffered grief because of it. According to his own account, he was struck by the similarities between Oedipus and Pharaoh Akhnaton who, as we have seen, supposedly lived about 1300

B.C. Velikovsky arrived at a controversial conclusion, Akhnaton and Oedipus were the same man.

Unfortunately the two, who were really the same, were separated by many centuries. Obviously something was seriously wrong with historical dating. It occurred to Velikovsky that the history of Egypt was in dire need of revision. The result was a ten-year study that included history, legend, mythology, geography and, surprisingly, cosmology. A Jew and a Hebrew scholar he was, of course, familiar with the story of the exodus. He became aware of certain well-known Egyptian manuscripts which describe events that very much resemble the plagues of Egypt. Somehow no one had ever connected the two. And that was only the beginning.

Early in his studies he discovered that ancient nations world - wide spoke of "sun ages," repeated disasters that convulsed the globe. These disasters were always associated with the actions of planet-gods. One of these happened at the time of the exodus, about 1450 B.C. A number of early historians mentioned an enormous comet that caused great destruction. This comet, called "Typhon," he thought, was associated with the planet Venus, and it reportedly came from the planet Jupiter.

Velikovsky came to the following (debatable) conclusion. In the middle of the Second Millennium B.C., a huge comet was ejected from the planet Jupiter. This comet, the proto planet Venus, flew toward the sun in the ecliptic, the plane where the planets travel. It crossed the orbits of the inner planets, Mars, Earth and Mercury, whipped around the sun and entered into a highly elliptical orbit. The slow-moving comet moved into the path of the earth, which caught up with it.

As the earth began to approach the tail of the comet, a ferrous (iron based) dust filtered in from the skies. It colored the waters a bloody red. The dust became black soot that irritated the skin of men and animals alike. Ever so slowly, the earth moved closer. High in the atmosphere, carbon and hydrogen in the tail of the comet mixed with oxygen to form hydrocarbons (petroleum). Fires burned on high, and a torrent of hot, sticky bitumen poured down. Meteorites roared down, mixed with fire. They stripped trees and killed animals. Insects bred at a feverish rate. Swarms of locusts ate what was left.

The tail of the comet now enveloped the earth, which was disturbed in its motion. Hurricane force winds swept cinders through impenetrable darkness. The hurricane lasted a week. Frightened by the din and the pitch blackness, the Egyptians were unable to move from their place. The outer crust of the earth was arrested in its motion, resulting in a major earth shock. Towns collapsed, houses were overturned, temples swallowed up by the earth. The flower of Egypt died. The Israelites on the other hand lived in huts, and the angel of death passed them over.

Egyptian sources state that the earth "overturned." The axis of the earth evidently shifted, but how much is a matter of conjecture. In any event, Israel escaped under fantastic conditions. The prolonged darkness ended, an extended day followed. When they came to Pi-ha-hiroth, with the Egyptian army on their heels, the overhead comet pulled the waters in heaps. It stood like solid glass. All that night the Hebrews walked across the dried-out bottom of the sea toward freedom. The Egyptian army followed, only to meet their doom. When they were in the middle of the sea, a great bolt of lightning discharged between the two planetary bodies. The comet and the earth parted; the tides collapsed. The impact of the waters was so great that the Egyptians were bodily thrown into the sky. Egypt, in other words, was left defenseless. The army perished with its commander-in-chief. The land was ruined, the government powerless. Israel on the other hand walked toward freedom.

Caution

Our notions of reality are presuppositional. It is only human to assume facts that are basic to our understanding of life, and fit everything within that paradigm, that framework. Historians do it. Scientists do it, too. As a rule of thumb, it is believed with dogmatic certainty that history knows nothing about global catastrophes, that humanity developed through eons of gradual change and that evolution is a scientific fact beyond dispute.

Is that true? Velikovsky, although an evolutionist, claimed that the earth suffered a number of upheavals. He based his belief upon evidence from scripture, mythology and worldwide traditions of global disasters. How these catastrophes came about is another matter. Pagan nations blamed their gods of course. These gods had a dual nature. They represented the forces of nature, such as the wind, rain, light and darkness, and they had an astral counterpart. They were not only the sun and the moon, but also the planets. The planets, like the sun and the moon, were personifications of the gods. What is so strange about these astral deities is their inversed importance. We would assume that the sun and the moon were the most important gods. They were not. Ancient peoples feared the planet-gods, such as Jupiter, Saturn, Mars and Venus.

This made Velikovsky wonder, is it possible that the planets in historical times posed a threat to the earth, that for some reason they were thrown out of their orbits? He developed a theory to explain the dynamics of the solar system and possible perturbations in the motion of the planets: gravity is an electromagnetic phenomenon.[7] It involves the electrical property of attraction. The macrocosm behaves like the microcosm. It is a matter of electrical attraction and repulsion. The planets travel around the sun by *electromagnetic circumduction,* much as in atoms electrons whip around the nucleus. The sun is a spinning electromagnet that pulls the planets along in its magnetic grip. The planets are charged magnets, capable of capturing satellites in their own magnetic field. The system is inter-dependent. The sun and the planets affect each other. That at least provides a plausible explanation for planetary behavior.

Unfortunately he began with an impossible proposition. Whatever the origin of Venus, this much is sure, Venus, which has a density four times that of Jupiter, could never be an ejected chunk of the gas giant. The differences between the two planets are too great, particularly their atmospheric makeup. There simply is no scientific evidence to support Velikovsky's claim that Venus was ejected from Jupiter "in a violent explosion." That requires too much energy; enough to light up the gas giant like a sun.

He never proposed a viable theory. That is a real problem with his books. Rather than present it as a possible explanation of historical events, he wrote as if it was a proven fact which of course, it is not. At times it reads like popular science fiction; occasionally one notices a certain arrogance. Besides, myth, legend and the scriptures to him were all the same. On top of that, he frequently quoted the Bible out of context. In his defense it must be said that his loudest critics do exactly the same thing.

We must be cautious when we evaluate Velikovsky's theories. Did Israel leave Egypt under catastrophic conditions? Yes. Did Venus have something to do with it? Perhaps. Much as we appreciate his insight and unquestioned scholarship, we need to critically and sympathetically evaluate his ideas. Velikovsky was often brain-storming, and in doing so he tried to prove too much. He attempted to rationalize unusual historical events, and looked for natural explanations when that was not always warranted.

Then there was William Comyns Beaumont (1873-1956). This eccentric Englishman wrote several books about global catastrophes, collisions between planets and even a revision of ancient history. "The Riddle of the Earth" appeared in 1925, and "The Mysterious Comet" in 1932, long before Velikovsky began his studies in 1940. There are at least twenty-five points of close similarities. It is known that Velikovsky was familiar with the works of Beaumont, although he merely considered Beaumont's conclusions as confirming his own views.

Whatever the controversy, the Old Testament is not the only record of a catastrophe that leveled Egypt at the time of the exodus. Contrary to popular belief, there are extra-scriptural records that confirm the exodus account; they give wonderful insight in the Egyptian side of the story. For there are Egyptian witnesses, and they not only confirm what Exodus so clearly states, they paint a terrifying picture. It was much worse than a superficial reading of the Bible would lead us to believe. Egypt was ruined, the population nearly annihilated.

Ipuwer's Admonitions

There exists a well-known Egyptian record, known as the papyrus of Ipuwer, that constitutes a primary source. It is presently in the Museum of Egyptology in Leiden, the Netherlands. Nearly every book on Egyptian history mentions it, at least that part that deals with the anarchy that followed a great disaster. The first part of this fragmented papyrus is missing, but judging from its historical character, Ipuwer evidently addressed royalty. Sir Alan H. Gardiner, who translated the paper, thought Ipuwer was a sage who blamed a king for neglect of duty. For this reason he called it, *The Admonitions of an Egyptian Sage*. He considered it "one of the most curious and important pieces of Egyptian literature that have survived the ravages of time."[8]

F.O. Faulkner in a recent translation observed, "The actual manuscript, written on the recto of the Leiden papyrus No. 344 and probably of Nineteenth Dynasty date, is clearly a copy of a much earlier work, written in Middle Egyptian."[9] He thought it was written after the calamity of a preceding revolution or civil war. Yet Ipuwer's comments clearly describe the aftermath of a natural, rather than a military upheaval. He wrote about half a century after the Middle Kingdom, following the end of the 13th Dynasty. It involved a disaster of epic proportion. Apparently no one noticed the similarities between the calamities described by Ipuwer and the ten plagues of Egypt. Nonetheless, they are there for all to see. The Hebrew and Egyptian records agree in detail.

The land was left in ruins. The scriptural account bluntly states that Egypt was devastated by repeated blows of nature. Water turned into blood, fish died, vermin multiplied, animals perished in a plague and a hail of bolides, mixed with fire; the crop was ruined. Then the firstborn died. Exodus implies that it was not merely the oldest sons, but a great many other people as well, who perished in some terrible catastrophe. Finally the Pharaoh and all his army died when they pursued Israel.

Following the exodus, we know next to nothing about Egypt. Of course not. There was no Hebrew eye witness to record the aftermath. Yes, but we do have an Egyptian witness: Ipuwer. He records a great many things that explain certain relevant questions. The most important of these: what happened to Egypt? Why is Egypt never mentioned again until the Hebrew kings, more than four centuries later? Who ruled Egypt, and how did these rulers affect Israel? And what was the state of affairs in Egypt after the Hebrew slaves made their hurried escape?

Ipuwer wrote his laments in the aftermath of the ten plagues of Egypt. The record he left paints a bleak picture of death and destruction. The population was decimated, the land ruined and in a state of anarchy. It is easy to see why. The pharaoh and his army, including the commanders, the aristocracy, perished in the waters of the Red Sea. There was no military force to impose order, no government to maintain justice. The civil government had effectively been removed, and the starving populace resorted to looting. Civil restraint disappeared. The land was filled with bloodshed.

> The land is full of confederates, and a man goes out to plough with his shield. 1.10
> Indeed, the land turns round as does a potter's wheel; the robber is a possessor of riches and [the rich man is become] a plunderer. 2.5

In the context of Ipuwer's observations, it is obvious that he was thrown into a social order that stood on its head. It was a topsy turvy world where the servant reigned.

> Indeed, noblemen are in distress, while the poor man is full of joy. Every town says, "Let us suppress the powerful among us." 2.5

That constitutes the bulk of Ipuwer's complaints. He was a scribe, a man of means, who helplessly watched his world collapse around him. Yet he provides tantalizing glimpses of a natural catastrophe, a stupendous upheaval of nature that ruined the once-fruitful nation.

A comparison with the scriptural account confirms the accuracy of the exodus account and its underlying message. The ten plagues taught a lesson to the Egyptians and Hebrews alike. They were aimed at the gods of Egypt beginning with Egypt's deity on earth, the pharaoh.

To the Egyptians the pharaoh was not merely Chief Executive, he was divine. That was the mind set of paganism in general. There were no such things as church and state; the ruling class was the priesthood. Loyalty to a national deity secured political stability and, one might add, the position of those in power. The king was also priest or even better, deity. In the Second World War the Japanese believed their emperor divine and would do anything he said. So it was with the pharaoh. And now the priesthood with its god helplessly endured the onslaught that was about to descend upon them.

For all his questionable fame, the identity of this pharaoh until now was never known. It is believed that he was either Amenhotep, Thutmose or Ramses II. We can say with certainty that none of these pharaohs were involved. It will be shown beyond doubt that they lived much later and that Ramses is mentioned in the scriptures by a different name. All the time scholars have been looking in the wrong place. The exodus occurred about a half a century after the end of the Middle Kingdom, at the beginning of the Second Intermediate Period, not during the New Kingdom, as is generally assumed. It will enable us to find the pharaoh of the oppression.

The Nile

Then there was the river Nile, the abode of many gods. Without the Nile, there would be no Egypt. The only river in the world to flow north begins deep in Africa, in Lake Victoria. It gave life to both the southern and northern kingdoms of Egypt.

Not only was the economic fortune of Egypt dependent upon the river, but the psychological welfare of the people largely depended on the faithfulness of the Nile River. The Nile dominated the agriculture of Egypt; this affected the form of her calendar which was divided into three seasons, each with four thirty-day months, with five "intercalary" days at the end of the year. The Nile not only provided a means of transportation for the Egyptians and irrigation for their crops, but it supplied the marshes for pasture and for hunting wild game so often depicted in Egyptian paintings. The river contained a wealth of fish, caught both by the line and the net (cf Isa 19:8) [10]

It has been a source of confusion to many that God would harden pharaoh's heart for the purpose of punishing him. Was that fair? It was just. The very challenge was like waving a red flag in front of a bull. Pharaoh's heart was hostile to begin with, and God used this to punish Egypt. Yet God did give a fair warning; Moses performed miracles before the Egyptian court by changing Aaron's staff into a snake, which the pharaoh countered by having his wise men do the same thing. True, Aaron's snake swallowed those of the sorcerers, but that did not deter the pharaoh. He should, because the Cobra, the symbol of royalty, was the tutelary spirit of the royal family.

Moses and his brother Aaron told pharaoh, "Let my people go." The pharaoh refused. Of course he did. How could he, a demigod, give in to the ambassador of slaves? Soon he faced the dire consequences. The life-giving Nile, the abode of many gods, became a river of blood. What caused it is anyone's guess, but it could have been iron oxide that filtered in from space. When it hit the waters it turned into a crimson red. It was not confined to the Nile. Water changed into blood, or something very much like it. It happened in Greece as well.

Blood

The Lord said to Moses, "Take your staff and stretch out your hand over the waters of Egypt - over the streams and canals, over the ponds and all the reservoirs - and they will turn into blood. Blood will be everywhere in Egypt, even in the wooden buckets and stone jars." Moses and Aaron did just as the Lord had commanded. He raised his staff in the presence of Pharaoh and his officials and struck the water of the Nile, and all the water was changed into blood. The fish in the Nile died, and the river smelled so bad that the Egyptians could not drink its water. Blood was everywhere in Egypt.

Exodus 7:19-22

The life-giving Nile became a sewer. Water everywhere became blood, or at least resembled it closely. It was so bad that the Egyptians could not drink the water. They were dying of thirst. That sounds incredible, but it is confirmed by an impeccable source. Ipuwer reports the exact same thing.

> Indeed, the river is blood, yet men drink of it. Men shrink from human beings and thirst after water. 2.10

What made things worse, fish died in the polluted waters. The Egyptian economy depended to a large extent on fishing. The dead and decaying fish not only produced an appalling stench, it created a health hazard as well. Worse, crocodiles were forced to leave the polluted waters and came ashore to devour the dead fish - and men. It was bad enough that the patron gods of fish were of no help, now the crocodile, a sacred animal, became an acute and deadly threat.

> Indeed, crocodiles [are glutted] with the fish they have taken, for men go to them of their own accord; it is destruction of the land. Men say: "Do not walk here; behold, it is a net." Behold, men tread [the water] like fishes, and the frightened man cannot distinguish it because of terror. 2.10

The translator adds that the *fish* are "a figure for the corpses the crocodiles have eaten." The context supports this interpretation. Egypt had recently been hit by a catastrophe that decimated the population, and the crocodiles feasted on the dead bodies. Now that they were ashore instead of in their native habitat, they attacked the terrorized population.

Frogs

Then followed a plague of frogs. Maybe frogs suddenly multiplied because their natural enemies were gone. In any event, they came out of the rivers and marshes and were everywhere. It must have been a nightmare to slip over the slimy creatures and to see them crawl all over. Then they died by the millions and were piled up in great, reeking heaps. There is an odd side note. The croaking of the frogs was a welcome sound to the ears of Egyptian farmers. It indicated that the Nile floods had inundated the marshes; the crops would be good. Because of that, the frog was associated with the goddess of fertility, Heqt, wife of the great god Khnum, the guardian of the Nile sources. Heqt also assisted women in childbirth. But Ipuwer informs us that Heqt failed women altogether.

> Indeed, women are barren and none conceive. Khnum fashions (men) no more because of the condition of the land. 1.10
> Men desire the giving of birth, but sadness supervenes, with needy people on all sides. — — Seed goes forth into mortal woman, but none are found on the road. 12.1

The translator added in a footnote, "Perhaps meaning that impregnation of women no longer produces offspring." The fertility goddess was of no use. Whatever the reason, women became barren; childbirth was at least greatly reduced and as a consequence the population was not being replenished. It should have been, because people died in the prevailing anarchy and epidemics. As a result the generations that followed were seriously diminished and unable to re-establish the strength of Egypt.

Israel and Egypt

Gnats

Then came a plague that tortured all Egyptians alike. From the dust and sand of Egypt came gnats and mosquitoes; swarms of them. We all know how pesky gnats are, and mosquitoes are carriers of diseases. Conditions were ideal for the proliferation of insects. Dead fish and frogs abounded, and the charged atmosphere was a breeding ground for gnats. They were more than a nuisance; they sickened the population and defiled the Egyptian priesthood.

> The priests in Egypt were noted for their physical purity. Daily rites were performed by a group of priests known as the *Uab* or "pure ones." Their purity was basically physical rather than spiritual. They were circumcised, shaved the hair from their heads and bodies, washed frequently, and were dressed in beautiful linen robes. In the light of this it would seem rather doubtful that the priesthood in Egypt could function very effectively, having been polluted by the presence of these insects. They, like their worshipers, were inflicted with the pestilence of this occasion. Their prayers were made ineffective by their own personal impurity with the presence of gnats on their bodies. [11]

Heredotus remarked how the priests kept themselves pure.

> Priests shave every part of their body every other day, to stop themselves getting lice or in general getting at all unclean as they minister to the gods. The priests wear only one garment made out of linen, while their shoes are papyrus; they are not allowed to wear any other clothing or footwear, and they wash with cold water twice every day and twice at night too.[12]

It is abundantly clear from Ipuwer's remarks that the priesthood was humiliated. In fact, he said as much. Obviously the priests could not wash themselves in the dirty water, and on top of that something very strange happened, people suffered hair loss.

Indeed, men are alike Ibises (herons). Squalor is throughout the land, and there are none indeed whose clothes are white in these times. 2, 5

Indeed, hair [has fallen out] for everybody, and the man of rank can no longer be distinguished from him who is nobody. 4.1

The distinguishing marks of the priests, bald heads and clean clothes, suddenly were not so distinguishing anymore. All had bald heads and dirty clothes. That certainly sounds strange, but there is a historical precedent. It happened in modern times, in 1783, when a volcano erupted in Iceland.

> In late May an eerie, bluish haze appeared over the Icelandic volcano Mount Skaptar, and a series of tremors that began on June 1 sent many families into tents for fear their stone houses would collapse. Then on the morning of June 8, the Lakagigar fissure, a fifteen-mile-long rip in the earth's crust, tore open, and for two months spewed forth lava at a prodigious rate.
>
> One river in Iceland disappeared entirely as a new river of liquid rock, steaming with poisonous gases, eventually filled and overflowed the six-hundred-foot-deep riverbed, creating a fifteen-mile-wide delta in the coastal lowlands. On July 29 a second eruption replaced yet another river. — — —-
>
> Ash obliterated the summer sun, and a similar noxious blue cloud spread over Iceland, eventually reaching as far as North Africa. Livestock began to sicken, the hides rotting from their bodies. Soon humans developed boils and deformities on their bodies; their hair began to fall out, their eyes stung, and their gums swelled.
>
> In the infamous "Haze Famine" that followed, trees, grasses, crops, and wild life withered and died, while fish disappeared from the poisoned coastal waters. As starvation set in, horses were seen eating each other, and people resorted to chewing on rope or the raw hides of animals for nourishment.
>
> Now even the horses are practicing cannibalism. [13]

These symptoms closely resemble the plagues of Egypt, including persistent darkness. Day turned into night. It follows that they must have had a similar cause. It came from the skies. Poisonous gases and dust entered the atmosphere, gases that killed fish and sickened livestock, and caused hair to fall out.

A volcanic explosion did take place at the time of the exodus. The island of Crete was the home of the Minoan civilization. A great catastrophe occurred at the close of the Middle Minoan II; Knossos was virtually destroyed. North of Crete is the island Thera, a large volcano. Around 1500 B.C. the top of this volcano blew off, leaving a huge caldera. In an explosion, worse than Krakatoa, fifteen cubic miles of rock was hurled into the stratosphere. Volcanic ash obliterated sunlight, a tremendous tsunami wave flooded coastal lands around the Mediterranean. Superheated gases created deadly fire storms. Whole populations were decimated in a great cataclysm.

This happened at the end of the Egyptian Middle Kingdom, and coincided with the exodus. The phenomena that accompanied the volcanic eruption of Mount Skaptar could have easily been duplicated in the explosion of Thera. Many though not all of the plagues described by scripture and Ipuwer fit a volcanic eruption. The darkness, ash and stones falling from the sky, and poisonous gasses speak of volcanic activity. Water turning into blood and a hurricane lasting a week is another matter. Nor was it a strictly local phenomenon. It was not limited to the Mediterranean, there are worldwide reports of darkness and floods and exploding volcanoes. The Indus valley was ruined, lake dwellings in Europe devastated. We find much the same in ancient Egypt in the physical devastation of the plagues that followed. Meanwhile both man and animal were tortured by deadly enemies, flies and disease.

Flies

It makes sense that the plague which followed would involve flies and pestilence. Considering the unsanitary conditions with dead fish, frogs, filthy water and an appalling stench, flies were bound to proliferate, and they did. The charged atmosphere and a near-perfect breeding ground provided ideal conditions for insects to germinate.

> Then the Lord said to Moses, "Get up early in the morning and confront Pharaoh as he goes to the water and say to him, 'This is what the Lord says: Let my people go, so that they may worship me. If you do not let my people go, I will send swarms of flies on you and your officials, on your people and into your houses. The houses of the Egyptians will be full of flies, and even the ground where they are."
>
> Exodus 8:20, 21

The blood sucking dog fly (so identified by the Septuagint), always was a problem in Egypt. It caused blindness. The fly Ichneuman was considered the manifestation of the god Uatchit. It lays its eggs on living things for the larvae to feed, causing infectious diseases. Flies were quite common, but this was a catastrophe; they came in swarms so bad that the pharaoh could not stand it anymore. He promised to let the Israelites travel some distance, but once the plague was gone, he again changed his mind. But insects such as flies and mosquitoes cause pestilence, and Ipuwer, as we have seen, reported just that: "Pestilence is throughout the land." (2.10) There was a miraculous element; Goshen, where the Israelites lived, was not affected.

Livestock

Horses and cattle were important to the Egyptians. They worshiped the Apis bull, and to a large extent depended on cattle for their livelihood. Horses, bulls and mules were the engines of industry, and the engine died.

> Then the Lord said to Moses, "Go to Pharaoh and say to him, 'This is what the Lord the God the Hebrews says, 'Let my people

go, so that they may worship me.' If you refuse to let them go and continue to hold them back, the hand of the Lord will bring a terrible plague on your livestock in the field - on your horses and donkeys and camels and on your cattle and sheep and goats. But the Lord will make a distinction between the livestock of Israel and that of Egypt, so that no animal belonging to the Israelites will die.'"
The Lord set a time and said, "Tomorrow the Lord will do this in the land." And the next day the Lord did it. All the livestock of the Egyptians died, but not one animal belonging to the Israelites died.

Exodus 9:1-6

Obviously not all animals were wiped out, rather animals of all kinds died. It made cultivation of the land and transportation impossible. The result was famine. Ipuwer reports that the population was starving. In the light of this plague and what followed, it is quite evident that food supplies were cut off. Worse, political and economic instability made men fear for the future. Why sow when someone else would reap?

> -the land is full of confederates, and a man goes out to plough with his shield. Indeed, the plunderer [...] is everywhere, and the servant takes what he finds. Indeed, the Nile overflows, yet none plough for it. Everyone says, "We do not know what will happen through the land." 1.10

This plague took dead aim at the sacred cow, the Apis bull, associated with the god Ptah. Throughout Egypt, the cow and the bull were worshiped. It becomes quite understandable why the temple cult of the Hebrews would be distasteful to the Egyptians. Bulls were of great importance in Israel as well, only they were objects of sacrifice rather than worship. Their blood was sprinkled over sacred vessels, something the Egyptians could never tolerate. These animals represented deity, and now they died of killer diseases.

Another deity whose worship would have been affected by the impact of this plague was Hathor, the goddess of love, beauty and joy represented by the cow. The worship of this deity was centered mainly in the city of Denderah although its popularity is witnessed by representations both in upper and lower Egypt. [14]

It was an infectious disease and fatal, and for this reason it is believed that it probably was anthrax. Anthrax mostly affects cattle, and is sometimes transmitted to man. Important, considering the plague that followed. It can cause boils or, if anthrax spores are inhaled, can result in lung inflammation. It can even be intestinal, if contaminated meat is improperly cooked. Any of these could have been involved in the plague of boils that affected humans.

Boils

As we have seen, in the haze famine of 1783 animals and humans alike developed skin sores. Something of the kind happened to Egypt.

> Then the Lord said to Moses and Aaron, "Take handfuls of soot from a furnace and have Moses toss it into the air in the presence of Pharaoh. It will become fine dust over the whole land of Egypt, and festering boils will break out on men and animals throughout the land."
> So they took soot from a furnace and stood before Pharaoh. Moses tossed it into the air, and festering boils broke out on men and animals. The magicians could not stand before Moses because of the boils that were on them and on the Egyptians. But the Lord hardened Pharaoh's heart and he would not listen to Moses and Aaron, just as the Lord had said to Moses.
> Exodus 9:8-12

There is a certain irony. The soot came from furnaces that provided the bricks, used in building Pi-Thom and Ramesse, cities built with Hebrew slave labor. The plague fits a pattern of pollution and unsanitary conditions. The dust that changed water into blood became soot that irritated the skin and darkened the skies. Obviously the Egyptians were unable to bathe in the foul water, and so they became dirty, conditions prevalent in war or natural calamities. As a result they developed skin diseases. They were covered with boils, and it does not say that they were healed, least of all by Egyptian deities.

> This plague, like previous ones, most assuredly had theological implications for the Egyptians. While it did not bring death, it was serious and painful enough to cause many to seek relief from many of the Egyptian deities charged with the responsibility of healing. Serapis was one such deity. One is also reminded of Imhotep, the god of medicine and the guardian of healing and sciences. The inability of these gods to act in behalf of the Egyptian surely must have led to deep despair and frustration.[15]

In the wake of the Second World War, the liberated people of Europe suffered skin diseases. There was no soap, no hot water, certainly no showers, and so they developed eczema or dermatitis, a skin disease. It is caused by irritants such as dirt, acids or alkali. The Egyptians suffered just as much, if not more. In the prevailing unsanitary conditions and the irritating dust that fell from the sky, they developed boils and eczema. On top of that, they may have suffered anthrax as well, inherited from their cattle. Worse was to come, and in keeping with previous plagues, wrath poured down from heaven. It involved a fire storm.

Hail

Following a pattern of intensifying plagues, wrath poured down from heaven. Gravel, mixed with burning gases roared down from on high. It was worse than anything that came before. An appalling hail of stones - meteorites - "with fire attached," according to a more literal translation, rained ruin. However, the Egyptians had ample warning. Moses cautioned pharaoh that hail would fall all over Egypt and kill any man and cattle out in the field.

> Those officials of Pharaoh who feared the word of the Lord hurried to bring their slaves and their livestock inside. But those who ignored the word of the Lord left their slaves and livestock in the field.
> Then the Lord said to Moses, "Stretch out your hand toward the sky so that hail will fall all over Egypt - on men and animals and on everything growing in the fields of Egypt." When Moses stretched out his staff toward the sky, the Lord sent thunder and hail, and lightning flashed down to the ground. So the Lord rained hail on the land of Egypt; hail fell and lightning flashed back and forth. It was the worst storm in all the land of Egypt since it had become a nation. Throughout Egypt hail struck everything in the fields - both men and animals; it beat down everything growing in the fields and stripped every tree. The only place it did not hail was the land of Goshen, where the Israelites lived.
>
> Exodus 9:22-26

This was no ordinary lightning storm, not even an extraordinary one. No electrical storm covers a whole nation, and the hail, "stones of barad," was not ice but gravel - meteorites. Inflammable gases and naphtha (petroleum or gasoline) mingled with the stones, burst into flames and burned whatever was left standing. It was not necessarily organic petroleum; it could have been produced in the depth of space. Methane is abundant in the solar system, and its derivatives interacting with hydrocarbons could produce petroleum. It follows that the atmosphere must have been saturated with hydrocarbons, most noticeably in a heavy cloud cover. Something of the kind happened when Egypt was struck by "hail and fire streaming down to the ground."[16]

Oil and its derivatives, such as petroleum, are lighter than water and will float on its surface. Rabbinical tradition speaks of water burning at the plagues of Egypt. The apocryphal Book of Wisdom, which dates from about 100 B.C., retains the memory of burning water during the plague of hail.

> For the wicked who refused to know you
> were punished by the might of your arm,
> pursued by unwonted rain and hailstorms
> and unremitting downpours
> and consumed by fire.
> For against all expectation,
> in water which quenches anything,
> the fire grew more active,
> for the universe fights on behalf of the just.
> For now the flame was tempered
> so that the beasts might not be burnt up
> that were sent upon the wicked,
> but that they might see and know
> they were struck by the judgment of God.
> For again, even in the water,
> fire blazed beyond its strength
> so as to consume the produce of the land.
> Wisdom 16:16-19 (NASB)

Jewish tradition recalls hailstones mixed with fire, and the devastating effect it had not only on the land, but on the Egyptians as well.

> As a rule, fire and water are elements at war with each other, but in the hailstones that smote the land of Egypt they were reconciled. A fire rested in the hailstones as the burning wick swims in the oil of a lamp; the surrounding fluid cannot extinguish the flame. The Egyptians were smitten either by the hail or by the fire. In the one case as the other their flesh was seared, and the bodies of the many that were slain by the hail were consumed by the fire.[17]

It was by far the worst plague. Trees were stripped bare, animals in the fields were killed and grain burned. The land was in pitiful condition. It is reflected in Ipuwer's complaints. He speaks of fire burning buildings and trees being stripped.

> Indeed, gates, columns and walls are burnt up, while the [hall] of the palace stands firm and endures.
> Behold, the fire has gone up on high, and its burning goes forth against the enemies of the land. 7.1
> Indeed / that has perished which yesterday was seen, and the land is left over to its weakness like the cutting of flax. 4.1 / 5.10
> Indeed, trees are felled and branches are stripped off. 4.10
> Indeed, everywhere barley has perished and men are stripped of clothes, [spice], and oil; everyone says: "There is none." The storehouse is empty and its keeper is stretched on the ground; a happy state of affairs! 6.1
> Indeed, all animals, their hearts weep; cattle moan because of the state of the land. 5.5
> Behold, cattle stray and there is none to collect them, but everyone fetches for himself those that are branded with his name. 9.1

Gardiner explains that the "fire" was not started by men but fell from the sky, and that it meant something disastrous. "That has perished which yesterday was seen" means it perished overnight. The hail stripped trees bare and destroyed the barley crop. Cattle in the field were killed or got lost. Scripture goes on to say that the flax and barley were destroyed, but the wheat and spelt were not.

> The only crop destroyed during this plague were those of the flax and barley which indicates that this occurred late in January or early in February. Barley was a very important crop to the Egyptians. Flax was widely cultivated, especially since the Egyptians did not like woolen materials, which were worn by the nomads. The flax ripened about the same time as barley and was usually cut in the month of March. Wheat harvest was approximately one month later in the early part of April. Verse 32 indicates that the wheat and the "rye" (better translated "spelt") were not harmed by this plague even though they were probably

growing at the time. Spelt is an inferior kind of wheat ordinarily raised in Egypt as an after crop.[18]

It must have been galling for the pharaoh to see officials of his own court listen to Moses rather than to him, Ra's manifestation on earth. His power was waning. Maybe that is why, despite repeated disasters, he still refused to listen. As a result the land was devastated even worse. The charged atmosphere made insects breed at an unprecedented rate. They came from the depth of Africa.

Locusts

Following all these calamities Moses warned the pharaoh that locusts would come; they would cover the ground and enter houses, and eat everything that was left. This time pharaoh allowed a limited number of Hebrews to go; only the very young and very old. Moses said, "No deal," and the pharaoh drove them from his presence.

> So Moses stretched out his staff over Egypt, and the LORD made an east wind blow across the land all that day and all that night. By morning the wind had brought the locusts; they invaded all Egypt and settled down in every area of the country in great numbers. Never before had there been such a plague of locusts, nor will there ever be again. They covered all the ground until it was black. They devoured all that was left after the hail - everything growing in the fields and the fruit on the trees. Nothing green remained on tree or plant in all the land of Egypt.
> Exodus 10:13-15

The Egyptians feared the locust, so much so that they worshiped the locust god. To this day, locusts are the scourge of Africa. Untold millions of these voracious insects appear in hordes so great that they darken the sky. Trees and vegetation are stripped bare; nothing is left in their wake. This dwarfed everything that came before or since. Maybe insects bred feverishly in the electrically charged atmosphere;

maybe their natural enemies did not keep them in check. At any rate, the land was stripped bare; there was nothing left to eat, including barley. Ipuwer repeatedly mentioned starvation. The Egyptians were desperate.

> Indeed, [men eat] herbage and wash (it) down with water; neither fruit nor herbage can be found (for) the birds, and [. . . .] is taken away from the mouth of the pig. No face is bright which you have (...) [for] me through hunger. Indeed, everywhere barley has perished and men are stripped of clothes, [spices] and oil; everyone says: "There is none." The storehouse is empty and its keeper is stretched on the ground, a happy state of affairs! 6.0

The starving population literally ate pig food; Ipuwer's laments are replete with references to hunger, a peasant revolt, mobs storming food supplies and taking it from the rich. It fits the picture of anarchy following a national calamity. It involved a natural disaster with references to darkness and a super storm.

Darkness

Of all the gods of Egypt, Ra was the most prevalent. Ra was the sun god, and the pharaoh was the deity personified. The sun god disappeared; it was removed from the sky. This was no ordinary darkness. It was pitch black; no one was able to see anything at all. Ra failed Egypt altogether.

> Then the LORD said to Moses, "Stretch out your hand toward the sky so that darkness will spread over Egypt-darkness that can be felt." So Moses stretched out his hand toward the sky, and total darkness covered all Egypt for three days. No one could see anyone else or leave his place for three days. Yet all the Israelites had light in the places where they lived.
>
> Exodus 10:21-24

Israel and Egypt

The exodus narrative leaves the impression as if it merely became very dark, but numerous extra-scriptural sources, both Jewish and Egyptian, make it clear that much more was involved. They mention a cinder storm that blotted out all light. This lasted at least a week. The first few days there was still some light, but as the gale became a roaring hurricane all light was extinguished. In the pitch blackness, the terrified Egyptians were unable to leave their homes or even to move. As the storm let up, a dim light eventually dawned. As we will see, there are several Egyptian references to just such an event. Jewish legend speaks of it as well.

> The last plague but one, like those which had preceded it, endured seven days. All the time the land was enveloped in darkness, only it was not always of the same degree of density. During the first three days, it was not so thick but that the Egyptians could change their posture when they desired to do so. — — On the fourth, fifth and sixth day, the darkness was so dense that they could not stir from their place. They either sat the whole time, or stood; as they were at the beginning so they remained until the end. The last day of darkness overtook the Egyptians, not in their own land, but at the Red Sea on their pursuit of Israel.
>
> The darkness was of such a nature that it could not be dispelled by artificial means. The light of the fire kindled for household uses was either extinguished by the violence of the storm, or else it was made invisible and swallowed up in the density of the darkness. — — None were able to speak or to hear, nor could anyone venture to take food, but they lay themselves down in quiet and hunger, their outward senses in a trance. [19]

Of course we wonder, what caused this storm of darkness in the first place? It could have been a cosmic event. If the earth in the presence of a planetary body gradually overturned, the earth would move under the atmosphere, and great windstorms would result. The evidence is obviously circumstantial, but a case can be made. Worldwide there are reports of a very long night, and in other places to an equally long day. The darkness involved hurricane force winds that lasted nearly a week. And although a gloomy light eventually penetrated, a dark pall remained for decades. It was under these dramatic circumstances that Israel prepared to leave Egypt, the house of bondage. But before the final devastating plague struck, God instituted the Passover.

The Passover

Considering the circumstances, the institution of the Passover is remarkable for its detailed instructions. It must have been a very important matter indeed to establish a feast such as this. It consists out of two parts: the initial ritual such as dictated by the need of the moment, and additional instructions for future celebrations. The Hebrews were to choose a male lamb, keep it four days for inspection, and then slaughter it. They were to take the blood of the lamb and brush it on the lintel and the sides of the door frame. In other words, they made the sign of a cross. They were to eat the meat roasted over a fire, along with bitter herbs, commemorating bitter years of slavery, and unleavened bread. Any leftovers must be burned. They were to eat it in haste, ready to go. That night the Lord would judge Egypt, but the angel of death would "pass over" any house with the blood of the lamb.

> On that same night I will pass through Egypt and strike down every firstborn - both man and animals - and I will bring judgment on all the gods of Egypt; I am the LORD. The blood will be a sign for you on the houses where you are; and when I see the blood, I will pass over you. No destructive plague will touch you when I strike Egypt.
>
> Exodus 12:12, 13

Obviously there was an object lesson. God was telling them something: Israel was saved by the blood of the lamb. This was established in the lasting ordinance of the Passover feast. Prominent is the prohibition of any yeast whatsoever, including bread. Only unleavened bread (crackers) was to be used, which Jews do to this day. In retrospect we can see why. The lamb was symbolic of the great sacrifice, accomplished by Christ, the Lamb of God, on the cross. His was the true and all-sufficient payment that satisfied the wrath of God. Those covered with his blood escape damnation. When the angel of death comes, will he find the blood of the lamb on the door post of your life? No leaven was allowed; leaven stands for the sin that permeates human life.

What makes it altogether interesting is the timing. The Passover preceded the deliverance of slavery and entrance into the Promised Land. It was prophetic of the real deliverance from the slavery of sin and God's wrath, and entrance into God's Promised Land. There is nothing mystical about these things; they are real, just as real as the judgment that overcame Egypt, and it was disastrous.

The Firstborn

The night the Angel of the Lord smote the houses of the Egyptians, the "firstborn" of the Egyptians died. That sounds incredible, but it may involve a play on words. In an attempt to rationalize the exodus account, Velikovsky reasoned that *bkhor* "first-born," is a corruption of *bchor*, meaning "chosen." These two words often are mentioned together, for instance in Psalm 104:36.

> Then he struck down all the firstborn (bkhor)
> the first fruit (bchor) of all their manhood.

The implication is that the flower of Egypt was killed, including the firstborn. It could never be a corruption of the text, as Velikovsky supposed. The scriptures simply do not allow for that. Not only does it explicitly mention specific cases of firstborn Egyptians, the language is in many cases very similar to that, used by Ipuwer.

> At midnight the LORD struck down all the firstborn in Egypt, from the firstborn of Pharaoh, who sat on the throne, to the firstborn of the prisoner who was in the dungeon, and the firstborn of all the livestock as well. Pharaoh and all his officials and all the Egyptians got up during the night, and there was loud wailing in Egypt, for there was not a house without someone dead. Exodus 12:29, 30

Scripture always proclaims God the ultimate sovereign, and for this reason all events are said to be his doing. However, it is also abundantly clear that he ordains not merely the end, but also the means to achieve that end. The agency involved in the destruction of Egypt was an earthquake. The early church fathers, who had access to ancient manuscripts, reported as much. Jerome wrote, "In the night in which the exodus took place, all the temples of Egypt were destroyed either by an earth shock or by the thunderbolt."

Eusebius spoke of "hail and earthquake by night," and said that the houses collapsed, and most of the temples.[20] This is implied in Exodus 12:12, "I will bring judgment on all the gods of Egypt, I am the Lord." Queen Hapshetsut said the temple of the goddess Ques was swallowed up by the earth. Just how deadly serious this threat really was, is related by none less than Ipuwer. His laments confirm the exodus account, extreme though it may seem. They also report phenomena, consistent with a severe earthquake.

> Indeed, gates, columns and [walls] are burnt up, while the [hall] of the palace stands firm and endures.
> Indeed, the ship of [the southerners] has broken up; towns are destroyed and Upper Egypt has become an empty waste. 2.10
> Indeed men are few, and he who places his brother in the ground is everywhere. 2.10
> Indeed, laughter has perished and is [no longer] made; it is groaning that is throughout the land, mingled with complaints. 3.10

> Indeed, the children of princes are dashed against walls, and the children of the neck (in arms) are laid out on the high ground. 4.1
> Indeed, those who were in the place of embalmment are laid out on the high ground, and the secrets of the embalmers [are thrown down because of It.] 4.1
> — — the residence is thrown down in a moment. 7.1
> Behold, Egypt is fallen to / pouring of water, and he who poured water on the ground has carried of the strong man in misery. 7.3

We are dealing with two different accounts - from different perspectives, of the same events. Even the wording is the same. They speak of houses collapsing, people dying, and coffins being pushed out of the ground in a violent earthquake. This is known to have happened in modern times. When the Israelites left Egypt they took the bones of Joseph along. According to rabbinical sources the coffin of Joseph was thrown out of its grave. Ipuwer said that the embalmed dead were removed from their graves. The collapsed palaces, temples and buildings all indicate a violent earthquake. Ipuwer's laments refer to loud noises (*years of noise*), associated with booming readjustments of strata, far below the surface of the earth.

> Would that there were an end of men, without conception, / without birth! Then would the land be quiet from noise and tumult be no more. 5.10/6.1
> The land has not fallen [. . .] the statues are burned and their tombs destroyed
> [. . .] he sees the day of [. . .] . He who could not make for himself <. . .> between sky and ground is afraid of everybody. —-
> Authority, knowledge, and truth are with you, yet confusion is what you set throughout the land, also the noise of tumult. 12.10

Hidden in Ipuwer's laments are references to Egyptian gods that bewail the hail of fiery stones, the roaring darkness and the shaken earth. It involves a trio of deities, Shu and his offspring, Geb and Nut, gods of earth and sky. Nut, the vault of heaven, was the daughter of the air god Shu. She is portrayed as standing on hands and feet in a semi circle, supported by Shu, who separated Nut from the earth god Geb. Nut was believed to be the mother of the gods Isis, Osiris, Nephths and Set, representing fertile and barren couples. The latter appear to be largely astral deities. The three related gods obviously were destroyed with their temples, worthy victims of Yahweh the God of Israel who said, "I will judge the gods of Egypt."

Invasion

What the scriptures do not refer to, at least not here, is something repeatedly mentioned by Ipuwer: Egypt was invaded by Bedouins. Arabs walked in and took over. To the extent that we are able to reconstruct Ipuwer's times, an amazing picture emerges. Not only was Egypt devastated by a great disaster that took innumerable lives, the nation was invaded by hordes of ruthless Arabs, and the Egyptians were unable to do a thing about it. Ipuwer's laments echo a sad refrain. Egypt lost its sovereignty.

> [the tribes of the desert] have become Egyptians everywhere. 1.5
> Indeed, the desert is throughout the land, the nomes are laid waste, and barbarians from abroad have come to Egypt.
> Indeed, men arrive […] and indeed, there are no Egyptians anywhere. 3.1
> Today [he who is afraid] … a myriad of people; .. the statues are burned and their tombs destroyed. 12.5.10
> .. in their midst like Asiatics […] Men<..> the [state] thereof; they have come to an end of themselves; none can be found to stand up and protect themselves.
> What has come to pass through it is informing the Asiatics of the state of the land; all the desert folk are possessed with the fear of it. 14.1, 15.1

Egypt's worst fears came true. Asiatics (Arabs) discovered the terrible plight of the once-powerful nation. They walked in and took over without a fight, for the simple reason that Egypt had no army. There were not enough Egyptians left to put up a defense. In the anarchy that followed, serfs used the opportunity to loot public places. Mobs rifled through court records and stole food supplies.

> Indeed, public offices are opened and their inventories are taken away; the serf has become an owner of serfs.
> Indeed, [scribes] are killed and their writings are taken away. Woe is me because of the misery of the time!
> Indeed, the writings of the scribes of the [cadastre] are destroyed, and the corn of Egypt is common property.
> Indeed, the laws / of the council chamber are thrown out; indeed men walk on them in the public places, and poor men break them up in the streets.
> Indeed, the great council-chamber is a popular resort, and poor men come and go in the Great Mansions. 6.5, 6.10

That could happen only after civil authority had broken down. No government allows the public to rob city hall. The land was in a state of anarchy. The poor walked into the ruins that once were government buildings and helped themselves to deeds of property. It was literally a land where the servant reigned. Nobodies suddenly lived in mansions, the wives of nobility in want. Class distinction disappeared, and with it the cement that made a once-great nation what it was. That was the enemy within. And then there was a hidden enemy, disease.

Pandemic

In the aftermath of the plagues, Ipuwer gave an eye witness account of prevailing conditions. He must have written his laments within months of the exodus. The picture he penned depicts a scene of murder, mayhem and appalling desolation. Innumerable people died. That makes us wonder about demographics: how was the population of Egypt affected? A superficial reading of scripture leaves the impression that the firstborn alone died, but that otherwise the Egyptians escaped rather unharmed.

That obviously is an erroneous notion, even in the light of the biblical account. As a result of the last plague, "there was not a house without someone dead." The Egyptians begged the Hebrews to leave. "'For otherwise,' they said, 'we will all die'" (Ex 12:30, 33). The implication is that more than the firstborn died. As we have seen, Velikovsky thought "firstborn" was a corruption of "first fruit," but it is more complicated than that. A great many people died, "the flower of Egypt." Josephus said that many Egyptians died of the diseases that accompanied the plagues.

Ipuwer's laments leave no doubt that many Egyptians perished; only a few men were left. Nor were the end of the plagues and the departure of Israel the final chapter in Egypt's suffering. In the anarchy that followed, gangs murdered hapless travelers and farmers. Far worse was the medical state of the land; epidemics decimated the population. Conditions were ripe for communicable diseases to wreak havoc.

All accounts indicate that it was dark; the sun was not visible, so it must have been much colder than usual. With food in short supply and cold prevailing, the populace was likely to stay close together in search of food and fuel. There is safety in numbers. There is however a grave danger as well, lack of hygiene. The streams were polluted and grime was everywhere, which created ideal conditions for contagious diseases. Ipuwer said outright that epidemics were rife, and that people died left and right, long after the final plague.

> Indeed, [hearts] are violent, pestilence is throughout the land, blood is everywhere, death is not lacking — —-.
> Indeed, many dead are buried in the river; the stream is a sepulcher and the place of embalmment has become a stream. 2.5
> Indeed men are few, and he who places his brother in the ground is everywhere. 2.10
> Indeed, men arrive [. . . .] and indeed, there are no Egyptians anywhere. 3.1

People died of thirst and they drank from the river in the face of crocodiles. Rivers and streams were contaminated by dead bodies. Egypt could have been struck by a plethora of diseases: typhus, anthrax, smallpox and so on. The most likely disease however is cholera. It occurs when people share the same water for bathing, drinking and cooking, and conditions are unsanitary, which they obviously were

> The important fact about its spread is that it is passed out in the faeces and is transmitted by contamination, contamination of material entering the human body by mouth, that is contamination particularly of water but also of uncooked food by means of dirty handling or by flies and by means of contaminated linen and clothing. It is an infection of man only and so is spread along this line of communication.[21]

The Nile was a virtual sewer, water supplies were contaminated, flies were everywhere, food was in short supply and the Egyptians lived in filth, all of which rendered them susceptible to diseases. Historically epidemics have taken a terrible toll. The Justinian plague of A.D. 542 killed half the Mediterranean population. In the black death of 1348/50, a third of all Europeans died. In the thirty-year war, half the population of Germany perished. More people died of cholera than of bullets. Between the natural disaster that destroyed Egypt and the pandemic that followed, easily half of all the Egyptians could have perished. Archaeological digs at Tell el-Dab'a (Avaris) confirm that many Egyptians died at that exact time. Avaris had a mixed population of Egyptians and "Asiatics," believed to have come from Palestine. The Palestinians in all likelihood were Hebrews.

> The initial expansion of Tell el-Dah'a was checked temporarily by an epidemic. In several parts of the site, Bietak has found large communal graves in which many bodies were placed, without any discernible ceremony. Thereafter from stra-

tum F onwards, the patterns of both settlements and cemeteries suggest a less egalitarian society than before. — — —

At this point in the city's history, its identification with the textually attested Hyksos Capitol of Avaris becomes clear. [22]

The evidence indicates that the "Asiatics" (Hebrews) left in a hurry, suddenly, and leaving all their tools and belongings behind. Upon their departure invaders came and took over. Bedouins always pressured Egypt, but this time they entered the doomed nation without a fight (the decimated Egyptians were in no shape to defend themselves) and they suppressed Egypt more than four centuries. The Egyptians to the end were unable to throw off their cruel yoke; the population never increased. Epidemics as a rule never disappear altogether; they keep coming back in different forms. The Bedouins were not affected, or at least not to the same extent because they were nomads. They were more mobile and did not settle. The Egyptians called them Hyksos, King-Shepherds.

The Hyksos

Egyptian records indicate that following the disaster, Asiatic hordes swept in from the gloom of the desert. They were utterly cruel and suppressed the Egyptians for centuries to come. Its population depleted and racked by disease and anarchy, its army gone, Egypt was unable to withstand their onslaught. Josephus, quoting the Egyptian historian Manetho, said Egypt was overrun by invaders from the east.

> In the reign of Tutimaios, for what cause I know not, a blast of God smote us, and unexpectedly from the regions of the east invaders of obscure race marched in confidence of victory against our land. By main force they easily seized it without striking a blow. Having overpowered the rulers of the land, they then burned our cities ruthlessly, razed to the ground the temples of the gods, and treated all the natives with a cruel hostility, mas-

sacring some and leading into slavery the wives and children of others. Finally they appointed as king one of their number whose name was Salitis. He had his seat in Memphis, levying tribute from Upper and Lower Egypt, and always leaving garrisons behind in the most advantageous places. —— In the Sethroite nome he found a city very favorable situated on the east of the Bubastite branch of the Nile, and called Avaris after an ancient religious tradition. This place he rebuilt and fortified with massive walls. —— Their race as a whole was called Hyksos, that is "King Shepherds"; for *hyk* in the sacred language means "king" and *sos* in common speech is "shepherd."[23]

That accounts for the absence of Egypt in the days of the judges, which lasted more than four hundred years. Egypt was occupied by the Hyksos rulers who supposedly ruled four centuries earlier. The fall of the Middle Kingdom was identical with that of the Old Kingdom; in fact, they were the same. Breasted reports that the Old Kingdom came to an end in an orgy of destruction. Temples were pillaged and violated, mortuary monuments destroyed, works of art systematically vandalized. The invaders shattered splendid granite statues of kings, all of which agrees with Manetho's report. Ipuwer said as much. The end of the Old and Middle Kingdoms were too much alike to be coincidence, it was the same kingdom.

One wonders, how could the Hyksos walk into Egypt, confident of victory and take over? Manetho said it happened following "a blast of God," a natural disaster. The answer is there for all to see. Egypt was defenseless. The army perished to a man, including infantry and cavalry, with no reserves to defend home territory. The pharaoh and all his officers were dead. Then the Bedouins came. Josephus said that the Hyksos, according to some, were Arabs. Gardiner made an interesting observation.

> The word Hyksos undoubtedly derives from the expression *hyk-khase*, 'chieftain of a foreign hill-country' which from the Middle Kingdom onwards was used to designate Bedouin

Sheiks. Scarabs bearing this title, but with the word for 'countries' in the plural, are found with several undoubted Hyksos kings — —. It is important to observe, however, that the term refers to the rulers alone, and not, as Josephus thought, to the entire race.[24]

The Hyksos, in other words were Bedouin Sheiks. They were Arabs, not Palestinians. They became the Hyksos kings who supplanted the Egyptian pharaohs. Following the departure of Israel, a blanket of silence falls over Egypt. The scriptures mention no pharaoh, no Egyptian incursion, not even a hint of trade. Egypt vanishes from the pages of holy writ until the days of the Hebrew kings, 450 years later. The scriptures assume throughout that the Egyptians disappeared from the scene, and were of no consequence. So Israel left at the beginning of the Second Intermediate Period. They left after the collapse of the Thirteenth Dynasty, shortly before the rule of the Hyksos pharaohs. How they got away is nothing short of miraculous, and it sealed the doom of Egypt.

The Strait of Tiran

When the Israelites left Egypt they did not, as one would expect, head straight for Canaan, rather they were ordered to move south into the Sinai Peninsula. They skirted the Gulf of Suez and marched toward the south, bypassing military bases, rounded the base of the peninsula and moved back toward the north (Ex 14:1) on the eastern side near the Strait of Tiran, toward the Gulf of Aqaba.

The Egyptians at first obviously did not pay much attention to the fleeing slaves. They had problems of their own, and for all they knew the Hebrews merely traveled a few days toward the east to sacrifice to their God. But when scouts looked in the east for their slaves, they were nowhere to be found. Then word came that they had moved into the Sinai instead. The Sinai? They were trapped. After them!

It must have taken at least a week before the pharaoh learned about it. Then there were military logistics. You cannot assemble an

Israel and Egypt

army overnight. With communications broken down it must have taken at least another week before the pharaoh was able to muster cavalry, ten thousand chariots, and infantry, sixty thousand foot soldiers. Keep in mind that darkness prevailed and that no stars were visible for orientation on their march. But at last he got his army moving after his indispensable slaves.

Israel was at least two weeks ahead, and was able to travel any time because of the light-giving cloud. Scripture reports that the Egyptians caught up with them at Pi-hahiroth. Where was that, and where was the Sea of Passage? The sea is called the Red Sea. The Hebrew word is usually read Yam Suph, meaning *Sea of Reeds*. However, it can also be read Yam Soph, meaning *Sea of Lands End*.

Scripture leaves no doubt about the identity of Yam Soph: "King Solomon also built ships in Ezion Geber, which is near Elath in Edom, on the shore of the Red Sea (Yam Soph)." (1 Kings 9:26) Elath is on the shore of the Gulf of Aqaba. Pi-hahiroth is believed to mean two parting canals or waters. That could have been the Strait of Tiran, which connects the Gulf of Aqaba with the Red Sea.

The Egyptians caught up with Israel at Pi-hahiroth, north of modern day Sharm al Sheikh. When the fleeing slaves found themselves blocked by mountains to the west and north and the Egyptian army to the south, they cried out in terror. The cloud moved south where it enveloped the Egyptians in darkness, but it provided light for Israel. Then Moses stretched his staff over the Strait of Tiran; the waters parted and an underwater land bridge appeared. It is a submarine passage, a few feet below sea level, that connects the Sinai Peninsula with Saudi Arabia, ten miles away. It is still there, a string of reefs, popular with divers.

There was no need for Israel to clamber down a steep slope to the sea bottom and up again on the other side. The Gulf of Aqaba is two thousand feet deep - except at this exact spot. Isaiah said God provided a road through the sea (Isa 51:10). The surface of this passage is flat rock, wide enough for a whole nation to escape, and smooth enough to make travel easy. The pharaoh evidently thought so too, for he ordered his army to follow his escaping slaves. Alas, he walked right into a trap. The memory of the passage survived in the Psalms.

> Come and see what God has done,
> how awesome his works in man's behalf!
> He turned the sea into dry land,
> they passed through the waters on foot.
> You brought us into prison
> and laid burdens on our backs.
> You led men ride over our heads,
> we went through fire and water,
> but you brought us to a place of abundance.
>
> Psalm 66:5, 6, 11, 12

The sea returned with a tremendous roar. The collapsing walls of water threw the trapped Egyptians high into the air, over the heads of the astounded Hebrews. The Jewish historian Josephus, too, mentions darkness and great lightning. Israel went not only through water, but also through fire. David recounted similar experiences. A traumatic event like that is forever etched into the memory of a people. The story was passed on from father to son, and the psalmist cast it in poetic mold.

> The earth trembled and quaked
> and the foundations of the mountains shook,
> they trembled because he was angry.
> Smoke rose from his nostrils,
> consuming fire came from his mouth,
> burning coals blazed out of it.
> He parted the heavens and came down,
> dark clouds were under his feet.
> He mounted the cherubim and flew;
> he soared on the wings of the wind.
> He made darkness his covering,
> his canopy around him -

the dark rain clouds of the sky.
Out of the brightness of his presence clouds advanced,
with hailstones and bolts of lightning.
The Lord thundered from heaven,
the voice of the Most High resounded.
He shot his arrows and scattered the enemies,
great bolts of lightning and routed them.
The valleys of the sea were exposed
and the foundations of the earth laid bare
at your rebuke, O Lord,
at the blast of breath from your nostrils.

Psalm 18:7-15

This is anthropomorphic language; it ascribes physical attributes to God to make a point. As Israel crossed the Strait of Tiran, the bottom of the sea was rocked by earthquakes. A rain of meteorites blazed through the sky, deep darkness was lit up by great bolts of lightning, thunder roared with tremendous noise. Whatever the cause of these extraordinary events, the psalmist maintains it was all God's doing. It has all the marks of divine intervention. No way could mere coincidence account for the annihilation of the pharaoh and his army, while Israel escaped toward safety across a submarine road that just happened to be there. It certainly was more than a number of fortunate events.

The Naos

References to events surrounding the exodus appear in an obscure tale, found on a shrine dating from Ptolemaic times, written a thousand years after the fact. The text was translated by F.L. Griffith in 1890 in English, and by Georges Goyon in 1936 in French. Following Griffith's translation, this "naos," found in Al Arish, mentions the primeval god Ra, also called Atum, the creator, and his offspring Shu and Tefnut, the first couple, who produced Geb and Nut, the gods of earth and sky. [25]

A naos was a wooden box used for temple purposes that contained religious artifacts. It was the model for the Ark of the Covenant. They were made of stone as well, and often were inscribed with historical data. This particular shrine was made of stone. (When it was found it was used as a cattle trough.) The story is a magical tale, based upon actual facts. It deals with a king who died in some kind of terrible catastrophe that involved prolonged darkness and a tempest. His successor was ousted by Asiatic invaders.

"The majesty of Shu" invited the nine gods to accompany him to the eastern horizon to see his father Ra-Haharkhis (*Ra of the horizon*) and order a temple built. The plan is mentioned in detail, and the temple being finished, unwelcome invaders appeared.

> Then the children of the dragon Apep, the evil-doers [of Usheru?] and of the red country (*the desert*) came upon the road of At Nebes invading Egypt at nightfall …… now these evil-doers came from Eastern hills [upon] the roads of At Nebes.

At Nebes was the mythical mountain where the sun rose, and Apep was Apopi, the terrible demon-god who ruled over chaos and the night, the Hyksos Seth. The text then mentions the fortifications that had been built to stop Asiatic (Arab) invaders, but something evidently went badly wrong. The invaders came at time of darkness and the king, heroic though he may have been, was in trouble.

> Now it came to pass that the majesty of Shu obtained the whole land, none could stand before him, no other god was in the mouth of his soldiers? [but sickness came upon him?] ..... confusion seized the eyes? he made his chapel ....evil fell upon this land, a great disturbance in the palace, disturbed …. Those who were of the household of Shu.

"The majesty of Shu departed to heaven with his attendants." The king obviously faced a major crisis. The text mentions sickness and a cataclysm, so severe that the king and his attendants died. The implication is that they were killed. His son in the person of the god Seb (or Geb) was very much concerned with the wellbeing of his mother Tefnut who, it turned out, was in the palace.

> Then the majesty of [Geb met her] he found her in this place which is called Pekharti? (*Goyon: Pi-Kharoti*): he seized her by force: [the palace was in great affliction]. Shu had departed to heaven: there was no exit from the palace by the space of nine days. Now these [nine] days were in violence and tempest: none whether god (*royalty*) or man could see the face of his fellow.

It does not take a genius to see that this deals with the plague of darkness. A tempest roared in a prolonged pitch black night. Geb assumed the throne and 75 days later proceeded north. However he was in for an unpleasant surprise.

> Shu had flown up to heaven, the great chief of the plan at the head of his city?? The prince of the hills…came? He went not to Heliopolis: moreover? Certain Asiatics carried his scepter, called Degai, who live on what the gods abominate.

Now that the king was dead and the devastated land in a state of chaos, invaders overran the fortifications. "Prince of the hill" was the designation of a Bedouin Sheik. A Hyksos king, accompanied by Arabs who "carried his scepter," became the defacto ruler. "What the gods abominate" was their cattle: Egyptians despised shepherds, and the Hyksos were a shepherd people. Judging from the context, Geb returned to the temple.

> He discussed the history of this people with the gods who attended him [and they told him] all that happened when the majesty of Ra was in At Nebes, the conflicts of the King Tum in this locality, the valour of the majesty of Shu.

This is the only time the story mentions the actual name of a king. Tum, or Thoum, is a variant of Atum, the chief deity. It is reasonable to assume that "Shu" is the mythical name for King Tum. The Egyptians believed that the gods once reigned among men as kings. The gods reminded Geb of the great deeds of Shu after his coronation, when he placed the Uraeus, the serpent-crown, on his head. Geb decided to crown himself, with disastrous results.

> Then said the majesty of Geb I also [will place] her upon my head even as my father Shu did. Geb entered Per Aart (*a wig*) together with the gods who were with him: then he stretched forth his hand to take the case in which [Ankhet] was: the snake came forth and breathed its vapour upon the majesty of Geb, confounding him greatly: those who followed him fell dead: his majesty? Burned with this venom? His majesty proceeded to the north of At Nebes with this burning of the Ureaeus Hert Terp. (*Goyon: his face was burnt*).

The order of events obviously is confused. Geb was wounded, probably burned, and all his companions were killed. How it does not say, but the similarities with the fate of his father are significant. Many years later his Aart (wig) was taken to a great lake, also called a whirlpool to wash it, where it turned into a crocodile. Whirlpools are mentioned many times. They refer to the primeval deep where Atum created the world. The deity defeated the invaders.

> Now when the majesty of Ra Harmachis [fought] with the evil-doers in this pool, the place of the Whirlpool, the evil-doers prevailed not over his majesty. His majesty leapt into the so-called Place of the Whirlpool? His legs became those of a crocodile, his head that of a hawk with a bull's horn upon it: he smote the evil-doers in the Place of the Whirlpool? In the place of the Sycamore: the Aart of Geb also in its turn did after this sort.

Israel and Egypt

The majesty of Geb then returned before all the gods in his "castle of Ruling the Two Lands" in the Land of Henna, which Goyon translates as "Hy-Tayou." That was Itj-Tawy, the palace of the 12th and 13th Dynasty pharaohs. The "Land of Hennep" has been identified as the Fayoum, part of the biblical Goshen. Geb asked the council of gods for advice, and promised to return Egypt to its former glory.

This is hardly a primary source. The memories of a long-ago disaster were cast in a sort of mythical tale with gods cast in the roles of forgotten rulers. These gods, like Egypt, were at first defeated but triumphed in the end. The tale has a happy ending. The king of the period, identified as Tum or Thoum, was killed. His successor was severely wounded and forced to leave. Bedouin Sheiks overran Egypt and ruled instead. Goyon identifies them as the Hyksos.

It is necessary to treat this story at some length because Velikovsky unfortunately misled well meaning people into believing it establishes both the location of the Sea of Passage and the identity of the pharaoh. It does nothing of the kind. There is not even a hint of the pharaoh pursuing fleeing slaves.

There is however a connection. The meaning of *Pi-Kharoti* and the Hebrew *Pi-hahiroth* though obscure, is believed to be the same, that of two parting canals or waters. Unfortunately we do not have the liberty to fit details into preconceived assumptions, based upon scant evidence. We can read between the lines, but it says nowhere that the pharaoh died in the whirlpool; far from it. Ra was the victor, pharaoh not the victim. The story is all about Tum's successor, cast in the role of Geb, and his run-in with the Hyksos evil-doers. It is a mythical tale, many centuries removed from the events, that speaks of a natural disaster and an invasion of foreigners.

Pharaoh Djedneferre Dedumose

In the naos story the only royal name mentioned is Tum or Thoum. That being a version of the god Atum, several candidates qualify. However, we should be able to identify the pharaoh who ran afoul on Moses and perished in the Strait of Tiran. The exodus occurred after the Middle Kingdom, in the final days of the Thirteenth Dynasty at the beginning of the Second Intermediate Period. Ipuwer wrote his laments in the literary style of the Middle Kingdom. The constant repetition of phrases confirms this; so do the references to "Great Houses."

As we have seen, the last dynasty of the Middle Kingdom was the 12th. It was found that the 13th Dynasty was merely a collection of kings who ruled simultaneously over several cities, and that this began already in the 11th Dynasty. In other words, the 13th overlapped the 12th, and after its demise took over. When it disappeared from the scene, Egypt disintegrated. But does it have the pharaoh we are looking for?

The pharaoh who led Egypt to its ultimate destruction must have ruled but a short time. Moses returned to Egypt because the men who were out to get him had died, so the pharaoh he dealt with must have only recently come to power. He must have been either the last or nearly the last of his line. A successor could have temporarily assumed a short-lived kingship, and summarily been ousted by the invaders. The last several pharaohs of the 13th Dynasty are known from the Turin list. Several may have very well ruled simultaneously.

Neferhotep I
Sihathor
Subekhotep IV
Subekhotep V
Laib
Ay Merneferre
Subekhotep VI
Neferhotep II
Sobekhotep VII
Dedumose
Semehemnit

Neferhotep I, Sihathor and Sobekhotep IV were brothers. Ay Merneferre ruled twenty three years, and he is the last pharaoh to be mentioned in monuments. As is so often the case, little is known about these rulers, but Egypt seems to have fallen apart shortly after the death of Ay.

> The true chronology of the 13th Dynasty is rather hard to ascertain, since there are few monuments dating from this period; many of the king's names are known only from an old fragmentary inscription or a little later in the period from scarabs. Merneferre Ay was the last king of the dynasty to be mentioned by name on monuments in Upper and Lower Egypt, and it seems that the eastern Delta broke away under its own petty kings about the time of his death. The confusion that followed is evident from the tales of woe in the contemporary papyri. [26]

The pharaoh of the exodus was Dedumose. He is the only choice. This obscure king was succeeded by a short lived successor who faded away. He was the last reigning monarch of the 13th Dynasty.

> By the Thirteenth Dynasty, the number of Asiatics, even in Upper Egypt, was considerable. They acted as cooks, brewers, seamstresses, vine dressers and the like. One official, for instance, had no fewer than forty-five Asiatics in his household. Such people were classed as "slaves," a comparatively new element in Egyptian society, but one that was destined to last a long time, as wholesale migrations and foreign wars brought many aliens into Egypt. [27]

Several kings of that period left monuments, a number of them with Semitic names. It was not at all uncommon for Egyptians to adopt these "Asiatics," who would enter the Egyptian mainstream, such as happened to Moses. Since the 12th Dynasty a large number of Asiatics occupied Egyptian soil, a Semitic people. A number of scholars say outright that they were Palestinians. It follows that the Asiatics who inhabited Egypt were largely the enslaved Hebrews. Archaeological digs confirm that an Asiatic people worked for the Egyptians.

> There is evidence from Tell-el Dab (*Avaris*) that a community of Asiatics, albeit very Egyptianized, existed there as early as the 13th Dynasty. So far however, this is the only convincing archaeological evidence for a population of Asiatics within Egypt (but living differently from the Egyptians), during the Middle Kingdom. There are also references in contemporary texts to "Camps of Asiatic workmen." ——- During the late 12th and early 13th Dynasties the site expanded enormously, including the emergence of a settlement populated by Asiatics. [28]

Of course the Hebrews were not the only enslaved laborers. There were other aliens, among them Syrian prisoners of war. The scriptures confirm this. When Israel left Egypt, many foreigners came along. The Mosaic Law recognized this, and made liberal provisions for them. They had good reasons to flee with the Hebrews: they were not Egyptians, they were Asiatics, too. Nonetheless, they were not the only ones to enter Egypt; Nubians (Ethiopians) did the same thing.

> A rather different immigration was also evident at the other end of the country. Nomadic warlike tribes from the eastern highlands of Nubia, particularly the Medjay, entered Egypt as mercenary soldiers, and took service with the Theban princelings. [29]

Nubia was conquered by Sestrosis (12th Dynasty). The reasons were economic as well as military; Nubia provided access to the gold mines of the Sudan. He gained control over Palestine and Syria as well. The 13th Dynasty therefore employed Nubians, particularly the Medjay, as mercenaries, and they enslaved Asiatics. That was the Egypt of Ipuwer. He frequently referred to slaves and Nubians, including the Medjay, and spoke of pyramids being built.

Everyone fights for his sister and saves his own skin. Is it Nubians? Then we will guard ourselves; warriors are made many in order to ward off foreigners. Is it Libyans? Then we will turn away. The Medjay are pleased with Egypt. How comes it that every man kills his brother? The troops / whom we marshaled for ourselves have turned into foreigners and have taken to ravageing. 14.10, 15.1

Verily, it is good when men's hands construct pyramids,
When pools are dug, and orchards planted with trees worthy of the gods. 13.10

The Egyptians always hired mercenaries, such as the Medjay. However, following the disaster at the Sea of Passage, where the whole army perished, Egypt suddenly was in a terrible plight. The population was decimated. There was neither time nor manpower to create another army. The impoverished Egyptians could not pay their mercenaries. Israel left Egypt loaded with gold and jewels, and the household slaves, by Ipuwer's admission, robbed their masters. So the mercenaries did the same thing, they "took to ravaging," they looted Egypt. It is the age-old problem of professional armies: who shall guard the guard? Not the king, because he is their prisoner, nor the people, because they are at their mercy.

Ipuwer lived at a definite time in Egyptian history, a time when Nubians and Medjay were mercenaries, Asiatics were slaves, pyramids were built and Bedouins invaded the nation, the final days of the 13th Dynasty. It was the end of that dynasty. There was a natural disaster of catastrophic dimensions; the pharaoh perished with his army, the land was ruined and in a state of anarchy. Arabian tribes overran Egypt, and the new king was deposed. Ipuwer said something very intriguing.

Behold, he who was buried as a falcon <is devoid> of biers, and what the pyramid concealed has become empty. 7.1

The translator explains that "he who is buried as a falcon" refers to the dead king, and "what the pyramid concealed" is the sarcophagus, the stone coffin. Ipuwer mourned the death of the reigning monarch who perished but was never buried. The bier, the funeral platform, was bare, the stone coffin empty. The biblical narrative confirms that the pharaoh died in the Sea of Passage. He drowned and the body was never found. Ipuwer goes on to say that the current king was "deposed by the rabble." He was ousted, but not killed.

> Behold, it has befallen that the land has been deprived of the kingship by a few lawless men.
> Behold, men have fallen into rebellion against the Uraeus, even the [- - - -] of Re, even she who makes the Two Lands content. 7.1

The Uraeus was the cobra-symbol of royalty. Similar statements and references to invading Bedouins paint a picture of terror and anarchy. We can imagine what happened. After the death of Dedumose Djedneferre, who perished in the Sea of Passage a successor, perhaps one of his sons, tried to rescue the situation and assumed the kingship. This did not last. Either the Hyksos or otherwise Hyksos sympathizers deposed him. Quite likely he escaped, but that was the end of that dynasty. All indications are that the survivors of the 13th Dynasty fled to the south. The 14th Dynasty consisted largely of viziers from the Delta who collaborated with the invaders. They briefly ruled along with the 15th and 16th, the Hyksos Dynasties.

That Dedumose was indeed the pharaoh, connected with the Hyksos and by extension the exodus, is confirmed by sources, unaware of the implications. Many scholars maintain that this particular pharaoh, the second to the last of the 13th Dynasty was the Tutimaios mentioned by Josephus when he quoted Manetho.

> At approximately that time an Egyptian king named Dedmose ruled from his ancient capital at Itj-tawy, near Memphis. He was probably the last independent king of the Thirteenth Dynasty and identical with the Tutimaios in whose reign, according to

Manetho, the Hyksos invaded the country and appointed Salitis as king.[30]

Dedumose is definitely identified as the king who was the last of the line before the Hyksos took over.

> Egypt again went through a period of slow decline when a series of "puppet" kings - Manetho's "60 kings of Diospolis" - ruled from Memphis and Lisht; they were dominated by a strong line of viziers. Despite this, an element of centralized control continued for over 100 years, and Egypt still exercised influence abroad. When the 12th Dynasty came to an end, a local dynasty broke away and ruled from Xois; this was the 14th Dynasty which continued to flourish after most of the country had submitted to the Hyksos —-. In the reign of "Tutimaios" - believed to be King Djedneferre Didumose - the Hyksos succeeded in gaining control of much of Egypt, and formed the 15th and 16th Dynasties.[31]

What about King Tum mentioned in the Naos story? He could be identical with Dedumose. His name relates to Pi-Thom (the abode of Atum), the city built by Hebrew slave labor. Djedneferre Dedumose being the last king of the 13th Dynasty, he was definitely associated with the Hebrews. But we cannot identify him by his name. After all, Atum and Ra were identical, therefore any name with either theophoric part could be used in proof. And that is asking too much. Velikovsky claimed the name of the pharaoh was Taoui-Thom, but he did that by linking "Thom" with part of "Hy-Tayou," an inadmissible construct that appears nowhere in the text.

Neferti

Basic to all these events is the presupposition that a natural disaster wiped out Egypt. It is evident in the Naos tale, and very much so in the laments of Ipuwer. A similar account appears in "The Prophecies of Neferti," generally believed to have been political propaganda. It was written several centuries later, after the Hyksos were expelled, and was intended to make Amenhotep I look good.

During the reign of King Snefru, so the story goes, His Majesty asked for a man who would entertain him with flowing rhetoric. His courtiers recommended Neferti, who asked if he should speak of things present or future. "Of what shall happen," said the king, whereupon the Lector Neferti - with 20/20 hindsight - foretold things to come. Judging from the structure of his "prophecy," it is loosely based on Ipuwer's laments, with additional details.

> He brooded over what should happen in the land and considered the condition of the east, when the Asiatics raid and terrorize those at the harvest, taking away their teams engaged in ploughing. —-
>
> Perished are those erstwhile good things, the fish ponds of those who carry slit fish, teeming with fish and fowl. All good things have passed away, the land being cast away through trouble by means of that food of the Asiatics who pervade the land. Enemies have come into being in the east; Asiatics have come down into Egypt, for a fortress lacks another beside it *(editor: to support it so as to keep the barbarians out)*, and no guard will hear. Men will hold back and [look out] by night *(editor: I.e. will not venture out, but stare apprehensively into the darkness)*, the fortress will be entered, and sleep will be banished from my eyes, so that I spend the night wakeful. Wild game will drink from the river of Egypt, taking their ease on their riverbanks through lack of anyone to fear.[32]

This followed the pattern of a national calamity, hunger, want and an invasion of the foreigners, mentioned by Ipuwer. They were Bedouin Sheiks who conquered Egypt and terrorized the populace. Men were so few that wild game could drink from the Nile without being bothered. The seer went on to describe the plight of the land.

> Re must begin by refounding the land, which is utterly ruined, and nothing remains; ― —- . This land is destroyed and there are none who care for it; there are none who speak and there are none who act. Weeper, how fares this land? The sun is veiled,/and will not shine when the people would see; none will live when [the sun] is veiled [by] cloud, and everyone is dulled by lack of it.― —-
>
> Re separates himself from men; he shines, that the hour may be told, but no one knows when noon occurs, for no one can discern his shadow, no one is dazzled when [he] is seen; there are none whose eyes stream with water, for he is like the moon in the sky, (though) his accustomed times do [not] go astray, and his rays are in (men's) sight as on former occasions.[33]

Re was the sun god, and the luminary deity somehow lost its shine. For decades the sun was altogether invisible; only a dim light distinguished day from night. Gradually the heavy pall evaporated until finally the sun became visible, albeit like the moon. Like Ipuwer, Neferti went into great detail to describe the anarchy that followed the collapse of the empire. Fortunately a rosy "prophecy" followed. "A king of the south will come, Ameny by name." That was Amenhotep I who, according to this "back to the future" science fiction, would right all things and become the legitimate king.

So much for politics. But since it involves a collective recollection of the past, it is only fair to ask if there is any reference at all to the cause of these catastrophic events that are so clearly described. In every known case the results are mentioned, but not the cause. There are allusions to astral deities who caused havoc, (Venus plays an important role), but nothing hinting either at anything observed in the heavens or unusual weather conditions due to volcanic activity.

That sounds strange to our western minds, but ancient civilizations never made a connection between cause and effect. It was the result of their astral religion. They believed the planets were gods, not physical objects in outer space, and natural disasters were caused by warring deities. There is no mention whatsoever of the Thera explosion, nor of phenomena such as tidal waves and violent atmospheric disturbances that must have accompanied it. In any event, such references are reported in other sources and they refer to a cosmic agent rather than a terrestrial cause.

The Comet

A number of ancient authorities report that a comet appeared, and that this comet inflicted destruction. Pliny mentioned it in his "Natural History."

> A terrible comet was seen by the people of Ethiopia and Egypt, to which Typhon, the king of that period, gave his name; it had a fiery appearance and was twisted like a coil, and it was very grim to behold; it was not really a star so much as what might be called a ball of fire.[34]

Other authorities describe it as "an immense globe of fire, also a sickle, which is a description of a globe illuminated by the sun, and close enough to by observed such. Its movement was slow, its path was close to the sun. Its color was bloody: 'It was not of fiery, but of bloody redness'."

This comet was connected with the exodus. This is important. Velikovsky found a book by Helvelius (1668) that referred to earlier scholars. "In the year of the world 2453 (1495 B.C.), according to certain authorities, a comet was seen in Syria, Babylonia, India, in the sign Jo, in the form of a disc, at the very time when the Israelites were on their march from Egypt to the promised land. So Rochenbach."[35] Velikovsky was able to locate a copy of Rochenbach's book (only three are known to exist), which was based upon ancient manuscripts, and he found this (in Latin).

> In the year of the world two thousand four hundred and fifty-three, as many trustworthy authors on the basis of many conjectures have determined, a comet appeared which Pliny also mentioned in his second book. It was fiery, of irregular circular form,

with a wrapped head; it was in the shape of a globe and was of a terrible aspect. It is said that King Typhon ruled at that time in Egypt. – Certain (authorities) assert that the comet was seen in Syria, Babylonia, India, in the sign of Capricorn in the form of a disc, at the time when the children of Israel advanced from Egypt toward the promised land, led on their way by the pillar of cloud during the day and by the pillar of fire at night.[36]

But was that "comet" the proto-planet Venus? Strange as it may sound, the evidence is surprisingly good. For eye witnesses to say it was a globe and a "ball of fire," it must have been huge. The mass of this object was large enough for gravity to make it a sphere; it must have been planet-sized. It was a planetary body with cometary characteristics. It had a cometary tail which, as we will see, means it was an electrically charged body. The wrapped head and fiery appearance point in that direction as well. Assuming that was the case, it explains the frequent references to fire and lightning at the Sea of Passage. It could have involved electrical discharges between the earth and the charged globe.

Yet it was not a comet. A comet is after all is either a large block of ice or an iron-nickel-based boulder, which does not fit the description of this object at all. Since its movement was slow and near the sun, it could not possibly be one of those high-speed missiles that whip past the earth in their elliptical path around the sun. A comet that approaches the sun is too small to be observed, and eventually will be drawn into the fiery inferno.

These ancient records certainly were based on eye witness accounts. It involved facts they could have never made up. The "comet" was pictured as bloody red with twisted coils, as if it had a wrapped head. That fits the description of a newly formed planet, still red-hot and electrically charged. Evidently it was called a comet because it had a cometary tail. There are good reasons why a recently formed (and therefore hot) planetary body would have a visible tail, but more about that later.

Space-age research knows of only one planet that fits that description, and that is the planet Venus. The surface of Venus is a fit description of hell. It is red-hot, like the coals of a grill, literally a lake of sulfur, and its atmospheric pressure is ninety times that of the earth, enough to crush a nuclear submarine. What really makes Venus so different from a "normal" planet is its cometary tail. Venus has the distinction of being the only planet with a magneto tail, magnetic filaments that make up the tails of comets. That is what ancient people recorded: a ball of fire that had a visible tail and looked like a hairy star. They believed Ishtar or Typhon was a goddess with long flowing hair. The early Chaldeans called Ishtar (Venus) the bright torch of heaven. It was clearly visible in broad daylight. We are therefore reluctantly forced to conclude that this "comet" could indeed have been the proto planet Venus.

Typhon

Legend and mythology frequently mention Typhon, the dragon who was defeated in heavenly battle. Typhon was the Greek name for Seth, revered by the Hyksos, and Seth was the astral personification of the planet Venus. There is a problem involved in this. In mythology there is an ever present danger of subjective interpretation. It is possible to read things into these stories that never happened. On the other hand, it is also possible that myths represent the memories of extraordinary events, and the greater the similarities between myths, the greater the likelihood that they tell a real story.

In "The City of God," Augustine made an interesting observation. He reasoned that the Greek gods, such as Mercury, Atlas, Gaia and Hercules had all been famous people who after their death had been deified. Perhaps. Pliny said that Typhon was the king of Egypt when a comet appeared. Since Typhon was the Hyksos god Seth and the Egyptian Apopi, it makes sense that Typhon was the Hyksos Pharaoh Apop. Augustine went on to say this. (Book 18, Ch.8)

Israel and Egypt

Minerva was far more ancient than these, for she is reported to have appeared in virgin age in the time of Ogyges at the lake called Triton, from which she is also styled Tritonia, the inventress truly of many works and the more readily believed to be a goddess because her origin was so little known. For what is sung about her having sprung from the head of Jupiter belongs to the region of poetry and fable, and not to that of history and real fact. And historical writers are not agreed when Ogyges flourished, in whose time also a great flood occurred - not the greatest one from which no man escaped except those who could get into the ark, for neither Greek nor Latin history know it, yet a greater flood than that which happened afterward in Deucalion's time.

The Latin Minerva was the Greek Athena, and both were Venus. Deucalion was the Greek Noah. Lake Triton was a vast marsh in Northern Africa, in what is now the Sahara desert. It is certain that this area until the middle of the Second Millennium B.C. was a savannah. Indications are that it was under Egyptian control. There is still such a lake, measuring 30,000 square miles, in Central Africa. Then a disaster struck. The lake emptied into the Atlantic Ocean and only the sandy bottom was left, the Sahara desert. This only added to the economic deprivation of the Egyptians. Minerva lived then, which was the age of Ogyges, of whom we will hear shortly. In his days the tidal wave of the Thera explosion inundated coastal lands.

In view of this it is quite likely that climatic conditions changed. So did geography. In Genesis chapters 12 and 13 we find a rather startling account of Abraham's whereabouts. He moved his flocks to the Negev. He might have just as well had them graze on the moon - in our day and age. The Negev could have never been the waste desert that it is now, searing hot and inhospitable. It was a steppe that suffered the same fate as North Africa. In all likelihood the Sinai Peninsula and Arabia Felix, including Midian, were equally affected. We may never know how disastrously the catastrophe of the exodus affected that part of the world. Evidently it was bad enough for the

Amelekites to be uprooted and migrate to more hospitable places. But that large tracts of land were laid waste cannot be doubted.

The comet that appeared was called Typhon, Pallas Athena and Minerva. According to Latin legend, Minerva or Venus was not born, but sprung full fledged from the head of Jupiter. Pallas was another name for Typhon. So was Seth, venerated by the Hyksos. The mythologies of various nations do not always identify Typhon the same way. Nonetheless, they are in many ways very similar. There is a pattern. Typhon, the many-headed dragon, was visible in the sky. It pelted the earth with fiery arrows. A planet-god, either Jupiter or Venus, fought and defeated the dragon which fell to the earth and was locked up underground. In Greek mythology Phaeton (Venus) drove his fiery chariot too close to the earth and turned Africa into a desert. Zeus (Jupiter) struck him with a thunderbolt and Phaeton plunged into Eridanos, the river of the underworld.

What does this mean? The picture is familiar to us from Revelations 12, but that does not prove anything one way or the other. It employs imagery that people knew from folklore. Something of the kind is described in Isaiah 51:9, 10, associated with the crossing of the Red Sea.

> Awake, awake! Clothe yourself with strength
> O arm of the Lord;
> awake, as in days gone by,
> as in generations of old.
> Was it not you who cut Rahab to pieces,
> who pierced that monster through?
> Was it not you who dried up the sea,
> the waters of the great deep,
> who made a road in the depths of the sea
> so that the redeemed might cross over?

It is the picture of a menace that threatened Israel at the time of the exodus. Velikovsky believed it involved a cosmic drama that caught the imagination of ancient peoples. Admittedly his assump-

Israel and Egypt

tions (presented as fact) are far-fetched and often untenable. For instance he claims that the earth and the proto planet Venus came close enough to affect each other's gravitational fields. As the earth drew close to the comet, the two charged globes repelled each other. The comet now followed the earth, which overturned. The incandescent globe was seen moving in the opposite direction. Meanwhile the tail of the comet became entangled with the globe, which resulted in violent discharges. It looked as if a many-headed dragon battled the planet-god. These enormous bolts of lightning tore the tail apart, and as a result meteorites pounded the earth, which became shrouded in the gases of the tail. It looked as if the planetary deity defeated the serpent and cast it to the earth.

That was not the end of the story. The comet followed the earth and after a period of about two months again came close. This could not be seen because of the cloud cover, but it coincided with the time of the lawgiving at Mount Horeb. The results were frightening. According to Deuteronomy 5:23, "the mountain was ablaze with fire," and was rocked by earthquakes. "It trembled violently and smoke billowed up, like smoke from a furnace." (Exodus 19:16-19). Not much later the comet disentangled itself from the gravitational attraction of the earth and moved away.

So much for Velikovsky's theories. Could it have happened that way? No. For Venus to come that close would have meant the end of the world. Besides, the earth could have hardly overturned, at least at the time when Israel crossed the Sea of Passage. If that happened, it must have been during the plague of darkness, when a hurricane howled in pitch blackness. Furthermore the location of the Sea of Passage was the Strait of Tiran, not some inland lake. It is very difficult to believe that the water, attracted by the nearby comet, was pulled up in great heaps. How could that possibly provide a road through the sea? One gets the distinct impression that the water was pushed down rather than pulled up. Besides, the Gulf of Aqaba opens up to the Red Sea and hence to the Indian Ocean. If waters that deep were suddenly removed by pulling it sky high, an enormous wave would have filled the vacuum in no time, obliterating everything in its path. No one would have been able to cross the Sea of Passage at all.

The identification of the cloud with Venus is highly questionable. Its movements could not coincide with the zigzag path of Israel. The cloud was more than a natural phenomenon, it was supernatural. It was a theophany, a divine manifestation, just like the burning bush, encountered by Moses.

Equally suspect is Velikovsky's appeal to the scriptures. Maybe phenomena such as these occurred, but the scriptures nowhere support his claims that this happened at the Sea of Passage. "According to the scriptures, the waters climbed the mountains and stood above them, and they mounted to the heaven," he wrote.[37] But when we read the pertinent quotations, it turns out they have nothing to do with the exodus. The book of Job does not apply because the story occurred at a much earlier time. The Psalms quoted (or misquoted) are these.

> He set the earth on its foundations;
> it can never be moved.
> You covered it with the deep as with a garment;
> the waters stood above the mountains.
> But at your rebuke the waters fled,
> at the sound of your thunder they took to flight;
> they flowed over the mountains,
> they went down into the valleys,
> to the place you assigned for them.
> You set a boundary they cannot cross;
> never again will they cover the earth.
>
> Psalm 104:5-9

This psalm deals with the providence of God. This particular passage speaks, not of the exodus, but of the deluge, the flood of Noah. It employs the language of Genesis 9:11. "Never again will all life be cut off by the waters of a flood; never again will there be a flood to destroy the earth." Velikovsky's use of Psalm 107 is an outright misrepresentation. This psalm speaks of God's goodness, and how he helps those in distress, in this case sailors on the high seas, facing mountain-high waves and scared to death.

> Others went out on the sea to ships,
> they were merchants on the mighty waters.
> They saw the works of the LORD,
> his wonderful deeds in the deep.
> For he spoke and stirred up a tempest that lifted high the waves.
> They mounted up to the heavens and went down to the depths,
> in their peril their courage melted away.
> They reeled and staggered like drunken men;
> they were at their wits end.
> Then they cried out to the LORD in their trouble;
> and he brought them out of their distress.
> He stilled the storm to a whisper;
> the waves of the sea were hushed.
>
> Psalm 107:23-29

Psalm 78:12, 13 does mention the events at the Sea of Passage, but nowhere intimates sky-high mountains of water.

> He did miracles in the sight of their fathers in the land of Egypt,
> in the region of Zoan.
> He divided the sea and led them through;
> he made the water stand firm like a wall.

It sounds rather as if they were walking on a hollow road, with walls of water to the right and the left, as Exodus 14:22 plainly states. And then there is Psalm 33:7, which merely says that God has assigned the waters to be stored in oceans. "He gathers the waters of the sea into jars. He puts the deep into storehouses."

How, we ask, can these things possibly be applied to the events surrounding the exodus? They cannot. And Velikovsky's theories about Mount Horeb fall flat in the face of known facts, the reason being that Mount Horeb is not in the Sinai Peninsula, but in present day Saudi Arabia, the Midian of Moses' long sojourn.

Jabul al Lawz

Following the miraculous escape across the Strait of Tiran, Israel traveled on to Horeb, the mountain of God. Until recently no one knew exactly where the sacred mountain was located. Then two American adventurers, at the peril of their lives, found creative ways to enter Saudi Arabia in search of the elusive mountain. What they found changed their lives; it confirmed the biblical account of the exodus in detail. [38]

The Israelites found themselves in a barren desert where nothing grew and, unlike Egypt, water was nonexistent. Then at last - a well. It turned out the water was bitter. However, the Lord told Moses to throw a stick into the water, which miraculously became sweet. It fits exactly. East of the Gulf of Aqaba, alkaline flats stretch out for miles. Alkaline renders water bitter. To this day there is a single well, filled with bitter water. As they traveled on, Moses found himself in familiar territory. After a few days they arrived at present-day Al-Bad, an oasis with twelve springs of fresh water, shaded by palm trees, the biblical Elim (Ex 15:27). Local Arabs insist that the nearby caves once were the home of the prophet Musha (Moses).

But Israel was called to meet God at Mount Horeb, so they moved on, only to again run out of water. They complained bitterly, which is why that place was called Massah and Meribah (testing and quarrel), because they put God to the test. The Lord told Moses to walk on ahead to Mount Horeb with some elders. There Moses struck a rock with his staff, and water rushed out. That rock is still there, a sixty-foot boulder atop an outcropping. A geyser erupted from an aquifer and split the granite rock right down the middle. Water gushed with abandon. It formed a large creek that kept flowing and eventually filled a lake, large enough to supply a million people with cattle for a year. The dried-out bed of a creek is still visible. So are the outlines of the lake it once filled. There even is a very old cedar tree. Could this be the burning bush where God spoke to Moses?

Israel and Egypt

Jabul al Lawz, the Arabian name for Mount Horeb, is 8,465 feet (2,380 meters) high. Isolated and shunned by Arabs, after all those centuries the site remains intact. To the east, where Israel camped, are piles of rock, spaced four hundred feet apart; these are the markers that kept the people a safe distance from the sacred mountain (Ex 19:12). Scripture records that Mount Sinai shook and that smoke and deep darkness covered the top. A feature, unique to Jabul al Lawz is its top: it is burned black, as if it was once exposed to intense heat. A number of geologists studied the features of the molted rocks, and suspect the mountain was once much higher than it is now. The top evaporated in the intense heat, and only the black dome is left to testify to the awesome spectacle.

There are other man-made structures: altars. Moses ascended mount Horeb to receive the law. He was gone a long time. The people became restive, and after five weeks took matters in their own hands. They demanded that Aaron make them a golden calf (actually pictures engraved in rocks, Egyptian fashion), erected an altar and proclaimed these idols their gods. Moses came down from Mount Horeb and in a rage smashed the two tablets of the law. He ground the golden calf to dust, threw it in the brook that flowed from the split rock and made the people drink it. The Levites took swords and went through the camp killing the worst offenders; three thousand in all. Thousands more died of the plague.

We stand amazed at the severity of the sentence. Yet the physical evidence of its reality is there. Near Jabul al Lawz stand the remains of a huge altar made of rocks, covered with pictures of bulls, the Apis bulls of Egypt, held up in sacrifice. Nor is it the only altar. The Levites constructed an altar of sacrifice made of rock. It is still there, near mount Horeb, built in a V-shape. With it are twelve pillars, one each for the twelve tribes of Israel. (Ex 24:4). In addition there is a burial site. The stone markers are pre-Islamic.

Mount Sinai, the traditional site in the Sinai Peninsula, hardly satisfies the demands imposed by the exodus. There is by far not enough space available for perhaps a million people to camp there. Mount Jabul al Lawz however, overlooks a vast plain, large enough to house that many people with cattle. Add to that the previously mentioned lake, formed by the water that streamed from the split rock, and we have exactly the right spot. It suddenly becomes intelligible why Moses' father-in-law Jethro would appear on the scene. They were in Midian, on Jethro's grazing grounds. Moses was reunited with his wife and children, and told Jethro all that the Lord had done for Israel. It is of more than passing interest to note that Jethro advised Moses to adopt a system of representative government that ultimately was incorporated in the Constitution of the United States.

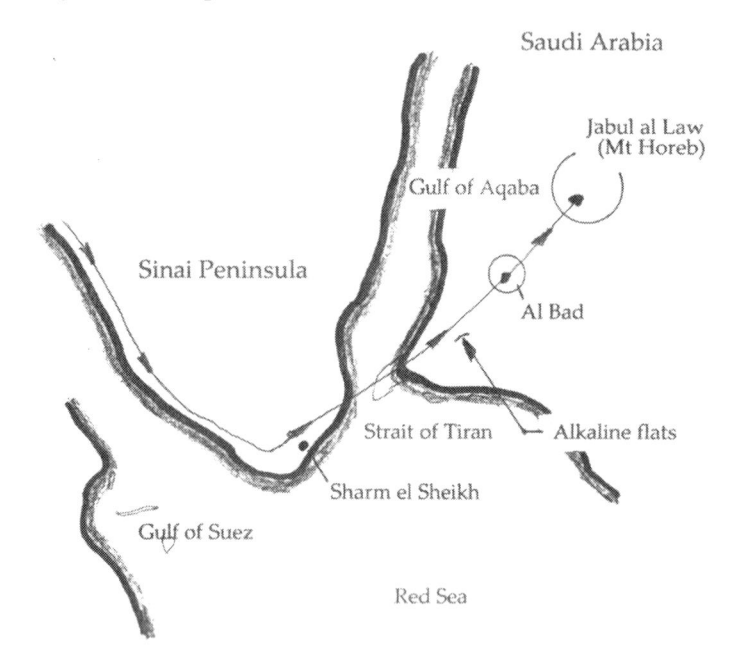

The Route of the Exodus

The Ten Commandments

The giving of the law at Mount Horeb is a landmark in human history. For this reason it is certainly worthy of our attention to consider what was said and what happened. Velikovsky thought he had an explanation. After the crossing, the proto-planet Venus followed the earth and after about six weeks again came close; so much that it stood straight overhead mount Horeb. It caused the earth to quake, set the mountain ablaze, and providing sounds, interpreted by Moses to be the ten *words* or commandments. "It was a perfect setting for hearing words in the voice of nature in an uproar. An inspired leader interpreted the voice he heard, ten long, trumpet-like blasts."[39]

That certainly is quite a string of coincidences. One cannot help but wonder, how could anyone that close to the mountain survive? Everyone must have been burned to cinders. On top of that, the theory is refuted by the facts. Of all the mountains in Midian, only the top of Jabul al Lawz is blackened. There is no evidence whatsoever of any adjacent terrain being affected; it was strictly local. It sure was convenient to have an inspired leader around at the right time in the right place. The notion sounds rather farfetched, even more so if we keep in mind that Moses was hardly the ideal representative of the great truths he pronounced. The man who reputedly said, "You shall not kill," had done so himself, and everyone knew it. Besides, Moses did not interpret these *words* for the people; they all heard it in plain language.

Nor was it the sort of thing an inspired leader would make up, the reason being that the giving of the law followed the pattern of a suzerain treaty. An overlord or suzerain would enter into a covenant, a formal contract, with his subjects, and stipulate the terms of that contract. He would begin by reminding them who he was and what he had done for them, followed by the terms of the covenant. If they would abide by the terms, they would enjoy his protection. That is the format we find in the Ten Commandments. (Ex. 20:1-17)

- The preamble:

I am the LORD your God who brought you out of Egypt, out of the land of slavery.

- The first four *Words* deal with man's relationship to God.

    1. You shall have no other God before me.

2. You shall not make for yourself an idol — — . You shall not bow down to them or worship them, for I, the LORD your God am a jealous God.
3. You shall not misuse the name of the LORD your God.
4. Remember the Sabbath to keep it holy. — — On it you shall not do any work.

- The fifth commandment is a transition. It deals with God and man.

5. Honor your father and your mother, so that you may live long in the land the LORD your God is giving you.

- The final five deal with man and his fellow man.

6. You shall not murder.
7. You shall not commit adultery.
8. You shall not steal.
9. You shall not give false testimony against your neighbor.
10. You shall not covet your neighbor's house. —

It was all said from the perspective, not of an inspired leader, but a sovereign ruler. It left Israel with a sense of dread. Their God was indeed a consuming fire. He was merciful as well, otherwise he would have never revealed himself in the first place, but the people must understand who they were dealing with. It gave them a standard for absolute truth and core values. Yes, there are moral absolutes that cannot be ignored. Any violation of these truths leads to anarchy and disintegration. A society that brushes these things aside does so at its peril. Western law is based upon the Ten Commandments.

Within the historical context it is of considerable value to note that the law and the temple ceremony grew from local soil. Israel was familiar with the religion of the Egyptians; the Aaronic priesthood clearly derived and adopted its ceremonies from Egypt. The Ark of the Covenant, the center piece of the temple ceremony, was a "naos." It was a shrine that contained the presence of deity.

> The shrines of the gods each contained a statue of the deity worshiped in the temple. They were mostly made of wood, since they were carried on the barques of the gods in processions, but stone and precious metals were also used. — — Almost all shrines were richly decorated with hieroglyphics and pictorial representations. The height of a naos seldom exceeded the height of a person, except for the naos of Mendes, which was seven meters high and four meters wide.
>
> The shrine that contained the deity stood, as a rule, in the rearmost corner of a chamber of the temple, which was accessible to only a few priests. The plinth (base) often shows representations of kings carrying the sky, since the naos embodied the space of the sky. If the shrine was opened, then symbolically the entrances to the sky were opened to the field of power held by the deity as represented by the statue.[40]

The statues of the gods were frequently carried along in procession, but the most sacred of these were always carried along in a naos on a barque that resembled a Nile boat. "During the procession, the barques were carried by the deity's priests on their shoulders."[41] The naos, in other words, was the model of the Ark of the Covenant. It makes sense that the Almighty would design for Israel a form of worship, adopted from that culture, something his people could understand. The Hebrews after all were born and raised in Egypt. They were familiar with the Egyptian temple cult and the naos; they knew that it stood for a divine manifestation of sorts. An idolatrous polytheistic cult was modified to mold an entirely different religion, used in the worship of a single transcendent God. The rituals employed in this religion involved a system of sacrifices that spoke of redemption; they foreshadowed the supreme sacrifice.

The Egyptian temple merely housed the naos, which contained the deity. The Hebrew cult resembled this setup, but it was fundamentally different. The tabernacle included the holy place and behind that the most holy place, which contained the Ark of the Covenant. The tabernacle was the place where God chose to dwell among his people, and it provided access to him. Worshipers were allowed to enter the outer court, the priests performed their functions in the holy place, and once a year, on the Day of Atonement, the High Priest would enter the holy of holies. It was the throne room of the Almighty.

The Ark of the Covenant was not to be touched because it was holy. It was made of acacia wood, and it was covered with pure gold. The lid was covered by two cherubim, symbolizing guardian angels. They guarded the stone tablets from human sight; to gaze directly upon the law with its demand for perfect purity meant instant death. It was the mercy seat, where the High Priest on the Day of Atonement would sprinkle the blood of a spotless lamb. The sins of the people were wiped away. It was all symbolic and foreshadowed the real presence of God on earth, and the final and all-sufficient atonement he would make when he shed his own blood.

The book of Hebrews makes it clear that the sacrifices of the Aaronic Covenant were provisional. Once the great sacrifice was made, the Old Covenant became obsolete and disappeared with its priesthood. The Romans under Titus A.D. 70 besieged Jerusalem and destroyed the temple with its sacrificial system. Every single Aaronic priest was killed. The Ark of the Covenant evidently had long since disappeared. It served its purpose, and it is of no consequence what happened to it.

Manna

The exodus account mentions several unusual natural phenomena with supernatural characteristics. They are the cloud that directed Israel, the emergence of the submarine road across the Strait of Tiran, manna, the heavenly bread, and the temporary if limited absence of entropy. All those years Israel wandered in the desert without having to worry about shoes and clothing. "During the forty years that I led you through the desert, your clothes did not wear out, nor did the sandals on your feet." (Deut 29:5}

These things defy a rational explanation. It involves the Supernatural: God intervened in the affairs of man. Miracles did not happen in haphazard fashion. They were few and occurred at crucial times in God's dealing with his covenant people. The cloud was a theophany, a divine manifestation. The crossing of the Sea of Passage was a miraculous deliverance; manna and the limited lifting of entropy dealt with providential care.

Of these the manna more than anything provokes our wonder. What was it and where did it come from? The story appears in Exodus ch. 16. When the people complained about lack of food, the Lord showed his glory. He provided quail (still prevalent there), and the next morning dew covered the ground. When it evaporated, a fine frost covered the ground. It tasted like honey and was baked into cakes. There was enough for everyone to eat the allotted amount, with provisions to gather nothing on the Sabbath. Double the amount fell on Friday, and nothing on Saturday.

It is very difficult indeed to find a natural cause not only for the manna, but also for these specific times and circumstances. Velikovsky thought he had a solution. The cloud cover was saturated and in the cool of the night it probably discharged its compounds of carbon and hydrogen in a sweet dew. This (disputed) explanation may or may not be true. However, it has problems all its own. The manna must necessarily fall everywhere including the camp, which was bound to be messy. In fact it fell outside the camp. Then there is the cyclical order whereby double the amount fell on Friday and none on Saturday, the Sabbath. Besides, when some gathered too much during the week it spoiled, but that never happened over the weekend. Clearly there is a supernatural element that defies a purely natural explanation.

The same care is expressed in Deuteronomy, where Moses reminded the people that all those years their clothes and sandals did not wear out. Considering the circumstances that makes sense. Israel was isolated in a desolate waste, and they could never fix or replace worn out sandals and clothing. For this there is no rational scientific explanation.

In a larger sense these events were a model of things to come. The Passover lamb was a picture of the ultimate sacrifice. The cloud prefigured the presence of God on earth. The miraculous crossing spoke of deliverance from the slavery of sin and entrance into the Promised Land. Manna was the food from heaven that sustained God's people, just as Christ by his very presence is the real food that satisfies our needs. And in the wilderness of this world God provides in unexpected ways. Western civilization with its Greek mind set may not always find logic and mathematical precision. But has not God provided our needs in ways we never dreamed of? Whatever the origins of manna, it still involved providential care.

Amelek

There is a remarkable interlude. Hordes of Arabs, uprooted by the same disaster that devastated Egypt, left their ancestral home in southern Arabia. They were the Amelekites, an ancient people mentioned in Genesis 14. They already existed in the days of Abraham; they were not, as is sometimes believed, his descendants. They obviously could have never met Israel in the triangle of the isolated Sinai Peninsula, since they came from Arabia, and the Sinai was Egyptian territory. Rather they were surprised to unexpectedly find a large nation in their flanks as they moved north toward Egypt and Palestine through Midian. This happened shortly before Israel reached Mount Horeb.

They attacked Israel and soon were engaged in a fierce battle. Moses, Aaron and Hur, the father of Joshua, went up the top of a hill. As long as Moses raised his hands to heaven, Israel was winning; however, when he became tired and his hands came down, the Amelekites gained, until finally Aaron and Hur held his hands up, and Israel under Joshua won the final victory. It left them with an undying hatred against the cruel and inhuman Amelekites. This was quite unlike their feelings toward the Egyptians who had oppressed them, but had been hospitable as well. Amelek was another story.

> Then the LORD said to Moses, "Write this on a scroll as something to be remembered and make sure that Joshua hears it, because I will completely erase the memory of the Amelekites from under heaven."
> Moses built an altar and called it The LORD is my Banner. He said, "For hands were lifted up to the throne of the LORD. The LORD will be at war against the Amelekites from generation to generation."
>
> Exodus 17:14, 15

There can be no doubt about it, Amelek was utterly evil; so much so that God promised to ban the memory of Amelek from the earth. In the memory of the Jewish people, Amelek has a terrible reputation. These Arabs moved to Egypt, which they conquered without a fight. According to a Jewish legend they obtained lists of names from Egyptian records and called on the Israelites, whom they murdered. They would cut the limbs of wounded captives and fling them to the sky to defy God in heaven.[42]

There are Arab traditions that the Amelekites were once Egyptian pharaohs. They were the Hyksos, the Bedouin Sheiks who ruled northern Egypt during the Intermediate Period. This explains why the Old Testament never mentions Egypt until the days of King Saul, more than four hundred years later. The scriptures assume throughout that Egypt disappeared from the scene and was of no consequence. Rather Amelek suddenly became the feared enemy.

Israel remained at Mount Horeb about a year, then they left for Canaan. However, they first sent out spies to gather intelligence about the land they were about to conquer. The spies explored Canaan from one end to the other; they came back with good news and bad. The land was indeed good, they said, but the people who lived there were too strong. There were giants; not merely tall men, but monsters like the Nephilim giants mentioned in Genesis.[43] They also reported Hittites, Canaanites - and Amelekites. That was a surprise. In an earlier list the Amelekites were absent (Ex 3:17). According to Arabic sources the Amelekites came in waves. Some invaded Egypt, others occupied the southern part of Palestine. Israel could never defeat them, the spies said.

Caleb and Joshua, two of the spies, would not hear of it. "Do not rebel against the LORD. And do not be afraid of the people of the land, because we will swallow them up. Their protection is gone, but the LORD is with us. Do not be afraid of them." (Numbers 14:9). Since the 12th Dynasty, the Canaanites enjoyed a certain protection from the pharaohs, but now that Egypt had been disposed, they were vulnerable.

However, generations of slavery caught up with Israel. They were freed slaves, yes, but they still had a slave mentality. They had always been told what to do and could not fend for themselves; things had to be done for them.

> That night all the people of the community raised their voices and wept aloud. All the Israelites grumbled against Moses and Aaron, and the whole assembly said to them, "If only we had died in Egypt! Or in this desert! Why is the LORD bringing us to this land only to let us fall by the sword? Our wives and children will be taken as plunder. Wouldn't it be better for us to go back to Egypt?" And they said to each other, "We should choose a leader to go back to Egypt."
>
> Numbers 14:1-4

That agrees with the Hyksos policy to enslave women and children and massacre the men. It was a bleak prospect. Better go back to Egypt and the security of the plantation system. Of course had they done so, they would have been welcomed by the Amelekites. Moses interceded for the people, and the nation was spared. But except for Caleb and Joshua, not one of that generation would see the Promised Land; they would die in the desert. "Since the Amelekites and Canaanites are living in the valleys, turn back tomorrow and set out toward the desert along the route to the Red Sea." (Num. 14:25) The

Red Sea was Yam Soph, the Gulf of Aqaba. Israel had a belated change of heart. Against Moses' advice they attacked the high hill country. "Then the Amelekites and Canaanites who lived in that hill country came down and attacked them and beat them down all the way to Hormah." (Num 14:45)

For forty years Israel roamed in "a barren wilderness, through a land of desert rifts, a land of drought and darkness, a land where no one travels and no one lives." (Jeremiah 2:6) The cloud cover lasted for decades; the desert was always dark. It was also a dangerous place. Rifts opened in the desert and fires erupted. Maybe the unsettled strata and petroleum had something to do with it. Fire from the Lord and gaping chasms overtook the rebellious. Israel survived; a new generation learned to deal with the hardship of life.

Until now it was believed Israel's sojourn in the desert and the consequent conquest of Canaan occurred during the Iron Age. That age belongs, not to the invasion of Palestine, but to the exile. Israel left Egypt at the end of the Early Bronze Age, and conquered Palestine at the beginning of the Middle Bronze period. When seen in that light, the facts fit the scriptures exactly. Archaeological findings and pottery dating from those times bear this out.[44] When at last the Hebrews entered the Promised Land, they realized that a major political power shift had taken place. Egypt had disappeared; instead Amelek became a contentious power. That is very much evident from the mishaps of Balaam.

Balaam

In Numbers chapters 22-24 we find the story of Balaam, a diviner of sorts. Balaam descended from a pocket of believers that survived in Aram (Syria). However, his beliefs were severely contaminated, he dabbled in augury. Balak, king of Moab, called on him to curse Israel. Balaam, torn between greed and fear, informed Balak that he could say only what God made him say. Eventually he came, never knowing he risked his life until his donkey told him so. Balaam's oracles reveal not only how powerless he was, but also the political realities of the day. In blessing Israel he said,

> How beautiful are your tents, O Jacob!
> Your dwelling places, O Israel!
> Like valleys they spread out,
> Like gardens beside a river,
> Like aloes planted by the Lord,
> Like cedars beside the waters.
> Water will flow from their buckets,
> Their seed will have abundant water.
> His king will be greater than Agag,
> Their kingdom will be exalted.
>
> Numbers 24:5-7

Who was Agag, or Agog, the greatest king of that time? That becomes evident from the oracle that followed.

> "I see Him, but not now;
> I behold Him, but not near;
> A star will come out of Jacob;
> A scepter will rise out of Israel,
> And crush the foreheads of Moab,
> The skulls of the sons of Sheth.
> Edom will be conquered;
> Seir, his enemy, will be conquered,
> But Israel will grow strong.
> A ruler will come out of Jacob
> And destroy the survivors of the city."
> Then he looked on Amelek and he took up his oracle and said:
> "Amelek was first among the nations,
> But he will come to ruin at last."
>
> Numbers 24:17-20

The premier nation was not Egypt, as one would expect, but Amelek, and Agog was their king. That Agog was indeed a Hyksos Pharaoh is confirmed by the list of Hyksos kings, provided by Sir Alan Gardiner. These were the famous rulers.

Akernenra Apopi
Nebkhepeshre Apop
Sewesenre Khayan
Aweserre Apopi

The Egyptian Apop or Apopi is identical with the Hebrew Agog. In ancient Hebrew the letters p and g are nearly the same. Agog the Amelekite was Apop the Hyksos Pharaoh. The Egyptians called the Asiatic invaders Apopi, after the demon of darkness. "Apophis was considered the counterpart to the sun god and symbol of the dark powers — Apophis was often equated with Seth, the enemy of the gods and ruler of the destructive forces."[45] Seth was the god of chaos and destruction in the cosmic and social order. In the astral realm Seth was the planet Venus. Scholars noted that the conflict in the First Intermediate Period (which as we have seen was identical with the Second) was between followers of the god Horus in the south and Seth in the north. Seth was the god of the Hyksos.

Khayan was also known as Khian. Balaam called Amelek "first among the nations" because it was the current world power. They conquered Egypt and controlled Palestine and Syria. It is quite understandable that the Israelites chose to invade Palestine from Trans Jordan in the east, away from the Hyksos fortress Avaris. They could do this without fear from the Hyksos overlords. The Amelekites were rather indifferent about the internal affairs of Palestine. They were robber barons who occasionally raided Canaan, but no more.

A Star

Something else needs to be mentioned. There is something odd, something out of the ordinary about the imagery of Balaam's oracle. He used a poetic device to impress upon his listeners just how badly the enemies of Israel would be beaten.

A star will come out of Jacob;
A scepter will rise out of Israel.

Planets, Ages and Empires

He will crush the foreheads of Moab,
The skulls of all the sons of Sheth.

> Numbers 24:17

The picture of a scepter is clear enough. A king would come out of Israel who would ruin Moab and Edom. That was King David, four hundred years in the future. But why would Balaam mention a star? Stars do not threaten anyone. They are so tranquil that children fall asleep thinking of it.

Twinkle, twinkle, little star,
How I wonder what you are.

But that is not what Balaam said. He compared the future king with a star that brought fear and destruction. Now how could Balaam possibly impress his audience with the notion of a destructive star unless such a feared prodigy was visible in the sky? Otherwise, the imagery would have been meaningless.

Strange as it may sound, such a phenomenon may have occurred. No less an authority than Augustine mentioned it. In "The City of God," he attempted to prove that changes can take place in the order of nature. In Book 21, Ch. 8, relying on ancient sources, he said this.

> From the book of Marcus Varro, entitled "Of the race of the Roman People," I cite word for word the following instance: "There occurred a remarkable celestial portent; for Castor records that in the brilliant star Venus, called Vesperugo by Plautus and the lovely Hesperus by Homer, there occurred so strange a prodigy, that it changed its color, size, form, course, which never happened before nor since. Adrastus of Cyzicus, and Dion of Naples, famous mathematicians, said that this occurred in the reign of Ogyges."

Ogyges, mentioned before, was the Latin name for Agog, who then was the greatest of all kings. Yet Augustine's story does not seem to make much sense. Venus, the morning or evening star, is a bright spot of light without a discernible shape. It is difficult to see how it could have been observed to change color, size, form and direction. There is an unconventional explanation. Venus may have been in an irregular, highly elliptical orbit that made it come perilously close to the earth. As it came nearer it grew in size and lit by the sun had a crescent shape that changed while it moved past the earth, after which it shrunk until it disappeared.

We could hazard a guess. After decades of gloom, the clouds dissolved and the sky became visible. A fearful sight appeared. A blazing star, mentioned by many peoples, was visible in broad daylight. It circled the sun in a highly elliptical orbit that crossed the path of the planets. This "star," which according to Augustine was Venus, had been seen before the great disaster and instilled fear. Venus was called the bright torch of heaven; it had a cometary tail. Nor was that the end.

The Miracle of Joshua

Some ten years after Israel began its conquest of Canaan, Joshua fought a battle with five Amorite kings. After an all-night march, he caught them by surprise and routed them. The Israelites pursued them all day, and then something very strange happened. While on the Ascent of Beth Horon, a long valley, a hail of meteorites killed a large part of the fleeing army. Numerous sources relate that the corridor was rendered impassable because it was filled with large rocks.

> On the day the Lord gave the Amorites over to Israel, Joshua said to the Lord in the presence of Israel:
> "O sun, stand still over Gibeon,
> O Moon, over the Valley of Aijalon."
> So the sun stood still and the moon stopped, till the nation avenged itself on its enemies, as it is written in the book of Jashar. The sun stopped in the middle of the sky and delayed going down about a full day. There has never been a day like it before or since, a day when the Lord listened to a man. Surely, the Lord was fighting for Israel.
>
> Joshua 10:12-14

What could possibly cause the sun to stand still in the sky? It was the Lord, yes, but the Almighty has always had a way of using means. The earth could have hardly been stopped in its daily rotation. Instead the axis of the earth may have tilted in the presence of a planetary body. That would have extended daylight several hours (eighteen hours, according to rabbinical sources).

If indeed the planet Venus was then a comet that crossed the orbits of the planets, it could have come close enough to tilt the axis of the earth. Even though destructive, the impact was not as severe as the global disaster fifty years earlier. Assuming that was the case, it must have passed farther away than before. Rabbi Rashi maintained that the stones that fell from the sky were the same as the ones that hammered Egypt during the 7th plague. It follows that they must have been meteorites, "stones of barad." Could it be that the sighting of Venus as reported by Augustine happened at this time?

Jericho

When Israel entered Canaan, their first conquest was Jericho. Having marched around the city every day for a week they finally surrounded it, and the moment they stormed it an earthquake hit. The walls collapsed outward; Joshua and his army walked in, killed everyone except Rahab the inn keeper and her relatives, and burned Jericho to the ground. Naturally, this story was met with disbelief - until archaeologists began digging. They discovered the walls had fallen in an earthquake and that a large supply of grain, stockpiled for a long siege, had been burned. In other words, the city fell before any grain was used.

Contrary to general belief, Israel did not enter Canaan during the Late Bronze Age, but at the end of the Early Bronze Age (EB III), the exact time when Jericho fell to invaders. The break was abrupt and total, and came with catastrophic suddenness. It was found that a semi nomadic people conquered Canaan and annihilated or otherwise absorbed the original population. These people entered Palestine by crossing the Jordan and captured cities such as Jericho, Ai, Gibeon and Lachish, all of it at the end of the Early Bronze Age. It followed the exact record of Israel conquering the Promised Land.

An unexpected surprise awaited archaeologists. Israel supposedly entered Canaan during the reign of Ramses II, or perhaps Merneptah, long after the Hyksos. But pottery, found in the ruins of Jericho, dated from the beginning of the Hyksos period. Of course, in the reconstructed version of history this is exactly what we would expect. The Hyksos began their rule forty years earlier, when they walked into a prostrate Egypt and occupied southern Palestine. Their dominion extended beyond Syria-Palestine to the Euphrates, and it seems the only nation to challenge them in any fashion was Israel. The conquest of Canaan was long and bitter and beset with failures. Joshua turned out to be a capable General. He established Israel in the Promised Land, and left it to his successors, the judges, to finish the task.

The Judges

The civil government of Israel was unlike any other nation. The nation was organized in a loose federation of autonomous tribes, ruled by elders. There was no central government, and necessarily no despotic king. Rather the twelve tribes were ruled by judges. Repeatedly a leader would come to deliver Israel from cyclic apostasy and oppression.

Who were the enemies of Israel? The Amelekites, Midian, the Canaanites, the Philistines. And Amelek was the power behind it all. The Song of Deborah speaks of the deeds of the tribes, and who fought the Canaanites. Some of their enemies "came from Ephraim, whose roots were in Amelek." The Amelekites established a garrison in Ephraim at a strategic location, whence they maintained control. The record states that they built strongholds such as Carchemish on the Euphrates, Gaza and Shahurem in southern Palestine. Amelek and Midian were related; they came from different parts of Arabia, and they worked together. The story of Gideon records how the

Amelekites and Midianites impoverished Israel by running their cattle through recently planted crops. They were indeed a shepherd people, bent on destruction.

The Philistines, according to rabbinical sources, were not the descendants of the original inhabitants of the Mediterranean coast who lived in the days of the patriarchs. Following the disaster of the exodus they left Cyprus, occupied the coast and were called after the former occupants. The newcomers were closely associated with Amelek. They intermarried and eventually became a mixed race. There is a curious side note. There were giants in Palestine; not merely tall people but "Anakim," perhaps a strain of the Nephilim that continued after the flood. Most were killed by Israel, but a few survived and found refuge with the Philistines. For all their size and strength they were no match for the invading tribes.

Still, Israel was not able to drive the Canaanites from the plains, the "Shepelah," (Judges 1:27-36) and to a large extend established themselves near the mountains. The Canaanites were the vassals and collaborators of the Amelekites who supported them in return. The Judges ruled about four hundred years, then the Israelites chose themselves a king. That coincided with an uprising in Egypt; the pharaohs of the south finally threw out the hated Hyksos, and the kings of Israel finished them off.

The Purpose

Now that we have seen that the history of Israel closely agrees with that of Egypt, a number of questions must be asked. Why would God move heaven and earth to move an enslaved people out of Egypt to Canaan and why was Egypt suppressed by the Amelekites some five centuries? Five hundred years is a long time. For all fact and purpose Egypt was removed from world history.

To some extent the exodus was symbolic of the great deliverance. The idea is that of paradise restored. God led his people back to the Promised Land. In a more immediate sense, the fantastic events that accompanied the exodus deeply impressed the twelve tribes. The memory of the miraculous deliverance, forever etched into the memory of the Hebrews, convicted them of a high calling. They were chosen by God.

It is also certain that Egypt was temporarily removed from the scene for the sole purpose of allowing Israel to get set up in Canaan to establish the worship of the One Holy God, Yahweh. Once the Egyptians recovered, they would have been sorely tempted to raid Palestine and haul their former slaves back to the brick kilns. Also the pharaohs would have probably resented the notion of a deity, higher than the representative of Ra on earth. Dictators have always hated the Judeo-Christian religion for just that reason. The Hyksos Pharaohs had no such delusions. They were robber barons who occasionally raided Canaan, but no more.

Another reason is that the Hebrews grew up in Egypt and picked up their religion. Make no mistake about it, the Hebrews were idolaters, and they kept it up in the Promised Land. The twentieth chapter of Ezekiel makes that very clear. This involved a continual struggle between Israel and the Lord. This is the symbolic meaning behind the name change of Jacob. His name was changed to *Israel*, meaning "striving with God." As we will see, Israel and Judah did not put their faith in God; they relied on Egypt for aid. Egypt had reasons to regret this, for the Almighty eventually made it "the lowliest of kingdoms." "Egypt will no longer be a source of confidence for the people of Israel but will be a reminder of their sin in turning to her for help. Then they will know that I am the Sovereign Lord." (Ezekiel 29:16) Which is exactly what happened; ever since Egypt has been the lowliest of kingdoms.

Israel was delivered from slavery in a miraculous fashion. This was done for a reason. The only gods they knew were Egyptian idols, and there were many, but they never knew the God of their fathers. In the events surrounding the plagues of Egypt, the wondrous events at the Sea of Passage and the Mount of lawgiving, they saw that this Almighty God was not to be trifled with. Yahweh was altogether holy, righteous, just and merciful. In other words, unlike Egypt's plethora of deities, this One God was for real, and he set before them a set of moral and ethical standards that were alien to the pagan religions around them. They were set apart for that purpose. "You will be for me a kingdom of priests and a holy nation," (Ex.19:6) a nation that eventually would bring forth the Messiah.

Catastrophism

No doubt this reconstruction of history is revolutionary and controversial, even more so because it involves cosmic catastrophes. Nonetheless, the scriptures describe events that are clearly catastrophic in nature. In view of its historical and religious importance, we must stop to evaluate the events, described in Hebrew and Egyptian sources. There was a major catastrophe that led to the collapse of Egypt and the deliverance of Israel. That much we know. It is only rational to ask what could possibly be the nature and cause of this disaster. There are many instances in the exodus account that indicate trouble came from the sky.

Was it, as Velikovsky thought, because the proto planet Venus came dangerously close or was it the result of the volcanic explosion that blew up the island Thera, or were the two related? Thanks to recent advances in plasma research and unexpected discoveries in the makeup of the universe, we are in a better position to judge whether or not Venus could have played a role. For that matter, certain strange events that occurred in the days of the Hebrew kings may be explained as well. It is time to look at an altogether different theory.

Chapter Two

Venus

Dynamics

Opponents of Velikovsky's theories have a legitimate point. The planets move according to Newton's law of gravity and inertia, which balance each other to assure a circular orbit around the sun. In addition there are laws dealing with energy preservation, meaning that the planets do not suddenly behave erratically. The driving force behind planetary motion is inertia. If for some reason that is changed, the movement of the planet is affected. This is where Velikovsky's theories beg an explanation. If the earth and Venus were disturbed in their path, how could they resume their regular motion? The case of Venus is more complex. How could it begin as an errant comet and then be captured in a nearly circular orbit, and if Venus is a new member of the solar system, how could it have possibly come into existence? These things seem to defy not only the laws of gravity and inertia, but of celestial mechanics as well.

Velikovsky was aware of this, and so he attempted to find a solution - not entirely successfully, but enough to point in the right direction. Myth and folklore, and for that matter straightforward reports, reveal a pattern of planetary behavior that points at an electrically charged solar system. There are repeated reports of electrical discharges between planets. If indeed the planets occasionally came close, they were repelled because they were magnetically charged. It is true that gravity and inertia have a place in celestial mechanics, (that is why satellites remain in orbit), but they are not the only forces that move planets, suns and galaxies. Velikovsky reasoned that the sun and the planets must be electrically charged, and that electromagnetism plays a role in the dynamics of celestial motion.

> Thus, celestial mechanics does not conflict with cosmic catastrophism. I must admit, however, that in searching for the causes of the great upheavals of the past and in considering their effects, I became skeptical of the great theories concerning the celestial motions that were formulated when the historical facts described here were not known to science. The subject deserves to be discussed in detail and quantitatively. All that I would venture to say at this time and in this place is the following: The accepted celestial mechanic, notwithstanding the many calculations that have been carried out to many decimal points, or verified by celestial motions, stands only *if* the sun, the source of light, warmth, and other radiation produced by fusion and fission of atoms, *is on the whole an electrically neutral body*, and also if the planets, in their usual orbit, are neutral bodies.
> Fundamental principles in celestial mechanics including the law of gravitation, must come into question if the sun possesses a charge sufficient to influence the planets in their orbits or the comets in theirs. In the Newtonian celestial mechanics, based on the theory of gravitation, electricity and magnetism play no role.[1]

He approached the mystery surrounding gravity in terms of magnetic attraction: gravity is an electromagnetic phenomenon. Furthermore he maintained that the sun and the planets generate magnetic fields which, depending on their intensity, cause satellites to orbit. He thought the magnetic field of the sun must extend well beyond the solar system; the moon must be within the magnetosphere of the earth. At the time he was ignored and laughed at, but with the coming of the space age his claims turned out to be prophetic. These things are taken for granted now, and few realize that it was proposed by an outsider long before it was accepted as factual.

There are aspects about gravity that Velikovsky mentioned but did not elaborate on. In his time already it was realized that gravity must act instantaneously, otherwise it would not work. Its effect decreases by the square of the distance, but it nonetheless acts in no time at all. This leads us to another puzzle. If the planets orbit the sun solely in terms of gravity and inertia which somehow perfectly balance out, then sooner or later the gravitational attraction of the planets would cause them to affect each other. The movement of the solar system would become chaotic. But no, the planets move around the sun as if pulled by a steel cable; gravity plays hardly any role at all. These considerations combined with discoveries in the field of plasma led a number of scientists to consider a wholly new approach. As Velikovsky supposed, basic, fundamental assumptions were questioned.

Now we must keep in mind that scientists are human and prone to errors. They are anything but perfect and particularly in the field of astronomy their notions often sound like science fiction. The story is told of a small airplane with three passengers on board; a world renowned scientist, a minister and a boy scout. While flying at 10,000 feet over rough terrain, the air craft suddenly developed engine trouble and the pilot ordered everybody to bail out. Then it turned out there were only three parachutes on board. "The airline cannot do without me, I am indispensable" the pilot observed. He grabbed a parachute and jumped. "I am the smartest man in the world," the scientist said. "Science cannot survive without me." He harnessed himself in his gear and followed the captain. So the minister and the Boy Scout were left with one parachute between them. "Well, my boy," the minister said, "You have your life before you. I am old and I have peace with the Lord, take the parachute." The Boy Scout smiled. "Don't worry Pastor," he said. "The smartest man in the world just jumped with my back pack."

When we read learned comments by scientist, it is well to keep this in mind. Newspapers cite the opinions of scientists with the certainty of "Thus says the Lord." Much as we appreciate their valuable contributions, they often come with notions that are, to put it mildly, debatable. It is certainly true, as Velikovsky's critics maintain that he frequently based his theories on conjecture and ill founded assumptions. Yet they themselves often do the exact same thing. In trying to explain away historical observations they come with ad hoc explanations and assumptions they cannot possibly prove, and often make no sense.

Then there is the pervasive notion, first proposed by Kant and soon refuted, that the universe always existed and that it is infinite. Are you sure you have a parachute? It is nonsense on the sight of it. For something to have always existed and to be without limits it must be eternal, without beginning and necessarily without end. Since the eternal is infinite, it has no limits and therefore cannot be measured. You cannot be partially pregnant. Matter, energy and time are related, and they all have their limits; they can be measured and are necessarily finite. They cannot have always existed any more than they are boundless, and that can only mean the space/time continuum was called into being. It was called into being by an Infinite, Eternal Being, in full accord with the law of causality.

What made science possible? The Greek for all their wisdom and insight had no science. They were great mathematicians, but never experimented. Why not? In Greek thinking the world was chaotic, a shadow of the real thing in heaven, where capricious gods frolicked. No one looks for order in chaos. It was not until the latter part of the Middle Ages that scientific thought emerged, very much the result of Christian thinking. Creation is just as real as the Creator who made it. Since God is a God of order and everything he made is good, we can expect order. Man is called to subdue the earth and to rule (not destroy), meaning among other things he has to acquire knowledge, that is science. Men of science presumed order and hence developed the scientific method. The school for science is not philosophy, but the laboratory. Every time that has been done, science has made remarkable progress. Who knows, new findings may literally throw new light on the nature of electricity, magnetism and light.

The Force

Science fiction fans know all about "the force," that mystical (New Age/Hindu) energy field of George Lucas' Star Wars universe. A number of scientists maintain that a force of sorts does exist, albeit without the mystical qualities of Lucas' wizard religion. There is a growing consensus that the universe is driven by an electrostatic force that acts instantaneously, or nearly so.

The New York physicist Ralph Sansbury conducted an experiment, based upon a new classical physics theory which postulates that the electron is neither a fundamental particle nor an electromagnetic wave, but has structure. He assumed the electron has particles, which he dubbed subtrons, that travel at speeds, far in excess of the speed of light. It means that magnetism and light travel in no time at all. Naturally this is being hotly disputed, but it deserves attention.

Sansbury rigged a laser, capable of firing a burst of light lasting ten nano seconds, and aimed it at a receptor forty feet away. Light is supposed to travel at a speed of one foot per nano second. Sansbury placed a fast-moving electronic shutter in front of the receptor in the closed position. He then fired the pulse of light, opened the shutter just before the photons supposedly reached it - and the receptor saw nothing. It was as if the light had never been fired.

The explanation lies in the electrostatic force involved. For the detector to "see" the light pulse, it needed to be exposed to the excited electrons in the laser the very moment the burst of light was fired; instead the shutter blocked the pulse of light and the receptor "saw" nothing. The speed of light, which is the same under all circumstances, has nothing to do with speed. It is rather the amount of time it takes for a detector (such as our eyes) to register a signal. Light in other words, does not travel at all. It is an instantaneous electrostatic force. It implies that we see the stars as they are now, and not eons ago, and that theoretically space travel is possible.

> The fallout from Sansbury's idea, if proven, is prodigious. To begin, for the first time we have a truly unifying theory where both magnetism and gravity become a derived form of an instantaneous electrostatic force. The Lorentz contradiction-distortion of space time and mass is unnecessary. Electromagnetic radiation becomes the cumulative effect of instantaneous electrostatic forces at a distance and the wave/particle (photon) duality disappears.[2]

Laboratory experiments are falsifiable, meaning they can be proven wrong, something required for a scientific theory. It should be easy for critics to duplicate Sansbury's test, under better conditions, and find out whether or not he was correct. If proven true, it means light does not travel at all, it is instantaneous. It also proves basic assumptions wrong. What drives the universe is not gravity, but an electrostatic force. Light is an instantaneous electrostatic phenomenon; there are no such things as electromagnetic waves.

> Amperes' formula for the magnetic field due to a current carrying wire can be derived from the classical model. The Lorentz contradiction-dilation of space-time and mass variations is avoided. Space returns to the classical "real world" of three dimensions with no connection to time. The difficulty in explaining how electromagnetic waves can be transmitted without an ether is avoided. It is the cumulative action of instantaneous electrostatic forces at a distance. A reinterpretation of the wave-photon duality is possible. The role of polarization of light in Einstein's photoelectric effect is explained by the model.
> Gravity is a result of weak electrostatic polarization of nucleons in a massive body and can therefore be modified by varying the charge on that body.[3]

Venus

Whatever the origin of this mysterious force (and there are numerous suppositions), it evidently traverses space in no time. For all fact and purpose it acts exactly like gravity, instantaneously. That makes sense, if indeed gravity is an electromagnetic phenomenon. But how do electrical current traverse space? Electricity after all needs a conductor. That conductor is abundantly available in space, it is called plasma.

Plasma

In his controversial book, "The Big Bang never happened," Eric J. Lerner postulates a universe, entirely different from that accepted by main science. It is a plasma universe, driven by electricity and magnetism. To the extent that the author sticks to the subject, half his book is excellent. The other half has nothing to do with the subject matter; he pushes bad religion. Nonetheless, he offers convincing proof that the universe could have never exploded into existence. Rather tremendous electrical forces shape the galaxies and feed them.

The theories of electromagnetism were developed largely during the Nineteenth Century. An electrical current running through a wire will create a magnetic field around the wire. A magnet near the wire will be pulled around it, the principle of the electric motor. It did not take long for scientists to realize the opposite has similar results: a wire passing through a moving magnetic field creates electricity; the concept behind the generator. Faraday saw that magnetic fields move through space and that they move in curved lines. Maxwell developed the laws of electromagnetism, and other scientists discovered the electron which carries the negative charge. It was found that electrons move around the proton, which is nearly two thousand times heavier than the electron, and constitutes the core of the atom.

Velikovsky supposed electromagnetic forces play a role in celestial mechanics, although he did not know how. Help came from an unexpected source; electrical engineers unwittingly came to his rescue. This of course is a field totally ignored by astronomers, among other things because electrical fields cannot be seen, and it is an area of expertise outside their domain. Plasma science, which is related to electromagnetism, was begun by two Scandinavian engineers who were fascinated by the northern lights. What causes the aurora, that colorful ever moving curtain in the sky?

Kristian Birkeland, a Norwegian scientist, noticed something similar in the cathode ray tube, a partially evacuated tube coated with fluorescent material. When an electrical charge was applied, the tube began to glow. Birkeland reasoned that something of the kind happened in outer space. He noticed that electrons follow magnetic lines. If the sun emits electrons, he reasoned, they quite likely would follow the magnetic lines of the earth.

Birkeland knew that electrons are attracted to magnets. The earth is a huge magnet. He reasoned that the sun emits charged particles that upon reaching the earth follow the earth's magnetic field. When they reach the poles, they spiral down. As these electrical currents develop mutually attractive magnetic fields, they merge into spiraling filaments that create the aurora. The northern lights therefore are nature's cathode tube. Laboratory experiments confirmed the theory. He concluded that electrical currents and magnetic fields move through very thin conductive gasses in outer space. How that worked he did not know. It was left to future scientists to work these ideas out.

Unfortunately Birkeland's work was ignored for half a century, thanks to the notion that mathematics rather than the laboratory is the proper domain of science. Meanwhile another Scandinavian, the Swede Hannes Alfven (pronounced Alfvain) picked up where Birkeland left off. Alfven, like Birkeland, was fascinated by the northern lights. When he learned that Birkeland explained the aurora as electrical currents flowing through gasses, he conducted laboratory experiments to find the answer. By that time the American chemist Langmuir conducted experiments with ionized gasses and found that such gasses, which he called plasma, carry electrical currents. It is applied, for instance, in neon lights.

Actually plasma is not a gas at all and certainly does not behave that way. Plasma is gas that is ionized; it has electrons stripped from the atoms, which renders it capable of carrying electrical currents. Alfven discovered that electrical currents flowing though plasma do not travel in straight lines. These currents create magnetic fields that twist it into braided vortexes; they are pinched together and visibly snake through plasma, like miniature tornadoes. They have since been dubbed Birkeland currents. Alfven concluded that a natural phenomenon like that must exist in space, and that the universe is filled with plasma, magnetic fields and electrical currents. At first that was fiercely denied, but the space age proved him right. For his work in the field of plasma science he received the Nobel Prize.

These discoveries have far-reaching consequences, so radical that few scientists are willing to face the implications. The universe is not at all a pure vacuum, it is filled with plasma (ninety-nine percent of all matter in the universe is plasma) and electrical forces, and that can only mean it is essentially an electric universe. It is not governed by gravity, the weakest force known to man, but electricity, the most powerful. Electrical forces are ten-trillion-trillion-trillion times more powerful than gravity.

There is by far not enough matter in the universe to account for the required gravity. If we scale down the sun to a particle of dust, the nearest star, another dust particle, is more than four miles away. Astronomers out of sheer necessity dreamed up "dark matter," so-called because it has never been seen, and gravity wells such as black holes, which exist only in the imagination of mathematicians. The theory of an electrically charged universe on the other hand provides an intriguing solution to the behavior of the nearest star, our sun.

The Electric Universe

What is the sun? Every time this question was raised, men have tried to explain the nature of that blinding star in terms of current technology. So the sun at first was a huge bonfire, then it was a pile of burning coal, then a huge gas ball, and now a nuclear furnace. However, nuclear explosions emit neutrinos, which are lacking in the sun; also the strange phenomenon of sun spots begs for an explanation. In addition, the corona is extremely hot, two millions degrees, much more than the surface of the sun. Besides, it moves faster than the sun itself, when the opposite should be the case.

The sun behaves very much like a plasma arc in welding, with the same blinding blue white light. It does not burn up internal energy sources, rather it is constantly being fed from the outside. It is a virtual electrode. Enormous amounts of electrical energy stream toward the sun, plasma being the conductor. This huge ball of charged plasma and gases which throughout has the same density, has an electrical atmosphere. The surface (photosphere) is about 5800K. As positive Ions enter the chromosphere the temperature drops to 4000K, but they then accelerate into the corona, where they arc into the blinding light that makes the sun. Sun spots are the result of holes in the corona. Rather than the product of so-called flux tubes from the interior of the star that cut off energy, they may merely be the result of lower current density.

All this of course requires an electrical source. Alfven explained how such vast currents could flow across the universe. He demonstrated that currents do not move in straight lines like the neat electrical wires we employ. It is much more complex than that. Space is neither the perfect isolator that will not allow currents to pass nor the perfect conductor that allows currents to flow without restrictions. Plasma is not a perfect conductor, it has ohmic loss, and that is where things become complicated. An electrical current produces a magnetic field, which affect not only electrons but also plasma.

> When a current flows through a plasma, Alfven shows, it must assume the form of a filament in order to move along magnetic field lines. The flow of electrons thus becomes force-free: because they move exactly along the lines of a magnetic field, no magnetic forces act on them. In a force-free filament, the electrons in effect cooperate to minimize the difficulty of flowing. Those along the center of the filament flow in straight lines, producing a spiral magnetic field along which inner electrons flow. Together,

the electrons move in a complex pattern of helical paths with increasingly steep pitch as they approach the filament's axis.

In Alfven's new view inhomogeneity - produced by the formation of filamentary currents - is an almost inevitable property of plasmas, and thus of the universe *as a whole*. The universe, thus, forms a gigantic power grid, with huge electrical currents flowing along filamentary "wires" stretching across the cosmos. Not only are current and magnetic field thereby concentrated into the spiraling filaments, but the plasma itself is pinched together by magnetic fields, sucked into an electro-magnetic tornado.[4]

The sun is a ball of lightning, and necessarily electrically charged. It has a magnetic field that reaches beyond the outer planets, and pulls the planets along in a fixed orbit. This counteracts the natural tendency of gravity and inertia to affect the motion of planets by mutual attraction. Left to themselves the planets are bound to pull each other out of orbit, which eventually would cause the solar system to become chaotic. The magnetic grip of the sun prevents that. The planets are affected because their electric charge is opposite that of the sun. They are enveloped by a magnetosphere and a plasmasphere that, like a cometary tail, is blown away from the sun. They move in harmony because the solar system has electrical equilibrium. Every planet that is, except Venus.

This explains the appearance and behavior of comets. These iron-nickel boulders originate outside the solar system. We would expect meteors to be rough and jagged, but close-up photos show surprising features. They look like enormous potatoes, slowly rotating and pitted with craters. How come they are rounded and why are they pockmarked?

Comets are strangers in the solar system. As their elliptical orbit speeds them back to the sun, they are affected by its electrical field. Dr. Donald E. Scott in that fascinating work "The Electric Sky," explains how.

Because comets spend much more time in the outer (lower-voltage) reaches of their orbits than they do in the near- (higher-voltage) region, they reach voltage equilibrium with the low voltage of the sun's outer plasma. As a comet approaches the inner range of its orbit, the voltage difference between it and the solar plasma through which it is traveling rapidly increases. As current flows to the comet in response to this voltage difference, the well-known cometary effects appear – a tail and coma plasma sheath in glow mode surrounding the comet nucleus and jets (plasma arc discharges sometimes pointed in the direction of the sun) that produce the craters observed on comet surfaces.[5]

Comets are subject to severe electrical charges. Their ragged edges are arced away, which is also why they have craters. The electrical nature of the universe provides an answer to a suggestion made by Velikovsky. Quoting ancient sources, he suggested that comets are born from near-collisions between planets. Exactly how that happened he did not say because he did not know, and critics laughed at it without bothering to investigate the matter. Yet it is possible. It is a result of the electrical nature of the solar system. When planets for some reason come close to each other, their plasma sheaths interact, resulting in planetary electrical discharges.

The power of a lightning strike is incredible. It will dig furrows and blow the earth sky high. What if that happens on a planetary scale? The evidence is much closer than we would think. The planet Mars (which lacks a magnetic field), has telltale signs of planetary lightning strikes. The surface is marked by rilles, hundreds of miles long, with patterns that could have only been made by electrical discharges. All indications are that Valles Marineris, the 2500 mile rift that dwarfs the Grand Canyon, was scooped by an electrical arc that blew millions of tons of soil into space. Much of the rubble fell back on the surface, which is covered with rocks. Much remained in space as meteorites, some of which ended up on the earth.

If indeed the universe is governed by electricity, it follows that the solar system is powered by both electromagnetism and gravity/

inertia. It also means that the strange phenomena ascribed to Venus are theoretically possible. The earliest reports of Venus describe it as a planetary body with cometary characteristics. It had all the makings of an electrically charged planet, red-hot, with a cometary tail. That is not at all what we would expect, but Venus is indeed different. It stands to reason that this could only happen in an electric universe. It also provides a plausible explanation how star systems develop.

> The view is that diffuse hydrogen and dust is efficiently scavenged and compressed by the well-known magnetic pinch effect of an electric current flowing along the arms of a galaxy. At some point gravity takes over and stellar objects are formed. Beyond a certain size proto stars become electrically unstable and "fission," spitting out some of the core and giving rise to one or more companions. This explains the predilection for stars to be found in pairs or multiples. Not all of the matter ejected from the core of a proto star may coalesce into a companion star. It may be in the form of one or a number of gas giants. (The recent discovery of a Jupiter-like body orbiting very close to a nearby star argues strongly for this model and against the standard theory). A gas giant, in turn, due to either internal or external electrical disturbance may fission, spitting out its core, to give rise to the highly condensed planets, moons, asteroids, comets etc.[6]

The Creation account relates how "In the beginning God created the heavens and the earth. Now the earth was formless and empty, darkness was over the surface of the deep, and the Spirit of God was hovering over the waters. And God said, "Let there be light," and there was light."

Let's assume that God initially called into being the Universe, a space/time continuum which obviously had a definite beginning. It was essentially a plasma universe. Let us further assume that all the raw material was there and that God fired up the Universe with an instantaneous electrical charge, which resulted in a burst of light.

The plasma, first in blinding white arc stage, gradually was reduced to a glow mode such as found in neon light, and eventually attained the dark mode prevalent now. The wording of Genesis creates the distinct impression that light is an instantaneous phenomenon.

It is well known that electricity has a tendency to create a rotary motion. It is evident in Birkeland currents. Who knows, maybe electrical storms generate tornadoes for just that reason. Star systems and galaxies could swirl into being, lined in enormous grids, plasma being the conductor of the electrical currents that power the stars. God formed order out of chaos.

This, of course, is not necessarily what catastrophists believe, but it is an interesting proposition. In any event, observations by the Hubble telescope indicate gas giants have been ejected by stars, which lend credence to the theory of an electric universe.

The Big Bang

To conventional science, this sounds like heresy. It is believed that the universe is governed by gravity, the weakest known force, so weak there is not enough matter in the observed universe to keep the galaxies together. For this reason, and out of sheer necessity, mathematicians conjured neutron stars, black holes and black matter, things never observed. The theory of an expanding universe and by extension a Big Bang that started it all, arose from a curious astronomical observation. As astronomers looked farther into the universe, they noticed a red shift. The greater the distance, the more light appears in the red spectrum. It was assumed that this red shift was the result of the Doppler Effect.

It is the well-known phenomenon of a ringing bell sounding high when a train approaches the source, and suddenly sounding lower once the train shoots past it. Sound waves are first compressed, then elongated, making it sound lower. The same thing appears to be the case in the universe. Distant galaxies move away at ever increasing speed; the light they emit therefore appears in the lower, the red spectrum. Beginning with this assumption, it follows that the galaxies must have started in a huge explosion, the Big Bang. This, of course, led to a dilemma. Where did that original minuscule ball of matter come from, and how did it destabilize? As one wit once put it, "In the beginning there was nothing, which exploded."

The Big Bang theory is fraught with difficulties. If indeed the stellar systems were blown into space, they should be rather evenly distributed, and they are not. Galaxies are strung out in irregular bands; there are clusters of galaxies lined up in enormous grids. They are so far away that the twenty some billion years assigned to the age of the universe is totally inadequate. It would have taken them at least one hundred billion years to get there. But once theories are established in the minds of men they become fact, whether or not there is real evidence.

The eminent astronomer Halton Arp thought otherwise. In his controversial (and technical) book "Seeing Red," he showed convincingly that red shifts have nothing to do with movement. Bright galaxies of the Seyfert class emit a perpendicular vortex of excess electrical energy that creates a rotary motion. Such a vortex begets a quasar - a nascent galaxy that is electron-deficient relative to the parent galaxy. As a result it emits light in the low spectrum, red. As quasars develop a higher electrical charge, they become brighter, a blue shift. The electrostatic force acting instantaneously, this shift occurs instantly across the whole galaxy. The red shift astronomers observe are quasars, not runaway galaxies. The universe is not expanding. There never was a big bang. However, the notion of an electric universe inspired some of Velikovsky's disciples to consider a number of options, and they are different to say the least. They are hardly factual, it is merely a hypothesis.

Saturn

The Saturn theory maintains that the world before the deluge was entirely different from what it is now, as was the solar system. It is believed that the planets did not follow individual orbits around the sun at ever increasing distances as they do now, rather they were very close and lined up in a polar array. If that was the case, the generation before the flood witnessed an awesome firmament. Facing north toward what is now Polaris, the north pole star, one would see first Mars, about the size of the moon, behind that Venus and behind it the awe inspiring giant planet Saturn, light-yellow and without rings. It was much larger than it is now, about the size of Jupiter. The system moved in tandem around the sun which, depending on the motion of the system, would cast a crescent shape on Saturn.

The role of Jupiter is uncertain, but it may have been hidden behind Saturn, which was much larger then. The system eventually destabilized. Mars moved close to the earth, resulting in that catastrophic event known as the flood. Jupiter disrupted Saturn, which caused Saturn to go nova; it exploded. Much of Saturn's atmosphere was blown away; the giant planet became much smaller, and it developed rings. Jupiter became the dominant planet. The system now entered an entirely different configuration; the planets began to orbit around the sun. Saturn was disowned, so to speak, by Jupiter; it entered a faraway orbit. Venus on the other hand moved inside the orbit of the earth.

Interesting, but the polar array theory is impossible to accept. The evidence is based upon highly subjective interpretation of mythology. Myth is believed to be an earthly story with an astral meaning. In early times, so the reasoning goes, the great god of paganism was Kronos or Saturn, the sun god. Once there was a golden age, the age of Kronos, when men lived very long lives in a virtual paradise. This was the antediluvian world. At this point the theory goes awry. There are numerous myths from many civilizations that mention someone who taught men the arts of civilization. This man was believed to be divine. In later times he was assigned the status of a god, usually the sun god such as Ra, Helios, Saturn, presumably because he enlightened mankind. To say that a luminary like the sun or perhaps Saturn instructed humanity is preposterous. Christianity knows such a person, but it would be folly to enlarge on that.

Nonetheless, there is ample evidence that humanity remembered an age of plenty, utterly unlike ours. There is even an implication in the Genesis account that conditions on earth before the flood - and by extension the solar system - were different from what they are now. It is implied in the divine decree following the flood. (Gen 8:22)

> As long as the earth endures,
> seedtime and harvest,
> cold and heat,
> summer and winter,
> day and night,
> will never cease.

In the context of the divine pronouncement it is clear that an altogether new world emerged, different from the world that preceded it. It is generally recognized that God instituted civil government to restrain the murderous anarchy that existed before the flood. An altogether different order was instituted to suit a new regimen. Seedtime and harvest, cold and heat, summer and winter are the result of a seasonal year. Evidently that was not the case before the flood. The antediluvial (pre-flood) world had an equitable climate; the temperature worldwide was around 75 degrees Fahrenheit. Food was readily available anywhere, and there were no weather extremes. The landmass was much larger than it is now. Much of the Pacific Ocean once was land, and the seas were much shallower.

The reference to day and night is intriguing. For some reason the nocturnal part of the earth evidently was to some extent illuminated. Something of the kind happens when the earth is covered with snow and the full moon makes the world look like a darkened day. Since the rainbow appeared after the flood, it follows that atmospheric conditions before the flood were different from what they are now. Some suggest the earth was protected by a water canopy that blocked harmful radiation. It may have diffused light sufficiently to produce a night glow.

If the primeval world was not seasonal, the axis of the earth was not slanted as it is now. It may have been nearly perpendicular to the ecliptic. Proponents of the Saturn theory point at pictures of Kronos

(Saturn) as it was lit sideways by the sun and variously had a crescent shape, sufficient to illuminate the earth. It is quite possible that the original system was disrupted by a catastrophic event. It could involve a near-approach between gas giants; planets could have been thrown out of their orbits.

What about the huge animals that once stalked the earth? They may have grown large because they lived a long time. Living conditions were ideal; plants and trees grew much larger as well. But how could dinosaurs move about in spite of their tremendous weight? Maybe they weighed less. If gravity is an electromagnetic phenomenon, the electrostatic potential of the earth may have been weaker than it is now. Earth's gravitational attraction was necessarily less, which made giantism possible. That is no scientific fact, but the puzzle remains whatever we assume.

The Saturn array theory has additional problems, mostly dealing with Venus, supposedly a young planet. For instance, it does not explain the highly unusual makeup of Venus; also it is difficult the imagine how it could so drastically change location. Nor does it account for the asteroid belt. The planets move in ever increasing distances from the sun. At the exact spot where there should be a planet between Mars and Jupiter there is an enormous asteroid belt instead. Four planetoids were identified. The gravitational pull of Jupiter scatters the asteroids.

There are two explanations. Either it is the remnant of an exploded planet or it is the residue of material that failed to form into a planet. The first solution is not popular because it involves a catastrophic event (heretical). The second has found more acceptance because it fits theories regarding the origin of the solar system. However, it does not explain how the combined mass of the asteroid belt (half the diameter of the moon) could account for the space it occupies. The space that requires a planet.

The Saturn theory being a mythological guess at best, it becomes necessary to re-evaluate the makeup of the original solar system. Assuming the planets circled the sun more or less in the same orbit they do now, there was an additional terrestrial planet inside the orbit of

Jupiter which the Chaldeans called Tiamat and the Greek Elektra. Then disaster struck.

Allen and Delair in their scholarly and well-documented book "Cataclysm," present evidence that not so long ago a cosmic catastrophe changed the face of the earth. Around 9500 B.C., they assert, a global disaster nearly wiped out humanity. Their application of ancient historical records is flawed, and their interpretation of scripture nonsense. For all their criticism of Velikovsky, they plagiarize Zachiria Sichin's follies. However, in their area of expertise they excel, and they submit compelling proof that the world before the flood was very different from what it is now. They present evidence that the earth suffered crustal warping, which produced huge mountain ranges. Great ice dumps formed at the poles; herds of mammoth froze on the spot. Tidal waves moved toward the north, splintering and mangling forest and animals, and left the debris in the arctic wastes. They believe that the cause of the deluge was a cosmic visitor, which they identify as "Marduk." This was a fragment of the Vela supernova which, astronomically speaking was uncomfortably close. They thought Marduk was identical with Phaeton, a moon-sized object, electrically charged and the cause of the deluge.

This is a mistaken assumption. Marduk was Jupiter and Phaeton Venus; they are so identified repeatedly and unmistakably. Phaeton was the son of Helios, identified as either the sun or Saturn. The remnant of a nova explosion could hardly be moon-sized. To have a spherical shape it must have had much more mass than that. Besides, an object that small could never affect giant planets such as Jupiter and Saturn; it could not be seen at that great a distance, nor could a light giving body have a crescent shape, as they assert.

It is ill advised to dream up a scenario that makes Jupiter an intruder in the solar system. Instead there may have been a catastrophic encounter between the enormous gas giant and Tiamat that tore the doomed planet to pieces, not only under its gravitational stress, but with enormous electrical discharges as well. Remnants of this exploded planet still float between Mars and Jupiter. The core of

Tiamat evaporated, but the outer shell was blown into space. This huge string of rubble is now known as the asteroid belt.

It is unlikely that Marduk/Jupiter is an intruder from another solar system. Both Jupiter and Saturn are largely made up of the same gases, hydrogen/helium. Nor is it the parent of Venus. If anything, Saturn is a more likely candidate. The renown astronomer Gerard Kuiper assumed that Saturn once was the size of Jupiter.[7] Either it destabilized or Jupiter somehow came close and disturbed its electrical balance. This being the case, the gas giant fissioned in a nova explosion in a tremendous burst of light. From this fateful event an iron-cored sphere was born, the proto planet Venus. This fits quite well in the model of an electric universe, and it agrees with numerous sources that report a blinding light lasting a week at the time of the flood, until the deluge came. Rabbinical sources mention it, and the Tiamat legend speaks of it as well.[8]

This hardly qualifies as scientific fact; it is merely a working hypothesis. But it does explain a great many things about Venus that are strange to say the least. If this is more or less what happened, then Venus is a very young planet. In this paradigm it was born, not in a violent explosion on Jupiter, as Velikovsky supposed, but as a result of a disruption between two dark stars. As Saturn fissioned, it produced an iron-based planet that began not so long ago in a white-hot stage. Among the results are the rings of Saturn. Of course, we must be careful with this. By no means must it be thought that it is in any way necessary to accept these things as factual, nor is it needed to appreciate ancient history. We are always willing to consider the improbable. Yes, Venus is altogether different from all the other planets in the solar system. Just how different nobody knew until the space age.

Hell on Venus

Science fiction writers loved Venus. They envisioned a lush planet with continents and oceans much like the earth, only warmer. Their space craft were of course flying saucers, and an advanced civili-zation of humanoids flourished. Then came the space age, and all these visions vanished. When Russian and American space craft explored Venus, they encountered the fires of hell. The atmosphere of Venus is mostly made up of Carbon Dioxide (95%), argon and methane, and layers of clouds made up of corrosive sulfuric acid, several miles thick. The surface temperature is seven hundred forty degrees Fahrenheit, like that of a gas grill, hot enough to melt lead. The surface of Venus has rivers of flowing lava. The atmospheric pressure is ninety times that of the earth, enough to crush a nuclear submarine.

Venus, like the earth, is unique. There is nothing like it in the solar system. It has features that beg for an explanation. Why is it that the surface of Venus is in a molten stage, why is its atmosphere so dense, and what is the cause of the strange glow at the top of the mountains? It is believed that the high temperature of Venus is the result of a greenhouse effect, but that hardly rings true. It does not explain the makeup of the atmosphere, and it could never get that hot. There is nothing to stop the heat from radiating into space.

It also fails to account for the strange electrical phenomena that are evident all over the planet. The highest mountains are increaseingly bright at altitudes of more than 13,000 feet. It could very well be the familiar phenomenon of St Elmus fire, electrical charges that spark at high points. The same glow was detected by Pioneer probes at an altitude of seven miles. The Venera spacecraft registered continuous lightning discharges; as many as twenty five per second at an altitude of two to thirty-two kilometers (one to nineteen miles.) Venus receives much of its electrical energy from the sun. Ultra violet light in the ionosphere causes both the day and night side of the planet to glow. Strange enough, Venus has a magneto tail, twisted electrical currents that interact with the solar winds (plasma), Birkeland currents. It is forty five million miles long, enough to reach the earth at inferior conjunction.

The Babylonians, Aztecs and Incas all reported that Venus, the blazing star, had long flowing hair, that it smoked and that it appeared to have horns. Venus was most unusual among the planets, it had cometary characteristics. To a lesser extend it still does. Comets have plasma tails that flow radially away from the sun, the reason being that their electrical charge is not in balance with that of the sun. If that is the case, it follows that Venus has not yet achieved electrical equilibrium with the solar system. The age of planets is often measured by meteor impacts; Venus has very few, proof that it has not been around very long. There is an odd note: Venus is in resonance with the earth. The same side faces us at every inferior conjunction.

The upshot is that Venus could indeed be a young planet with a high electrical potential, and that the reports of ancient peoples about a cometary, burning planet in all likelihood are accurate. However, Venus was known by other names, and very ancient peoples worshiped this planet several millennia before Christ, long before the exodus. How then could Venus be a young planet?

The Sumerians

The late Carl Sagan raised a valid criticism against the Venus hypothesis. He showed that the Sumerian civilization around 2400 B.C. worshiped Eanna, or Venus. Since they worshiped this deity, Velikovsky's theory of a young Venus collapses. It existed long before the exodus. However true that may sound, recent research in ancient history renders Sagan's criticism, no matter how sincere, invalid. It goes all the way back to the landing place of Noah's ark. That is generally believed to have been Agri Dagi, the traditional Mount Ararat in Turkey, although the evidence points at an area farther south. Scholars generally agree that "the mountains of Ararat" refers to the ancient kingdom of Urartu in present day Turkey-Armenia.

Exactly where the ark landed is a matter of often hot and not so civilized debate. Some suggest Northern Iran, but that theory is not very well supported by the facts. A more likely candidate is Mt. Cudi, (pronounced Mt. Judi) in East Turkey, 175 miles south of Mt. Ararat. It is true that some have made unwarranted claims, and there is always the possibility of a geological formation, but the evidence of a recently unearthed vessel is there. It is about the size of the ark as described in Genesis, with evidence of highly developed structural framing. We will let the experts argue the case.

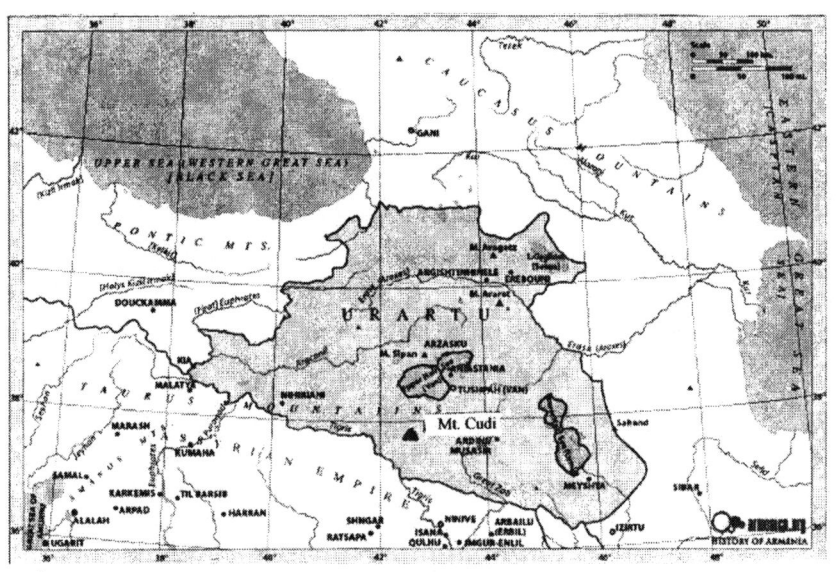

Source: www.armenica.org. historical maps/Armenia/kingdom of Urartu

If we take the scriptural account at face value, the flood of Noah occurred no earlier than 3000 B.C., and the ark settled in the mountains of Urartu. Once the human population increased (which may have taken a few centuries), the survivors journeyed to the south until they reached the plains of Shinar, also known as Babylonia. It makes sense that they would travel to a warm climate, build cities, settle and then move on. After Babylon was established, strong men such as Nimrod and Cush traveled north, built Nineveh and established the beginning of an empire.

Rather than replenish the earth, humanity chose to stay together until the confusion of tongues drove them apart. Velikovsky thought he found the primary cause; the planet Mercury flew close past the earth, resulting in electrical discharges that affected the mental capacities of the brain. Speech was altered. Fantastic though it may sound, the idea is not without merit. There are worldwide reports of this event (lightning plays an important role), and Mercury is associated with speech and memory. Mercury universally is the messenger. Nebo (Mercury) at that time was an important deity. The Egyptian Thoth was the messenger of the gods. The Greek Hermes is associated with language. That is where we get the technical word "hermeneutics," meaning principles of interpretation.

In any event, groups of peoples were on the move. They scattered far and wide. The descendants of Japheth moved toward the Mediterranean, Europe and the Caucasus. The Scythians came from the line of Japheth's grandson Ashkenaz. The descendants of Ham chose the road through Palestine toward Africa. Mezraim became Egypt. They also established Babylon and moved north to build Nineveh and the cities of Assyria; they occupied the Fertile Crescent. The scriptures do not mention this, but the Hamites may have moved east toward Asia as well. The descendants of Shem generally occupied the plains to the south of the Ararat mountain range, Arpaxad to the east and Aram to the west. This was rather a large area. Abraham in all likelihood originally came from an area north of Aram, in present day Turkey-Armenia.

One gets the distinct impression that the sketchy record of Genesis and the official history of the Sumerian civilization do not match. For the human race to re-establish itself, several centuries must have passed. People still lived a long time, so they likely had many children, meaning they could replenish fairly fast. Exactly when the flood occurred no one knows, but it could have hardly been the short time, derived from the ten-generation genealogical record, which amounts to about two hundred twenty years. Noah lived another three hundred fifty years after the flood, and Shem five hundred, meaning he outlived Abraham, which is impossible. It follows that the record has gaps. When it says that so-and-so became a father, it often means he became an ancestor. The record evidently mentions key men. It must have taken the earth and humanity some time to recover from the fearful devastation of the deluge, and it is therefore not unreasonable to place the flood fairly close to the year 3000 B.C. (The oldest known trees are five thousand years old.) All in all, we would hardly expect

Venus

a full-fledged civilization to appear as if it were, out of nowhere around 2400 B.C. It is very difficult to believe that an advanced civilization could have flourished in southern Mesopotamia, only to suddenly decline and vanish, not to be duplicated until fifteen hundred years later.

Displaced Empires

It is against this background that we look at a theory, proposed by Gunnar Heinsohn, professor of human sciences at the University of Hamburg, Germany, which drastically relocates kings and for that matter whole nations. His reconstruction is vast and sweeping.[9]

It amounts to this, the Third Millennium empires are ghost empires. Scholars of antiquity know nothing about a "Sumerian" civilization around 2500 B.C. Early Dynastic strata are often found underneath the Neo-Babylonian (Chaldean) levels of 600 B.C., and "Sumerian" royal graves dating from that era are virtual identical with those of Scythian princes fifteen hundred years later. A comparison with ancient China shows a very similar development, yet the Chinese culture did not really flourish until 600 B.C.

To understand the ramifications, we need to look at the histories of Babylon, Assyria, the Chaldeans and the Medo-Persians. Babylonia was more or less a city-state, coveted by the major powers of that time. The Table of Nations in Genesis 10 identifies these nations as Elam (Persia), Asshur (Assyria), Arphaxad (Chaldeans), Lud (Lydia) and Aram (Syria). They were descendants of Shem, and generally spoke Akkadian, a Semitic language.

The history of Assyria is fairly well known; it lasted from about 950 B.C. to the fall of its capitol Nineveh, 606 B.C. The first Assyrian king of name was Tiglath-Peliser II, who was succeeded by his son Asshur-dan II and his grandson Raman-nirari II. This king and his son Tukulti-Nibib II were also kings of Babylonia, and they raided nations in every direction including the Chaldeans, who lived in Northern Syria and Asia Minor. They subdued Syria and several

Mediterranean cities. Their successor Shalmaneser II attacked Damascus 854 B.C. and came in contact with the kings of Israel.

What concerns us is the identity of the persistent foes of the Assyians, the Chaldeans. This may sound strange, but for all their prowess virtually nothing is known about the Chaldeans from their own art and literature. Whatever is known about them comes from Assyrian, Greek and Hebrew sources. How is this possible? This will sound heretical to historians, but the Chaldeans did leave a literary legacy, only it is known by a different name, they were the Hittites.

During the late Eighteen Hundreds, pictographs were found in Asia Minor, Jerublus and Babylon, that were totally different from then-know scripts. However, an accompanying Egyptian text mentioned a people called *Kheta* or *Khatti*. Around 1870 it was decided that these must have been the Hittites, mentioned in the Old Testament. This was based less on scholarship than on phonetics, it sounds the same. The Hittites supposedly existed at the time of the Ramses Dynasty, 1500-1250 B.C.

No such pictographs were ever found in Palestine, and no ancient historian was aware of a "Hittite" empire, but that did not faze scholars. The biblical Hittites were descendants of Ham through Canaan. The art of the "Hittites" was very similar to that of the Babylonians around 600 B.C. All this is based on very confused and very mistaken assumptions. It makes much more sense if we look at the ancient tribes which the Greek called Chaldeans, so-called after their pantheon of gods, Khaldis. Their origins are shrouded in obscurity, but they probably were of Semitic ancestry, descendants of Arphaxad. They were "children of Khaldis," or Khaldeans.

Various Chaldean tribes lived in central Turkey in a geographic area which they called Hatti, much as we speak of "Europe." A sensational discovery awaited historians in 1906 when hoards of tablets slipped down steep hills from underneath the ruins of Boghazkoy, a very ancient city in central Turkey. Hugo Winckler and Makridi-Bey, two scholars, heard of it and came in person. They tried to read the tablets, which were unearthed by the thousands, and to their surprise found a copy of the treaty between Ramses II and Hattusilis, king of

Hatti. It was evident that Kheta and Hatti were the same. Surely, they found the records of the Hittite Empire. The problem was that the strata from which the tablets came belonged to a much later time, but Ramses reigned 1300 B.C. so that was the end of the discussion.

It turned out the Hittites were in many ways more advanced than the Babylonians who came after them, and the art and literature of both had much in common. Scholars were amazed that the 15th and 14th Century B.C. Hittite culture was so similar to that of the 7th and 6th Century B.C. Assyrian. The facts speak for themselves. The Hittites and Chaldeans lived in the same area, supposedly eight centuries apart. But the "Hittite" empire was unknown to the earliest historians, and the Chaldean Kingdom for some inexplicable reason vanished without a trace.

There was no Hittite Empire. The Assyrians, to quell any possible insurrection, deported whole populations to the far reaches of their vast empire, such as happened to the ten tribes of Israel. This explains why Chaldeans were found in the "Sealand" of southern Babylonia, near the Persian Gulf. Other Chaldean tribes may have been pushed into that direction as well. Around 700 B.C. these southern Chaldeans (the Bit-Yakim tribe) in cooperation with Elam under Merodoch-Baladan wrested Babylonia from the Assyrians. Merodoch-Baladan proclaimed himself king of Babylonia, which incidentally was not appreciated by the Babylonians. His kingdom included eight hundred cities. This power grab was short lived. The Assyrians suppressed the rebellion and devastated Babylon. Merodoch-baladan barely escaped to the marshes of southern Babylonia.

Two generations later the Urartu Chaldeans from Asia Minor following the death of Assurbanipal 627 B.C. under Nebopolassar began a sustained attack and succeeded in "liberating" Babylon. The Chaldeans made Babylon their prime city, but it was not the seat of their government. No Chaldean government records have ever been found in Babylon. They were kept in Boghazkoy, the ancestral home of the Chaldeans in central Turkey.

For all its glamour the Chaldean or Neo-(new) Babylonian Empire lasted less than a century. In other words, the Medan Kingdom overlapped that of the Chaldeans. After the death of Nebuchadnezzar, the most famous and well known Chaldean king, the empire fell apart. The native Babylonians were happy to get rid of the foreigners who ruled over them, and welcomed Cyrus the Mede with open arms. It is significant that the ancient historian Strabo mentioned a northern people that defeated the Assyrians.

> In ancient times Greater Armenia ruled the whole of Asia, after it broke the empire of the Syrians (Assyria), but later, in the time of Astyages, it was deprived of that great authority by Cyrus and the Persians.[10]

There can be no doubt that Strabo spoke of the Chaldeans who conquered the Assyrians, but in turn were defeated by Cyrus the Mede. They came from the north, not the south. This "Greater Armenia" could never be a hazy Hittite empire; Strabo clearly referred to the 7th Century Chaldeans. With this in mind we now consider the theories of Gunnar Heinsohn, mentioned before.

Phantom Empires

We need to approach this version of history with great caution. There are real problems with Heinsohn's theories, beginning with his appreciation, or lack of it, of Biblical history, which he dismissed as "fundamentalist." He is, to put it mildly, ignorant of Biblical studies such as only an Atheist can be. As we have seen, Abraham and his relatives hailed from "Ur of the Chaldeans." Heinsohn takes this to mean that Abraham lived at the time of Nebuchadnezzar, around 600 B.C. This, of course, is laughable. Nebuchadnezzar's empire was located in Iraq, but that does not mean he was Saddam Hussein.

Among other things, he believes that Abraham used coins (evidently the Shekel), when a monetary economy did not evolve until the days of the Chaldeans. But a Shekel in Abraham's days was a measure of weight (two Shekels equaled five ounces). When Abraham bought a cave to bury his wife Sarah (which archaeology found to be common practice at that time) as recorded in Genesis 23, he paid for it according to the weight of silver. "Ur of the Chaldeans" refers to the original home of the Chaldeans in what is now Armenia. It had nothing to do with the Sumerian civilization.

Considering the world of the patriarchs and that of the Judean kings, who lived at the time of Nebuchadnezzar, it is difficult to imagine a notion that ludicrous. It results in distortions that seriously mar his studies. However, Heinsohn did see a pattern in ancient history that clearly indicates a duplication of known civilizations, meaning humanity is much younger than is generally believed. As we have seen, the succession of the Mesopotamian empires was Assyrian – Babylonian - Neo Babylonian – Medo/Persian. The same order appears 1500 years earlier in Akkadian – Sumerian - Neo Sumerian – Martu/Amurru in the same theater of history. Heinsohn presents evidence that these empires were duplicated.

Around 2350 B.C., Southern Mesopotamia was conquered by the Akkadians under their first king, Sargon, the founder of the first known empire. This information is largely derived from tablets written in Akkadian after 700 B.C., believed to be copies of a much earlier record. The problem is that the Capitol city, built by Sargon and modeled after Babylon, has never been found; neither has the road network, mentioned in the tablets. The Akkadian Sargon captured Babylon and pillaged it, after which he announced himself king. But Babylon could have hardly existed at that time, or at least it could not have been that size. Only the Assyrian king Sargon could have said that, fifteen hundred years later. In truth, the lives of both Sargons are remarkably similar.

Assyria under Sargon captured Babylon. Assyria also had excellent roads. The Akkadian Sargon and his grandson Naram-Sin conquered "Magan and Heluhha," which in the 7th Century tablets always meant Egypt and Ethiopia. The first Mesopotamians known to have done that were Sargon the Assyrian and his grandson Essarhadon. These kings traded with Dilmun, the First Millennium name of India, which could have never been the case the Third Millennium B.C. They also had extensive trades with Kaptara, either Crete of Cyprus, islands in the Mediterranean, which did not happen until the Eighth Century B.C.

The Akkadians were supplanted by the "Neo-Sumerians." In excavations in Uruk the strata of this period coincide with the Neo-Babylonian or Chaldean strata, fifteen hundred years later. Surprisingly the Neo-Sumerians had a monetary economy, which did not develop until the age of the Chaldeans. It was common in Mesopotamia of the 8th Century. The Neo-Sumerian kings Ur-Nammu, Shulgi and Ibbi-Sin gave themselves titles like "King of the Four Quarters," which would seem rather exaggerated, but they are very similar to those used by the Neo-Babylonian kings Nabopolassar, Nebuchadnezzar and Nabonidus, who ruled a vast empire.

Ur-Nammu the Neo-Sumerian was involved in repeated hostilities with Egypt, which makes no sense, unless he was the same as the Chaldean Nabopolassar. Shulgi, a word meaning "crown prince," therefore was Nebuchadnezzar the Chaldean who, while crown prince, was invested with ruling power, and who defeated the Egyptians at Carchemish. The lives of the last Neo-Sumerian king Ibbi-Sin and the last Chaldean king Nabonidus are virtual mirror images. During the last ten years of their reigns both had a rival regent, both looked for protection in a fortress between the Euphrates and the Tigris without success. Their Capitol was captured but not destroyed and when taken alive, both were exiled to Persia. The Neo-Sumerians were conquered by the Martu/Amurru, the Chaldeans by the Medo-Persians.

The Persian Cyrus the Great mentions Martu kings and how they kissed his feet, although the Martu supposedly disappeared a millennium earlier. Both the Martu and Persians worshiped the dog, and iron mining mentioned in the Hammurabi period was six hundred years ahead of the Iron Age. Yet the Martu were able to chisel hard stone, such as dormite, which can only be done with iron. The Persians however did possess that technology. The political framework of the Martu was the same as that of the Persians. The empire was not a collection of allied cities, but a single state. The temple city Eridu, which ceased operation around 1700 B.C., nonetheless was still used in Persian times, and is mentioned as late as A.D. 170.

There are numerous cases where the records of two warring empires are juxtaposed. For instance, Merodach-Baladan left an account of his defeat by Sargon the Assyrian, but Sargon somehow failed to mention this. However, Sargon of Akkad described his victory over Lugalzagesi, identical with Merodach-Baladan's report. The battle was fought at "Dur," and both Lugalzagesi and Merodach-Baladan were late. Much was at stake. The Babylonian kingdom consisted of eight hundred twenty cities, eighty-eight of which were walled. Sargon of Akkad and Sargon the Assyrian both had a son (Sennacherib) who came to the throne by killing a brother, only to be assassinated himself. They are the same.

The Implications

The implications are revolutionary. The most important of these, recorded history goes back to about 2000 B.C. That is very recent indeed. Humanity is supposed to have been around for tens of thousands of years. That is based on suppositions rather than actual historical records. How odd. Why did it take so long for civilization to develop? Could it be that not so long ago an appalling disaster (etched world-wide in human memory) virtually wiped out mankind, and that the survivors did not recover until about 2000 B.C. or even later?

It also follows that the Genesis creation account was not at all derived from earlier pagan sources, such as the Gilgamesh account, rather it was the other way around. If the Sumerians were the Chaldeans, it makes sense that the Mesopotamian flood stories were so similar to the Greek tales of Deucalion. Greek and Sumerian mythology closely resemble each other.

There are however assumptions in Heinsohn's theory that must be challenged. Hammurabi and Darius definitely were not the same, as Heinsohn would have us believe. Their lives nowhere resemble each other. He ignores facts of history that are beyond doubt, facts attested by the Old Testament and ancient historians. Contrary to his assertions, the Medo/Persians came after the Chaldeans, not before, and the Medo/Persians did rule in Palestine. There is ample evidence of an extensive Persian road system in the northern Sinai.

Heinsohn's trust in the so-called Higher Critics with their destructive theories is seriously misplaced. He is leaning on a broken reed. Wellhausen's blatant assertions have long since been disproved by archaeology and scholarship. The Pentateuch is not a late production; it is an accurate account, based upon original manuscripts. Scholars may have mistakenly assigned certain kings to a wrong age, but the scriptures never do that. He is ill served with the applause of a mutual admiration society. He would be much better advised to cease that silly psycho babble about "deicide," as if religion was the result of mass hysteria that could only be released with ritual sacrifices. Welcome to European atheism. In a world without God it is impossible for Atheists to imagine that the belief in one God was man's original religion and not a late development, and that Abraham was a key figure in God's redemptive purposes.

However, the upshot is that the "Sumerians" of 2400 B.C. who worshiped Eana/Ishtar were in reality the Babylonians of Meredochbaladan, 710 B.C. When they reported seeing Venus, they did so long after the exodus, instead of a thousand years before. That is in general agreement with Venus' violent reputation and its sudden appearance, which was around the middle of the Second Millennium B.C., roughly the time of the Exodus.

The very makeup of Venus and its worldwide reputation indicates that there is something different about this planet. Velikovsky's theory does fit certain relevant facts. Among these is Augustine's strange reference to Venus' evident near approach to the earth, and the horrid veneration of the morning star, so prevalent among pagan nations.

Graham Hancock in his odd book "Fingerprints of the Gods" relates how horrified Catholic priests witnessed the bestial slaughter of Aztec prisoners of war. In an appalling ritual, Aztec priests dressed themselves in the flayed skins of their victims until pools of blood dripped on the ground, all of that to appease the feared astral deity Venus. They thought the end of the world was delayed by feeding Venus human sacrifices and so satisfy her. Yes, it is altogether possible that Venus is a young planet with a violent history. However, that lasted only a short time. There are reports of Venus shining like a torch, but it never approached the earth again. And so we return to the history of Israel and its neighbors.

Chapter Three

The Thutmose Dynasty

Ahmose

Egyptologists are disagreed how long the Hyksos pharaohs ruled. The great length of their reign ascribed by Manetho does not fit conventional dating at all. Historians are able to assign about a century and a half, but that's about it. This leaves them in a quandary. They know of no "blast of God" that would account for Egypt's demise; natural disasters are never even considered. So they soften Manetho's unequivocal statement. The Hyksos were Asiatics who gradually moved into Egypt, asserted themselves and took over. Naturally they could hardly be as cruel as Manetho made them out to be. For all we know they really benefited Egypt; the Egyptians merely did not like to be ruled by foreigners.

This is speculation, none of it accurate. Historians cannot discard primary sources, merely because these sources do not confirm their presuppositions. The record is clear; the Hyksos-Amelekites were ruthless. They tortured prisoners, smashed teeth, gouged out eyes, and cut off the limbs of their victims and flung them up to the sky to defy God in heaven. The Egyptians, like the Hebrews, hated them with a passion.

The Thutmose Dynasty

The Hyksos ruled more than four centuries and during all that time they left no art, no monuments, not even any writings. It was a destructive people. The famous Egyptologist Flinters Petrie reasoned that the Hyksos who invaded Egypt were primitive, but as they were exposed to the far superior Egyptian culture they gradually became more civilized. After about a century they adopted Egyptian customs, called themselves pharaohs, and generally imitated Egyptian ways. They could be designated the Arab Dynasty.

They captured Thebes, but ruled from Avaris in the Delta in northern Egypt. Avaris probably was el-Arish. They constituted the Fifteenth Dynasty, along with the Sixteenth Dynasty, largely Egyptian collaborators of the Delta. Northern Egypt was unable to revolt; the population never increased sufficiently in numbers to regain their strength and overthrow the oppressor. However, the princes of Southern Egypt, who constituted the Seventeenth Dynasty, ruled more or less independent from the Hyksos, and after four centuries found the courage to stand up to the usurpers.

The Hyksos king Apop sent Pharaoh Tao Sekenenre a complaint that noisy hippopotami in Thebes (400 miles away) kept him awake. That was a cryptic way of saying he was aware that Theban princes were scheming a revolt. Sekenenre was killed in battle, but by this time the Southern Kingdom was ready. The great liberator was Kamose, the successor of Sekenenre. Even at that, he relied largely on mercenaries from Africa. Over the objections of several southern rulers, he built ships and used horses and chariots to route the Hyksos. He returned to his Capitol a victor, but was not able to finish his great task, he died after six years.

It should be noted that the Intoyef princes played an important role in expelling the Hyksos. It is curious indeed that the same thing happened following the presumed First Intermediate Period, when the Intef princes re-established Egyptian sovereignty. That probably was not the case. It is likely that the Intoyef family was mistakenly looped back several centuries to begin the 11th Dynasty, the Middle Kingdom. This was the dynasty of Pharaoh Djoser and his Vizier Im/

Mentu/hotep. That the same family would do this twice in the course of six hundred years is unbelievable.

Ahmose, the founder of the Theban (18th) Dynasty, ruled twenty four years. He resumed the war with the Hyksos in the middle of his reign, and captured Avaris near the end. He fought and defeated the Nubians in the south who had been allied with the Hyksos, and then turned his attention to the north, where he ruthlessly slaughtered the Hyksos sympathizers of the Sixteenth Dynasty. No government appreciates collaborators. Yet the capture of Avaris was not the sole work of Ahmose; he had outside help. It came from an unexpected source.

Saul

As a result of the Egyptian revolt Saul, the first king of Israel, was able to defeat the weakened Amelekites. (1 Sam. 14:47) Shortly thereafter, the prophet Samuel told him to attack and annihilate the Amelekites. Odd, considering that Amelek supposedly did not account for much. Equally strange is the location; Saul attacked Egyptian territory.

> Samuel said to Saul, "I am the one the Lord sent to anoint you king over his people Israel; so listen now to the message from the Lord. This is what the Lord Almighty says: I will punish the Amelekites for what they did to Israel when they waylaid them as they came up from Egypt. Now go, attack the Amelekites and totally destroy everything that belongs to them. Do not spare them; put to death men and women, children and infants, cattle and sheep, camels and donkeys." So Saul summoned the men and mustered them at Telaim - two hundred thousand foot soldiers and ten thousand men from Judah. Saul went to the city of Amelek and set an ambush in the ravine. — Then Saul attacked the Amelekites all the way from Havilah to Shur, to the east of Egypt. He took Agag king of the Amelekites alive, and all his people he totally destroyed with the sword. But Saul and his ar-

my spared Agag and the best of the sheep and cattle, the fat calves and lambs - everything that was good. These they were unwilling to destroy completely, but everything that was despised and weak they totally destroyed.

1 Samuel 15:1-9

For God to put a whole nation under a ban, it must have been corrupt indeed. This was the second time Israel was called to exterminate a people. That was not at all customary. The law commanded them to be hospitable to strangers. But just as the Canaanites of old had been ripe for judgment, so Amelek, too, had filled the cup of iniquity to overflowing. The record shows that Egypt did the same thing.

Bible scholars are at a loss to explain why Saul took an army of more than two hundred thousand men to defeat a Bedouin tribe, and how that could affect all of Syria-Palestine. Havillah was generally the land of the Euphrates, north of Syria. *Shur* means *wall*; it refers to the wall of fortifications that protected Egypt along its eastern frontier. Why was that done at the border of Egypt (as if the Egyptians did not care), and how could that possibly be so great a strategic victory that Palestine was liberated all the way from the Euphrates to the fortifications of Egypt?

But Saul did not just fight an obscure Bedouin tribe, he faced the Hyksos. The city of the Amelekites was Avaris, the Hyksos stronghold, and the ravine was the bed of a river, the river of Egypt. It was known as the wadi of el-Arish, dry in the summer, a raging river in the winter. The Hyksos built several strongholds in the south of Egypt to protect themselves against attacks from the princes of the upper kingdom. Farther north in the southern part of Palestine they built Shahuren, on the Euphrates the newly founded Carchemish and in addition several forts in Palestine. Following a number of Egyptian victories, Saul gave the final blow to the once-mighty Hyksos Empire and captured their last king, Pharaoh Apop, alive. It was a victory of major proportions that altered the course of history. Egypt was restored to its role as a world power.

Yet what should have been Saul's finest hour became his worst failure. His victory was tainted. Egyptian records make it clear that a compromise had been reached. Saul captured Avaris, but somehow it was agreed to let a large portion of the Amelekites escape to the Hyksos stronghold Shahuren in southern Palestine. Saul's role, as usual, was flawed. Nobody has ever accused him of cowardice (he died in battle), but he failed as a leader of men. He allowed Agag to live and let much of the Hyksos go. It was like allowing SS death camp troops to escape and then parade Hitler to show off.

It could hardly be said that Saul had a soft heart. He did not hesitate to destroy whatever was second rate. When he chose not to take the high road and spared Agag (Apop), he lost the respect of his soldiers. Of course, Saul had an excuse. They spared the cattle of the shepherd-kings "to sacrifice to the Lord." Meanwhile he erected a monument in his own honor to commemorate the victory. Samuel was upset and angry. When Saul came with excuses, he said,

> Does the Lord delight in burnt offerings and sacrifices
> as much as in obeying the voice of the Lord?
> To obey is better than sacrifice,
> and to heed is better than the fat of rams.
>
> 1 Samuel 15:22

Samuel ordered Agag, king of Amelek, better known as the Hyksos Pharaoh Apop, to be brought forward. Agag thought he was safe, but Samuel told him,

"As your sword has made women childless,

so will your mother be childless among women." (1 Sam. 15:33) He put Agag to death, something Saul should have done. Samuel's pronouncement says something about the terrible reputation of the Hyksos-Amelekites. The execution was like that of the Nazi war criminals following the Second World War

We need to investigate the etymology of Hyksos. Manetho said it meant *shepherd kings*, but modern scholars, quite correctly, explain the word was derived from hyk-khase, meaning *Chieftains of a foreign hill-country* (Gardiner). Yet it is evident that the Hyksos were indeed a shepherd people. The Amelekites definitely were. Maybe Hyksos had a dual meaning. It is quite normal for words to stand for different things. Sometimes foreign words are adapted and changed to fit a need. For instance colonial England picked up the word *fellah* (servant) from India, and changed it to *fellow*, which has a totally different meaning. It merely sounds the same. Maybe the Egyptians did something of the kind. They evidently took the word Hyk-khase and made it Hyk-sos, because the invaders, although indeed Bedouins, were remembered as a shepherd people. At least that is how Manetho transmitted it through the Greek.

Velikovsky made an interesting observation. He thought Psalm 78, which recalls the plagues of Egypt, originally may have referred to king-shepherds rather than angels. Verse 49, speaking of God's judgment on Egypt reads,

> He unleashed against them his hot anger,
> his wrath, indignation and hostility -
> a band of destroying angels.

The "destroying angel" is mentioned with the final plague, but there is no mention of a "band of destroying angels." Velikovsky thought there may have been a corruption in the text. "A band of destroying angels" is derived from *mishlakhat mala̱khei-roim*. However, if we delete the single letter *a* (aleph), it becomes *mishlakhat malkhei-roim*, which renders it "Invasion of king-shepherds." It means the Lord sent his wrath in the form, not of *a band of destroying angels*, but *an invasion of king-shepherds*. We will leave this for competent scholars to judge. Whatever the case, Saul defeated the shepherd-kings but still failed his duty.

David

One wonders, if God hand-picked Saul to be king, was not that a poor choice? God gave Israel a king because they clamored for one.

So as a warning, God gave them a bad one. Saul looked every bit the gifted leader; unfortunately he wasn't. Throughout his career he exhibited poor judgment. It showed when he was facing a superior enemy, but was told to wait a week for Samuel who, being a priest would first make a sacrifice. When Samuel did not show up and his troops began to desert him, Saul took it upon himself to perform the sacrifice. It was a test of faith and he failed. (1 Sam. 13:1-15) Because of this, the kingdom was taken away from him and given to another. That was tragic, because his son Jonathan was everything Saul should have been. He would have made a good king. Instead the kingdom was given to David, "The man after God's own heart."

Unlike Saul, David was not at all impressive, but under pressure he turned out to be a magnificent leader. He was introduced to Saul's court when the king, who became seriously depressed, needed psychological help. David was known to be a great musician, so he was called to the court and quieted Saul. He is remembered for his fight with Goliath, one of a few remaining Anakim, or sons of Anak, also called Nephilim. It says something about David's personal courage that he took on a ten-foot giant with a slingshot. Saul was thankful, but his condition was such that he did not even recognize David. Even more important was David's trust in God. It served as an example that Saul so sadly lacked. Not that he was perfect; far from it. He was a man of great gifts and great faults. But he had a heart for God, and when faced with his sins, acknowledged it.

Interestingly David, too, had a run-in with the Amelekites. Which goes to prove that Saul's claim that he had killed the Amelekites was at best only partially true. Because of his great achievements, David became a general in Saul's army. Soon he became altogether too popular; the women sang,

"Saul has slain his thousands,
and David his tens of thousands."

Saul began to recognize in David the one whom Samuel said would succeed him. Several times he tried to kill David. Eventually David with a band of desperadoes went into hiding, fleeing Saul.

Several times it was within his power to kill Saul, but he refused because Saul was God's anointed.

To escape Saul, David did something he should not have done. He sought protection from the Philistines. The king of Gath gave him the town of Ziklag to live in, believing David raided Israel. He was mistaken; David raided the Amelekites, Philistine allies instead, and he left no prisoners. It was a spiritually dry period in David's life. However, it is generally believed that he learned metallurgy from his host. The Philistines knew how to make steel implements, skills David put to good use. In years to come Israel was able to make steel weapons. Then the Philistine kings assembled for a battle against Saul. They were offered David's services, but knowing his reputation they declined, so David returned, only to find his base city burned and wives and children abducted.

> David and his men reached Ziklag on the third day. Now the Amelekites had raided the Negev and Ziklag. They had attacked Ziklag and burned it, and had taken captive the women and all who were in it, both young and old. They killed none of them, but carried them off as they went on their way.
>
> 1 Samuel 30:1

That very much resembles the tactics of the Hyksos, described by Manetho. "They burned our cities ruthlessly, razed to the ground the temples of the gods and leading into slavery the wives and children of others." David and his men pursued the Amelekites and found an Egyptian who was dying of thirst and hunger. They gave him food and water and when he revived, David asked him, "To whom do you belong, and where do you come from?"

> He said, "I am an Egyptian, the slave of an Amelekite. My master abandoned me when I became ill three days ago. We raided the Negev of the Kerehites and the territory belonging to Judah and the Negev of Kaleb. And we burned Ziklag.
>
> 1 Samuel 30:13

He then led David and his men to the Amelekites. David defeated them and found wives and children alive and well. Meanwhile it would seem rather strange that an Egyptian would be the slave of an Amelekite. Was not Egypt a powerful nation and Amelek an obscure Bedouin tribe? But the Hyksos had enslaved the Egyptians for centuries and so this would be accepted as a normal state of affairs. The Hyksos-Amelekites presumably were aware of impending hostilities between Israel and the Philistines, and used the opportune moment to raid Judah in the south from their stronghold Shahurem. That the Hyksos were indeed Bedouins is evident from a sad chapter in our times. Muslim Bedouins attack Christians in Africa. They burn down their houses, slaughter the parents and sell the children into slavery. Such intolerance is not limited to Africa, but the tactics are unique.

King Saul was killed in the battle with the Philistines. David mourned the death of Saul and his son Jonathan, who had been a dear friend. After a long struggle with the house of Saul, David eventually became king. The scriptures are silent about the fall of Shahurem, but Jewish sources inform us that Joab, David's general, after a long siege finally captured "the city of Amelek." Egyptian sources say the siege of Shahurem lasted three years, and imply that an ally actually did most of the fighting. David captured Salem, the city of the Jebusites, which he called after himself, the city of David. But the venerated name stuck, and eventually the name was changed to Jerusalem. David reigned forty years, and was succeeded by his son Solomon.

Solomon

The political realities of Solomon's time were entirely different from those of Saul and David. Egypt was back on the scene. Saul had taken care of Amelek; David consolidated Israel's position, and Solomon, now king over many of the Asiatic provinces of the former Amelekite Empire, gave the new nation its splendor. Something very

The Thutmose Dynasty

similar happened in Egypt. Ahmose, the first pharaoh of the 18th Dynasty, was the great liberator. His successor Amenhotep I ruled twenty seven years. He consolidated Egypt's power by subjugating the Nubians.

His successor was Thutmose I, a powerful ruler who married into the royal family. His daughter was the future queen Hapshetsut. Modern scholarship limits his reign to eleven years, but during that time he accomplished much. Among his military exploits were a war in the south against Nubia, and an extended campaign in Syria-Palestine. Thutmose did not bother to challenge the kingdom of Mittanni, beyond the Euphrates. In fact it seems further north he ran into considerable resistance. He was succeeded by his son Thutmose II, who lasted only three years, and left a muddled political situation. His first two sons died, which left a young prince by a harem girl, Thutmose III. However, his wife and half-sister Hapshetsut was strong willed and assumed the rule of pharaoh.

By this time we are well into the reign of Solomon, and it becomes understandable what should come as a surprise, that after four hundred years of silence suddenly a pharaoh is mentioned. Solomon married the daughter of an unnamed pharaoh who, we are casually informed, "had attacked and captured Gezer. He had set it on fire. He killed its Canaanite inhabitants and then gave it as a wedding gift to his daughter." (I Kings 9:16). That pharaoh must have been Thutmose I, and his daughter may have been princess Nefrubity, the full sister of Hapshetsut.

Politically it made excellent sense for Thutmose to deed a strategically important city to a trusted ally. After all, he had good reasons to secure his flank in Palestine. The Philistines were Hyksos sympathizers, in fact related to them, and Thutmose had every reason to subdue them. The Canaanites had been collaborators as well, and it was essential to sack Gezer in central Palestine; it was strategically located on an important cross road. However, Thutmose could hardly afford a continued military presence in Palestine, so he gave it to Solomon "as a wedding present."

It is significant that this is the first time a pharaoh is mentioned following the exodus. It took more than four hundred years, which agrees exactly with the length of time Heredotus ascribed to the rule of the Hyksos. Following the Second Intermediate Period, when the Hyksos 16th and southern Egyptian 17th Dynasties coexisted, came the New Kingdom. Out of Thebes the Eighteenth Dynasty, the Thutmose Pharaohs arose, conquered all of Egypt, and began a new rule.

In the fourth year of his reign, Solomon began the construction of the temple and his palace. It took seven years to finish the temple, thirteen to finish the palace. Both were gold-plated. What is more, Solomon was a student of nature. He built botanical and zoological gardens, and sent ships far and wide to collect rare plants and animals. The scriptures list gold, silver, ivory, apes, baboons, almug wood and precious stones. Exotic plants and trees were not limited to his personal collection; Jerusalem was filled with myrrh terraces. It took his traders three years to make the return trip. Some speculate it involved global travel. The Hebrews were no sailors but Hiram, king of Tyre, entered into an alliance with Solomon. He provided the fleet Solomon needed in exchange for cities and a naval base at Ezion Geber at the Gulf of Aqaba.

Yet Solomon made terrible mistakes. In flat violation of the law he turned to Egypt for armaments: horses and chariots. And in erecting all those magnificent buildings he ignored Moses' admonition not to do so. If Israel chose a king, Moses warned, he must be native, not a foreigner, and he must obey the law.

> The king, moreover, must not acquire great numbers of horses for himself or make the people return to Egypt to get more of them, for the LORD has told you, "You must not go back that way again." He must not take many wives or his heart will be led astray. He must not accumulate large amounts of silver and gold.
>
> Deuteronomy 17:16, 17

Moses was wiser than Solomon. He had been in a position of royal authority himself, and he knew the temptations that came with it.

All that gold that glittered distracted from the real values of life, something Solomon afterwards realized. "Meaningless," he called it, "a chasing after the wind." (Ecclesiastes 2:26.) It made Jerusalem a target for aggressors. However, at that time Solomon's fame spread far and wide, and so he was visited by many dignitaries, among them a famous queen.

> When the queen of Sheba heard about the fame of Solomon and his relation to the name of the LORD, she came to test him with hard questions. Arriving at Jerusalem with a very great caravan - with camels carrying spices, large quantities of gold and precious stones - she came to Solomon and talked with him about all that she had on her mind. Solomon answered all her questions; nothing was too hard for the king to explain to her.
>
> I King 10:1-3

Books have been written about this queen, her country, who she was and what is meant with Sheba. Just as there is something mysterious about this queen, so Hapshetsut evoked wonder when she mentioned a strange country she visited which she called Punt. All these writings are educated guesses at best, and they are largely disagreed. There is however an easy and historically sensible solution, we need to look at the revised history of Egypt.

Hatshepsut, the Queen of Sheba

Following Thutmose I came Thutmose II, evidently a rather weak king. His wife, Queen Hatshepsut, was the daughter of Thutmose I as well, which made her a contender to the throne. So was Thutmose III, her stepson by a concubine. However, Hatshepsut was ambitious; upon the death of her husband she assumed the kingship, and Thutmose III (the lawful heir) became co-regent. Queen Hatshepsut left an important inscription that has been a source of contention. It deals with temples that had been ruined.

> The abode of the Mistress of Qes was fallen in ruin, the earth has swallowed her beautiful sanctuary and children played over her temple — I cleared it and rebuilt it anew — — I restored that which was in ruins, and I completed that which was left unfinished. For there had been Amu in the midst of the Delta and in Hauar (Avaris), and the foreign hordes of their number had destroyed the ancient works; they reigned ignorant of the god Ra.[1]

The temples collapsed and sank into the earth with the last of the ten plagues. Then the Hyksos came to finish the job. No doubt her predecessors had already begun rebuilding, but Hatshepsut, like Solomon, finished the grandiose task.

Hatshepsut was one of a very few Egyptian queens to be reigning monarch. Her rule, like that of Solomon, was not one of war and conquest, but rather one of peace and prosperity. The parallels between Solomon and Hapshetsut are striking. They built palaces and temples, both nations prospered, and both sent ships on trade missions. Apparently neither had reasons to fear attacks of predatory nations. They have something else in common. It involves an expedition. The Queen of Sheba, loaded with gifts, paid Solomon a state visit. Who was she? Josephus said she was the queen of Egypt

> There was then a woman, queen of Egypt and Ethiopia; she was inquisitive into philosophy, and one that on other accounts also was to be admired. When this queen heard of the virtue and prudence of Solomon, she had a great mind to see him.[2]

Egyptian records say as much. Hatshepsut sent an expedition to a mysterious country named Punt, which she called the divine land. To the Egyptians it was familiar territory. An official from the Old Kingdom said he visited Byblos in Syria and Punt eleven times. Punt must have been near Syria.[3] It was also called the divine land, and it is mentioned as east of Egypt. Palestine was called Retenu, and Retenu was Punt, the divine land. Palestine has always been considered the Holy land, just as Jerusalem always was a Holy City. It was a temple city before David, for Melchizedek, the priest-king mentioned in Genesis 14, was priest of God Most High, and he came from Salem, which under David became Jerusalem.

Hatshepsut or Hatshepsowe, was the Queen of Sheba (the Hebrew text merely calls her queen SHWA), and she visited Solomon in the ninth year of her reign, 938 B.C., in the latter part of his rule. It does not say that she came along, but considering the importance of the mission, it only makes sense that she did. Her sister was, after all, married to Solomon, and so an official state visit was agreed upon. Both obviously were quite prepared.

Scholars have long wondered about the identity and location of Punt. Queen Hatshepsut left detailed descriptions of Punt, or Palestine. Scholars were puzzled about the wide variety of fauna and flora she described. Plants, animals and birds of faraway countries are mentioned that could never originate in Palestine. They didn't. As we have seen, Solomon stocked his gardens with animals and plants, gathered from distant lands. 1 Kings 10 describes the visit of the Queen of Sheba, and mentions the exotic plants and animals that the ships of Hiram brought Solomon, besides gold and silver and precious stones.

Bas-reliefs of Hatshepsut, who supposedly lived six hundred years earlier, tell much the same story. Punt was filled with gold, and silver was common. The queen marveled at the myrrh terraces and expressed the same amazement as that, found in the scriptures. Hatshepsut gave gold and spices, and received myrrh, exotic trees and apes. She also received "her heart's desire," silver; rare in antiquity, but abundant in Israel. She returned to Egypt with her fleet, probably from a Phoenician sea port.

The queen was strong willed, and one of a very few women to be pharaoh. To accommodate the people, she would often appear in male clothing, and even assume masculine appearance. Jewish tradition reports that the Queen of Sheba looked masculine. When she approached King Solomon she raised her garments to keep it dry from what appeared to be water. "On her bared feet the king noticed hair, and he said to her: 'Thy beauty is the beauty of a woman, but thy hair is masculine; hair is an ornament to a man, but it disfigures a woman.'" [4]

Just how impressed Hatshepsut really was, is evident from the temple she erected in honor of her favorite god, Amon. The ruins of "The most splendid of splendors" still stand in Der el-Bahri. "Even now there is no nobler architectural achievement to be seen in the whole of Egypt," said Gardiner.[5] It was modeled after the temple of Punt, high on the side of a mountain, complete with myrrh terraces. She even had the trees of her expedition planted. The temple of Hatshepsut, in other words, was made in the image of Solomon's temple. It should give Bible scholars a fairly good idea what the temple in Jerusalem looked like.

Rehoboam

The long reign of Solomon, which began so promising, ended a failure. Things came altogether too easily for Solomon's own good. Having accomplished his grandiose building projects, he became a pleasure seeker. In flat disobedience of the law, he acquired himself additional wives, all of them pagan, and he magnanimously erected idols for them. That was the synergism, the mixing of two opposing doctrines that plagued Israel ever since. The One Holy God was no more tolerant of Israel worshiping idols than a wife of her husband fooling around with other women. For this, the house of David lost its universal kingship.

Solomon's son Rehoboam from the outset failed to appreciate the magnitude of the problems he inherited from his father. Those magnificent buildings had come at a price. Heavy taxation, labor conscription, the loss of tribal autonomy and a centralized government all took their toll. There was also the menace from the south; there had been a change of the guard in Egypt. The prophet Ahiah informed a promising young official by the name of Jeroboam that he would become king by default over ten of the twelve tribes of Israel. When Solomon heard of this, he tried to kill Jeroboam. The upshot was that Jeroboam escaped to Egypt, where he was warmly welcomed by King Shishak. He remained there until the death of Solomon.

It is believed that maybe Shishak was Soshenk, but Soshenk was the Pharaoh So who failed to come to the aid of Samaria, 622 B.C. (2 Kings 17:4). If we look at Hatshepsut's successor however, we arrive at a very different conclusion. Hatshepsut visited Solomon in the latter part of his reign. She was the reigning monarch, but her co-regent, crown prince Thutmose III, became increasingly restive. His disposition was not at all peaceful; he had war in mind. The fabulous riches of Jerusalem made it a target for greedy kings. King David left Solomon billions of dollars worth of gold and silver to build the temple. With the arrival of Jeroboam, Thutmose saw a golden opportunity to divide and conquer. Jeroboam became a collaborator in his plans.

The political scheming of Thutmose was to bear rich fruit. When after the death of Solomon, Rehoboam became king, delegates of the tribes came for redress. The new king was somewhat taken aback, but after three days he came back with his answer: I will be worse than my father. That did it. Ten tribes seceded and made Jeroboam king. Rehoboam was about to fight the rebel tribes, but a prophet told him not to start a civil war; this was from the Lord. Even so, "There was continual warfare between Rehoboam and Jeroboam." (2 Chronicles 12:15).

Rehoboam realized that Judah was in trouble. Suddenly he had an enemy to the north and a menace in the south. He fortified several cities and strengthened his defenses. In the northern kingdom, Jeroboam set up idols to keep the people from going to the temple in Jerusalem. In response to this, the priests and Levites came to Judah and settled there. Believers from all the tribes still made their annual trip to Jerusalem. Maybe Rehoboam thought this guaranteed the blessings of the Almighty; in any event, he showed his true colors and abandoned the law altogether. So did the two tribes, Judah and Benjamin, for they worshiped the Ashteroth (Ishtar) and even resorted to religious prostitution.

Shishak

If Rehoboam thought he had God trapped in his precious temple, he was sadly mistaken. He discovered the hard way what others found out before and since, that God works out things for a righteous purpose. Shishak, king of Egypt, invaded Palestine with a huge army. "He captured the fortified cities of Judah and came as far as Jerusalem," where the fearful King Rehoboam and his men took refuge. This campaign appears to have been twofold. Shishak first captured the fortified cities of Judah in the south, then he breached the defenses of the Judean Capitol. This marks the full-fledged return of Egypt on the scene. Shishak was an aggressor. He obviously had nothing to fear from the ten tribes of Israel; Jeroboam was a trusted ally who, to escape the wrath of Solomon, found refuge in Shishak's court.

> Then the prophet Shemiah came to Rehoboam and to the leaders of Judah who had assembled in Jerusalem for fear of Shishak, and said to them, "This is what the LORD says, 'You have abandoned me; therefore, I now abandon you to Shishak.'" The leaders of Israel and the king humbled themselves and said, "The LORD is just."
>
> 2 Chronicles 12:5, 6

They submitted and received a reprieve. They would not suffer God's wrath through Shishak, but they would be subject to him. That way they would discover the difference between serving the Lord and serving a foreign king. There was no siege. Shishak and his army walked in and looted the temple and the royal palace. They took everything. The Almighty cared no more about the treasures of the temple than the sham religion of Rehoboam. Which goes to prove that the trappings of a gilded church do not necessarily make it the house of the Lord.

It is certainly very unusual for an ancient city to surrender that easily. Nonetheless, the Egyptian record indicates that is exactly what happened. There is no mention of a siege. Who then was this Pharaoh Shishak?

Thutmose III

If Hapshetsut, queen of Egypt, was the "Queen of Sheba," it follows that her successor must have been the Shishak who subjugated Israel and Judah. Her stepson Thutmose III did just that. The coregency of Hatshepsut and Thutmose III lasted twenty-two years, from 947-925 B.C. There are reasons to believe her death was not altogether a natural one. Thutmose evidently was quite prepared for her untimely departure, for no sooner was the queen dead and buried than he mustered his army for an assault on Palestine.

It is easy to see why Thutmose succeeded so easily. Both the Egyptian record and scripture describe a confused political situation, engineered by Thutmose. Palestinian princes were fighting each other. The fractured nation of David and Solomon had lost its solidarity. The ten tribes, since called Israel, seceded under Jeroboam, but much of the new nations' religious loyalty was with Judah. Many of the northern princes sympathized with Rehoboam. That much is clear from the scriptures. The divided kingdom, now vulnerable, was an easy target for the pharaoh. His actions closely resemble those of Shishak.

Thutmose left a triumphant record of his heroics. Exactly where he fought his battles is an altogether different matter. Breasted translated the (damaged) inscriptions to read, "The wretched enemy of Kadesh has come and entered Mkty (Megiddo). He is there at this moment." But Birch had a different version. The pharaoh related how he "was discoursing with his brave troops telling that the vile (enemies) of Kateshu had come entered to Maketa; it was done at the moment."

The Egyptian army evidently executed a pincer attack. One army captured the strongholds of Judah in the south, the other headed north along the coast. Where did they go? Breasted thought Mkty was Megiddo. However, the picture that emerges does not fit Megiddo at all. Thutmose described his actions in detail. He decided on a daring strategy. His other army headed north, yes, but not to Megiddo. Thutmose told his stunned generals what he had in mind. Before them was a narrow pass, the "Ascent of Beth Horon," the northern approach to both Jerusalem and Jericho. His final object was *Aruna*. When his officers realized what he was up to, they nearly mutinied. The attack was almost suicidal. Surely the pharaoh could see that the gorge was so narrow that horses could merely go single file if at all, because of the steep incline. Besides, rocks were everywhere.

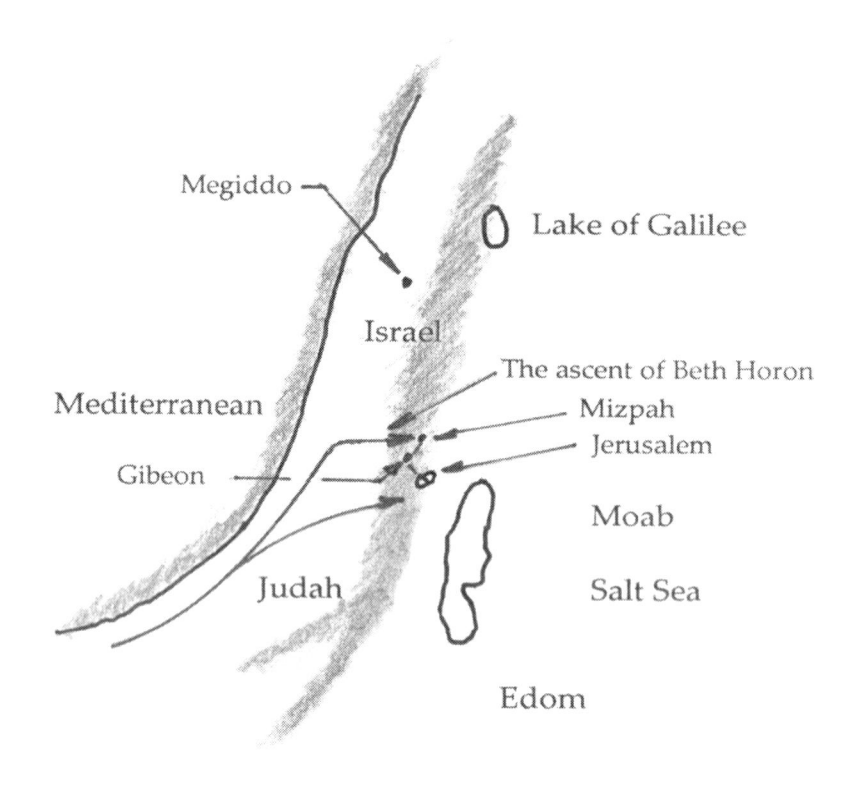

The Egyptian pincer attack on Jerusalem

Odd though it may seem, Thutmose understood their fears. Rather than force his will he put it up to a vote, and the generals reluctantly agreed to go ahead. He skirted the border of Judah, successfully crossed the treacherous and steep ascent between upper and lower Beth Horon, and unexpectedly attacked a town he called Mkty or Maketa, mentioned in Joshua 10:10. In the Septuagint Migdal, which is located north of Jerusalem, is called Magedo or Makedo. Migdal means "fortress." The enemy, caught totally unaware, fled headlong to Mkty, where the "wretched foe" of Kadesh was hauled up over the city wall by his clothes. The army stopped to loot the spoils of war, and the king of Kadesh escaped.

The Egyptians moved further south to Gibeon, where they encamped near a pool. This is where the Megiddo theory fails. Breasted was not informed about the topography of the Jezreel valley. When one of his students investigated the area he reported that the pass leading to Megiddo was much unlike the one, described by Thutmose. The Wadi Ara was wide, level and gradual, and a surprise attack was out of the question. A sentry would have seen the approaching army miles away. Besides, the identification of Aruna is beyond doubt; it was the temple mount of Jerusalem.

The story appears in the second book of Samuel, chapter 24. The nation was punished for an offense, committed by David. The angel of the Lord stood on the threshing floor of Araunah the Jebusite and the prophet Gad told David to build an altar there; the site was just north of the future temple of Solomon. Jebus later became Jerusalem. There was a rain-fed pool at Gibeon, and a road led to the threshing floor of Arauna the Jebusite. History proved the fears of Thutmose's generals well founded. Roman soldiers found the ascent impassible, and in the First World War General Allenby had to call off his attack on Turkish troops.

Thutmose succeeded however; he overran the temple, looted it and captured Jerusalem. His plan worked to perfection. For it is beyond doubt that he planned the whole thing. It is easy to see how, he knew the lay of the land. Hapshetsut personally visited Jerusalem. It only makes sense that Thutmose came along. It could have happened a number of different ways. In any event, he saw the riches of Solomon's gold plated capitol and planned ahead. That Mkty could have never been Megiddo is evident from the loot, taken by Thutmose; archaeology knows of no temple in that general area that could have possibly been that rich.

The scriptures call him Shishak, and it is believed that this must have been Soshenk. But Soshenk, who lived much later, was an ally, not an enemy. Shishak in all likelihood was derived from Thutmose's Horus name, Sheser-khau, or Shisher-ka. Following the triumphant return of his Palestinian campaign, which was the first of many, Thutmose made a list of all the cities he captured. Highest on the list was Kadesh, then Mkty, followed by 117 other names. Among these are the fortified cities, mentioned in 2 Chron. 11. It seems he simply walked in. This is all the more remarkably in view of the treasures he stole. The wealth of an advanced civilization was carried off to Egypt. But what was that nation and what that city? To this day historians are unable to identifying Kadesh.

Kadesh

Kadesh was the prime target of Thutmose's ambitions. It has always been a bone of contention exactly where this city was located. There are a number of cities by that name, but none qualify. It could not be that far away, for the Egyptians used four-wheel ox carts on their march. The Kadesh on the Orontes hardly qualifies. How could ox carts travel 250 miles over rough terrain? Besides, none of the places, mentioned by Thutmose fit that location.

It is certainly odd that Thutmose failed to mention Salem or Jebus on his list. Those were the names of Jerusalem, six hundred years earlier, when Thutmose supposedly made his move. Obviously, historians are faced with a perplexing problem, inherent in the names of foreign nations. Even today, cities and even nations go by very different names. If we were to look at the map of Europe, we would be hard pressed to find a country called Eastern Empire. Yet Oesterreich means just that. We know this nation as Austria, East of Germany (not Australia in the South Pacific). Only the Germans call their country Deutschland, not to be confused with Dutch, the language of the Netherlands (Holland); but the Dutch say Nederland.

If we have difficulties recognizing countries by their native names, how much more those of vanished civilizations? Historians were unable to find Kadesh somewhere in Syria-Palestine because that is what the Egyptians called it, not the natives. Kadesh is the Hebrew word c'desh, meaning holy. In the days of Thutmose the name of the city was not yet settled. It was called Salem, Zion, the City of David (Davidville), and "the city c'desh," the holy city, as in Isaiah 52:1

> Awake, awake, O Zion,
> clothe yourself with strength.
> Put on garments of splendor,
> O Jerusalem, the holy city. (The city c'desh)

Thutmose captured the holy city, Jerusalem. He may have called it Kadesh because he identified Jerusalem with the temple. Not only because that was his main target, but because Hatshepsut called her version of Solomon's temple *Djazair jdereru*, "the most splendid of splendors." That sounds very much like the "Holy of Holies," the inner sanctum of the temple in Jerusalem, and some scholars have indeed translated it so.[6]

It was the supreme c'desh, or Kadesh. The Egyptians identified Jerusalem with the temple in much the same way as we identify Washington, D.C. with the White House. It is easy to see why Thutmose need not worry about Megiddo; it was occupied by a collaborator who would gladly hand him the place. Jerusalem was another story. Thutmose wanted it badly for its monetary value, not its location: it was gold-plated. The City of David was a mountain fastness, isolated and out of the way. It was small, about thirty acres, with a population of about 4,500.

Karnak

Having emptied the temple and the palace, Thutmose carried the loot to Egypt. There, to immortalize his great accomplishment, he had the precious treasures reproduced on the walls of the temple of Amon in Karnak. The bounty was so great that he used a numerical system to catalog the displayed items. There are separate rows for gold, silver and copper items. These religious artifacts agree exactly with the ones, used in the tabernacle and the temple in Jerusalem and they tell a remarkable story. They were not used in pagan, polytheistic rituals; there is no image of any god at all. This temple was the house of a single God who must not be thought of in any physical fashion, nor be portrayed in any way. It was also free from any moral corruption, so prevalent in pagan temples.

Judging from the furnishings of this temple, a form of worship had been adopted from the culture of that time to suit a strictly monotheistic religion, that of Yahweh. The temple ceremony of this religion involved such items as show bread, incense, sacrifices, and altars to suit. They are pictured exactly as described in the Bible. Several items were portable, to suit a people on the move, as happened with the tabernacle in the desert. Altars, vessels, candlesticks, basins, priestly garments and even the three hundred shields, mentioned in 2 Chronicles 9:15 are displayed in detail. As if that was not enough, Thutmose came back to Jerusalem to confiscate Solomon's zoological gardens and had that reproduced as well. And so well-meaning authors believe Thutmose was a renaissance man with an interest in horticulture, not realizing they are looking at stolen art. Solomon's fears had come true.

> I hated all the things I had toiled for under the sun, because I must leave them to the one who comes after me. And who knows whether he will be a wise man or a fool? Yet he will have control over all the work into which I have poured my effort and skill under the sun. This too is meaningless. So my heart began to despair over all my toilsome labor under the sun. For a man may do his work with wisdom, knowledge and skill, and then he

The Thutmose Dynasty

must leave all he owns to someone who has not worked for it. This too is meaningless and a great misfortune.

Ecclesiastes 2:17-21

In retrospect, Thutmose has done us a great favor. True, the robber-king was motivated by greed. But it is an act of divine irony that he should leave for posterity iron clad historic evidence of biblical truth. How long now have we been told that the tabernacle never existed, that the Law of Moses was a pure fabrication, concocted centuries later, perhaps by Ezra, and that the riches of the temple in Jerusalem were greatly exaggerated. Yet *the altars, vessels and furnishings of Solomon's temple are displayed on the walls of a pagan temple in Egypt.* They are reproduced exactly as they are described in the books of Exodus, Leviticus, Kings and Chronicles.[7] The only thing missing is the Ark of the Covenant. In all likelihood it was removed before the arrival of the Egyptians. Something of the kind happened when Absolom made his power grab (2 Sam 15:24). It does however include a statue of Amon-Ra, a deity so magnanimously provided for Solomon's Egyptian wife, the daughter of Thutmose I.

Historians were amazed at the superior civilization that existed in Syria-Palestine about 1500 B.C., the time of Thutmose's conquest. A number of scholars observed with wonder that the language these Canaanites spoke was "almost identical with the Hebrew."[8] It was Hebrew, spoken by Hebrews. That civilization was Israel and Judah. In addition, every authority mentions a profound and beneficial influence on Egypt. The language absorbed Semitic words and the Egyptians became more gracious. The women became more delicate, the man's faces gentler. Strange, to say the least, in a pagan world. The Egyptians evidently were exposed to a more gracious civilization, and their attitude softened.

Now of course, this was not really the Syrian civilization of 1500 B.C. It was Israel some six hundred years later. It was serendipity, a side effect of God's redemptive purposes. Israel was chosen by God to be a channel of redemption. The Law of Moses with its high moral and ethical standard produced a people of dignity and purpose.

Israel influenced Egypt greatly and beneficially. When Thutmose looted the temple, he unwittingly imported a gracious disposition as well. As a result, Egyptian rule was relatively benign; Thutmose imposed rather peaceful conditions, not unlike the Pax Romana, the Roman peace at the time of Christ. This was, so to speak, the Pax Egyptana. Not that it was appreciated. Nobody likes to live under the heel of a foreigner, even if that boot is gentle.

The second year, following the Palestinian campaign, Thutmose attacked Syria, which he conquered. He listed no less than 330 captured cities. All in all, he conducted seventeen campaigns over a period of twenty years, with unforeseen results. When he crossed the Euphrates he ran into the kingdom of Mittanni, Indo-Europeans, which he subdued as well. Their relationship was friendly however. Thutmose initiated a policy of deporting captured princes to Egypt, where they were raised in the courts. By doing so, Egypt secured a ruling class. This is why eventually foreign princes were sympathetic to Egypt: they were raised there. It is known that princes from Mitanni intermarried with the Egyptians.

Amenhotep II

When Rehoboam submitted to the judgment, pronounced by Shemiah, the Lord decreed temporary submission to the yoke of Egypt. "I will not destroy them, but soon give them deliverance." (2 Chron 12:17). Rehoboam ruled seventeen years and his son Ahiah three years. Ahiah inflicted a defeat upon Jereboam, which would indicate that the influence of Egypt, Israel's overlord, was waning. As a result Asa, grandson of Rehoboam, began his rule with a ten-year peace. Asa was a God-fearing man. He tore down the altars of the foreign gods, built up the fortified cities of Judah and built a strong army, all of which was unacceptable to the Egyptians, who considered Palestine their turf.

The inevitable clash eventually came. "Zerah the Cushite marched out against them with a vast army." The size of this army was in the order of a million men, with three hundred chariots, the tanks of the day. Asa prayed to the Lord, engaged Zerah, and inflicted a great defeat. The Egyptians fled, leaving behind enormous spoil. It was a wondrous victory indeed. But who was Zerah the Cushite? Scripture does not identify him with a pharaoh, and the Ethiopian (Cushite) Dynasty came at a much later time.

After the death of Thutmose III, his successor Amenhotep II began his reign by suppressing an insurrection in Palestine and Syria. In his ninth year he returned to Palestine to harass and plunder a number of unimportant places. He left no record of a third campaign. There was Egyptian activity in southern Palestine; only it was not Amenhotep, but User-tabet, an Ethiopian general who battled in that general vicinity. The Hebrews evidently transliterated *User* to *Zerah*.

The campaign was a failure. There are scant records of meager spoils, and upon his speedy return Asiatics in a southern city revolted, something that would only happen following a defeat. It is quite understandable that this campaign went unnoticed. The pharaohs were notoriously biased reporters, and they were hardly inclined to admit to a defeat. All the same, it ended Egypt's foreign ambitions. Velikovsky maintains there is a Syrian record that speaks of just such a defeat, known as the Poem of Keret. It appears on tablets, found in the Syrian city of Ras Shamrah. It is worth our while to investigate his theory.

Ras Shamrah

Ras Shamrah is a village in Syria on the shores of the Mediterranean. In 1828 a peasant removed a stone in his field and discovered a hidden burial vault. It turned out to be part of an ancient maritime city called Ugarit. The pottery of the top layers was that of the Egyptian Middle Kingdom, and farther down that of the Hyksos Pharaoh Khian. Other cultures were identified: the Minoan age of Crete, and corresponding with it the Mycean age of Greece. Since ancient history is dated according to Egyptian chronology, the age was established as the Fifteenth Century B.C. A discrepancy surfaced. The burial vaults of Ras Shamrah are identical with those of Cyprus, six hundred years later and sixty miles away. But Egyptology ruled, and so this was discarded as just another curiosity.

Ugarit was a city of learning. Scribes wrote four different languages, among them Sumerian (Chaldean) and Akkadian, used in business and the courts. Akkadian tablets revealed another problem. The last king of Ugarit was Nikmed. Nikomedes is a distinctly Greek name. How could that be the case in the 15th Century B.C.? The Greek became prominent many centuries later. Ugarit was a maritime city with a diverse population, including a people called Jm'an, which the Assyrians called Jamanu or Ionians, Greeks. A third language was Khar, spoken by the Carians. These people lived in Syria and along the Mediterranean shores. Among the tablets was the Poem of Keret, mentioned above. It is an interesting piece of mythical literature, of considerable interest to scholars.

The fourth language was written in cuneiform, but scholars realized it was an alphabetical script. They substituted Hebrew letters and found they were reading Hebrew. Hebrew in 15th Century Canaan! And here all the time the higher critics of the Wellhausen School had pronounced the Old Testament a late fabrication. No such thing as Hebrew existed; it could not be, because alphabetical writing had not been invented yet. Or so we were told.

The biggest surprise was yet to come. The world of 15th Century Canaan was identical with that of 9th Century Israel. It never dawned on historians that something was wrong with their scheme of history. Rather they suddenly found proof that the authors of the scriptures had stolen their high moral values from the Canaanites. That hardly agrees with Biblical reports of gross immorality so utterly perverse that God ordered the Canaanites annihilated. Archaeological digs provide abundant proof that these people performed sex perversions in a pornographic religion. However, the literature and civilization of Ugarit which supposedly existed some five centuries before the kings of Judah and Israel, has fascinating parallels with the world of the Old Testament.

The Poem of Keret

Velikovsky claimed the Poem of Keret is based on a battle that very much resembles the activities of Zerah the Cushite. According to him two tribes of Israel, Asher and Zebulon are mentioned, in addition to Sidon, an ally of King Asa. What is this poem all about? It is essentially mythical literature that reflects Canaanite civilization. King Keret of Hubur (or Khuburu) suffered the slings and arrows of outrageous fortune. The only survivor of eight children, his seven wives either died or deserted him, and he had no children. While bewailing his plight, the god El appeared to him in a dream and told him to make war against the king of Udum. He must not ask for gold or silver, but demand that King Pubala of Udum hand him his daughter Hariya as wife. Keret assembled a vast army.

> Keret came down from the roof,
> He prepared food for the city,
> Wheat for Beth Hubur.
> He parched bread of the fifth,
> Food for the sixth month.
> The crowd mustered and came forth,
> The elite of the fighting men mustered.
> Then forth came the crowd together;
> His host was abundant in freemen,
> Three hundred times
> Marching in thousands like a rain storm,
> Even in tens of thousands as winter rain.
> After two, two marched,
> After three all of them.

It was an army of volunteers. The widow, the bachelor, even the sick helped; the blind man gave his blessings. The bridegroom, though exempt from military duty, joined. After three days they reached the shrine of Atherat, the goddess of oracles. Keret vowed if he would bring back Jariya as wife, he would give the goddess a third of his wife's weight in silver and a third in gold.

> They went a day, a second (day),
> A third, a fourth day.
> After sunset on the fourth day
> He reached Udum the Great,
> Even Udum Abundant in Water.

They took up position and watched the city six days. At sunrise of the seventh day King Pabil sent messengers with terms.

> Take silver and electrum,
> Gold in token of her value,
> And a henchman perpetual, three horses,
> A chariot which stands in the stable of thy humble servant.
> Take, O Keret, peace offerings in peace.
> Harm not Udum the Great,
> Even Udum Abundand in Water.
> Udum is the gift of El,
> The present of the Father of Men.
> Depart, O king from my house.
> Withdraw, O Keret, from my court. [9]

Keret demanded that Pabil's beautiful daughter be handed over to him. Pabil eventually agreed and Keret married Hariya, who bore him two sons and six daughters. But Keret never kept his vow with the goddess Asherat, who struck him with a deadly disease. The god El intervened however and healed Keret. At this point the remaining tablets are missing, so we can only guess how the story ended.

It is certain that this tale has nothing to do with Zerah the Cushite. There was no battle, no mention of any tribe of Israel, and no invasion of Southern Palestine. Besides, according to the scriptural account Asa fought his battle without allies. This is one of those cases where Velikovsky discovered meanings hitherto veiled. What is important however is the structure of this poem and other literary productions. The Canaanites were influenced by Hebrew poetry.

They used the same parallelism and metrical patterns we find in the Psalms and the prophets, notably Isaiah. In other words, the Canaanites of Ugarit lived in the days of the Hebrew kings, at least five hundred years later than is generally assumed.

A very similar discrepancy appears in Egypt in the so-called el-Amarna letters, which date from the reign of Pharaoh Akhnaton. The story of this pharaoh, regarded as a religious reformer, is one that needs to be told. Velikovsky the psychiatrist had a great interest in this distorted life. It is true that the life of Amenhotep IV (Akhnaton), son of Amenhotep III, closely resembles that of Oedipus. The story of Oedipus is told in a Greek tragedy; it is based upon much earlier historical events in Egypt. It involves a well-known royal family.

Oedipus

In the Oedipus legend, an oracle warned Laius, king of Thebes, and his wife Jacosta, that the son she was expecting would kill his father and marry his mother. The child was left to die in the desert, but was found by a shepherd and eventually adopted by the king of Corinth. They called him Oedipus (swell foot), because his feet were swollen. He grew up believing himself to be a prince, but by chance he heard the truth, and the curse that hung over his head. He left distressed, wandering through the world. When the driver of a chariot whipped him, he killed the driver and the passenger, his father Laius. He came to Thebes, where a sphinx asked a riddle, which he solved. The sphinx killed herself by jumping from a cliff. The people of Thebes, grateful that the monster was dead made him king, and he married the widowed Jacosta, his mother.

Unaware of their true relationship, Oedipus and Jacosta had two sons and two daughters. But the gods were displeased and sent a sign, a disaster. The oracle said that a crime had been committed. The king and the queen soon realized the truth. Jacosta hanged herself. Her brother Creon, who despised Oedipus, had him punished. Oedipus blinded himself and went into exile, accompanied by his daughter Antigone. Creon, the true ruler, arranged for Oedipus' sons Polynices and Eteocles to reign in turn every year.

Supported by Creon, Eteobles refused to return the throne to Polynices, who assembled a mercenary army and attacked Thebes. The two brothers met in mortal combat and killed each other. Creon, now king, ordered Eteocles buried with great ceremony in a rich tomb; he himself conducted the funeral rituals. He decreed Polynices be left as food for the birds, on pain of death. Antigone disobeyed Creon's order and buried Polynices anyway. She was arrested and sentenced to die in an enclosed tomb.

Akhnaton

Is the story of Oedipus based upon the biography of Akhnaton? Akhnaton was physically malformed. His head was elongated, his neck thin, his abdomen and thighs swollen. Oedipus means swell foot or swell leg. Akhnaton suffered from a rare disease called Lip dystrophy. Body fats disappeared from the upper part of his body, but increased in the lower parts. Akhnaton was a stranger to the Egyptian court. He spent his childhood away from Egypt. Upon the sudden death of his father Amenhotep III, his mother Tiy was briefly head of state until the arrival of her son, who was then called Amenhotep IV.

At that time the priesthood of Amon exercised great authority over the succession of the throne. The oracle at Heliopolis told the king whom the gods wanted to succeed him. Akhnaton called himself one "who survived to live long." It is quite possible that Akhnaton was the actual crown prince, but the oracle announced his brother Thutmose legitimate heir. Thutmose suddenly died however, and Akhnaton was next in line. If that was the case it becomes understandable why he had no use for the priesthood of Amon. Nor did Tiy appreciate her deceased husband. She was strong willed, not of royal descent, the daughter of a priest, and as Amenhotep in his old age grew unstable, she became more powerful. Late in life, Amenhotep had himself portrayed in women's clothes, unheard of for a pharaoh. He also "married" one of his own daughters and had a child by her, which soon died.

His son, Amenhotep IV, soon changed his name to Akhnaton, after the sun god Aton; he had no use for the Amon cult. Amon originally was the creator-god, later associated with Ra, the sun god. Aton on the other hand was not an astral deity but the sun disk, the physical sun. The religious reform of Akhnaton was anything but spiritual; it was wholly materialistic. He certainly was close to nature and in many ways humane. Unlike his father, a ferocious hunter, Akhnaton never hunted at all. He also put a stop to the brutal killing of prisoners of war and the cult of human sacrifice.

His break with the Amon cult came in his fourth year. He disowned the priesthood and closed the temples in Thebes. He also built a new Capitol, which he called after himself, Akhet-Aton. He re-established the Aton cult and built temples for the sun disk. He married Nefretete, the daughter of Ay, a priest and political strong man. Ay was also the brother of Queen Tiy. Tiy, the mother of Akhnaton, had a peculiar title; she was called "King's Mother and Great royal Wife." A queen always kept a harem for the king; a quaint Eastern custom. Tiy kept a harem in Akhet-Aton. Why would she do that after the death of her husband? In all likelihood both Akhnaton and Tiy inherited the morality of a civilization, very much unlike that of Egypt. The unpleasant truth is she married again, only this time to her own son, Akhnaton.

The Court of Mitanni

When the youthful Akhnaton left Egypt, where did he go? There is every reason to believe he grew up in the court of Mitanni which, as we have seen, was conquered by Thutmose III. This court probably involved a ruling class, perhaps of Mede extraction, that invaded Northern Syria. The Assyrians afterwards drove them away toward the western part of Asia Minor. There were family ties between the court of Mitanni and Amenhotep II. Some of the princesses of Egypt were Mittannian, one of them his mother. There is an Indo-Iranian style in the poetry of Akhnaton. He is pictured holding a light-ray emitting sun in his raised hands; that sun, so prevalent in his art, is the Vedic sun god Surya. Then there is another, more bothersome attribute. The Indo-Iranian culture of Mitanni had a unique approach to sexual mores; marriage between parents and children was considered honorable. Also, that of brother and sister of the same parents.

There are degrees of incest. In Egypt the royal line was continued through the female side. For this reason kings would marry close relatives, often a half-sister. The expression "my sister" could also mean "my wife." This is echoed in the Song of Songs, which indicates Egyptian influence. The practice was forbidden in the Law of Moses. Egyptian law was rather liberal, but the notion of a mother-son marriage was revolting. Historically this has always been true in all nations and all cultures - except the Indo-Iranian, such as Mitanni.

Akhnaton was about twenty-four years old when he came to the throne. He married Nefretete and had five daughters by her. The oldest was Meritate, who later married Smenkhare. The second daughter died at a young age. The third was Akhesapaaten, who became the wife of Tutankhamon. At first Akhnaton kept the marriage with his mother a secret, but not for long. Tiy settled in Akhet-Aton and soon everyone knew. It was difficult not to, for Akhnaton and Tiy appeared in public, quite undressed. They also had a daughter called Beketaten.

Akhnaton called himself the king "living in truth." People who reject moral restraints or live perverted lives think of themselves as true to their feelings and truthful. If Akhnaton thought the Egyptians would accept his life style as enlightened, he was mistaken. The Egyptians were not enlightened, they were appalled. Society on the whole tends to be tolerant of deviant behavior, just so it is kept private. But when it is demanded that perversions be accepted as normal, there will be a backlash.

That is what happened to Akhnaton. In the 12th year of his reign his wife deserted him, and Tiy became the great queen. Obviously this was the result of a power struggle. Nothing more is known of Nefretete, but her father Ay was furious at the humiliation of his daughter. That sealed the fate of Akhnaton. He ruled five more years, then Ay instigated a revolt. He had ample reasons to. Akhnaton was too involved with pleasure to give the kingdom much thought. Palestine was being raided without Egypt doing a thing about it. Tribute ceased; the empire was going to the dogs, but Akhnaton did nothing.

Then came an omen - perhaps the famine that struck Israel as well, and Akhnaton was deposed. He may have remained in Akhet-Aton a few more years, then he went into exile, evidently blind. The seat of the government was re-established in Thebes, the city of the restored Amon priesthood. Akhet-Aton was demolished, and that was the end of Akhnaton's religious reform.

Tut-ankh-amon

The greatest treasure ever found in Egypt was the burial vault of the youthful king Tutankhamon. Mural scenes suggest he died in battle against a Syrian-Ethiopian army after a reign of seven years. He was only seventeen years old when he died. The riches of his tomb defy belief. The question has been raised, why would a youthful ruler who had yet achieved nothing, receive such signal honor?

There is more. In the tomb of Tiy a damaged coffin was found. The body was that of a royal person, hurriedly prepared for burial. A beautiful love poem was found hidden under his feet. After considerable medical research it was found that this was Smenkhare, the older brother of Tutankhamon. It was also determined that both were sons of Akhnaton. One son was buried in splendor, the other in disgrace.

Smenkhare was a favorite son of Akhnaton. However, a bas-relief led competent scholars to the conviction that the father exhibited foul feelings for his son. Smenkhare ruled one year, then Tutankhamon, his ten-year old brother took over. Tay, his uncle was regent. When Smenkhare returned a year later, his younger brother, backed by Tay, refused to step down. Smenkhare, robbed of the throne, returned several years later with an army to capture Thebes. It is certain that both brothers died at the same time, very likely in this battle.

Their regent Tay, by this time an old man, became king. He personally conducted the funeral ceremonies for Tutankhamon. Of course, it was all his doing in the first place. What happened to the body of Smenkhare? It was found in the tomb of Tiy, hastily buried, a love poem under his feet. The famous Egyptologist Gardiner concluded that this poem was written by the sister of the prince. It was later found that this was Meritaten, his half sister and wife. She ignored Ay's decree that her husband should be left unburied, and hastily embalmed him in a tomb pit, but was caught in the act. The new king ordered the body buried in Tiy's tomb. Meritaten was imprisoned in a nearby pit where she died, close to her beloved Smenkhare. Of Tiy nothing else is known. She was not buried near her husband, Amenhotep III, as one would expect. Like Akhnaton, her body was never found.

Akhnaton supposedly was the first monotheist, long before Moses, because he never represented deity in any physical way. It is true that the belief in a single God did not originate with Moses. Archaeological evidence from the earliest civilizations indicates that mankind believed in one Supreme God; polytheism developed later. Monotheism survived in the Semitic peoples, beginning with the Arameans, followed by the Hebrews. Akhnaton was not at all a religious reformer, he was a sick pervert. Besides, he lived six centuries after Moses. Certain scholars seized upon Akhnaton's worship of a single deity because they thought this would undermine the scriptural account of divine revelation. They were wrong.

Literature

In Egyptian literature there are very interesting examples of writings that closely resemble the Hebrew Scriptures. A well-known case is that of Aknhanton's *Hymn to the Aten,* Aten being the sun disk. The similarities with Psalm 104 are striking. Both deal with a providential care for nature. To appreciate the flavor, we must quote these songs at some length.

> Whenever you set on the western horizon,
> the land is in darkness in the manner of death.
> They sleep in a bedroom with heads under the covers
> and one eye does not see another.
> If all their possessions which under their heads were stolen,
> they would not know it.
> Every lion who comes out of his cave and all the serpents bite,
> for darkness is a blanket.
> The land is silent now, because he who made them
> is at rest on his horizon.
> But when day breaks you are risen upon the horizon,
> and you shine as Aten in the daytime.
> When you dispel darkness and you give forth your rays
> the two lands are in festival,
> alert and standing on their feet,
> now that you have raised them up.
> Their bodies are clean, and their clothes have been put on;
> their arms are lifted in praise at your rising.
> The entire land performs its work:
> all the cattle are content with their fodder,
> trees and plants grow,
> birds fly up to their nests,
> their wings extended in praise for your Ka.
> All the kine prance on their feet;
> everything which flies up and alights,
> they live when you have risen for them.
> The barges sail upstream and downstream too,
> for every way is open at your rising.
> The fishes in the river leap before your face
> when your rays are in the sea.[10]

The hymn to the Aten merely regards Aten as the sun disk, a physical object that so happens to sustain life. Psalm 104 goes far beyond that; it extols the Creator who upholds nature.

The trees of the LORD are well watered,
the cedars of Lebanon that he planted.
There the birds make their nests;
the stork has its home in the pine trees.
The high mountains belong to the wild goats;
the crags are a refuge for the coneys.
The moon marks off the seasons,
and the sun knows when to go down.
You bring darkness, it becomes night,
and all the beasts of the forest prowl.
The lions roar for their prey
and seek their food from God.
The sun rises, and they steal away;
they return and lie down in their dens.
Then man goes out to his work,
to his labor until evening.
How many are your works, O Lord!
In wisdom you made them all;
the earth is full of your creatures.
There is the sea, vast and spacious,
teeming with creatures beyond number -
living things both large and small.
There the ships go to and fro,
and the leviathan, which you formed to frolic there.
Psalm 104:16-26

The similarities are obvious, and so are the differences. The *Hymn to the Aten* is a poetic report about the world as enlightened by the sun. Psalm 104 looks beyond the narrow interests of the farmer, and sees God as the Creator and sustainer of life; not merely of cattle, but of wild animals as well. We also notice the similarity in style. Hebrew poetry employed parallelism, a phrase followed by a similar a statement.

I looked all over, I searched everywhere.

Or it could be an opposite reply.
Yesterday it rained, but today the sun shines.

The Egyptians obviously did the same thing. In addition Hebrew and Egyptian wisdom literature closely resemble each other. The similarities between *The Instruction of Amenemope* and the book of Proverb are striking.[11]

Do not displace the surveyor's marker
on the boundaries of the arable land,
Nor alter the position of the measuring line.
Do not be greedy for a plot of land,
Nor overturn the boundaries of a widow.
                                  Amenemope, Ch. 6

Do not move an ancient boundary stone
or encroach on the fields of the fatherless,
for their Defender is strong;
he will take up their case against you.
                                  Proverbs 23:10

Beware of robbing the grain measure,
To falsify its fractions;
                                  Amenemope, Ch 17

The Lord detests differing weights,
and dishonest scales do not please him.
                                  Proverbs 20:23

The general tenor of Amenemope's instructions is very similar to Proverbs. It deals with honesty and character, and encourages personal responsibility. Equally intriguing are the *Song of the Harper* and the *Song of Solomon*; both are erotic love songs that closely resemble each other.[12]

The voice of the turtledove speaks out.
It says: day breaks, which way are you going?
Lay off, little bird, must you scold me?
I found my lover on his bed,
and my heart was sweet to excess.
We said: I shall never be far away from you
while my hand is in your hand,
and I shall stroll with you
in every favorite place.
He set me as first of the girls
and he does not break my heart.

Harper, 14

All night long on my bed
I looked for the one my heart loves;
I looked for him but did not find him.
I will get up now and go about the city,
through its streets and squares;
I will search for the one my heart loves.
So I looked for him, but did not find him.
The watchmen found me
as they made their rounds in the city.
"Have you seen the one my heart loves?"

Song of Songs 3:1-2

The Song of the Harper is made up of different fragments, and the Song of Songs is a single composition. Besides, it has a distinct message. Nonetheless, they are in many ways very similar. It follows that Hebrew and Egyptian wisdom literature are related. Who inspired who is hard to tell, but both clearly date from the same time. Since most of the Psalms and Proverbs date from the days of David and Solomon or shortly thereafter (not all Psalms were written by David), it follows that Akhnaton must have lived in the days of the Hebrew kings, not centuries earlier. It is generally agreed that the

Hymn to Aten and Amenemope's instructions were written in the early days of the New Kingdom, which must have been around 900 B.C.

The el-Amarna Letters

When Akhnaton built his Capitol Akhet-Aton, he had a library made to store copies of official documents, including those of his father, Amenhotep III. These archives were found in 1887 in a village called el-Amarna. They consist of tablets, written in Akkadian or Assyria-Babylonian, which was the international language of that time. Vassal kings of Syria and Palestine asked for protection against "Habiru" who raided their country. Since the pharaoh was Akhnaton, supposedly around 1400 B.C., there has been speculation that maybe this was a reference to invading Hebrews. It is now generally agreed that Habiru means pillagers. However, historians ran into a perplexing problem. The Capitol cities of the nations in Palestine were Urusalim (Jerusalem) and Sumur (Samaria).

It is difficult to see how these cities could have been known that early. Jerusalem at the time was called either Jebus or Salem. Samaria was not built until six centuries later by Omri, king of Israel (885-874 B.C.). Samaria received its name from Shemer, owner of the real estate where it was built. (1 Kings 16:24). It could also be read Sumur. It follows that the el-Amarna letters were written in the days of the ten tribes of Israel and the kingdom of Judah, three quarters of a century after the death of Solomon.

Samaria

Samaria was an important city in the trade of ivory. Much of it was exported to Egypt. It was also an administrative center for Egypt in Syria-Palestine. Samaria became the Capitol of the ten tribes of Israel because it was centrally located and easy to defend. But it stood for everything that was idolatrous in Israel and so the Lord pronounced doom.

> What is Jacob's transgression?
> Is it not Samaria?
> What is Judah's high place?
> Is it not Jerusalem?
> Therefore I will make Samaria a heap of rubble,
> a place for planting vineyards.
> I will pour her stones into the valley
> and lay bare her foundations.
>
> Micah 1:5-6

Samaria had a violent history. It was finally destroyed in the Christian era. But the soil was rich, so farmers dug up the ground, piled up heaps of rubble and unceremoniously dumped the foundation stones into the valley, where they are to this day. The hill where once stood Samaria is now covered with olive gardens, corn fields and fig trees.

At that time Israel was losing its religious identity, and with it the cement that bonded the ten tribes together. The king could not always rely on the loyalty of all the tribes. The kings of Judah and Israel were both subject to Egypt, but still enjoyed a measure of independence. They even had their own vassals. Judah subjected the kings of Arabia and the Philistines, and Samaria controlled Mesha, king of Moab.

The el-Amarna letters repeatedly mention "Mesh." The king of Sumur (Samaria) complained about him as a rebel. There were frequent wars between them, and a number of times Samaria was attacked. Once it was even captured. The king of Judah, true to his convictions, was not the only one not to call the pharaoh "my god," nor did he mention the name of his God. The name of the Lord was too hallowed to be mentioned. There are additional similarities.

The prophet Elisha warned a woman to leave Israel because the Lord had decreed a seven-year famine (2 Kings 8:1). The drought occurred in the days of Akhnaton, and the el-Amarna letters kept begging the king of Egypt for help, to no avail. As the years passed and

The Thutmose Dynasty

the famine grew more severe, no animal survived and women, according to rabbinical tradition, ate their own children. It was at this time that Ramoth-Gilead became important; it was the bread basket of that area, and it was not affected by the drought. In the el-Amarna letters it is called Iarimuta, and it is repeatedly mentioned. The combined forces of Judah and Israel were defeated in an attempt to capture it. Is it possible that this famine sealed the doom of Akhnaton?

Assyria

In 858 B.C., Shalmanezer III became king of Assyria. Shalmanezer was an aggressor, and it was under his leadership that Assyria began to expand. The kings of Assyria were utterly cruel. They are always spoken of with fear. The Ras Shamra letters mention how Ugarit was destroyed by fire, but it does not reveal the name of the enemy. The Hatti (Babylonians) are mentioned as well, and that agrees with the annals of Shalmanezer. The Assyrian king assimilated Babylon into the Assyrian empire. He mentions the cities of Nikdime and Nikdiera, and how its people fled before him on ships. He overtook them and "with their blood dyed the sea like wool." Nikdime evidently was "the city of Nikmed," Ugarit.

Two years later, Shalmanezer fought a coalition of twelve princes in the battle of Qarqar, Ahaz among them. Ahaz repeatedly warned the pharaoh of the danger, coming from the north. So did the princes of Syria. They reported how the king of Hatti burned cities to the ground, the exact tactics of the Assyrians. In the face of this terror, a number of Phoenicians left the coastal cities and Tyre, and founded Carthage in North Africa, which became an important trade center.

Appeals to Pharaoh Akhnaton were useless. He was too engrossed in his perverted fantasies. It is of considerable interest that the king of Hatti (Assyria) was unable to defeat his neighbor to the north, Mitanni. Mitanni, as we have seen, had friendly relations with the court of Egypt, and its king Tushratta, father-in-law of Akhnaton, informed the pharaoh that he had raided Hatti. Not so Akhnaton. The flower child-king sent Shalmanezer (whom he called Barraburiash) what amounts to a tribute. Keep in mind that these kings were supposed to have lived five hundred years earlier. The Assyrians were at the beginning of their imperial might, and we will meet them again, but for now we will merely look at the pharaohs.

With the death of Akhnaton and his sons, the Theban (Thutmose) Dynasty came to an end. Ay, an old man, had no heirs, and so the scepter passed to another dynasty, believed to have been the Ramessides. The revised chronology takes them off their exalted throne. They were not at all independent rulers, but benefactors of the Assyrians. In fact, they survived them. The Thutmose Dynasty saw the beginning of the Assyrian supremacy, the Ramessides the end. For all their fame they are known by different names in an obscure dynasty, and their opponents are well known to us from the scriptures. Still, their accomplishments were remarkable.

Chapter Four

The Ramessides

Ramses II

Following the Thutmose Dynasty comes perhaps the most famous line of pharaohs, the Ramessides. Now Ramses or Ra-messe, is actually a generic name. It means "House of Ra," Ra being the sun god. Where, we ask, does the Ramesside Dynasty fit into biblical history? Not in the days of the judges for sure, in spite of what the experts tell us. The Hyksos and Thutmose Dynasties were displaced by some five centuries. Just pushing them forward about four hundred fifty years puts them in their proper place.

Not so the Ramessides. They were merchant princes who lived much later. They were not a royal family, for the father of Ramses I was a "captain of troops," and he came from northern Egypt. His son Seti the Great fully established the dynasty, but it was the pharaoh who is known as Ramses II who stands out as a builder and explorer. Not only did he erect great monuments, he also had a canal dug to connect the Nile with the Red Sea, although the project was never finished. He himself recounted having sent ships to faraway seas.

Ramses II came to power about 1290 B.C. In the second year of his reign he marched his armies along the coastal plains of Palestine.

He was confronted by a local prince, but before the battle could be joined his adversary was fatally wounded by an arrow. The enemy fled, and Ramses marched on to northern Syria. Upon his return he took several Palestinian princes captive to Egypt. He also imposed a heavy tribute. Three years later, in his fifth year, he again led a strong army through Palestine to meet a mighty adversary, Hattusilis, commander of the Hittite army.

Hattusilis evidently was a physical dwarf, but a mental giant. After the death of his father, his brother Nergil became king. Nergil, aware of his younger brother's abilities, made him commander of his northern army. That turned out to be a good decision, for Hattusilis was victorious wherever he went. He became governor of the rebellious northern provinces, which he subdued. Now he faced the pharaoh.

The Poem of Pentaur

Thanks to the pharaoh's narcism, this campaign is known rather in detail. The Poem of Pentaur, so called after a copyist, was written to extol the heroics of Ramses II. It glorifies "the victory he achieved in the land of Khatti, Nahrim, Carchemish, Kody, the land of Kadesh." Since Kadesh, as we have seen, is the Semitic word for holy, it probably involves a holy city, that is a temple city.

The army was composed of four divisions; Amon, Re, Ptah and Sutekh, among them mercenaries called Sardan. It was a mighty display of arms, and everybody was impressed: "all countries trembling before him — bowing down through fear of his might." The army looked well nigh invincible. Alas, it wasn't. The bombastic king, overconfident after his easy victories, had too exalted an opinion of himself and the strength of his army, and he grossly underestimated the overwhelming force and superior generalship of the enemy.

The battle was joined by a river called –r-t, p–-r-t and variations thereof. Because of this, it was assumed that it was the Orontes. There is a place by the Orontes called Tell-Nebi-Mend, which seems to satisfy the description of the battle. The problem is that the

Orontes was called after a Bactrician general, 400 B.C. (It is a distinctly Persian name). Before that it was called Typhon. Frankly, there is no way to tell which river is meant.

There are other reasons to question the Orontes. If that is where the battle was fought, why did Ramses mention Carchemish on the Euphrates, much farther toward the northeast? The road traveled by the Egyptian army did not stop at the Orontes. To the north of Tell-Mend, a road leads from Hemath on the Orontes through Aleppo, el Bab and Arima to Carchemish on the Euphrates.

Ramses relates that the First Division, that of Amon which he headed, was north-west of Kadesh. The Second Division, called Re, crossed the river r--t, and the Third and Fourth Divisions, Ptah and Sutekh were south of Aromana (Arima). Their officers were south of Baw (el Bab). It follows that Kadesh must have been Carchemish. Car, or Cor, is a Carian word meaning holy, and Chemish is Chemosh, a Syrian deity. Carchemish was a temple city, dedicated to the worship of Chemosh. It is now the site of the city of Jerublus or Jarabulus.

The topography of Carchemish fits the description of the battle field exactly. Egyptian bas-reliefs show a walled city with two fords and towers; the top of the walls and towers have a triangular design. Behind the city is a large river. A small river loops along the front, creating an island. This nowhere resembles Tell-Nebi-Mend on the Orontes (it is a peninsula), but it fits Carchemish exactly. So do the archaeological digs of the city. Its walls had the same triangular design as that depicted on the Egyptian murals. Also, the Babylonian name of the Euphrates is Puratu; Prat in Hebrew, which fits p–r–t. The modern name is Al Furat.

The Battle of Carchemish

It soon became apparent that Ramses had made several awful military goofs. Not that he ever admitted to it. For beginners he himself, as Commander-in-chief, with the Amon Division was far ahead of the other units, out of touch, with no idea where the enemy was.

Had he sent out scouts, he would have discovered that the enemy was across the river hiding behind the city instead of a hundred miles away, as he had been led to believe. He complained bitterly about it. "This is a great crime that the governors of foreign countries and the chiefs of Pharaoh have committed without causing to be tracked down for them the fallen one of Khatti (Kheta) wherever he was, that they might report to the Pharaoh every day."

The Amon Division was setting up camp northwest of Carchemish when the pharaoh received intelligence about the unpleasant truth. Just then enemy chariots attacked the second (Re) Division as it was fording the river, and cut it in pieces. Ramses was still berating his officers when remnants of the Re Division burst through the camp with the enemy on their heels. The panicked Egyptians fled toward the north, leaving the pharaoh with mere bodyguards, surrounded by chariots. The poem went into high gear.

> Then his Majesty arose like his father Mont — ; he was like Baal in his hour. — Then his Majesty started forth in a gallop, and entered into the host of the fallen ones of Khatti, being alone by himself, none other with him. And his Majesty went to look about him, and found surrounding on his outer side 2,500 parts of horses (chariots) with all the champions of the fallen ones of Khatti and the many countries who were with him.[1]

Ramses here mentions the troops who had sided with the Hittites; they were troops of Syrian cities. The chariots of the enemy were stronger than those of the Egyptians. They were larger, and carried three men instead of two. The pharaoh speaks of himself as a fierce-eyed lion who single-handedly hurled the enemy into the river. Well, not exactly of course, but he did rally his men and again and again charged into overwhelming enemy forces.

After several desperate charges, Ramses succeeded in beating back the enemy. Fortunate for him, the Hittite cavalry unwisely stopped to plunder the camp. Just then a contingent of Egyptian allies arrived and annihilated the looting Hittites, which allowed

Ramses to escape. He at once sent for his remaining divisions. Hattusilis now threw in his reserves who engaged the Amon and Re Divisions or what was left of it, but the Egyptians held on, until late in the afternoon the Third Division appeared.

The Hittites were now caught between two armies and after severe losses retreated. A truce was agreed upon, but the Egyptian army was badly crippled and in the face of overwhelming enemy forces beat a hasty retreat. The Hittites "covered the mountains as grasshopper in their multitude." Ramses patted himself on his back: "The nations have seen me: they will repeat my name even in far away regions." There can be no doubt that his conduct had been courageous, but that did not change the outcome. The battle was a tactical defeat and a strategic disaster. All of Syria and Palestine came under Hittite control.

Hattusilis pursued the beaten army to the Egyptian border, but soon had to leave. Urgent domestic problems required his presence back home. He returned in record time. He was called to the royal court to defend himself against serious charges. A former ruler, now dethroned, accused him of a power grab. His military successes had made him altogether too popular. But his brother Nergil, the king, decided in favor of Hattusilis and made him king of the northern provinces.

Now that the Egyptians were temporarily powerless, the various peoples of Palestine did not pay tribute. It took Ramses three years to recover sufficiently, then he attacked Ashkelon and Gaza and put them under submission. Further attempts to recover Syria and Palestine proved pointless. The Hittites returned and attacked Egypt, but were repelled at the Wadi of el-Arish (the river of Egypt). After nearly two decades of fruitless fighting, both sides agreed upon a truce. A continuous war would benefit neither side. As a gesture of good will, Ramses agreed to marry the daughter of Hattusilis. To his credit, the treaty included a clause that extradited political refugees should receive humane treatment.

Necho II

We must ask an obvious question. Why is nothing of the kind recorded in the book of Judges? Could it be that this pharaoh, too, belongs in another era? It does have a familiar ring. Is there a pharaoh, somewhere in the Old Testament, who matches Ramses II? As a matter of fact, there is, and Greek sources have a good deal to say about him as well. Heredotus relates that Necho II, a king of the 26th Dynasty, was a man of considerable achievements. He was a general, builder and merchant. Among other things, he ordered a canal constructed to connect the Nile with the Gulf of Suez.

> It was Necho who made the original attempt to dig a canal through to the Red Sea; Darius of Persia, in a second attempt, completed it. —

Heredotus claims that a hundred-twenty-thousand men died digging. He goes on to report that Necho built a Navy and conducted a number of military campaigns in Syria. He was the first to discover that Lybia (Africa) was surrounded by water.

> King Necho of Egypt was the first to discover this, as far as we know; after he abandoned the digging of the canal from the Nile to the Arabian Gulf, his next project was to dispatch ships with Phoenician crews with instructions to return via the Pillars of Heracles (The Strait of Gibraltar) and arrived back in Egypt.[2]

This trip took two years, and the crew reported an unheard-of phenomenon, the sun shone in the north. Of course, they did not realize they had crossed the equator. Heredotus found this impossible to believe. Historians had problems of their own. How could Heredotus say Necho was the first to attempt digging a canal if Ramses II attempted that six hundred years before? Heredotus must have been mistaken; Necho must have picked up where Ramses left off. This could hardly be true. Heredotus was impressed exactly because Necho was the first to attempt such a great undertaking. He made the *original* attempt to dig a canal. It was the *only* attempt. There are no reports of anyone stumbling over this canal during the previous centuries. Besides, without proper maintenance it would only be a matter of time before it would be filled in by sand storms. So much about Heredotus. What do the scriptures say about Necho?

In 2Kings 23 and 2Chronicles 35, we read that Josiah, king of Judah, attempted to prevent Pharaoh Necho from marching up to the Euphrates. At the stronghold Megiddo, Josiah was mortally wounded by an arrow just as his army lined up, and the battle was over before it began. Necho continued to Riblah in Syria. Upon his return he dethroned King Jehoaz, whom he took captive to Egypt. He installed Jehoiakim as king instead, and imposed a heavy tribute. Three years later, in the fourth year of Jehoiakim, Necho marched his army toward Syria for a fateful battle with the Chaldeans

The Chaldeans

Chaldean tribes were scattered throughout Asia Minor and Babylonia. The Assyrian king Tiglath-Peliser III after a protracted war pushed them to the east and west of his empire. By the end of the Eighth Century B.C., Merodach-Baladan, whose main territory was near the Persian Gulf, captured Babylon. It involved much more than Babylon proper; his kingdom included some eight hundred cities. He called himself "King of the Chaldeans." That did not last. The Assyrians attacked and captured Babylon 707 B.C., but Merodach-Baladan made good his escape. It was not until 625 B.C. that the Urartu Chaldeans were able to defeat the Assyrians near Babylon. The combined armies of the Chaldeans and the Medes then attacked the Assyrians. The Scythians joined, and 612 B.C. Nineveh, the impregnable Capitol of Assyria, fell in a matter of months. The Chaldeans and Medes divided the fallen Assyrian empire between them. The Chaldean king Nebonassar made Babylon his Capitol, for good reasons.

Babylon was an ancient city-state in the plain of Shinar and the Capitol of Babylonia, the eastern end of the Fertile Crescent. It was the center of intellectual life in western Asia and especially noted for its study of the stars. Thus, Babylon became a center for magicians, sorcerers, diviners and other occult practitioners.

The Chaldeans are first mentioned in early Babylonian notices. The name appears in Assyrian notices after 883 B.C. Because of their proficiency in astronomy and skillful practice of astrology, the Chaldeans became a cast of astrologers. They were prominent in Babylon beginning in 625 B.C.

Thus the Chaldeans could be considered priests because of their involvement with the gods and fates. They acquired special powers from their knowledge of astronomy and their investment in occult magic.[3]

Pharaoh Necho watched the growing power of the emerging Chaldean Empire with increasing alarm. His dynasty was established by the Assyrians, and he had every reason to maintain friendly relations with his former ally. However, the demise of Assyria allowed him to take over Syria-Palestine. So it was that he marched his mercenary army northward to stop the Chaldeans and aid what was left of the Assyrian Empire. The Egyptians and Chaldeans met in a fateful battle. Odd though it may seem, this battle was never recorded in Egyptian annals. It seems it never happened. Fortunately, we know a great deal from an unexpected source; it is recorded in detail in the scriptures. Surprisingly it is not mentioned in the historical books, but in the prophets.

Jeremiah 46

The prophet Jeremiah records a battle that occurred 605 B.C., in the fourth year of Jehoiakim, which was the fifth year of Necho. The poem of Pentaur informs us that Ramses fought the battle of r--t three years after he first invaded Palestine, on the ninth day of the tenth month of the fifth year of his reign. Jeremiah gives "the message against the army of Pharaoh Necho which had been defeated at

Carchemish on the Euphrates River by Nebuchadnezzar in the fourth year of Jehoiakim, son of Josiah king of Judah." (Jer. 46:1)

> Prepare your shields, both large and small
> and march out for battle!
> Harness the horses, mount the steeds!
> Take your positions with helmets on!
> Polish your spears, put on your armor!
>
> Jeremiah 46:2-4

Moral was high, confidence abounded. It was all very impressive. But now what? The prophet feigned surprise.

> What do I see?
> They are terrified, they are retreating,
> their warriors are defeated.
> They flee in haste without looking back,
> and there is terror on every side,
> declares the Lord.
> The swift cannot flee, nor the strong escape.
> In the north, by the River Euphrates
> they stumble and fall.
>
> Jeremiah 46:5, 6

That was a synopsis of the campaign; its glorious start and humiliating end. A more detailed description followed. The prophet vividly recalled the pageantry and resentment of a foreign army marching across his country.

> Who is this that rises like the Nile,
> Like rivers of surging waters?
> Egypt rises like the Nile;
> like rivers of surging waters.
> She says, "I will rise and cover the earth;
> I will destroy cities and their people."

> Charge, O horses! Drive furiously, O charioteers!
> March on, O warriors -
> men of Cush and Put who carry shields,
> men of Lydia who draw the bow.
> But that day belongs to the Lord, the Lord Almighty -
> a day of vengeance, for vengeance on his foes.
> The sword will devour till it is satisfied,
> till it has quenched its thirst with blood.
> For the Lord, the Lord Almighty, will offer sacrifice
> In the land of the north by the river Euphrates.
>
> Jeremiah 46:7-10

The army of Necho, according to Jeremiah, besides the Egyptian contingent, had units of Cush, (Ethiopia), Put (Lybia) and Lydia for a total of four divisions. Egypt, Ethiopia and Lydia were part of greater Egypt, but Lydia was a more recent ally. It was located in modern Turkey, across the Mediterranean. The Sardans, mentioned by Ramses, were mercenaries. *Sardans* means "men of Sardis," Sardis being the Capitol of Lydia. The army of the Chaldeans was aided by the Syrians (Jer. 35:11). This is also known from history. Necho /Ramses claimed he had won a victory, and that "the nations have seen me: they will repeat my name even in far away regions." Jeremiah thought different: Egypt had been badly beaten.

> Go up to Gilead and get balm,
> O virgin daughter of Egypt.
> But you multiply remedies in vain;
> there is no healing for you.
> The nations will hear of your shame;
> your cries will fill the earth.
> One warrior will stumble over another;
> both will fall down together.
>
> Jeremiah 46:11, 12

The Ramessides

This marked the beginning of prolonged hostilities on Palestinian soil. Nebuchadnezzar pursued Necho to the border of Egypt and Jehoiakim, king of Judah, became his servant; Necho received no more tribute. Two months later Nebuchadnezzar hastily returned to Babylon. Hiram, king of Tyre and a relative, accused him of coveting the throne. Nebuchadnezzar refuted him, and was appointed king of Babylon instead. A few years later he had Hiram, an old man, executed. It is believed that Nebuchadnezzar succeeded his father to the throne, but that was not the case. His brother became king, and when he died, his son ascended the throne. Within a year the boy-king was either killed or exiled, and Nebuchadnezzar was king instead.

It is instructive to compare the actions of Ramses with those of Necho. Three years after his humiliating defeat, Necho recovered sufficiently to again invade Palestine. Ramses did the same thing. Necho, like Ramses, captured Gaza and Ashkelon in his eighth year (Jeremiah 47). This led Jehoiakim, an Egyptian sympathizer, to rebel against the Chaldeans, with disastrous results. Three years later, in the eleventh year of Jehoiakim, Nebuchadnezzar sent an army against Necho, who hastily retreated; Jehoiakim was taken prisoner and put to death. His son Jehoiachin was installed as king instead, but Nebuchadnezzar, suspicious of his loyalty, returned three months later. The youthful king came out to Nebuchadnezzar to show his allegiance and save his people. Nonetheless, Nebuchadnezzar sent him to Babylon, along with the nobility, including Daniel and his friends, and skilled craftsmen. There Jehoiachin remained a prisoner until the death of Nebuchadnezzar, thirty seven years later, then he was released.

Meanwhile Nebuchadnezzar installed Mattaniah (Zedekiah), Jehoiachin's uncle as king. The prophet Jeremiah, no friend of the Chaldeans, nevertheless counseled submission to Nebuchadnezzar. But a strong pro-Egyptian faction, fearful of Nebuchadnezzar, pinned its hope on Necho and after eight years rebelled. It was in vain. The Chaldean army returned and laid siege to Jerusalem. When Necho moved into southern Palestine, they withdrew to face the Egyptians. The Jews used this occasion to take back the slaves they had recently released. Because this involved the breaking of a solemn oath, the Lord told Jeremiah,

> I will hand Zedekiah king of Judah and his officials over to their enemies who seek their lives, to the army of the king of Babylon, which has withdrawn from you. I am going to give the order, declares the Lord, and I will bring them back to this city. They will fight against it, take it and burn it down. And I will lay waste the towns of Judah so no one can live there.
>
> Jeremiah 34:21, 22

It is generally agreed that the Egyptians and Chaldeans arrived at some kind of agreement. There was no battle; a war would benefit neither side. Any treaty must necessarily be recorded in the annals of the kings, that is the pharaohs. The record of Ramses agrees with that of Necho. Historical dating provides identical results. The three Judean kings ruled a total of nineteen years. Since hostilities began in the second year of Necho, any peace agreement must have been reached nineteen years later, in his twenty first year. The record stated that Ramses II signed a peace treaty with Hattusilis on the twenty-first day of the fourth month in the twenty-first year of his reign. The Egyptians ceded Syria-Palestine to the Chaldeans, which left Judah without help. Nebuchadnezzar came back to Jerusalem and after a siege that lasted a year and a half, breached the walls 586 B.C. The people of Jerusalem were carried captive to Babylon.

The message given through Jeremiah was clear. The Jews, rather than trust the Lord, had relied on Egypt instead. In a sense they had the slave mentality of the Hebrews who wanted to return to the flesh pots of Egypt after the spies gave a bad report of the Promised Land. They would rather pay protection money to Egypt than rely on Almighty God. The result was very much the same; they left the Promised Land. Jeremiah went on to foretell the fate of Egypt. "Pharaoh King of Egypt is only a loud noise; he has missed his opportunity." The Lord would send an enemy from the north who would inspire fear.

> Egypt is a beautiful heifer,
> but a gadfly is coming against her from the north.
> The mercenaries in her ranks are like fattened calves.
> They too will turn and flee together,
> they will not stand their ground.
>
> Jeremiah 46:20, 21

The meaning is that Egypt, so mighty in its appearance, was merely a pretty cow and anything but a strong bull. It would be pestered but not destroyed by a gadfly, the Chaldeans. The mercenaries she had hired were calves by comparison; their loyalty in doubt, they would fail her. The enemy, numerous as locusts, would cut Egypt down to size. Twofold punishment was ordained.

> The Lord Almighty, the God of Israel says: "I am about to bring punishment on Amon god of Thebes, on Pharaoh, on Egypt and her gods and her kings and on those who rely on Pharaoh. I will hand them over to those who seek their lives, to Nebuchadnezzar king of Babylon and his officers. Later, however Egypt will be inhabited as in times past," declares the Lord.
>
> Jeremiah 46:25, 26

The prophecy was fulfilled in stages. Nebuchadnezzar besieged and captured Jerusalem, and the city was leveled. The Jews were banished to Babylon, where they languished for seventy years, then a remnant returned. Zedekiah, king of Judah, was captured and taken before Nebuchadnezzar, who ordered his sons killed before his eyes; that was the last thing he saw, for the cruel Chaldeans cut his eyes out. He was taken to Babylon where he was imprisoned until the day of his death. The Jews who fled to Egypt were extradited to the Chaldeans under treaty obligation. Afterwards Egypt was devastated, but recovered.

Necho/Ramses

There are definite parallels between the poem of Pentaur and Jeremiah; he even employs several words and expressions used in the poem. This retrospective account of a battle and its disastrous outcome is unique in the scriptures. It makes us wonder, why would Jeremiah go into such detail about the defeat of a pharaoh? After all, Nebuchadnezzar was probably worse. It is possible that Jeremiah while in Egypt read the poem of Pentaur. Knowing how Judah had been fooled by the pomp of Necho, he saw that the pharaoh, although not necessarily lying, did not quite tell all of the truth. It has all the makings of a rebuttal. We can imagine that he felt an irresistible urge to set the record straight and in so doing left an account that placed a displaced pharaoh where he belonged, in the days of the Chaldeans.

Necho II was a replica of Ramses II. Both sent ships around Africa, they dug the same canal, and they fought identical battle at the same time in their reigns, with identical results. However, there is a major difference. Ramses posted his achievements all over Egypt, whereas Necho was mute. More than that, in the annals of Egypt he is unknown. It seems he never existed. How could this be? The pharaohs were professional braggarts, yet Necho waged wars, conducted enormous building projects, kept the mighty Babylonian king Nebuchadnezzar at bay - and modestly said nothing. Such reticence is impossible to accept from a pharaoh, certainly a man of Necho's achievements.

The lives of Ramses and Necho are so similar as to be the same. Necho's accomplishments are written in mighty monuments, but historians mistakenly assigned him to a much earlier time and called him Ramses. These monuments are remarkable for their sheer numbers and state of preservation, as if they belong to a much later age. The reference to Baal in the poem of Pentaur is an anachronism. Baal was a Semitic deity; the early Egyptians would have called him Seth.

Shortly after Ramses became king, he had commemorative tablets engraved at the Dog River near Beirut. They were cut in a rock next to a tablet of Essarhadon. The king of Assyria after all had defeated the Ethiopians, and his son Assurbanipal established the Ramesside dynasty. Ramses supposedly lived six hundred years before Essarhadon, yet their tablets are engraved on a rock a foot apart, as if somehow they belong together. That is not all. Pottery belonging to the age of Ramses II is often found in places that belong in the age of Necho II. This misalignment created a 650-year vacuum in world history; a black hole, in which nothing exists. This hole disappears when we realize that Ramses and Necho were one and the same. The imaginary Hittites of 1300 B.C., who are never mentioned by classical historians or scripture, were in reality the Chaldeans of 600 B.C., the Neo-Babylonian Empire. How then, does the dynasty of the Ramessides fit into Egyptian history?

Dynasties

Historical dating reads something less than inspiring (it is outright dull), but it does provide crucial information regarding nations and people, mentioned in the scriptures. All of a sudden a name like "Tirhaka" appears, and we wonder where he came from. History being offset by some six hundred years, it helps to construct a possible scenario what really happened. Although not necessarily accurate in all details, we nonetheless are able to get a fairly good idea where certain people fit. Much later than is believed, of course. It begins with the Theban or Thutmose Dynasty.

The last of the Thutmose Pharaohs was Amenhotep IV, who called himself Akhnaton. He was ousted in a palace coup by his father-in-law Ay. Akhnaton's sons Smenkhare and Tutankhamon died in battle, fighting each other. Ay, and old man, became the ruling king but left no heirs, and that effectively was the end of the Theban Dynasty and the Amarna period. The era that followed is known as the Third Intermediate Period.

Greater Egypt included the Upper and Lower (Ethiopian) Kingdoms and Lybia, west of Egypt. After the 18th (Theban) Dynasty of the Thutmoses came, not the Ramessides (19th), but the Lybian (22nd / 23rd) and Ethiopian (25th) Dynasties. The 24th Dynasty was a single king who ruled concurrent with the 25th. When Manetho made up his king list he first listed the native pharaohs and then the foreign rulers, even though that was not the actual order. The art and literature of the Lybian and Ethiopian Dynasties are very similar to that of the Theban Dynasty; so similar as to sometimes be confused with each other. They were separated by mere decades rather than centuries, as is commonly supposed.

The Lybian Dynasty from the beginning faced a serious threat. Already under Akhnaton and Ay, the Assyrians became a dominating power. This utterly cruel and violent nation sought to wrest control of Syria-Palestine from Egypt. In Israel the northern kingdom (the ten tribes) and Judah, the southern kingdom, were vassals of Egypt. Shalmanezer III began an all-out effort to subject Syria and Israel. He defeated a coalition of Syrian and Israelite troops under Ahab, who were aided by a contingent of Egyptian forces. However, Ay's palace revolt against Akhnaton and his subsequent death weakened Egypt's hold on Palestine.

A coup in Israel ended the house of Ahab, which was sympathetic toward Egypt. Instead the new king Jehu initiated a pro-Assyrian policy. Meanwhile the Assyrian king Shalmanezer instigated unrest among the princes of Palestine, which disrupted Israel and Judah and challenged Egypt. Jehu and his son Jehoash proved no match for the kings of Damascus (Syria). It was under Jehu's grandson Jereboam II that Israel attained its greatest strength. Jereboam's reign largely coincided with that of Uzziah, king of Judah, at a time when Assyria weakened. Both reigned a long time, about fifty years.

Following the death of Jereboam II, 753 B.C., the throne of the northern kingdom changed hands in a number of palace assassinations, until finally Pekah established his rule. By that time Assyria under Tiglath-Pelizer III (Pul) was making a comeback. Pekah refused to pay tribute to Assyria. So did Rezin, king of Syria. In the meantime Ahaz became king of Judah. He pursued a pro-Assyrian policy, which enraged Pekah and Rezin. Both inflicted serious defeats upon Judah. Ahaz begged Tiglath-Pelizer for help, and the Assyrian king was all too happy to help. He captured and destroyed Damascus, and killed Rezin.

The Lybian Dynasty

This left the northern kingdom wide open for an Assyrian assault. Following the death of Rezin, Hoshea deposed and killed Pekah. A few years later he refused to pay the crushing tribute to Assyria, and turned to Pharaoh So for help. Who was So? It is generally agreed that the pharaohs of that time were the Soshenks of the Lybian Dynasty. Soshenk I established his dynasty in the Delta during the reign of Jehu, king of Israel. He was succeeded by Orsokon I and II, and it was Soshenk II who reigned in the days of Hoshea.

Hoshea's appeal to Pharaoh Soshenk fell on deaf ears. The Egyptians never came. Shalmanezer V besieged Samaria, but Soshenk did nothing. After a siege that lasted three years, 723 B.C., Hoshea finally surrendered Samaria to the Assyrians, and that was the end of the ten tribes of Israel. By that time Sargon II was king of Assyria. He deported the remaining population into the depth of Asia and brought in peoples from Babylon and Persia.

In Egypt the weak Lybian pharaohs were challenged by the more powerful Ethiopian rulers. Nubian pharaohs, related to the Thutmose kings, ruled from Thebes simultaneous with the Lybians. However, they did not have widespread support, and a number of would-be pharaohs ruled independently. It was all very confused, and it weakened Egypt.

With the fall of Samaria, all of Palestine fell under Assyrian control. The last Lybian pharaohs became subject of the Assyrian overlords. Nonetheless, some still foolishly resisted. Around 715 B.C., when Hezekiah was king of Judah, Yamani seized control of Ashdod with the intent to instigate rebellion against the Assyrians. But neither Hezekiah nor the Ethiopian pharaohs, who by that time controlled Egypt, were willing to stick out their necks.

Yamani repeated Hoshea's mistake. Sargon destroyed Ashdod, the former Philistine city, and Yamani fled to Egypt, far south into

Ethiopia. However, the king of Ethiopia did not wish to offend Assyria, so he returned the unfortunate Yamani in shackles. The incident is mentioned in Isaiah 20, which foretells the fate of Egypt and Ethiopia. But Sargon could not afford to conquer Egypt. Dramatic events required his attention elsewhere. Abrupt changes in the order of nature caused tribes and nations to migrate to faraway lands. The Phrygians moved from Europe into Asia Minor. The Assyrians prevented them from further encroachment, but then the Cimmerians crossed the Caucasus into the Iranian Plateau. They were pushed farther west and south by the Scythians, who came from the steppes of Russia. Sargon stopped the Cimmerians, but 705 B.C. was killed in battle fighting them.

Sargon's son Sennacherib suppressed several uprisings in the north and then set his sight on Egypt. Four years later, 701 B.C., he attacked the cities of Judah and besieged Jerusalem. Hezekiah agreed to submit, and Sennacherib broke off the attack in exchange for an exorbitant tribute. He deported more than two hundred thousand Judeans. (Or so he said). His flank secure, he set out to attack and defeat Pharaoh Sethos. He proceeded to Pelusium, where he received official submission from the Egyptians.

There are reasons to believe Pharaoh Sethos ascended the throne by dubious means. Evidently there were three brothers, Sethos, Ramses Septah and Harmah, also known as Haremhab, who belonged to a priestly family. Ramses Septah married a princess who was able to trace her genealogy back to the Thutmose Dynasty. Her name was Tworse, and she was a queen in her own right. But Ramses Septah was an Assyrian sympathizer, so his brother Sethos had him killed. Tworse had a son by Ramses Septah, born after the death of his father. She was pharaoh until the birth of her son, whom she called Merneptah Sipteh. He instantly was pronounced pharaoh. Sethos later married the queen, something she did not mind at all. Sethos established his throne in Pelusium and appointed his brother Haremhab priest and governor.

Haremhab began his career under the last of the Lybian pharaohs, probably as a viceroy, and he remained an ally of the Ethiopian Pharaoh Tirhakah until 701 B.C. After Sennacherib defeated the Egyptian army, Haremhab went over to the Assyrians. Sennacherib recognized in Haremhab a trustworthy ally. He appointed his vassal pharaoh, and even gave his own daughter as wife. Haremhab proved to be a man after Sennacherib's own heart. He issued an edict that reflected the cruel treatment of Assyrian prisoners, so unlike the far more humane Egyptian laws.

The Ethiopian Dynasty

About 688 B.C. Tirhakah, now Haremhab's enemy, returned from Ethiopia, conquered Egypt and reinstalled Sethos. Haremhab fled, and the following year Sennacherib set out for his second and fateful campaign against Egypt and Judah. On his way to Egypt, Sennacherib demanded submission from Hezekiah, king of Judah, but Hezekiah was determined to oppose the rapacious Assyrians. Sennacherib decided to take Jerusalem by storm, and readied his army for an assault. The night before the attack, the night of the Passover, the Assyrian army was scorched to death by a conflagration. A hundred eighty-five-thousand men died in a single moment. Sennacherib survived, badly burned, and beat an inglorious retreat to Nineveh. Four years later he was assassinated by two of his sons.

Sennacherib was succeeded by Essarhadon, who spent the first several years of his reign subduing rebel vassals. In his tenth year, 671 B.C., he marched against Egypt, pillaging and burning several Phoenician cities along the way. After several bloody battles he finally defeated Tirhakah, the Ethiopian king, and burned Memphis. Tirhakah fled, leaving his wife and children behind. They were captured and deported to Nineveh. Essarhadon went on to defeat all the Ethiopians in Egypt, and appointed twenty new Egyptian kings and governors, after which he returned to Assyria.

But Assyria was far away, and Ethiopia very near, so a few years later Tirhakah returned to seize northern Egypt. The Egyptian rulers who had been appointed by their Assyrian overlord did not resist, but asked Essarhadon for help. When Essarhadon heard of Tirhakah's conquest, he assembled a mercenary army and hastened to Egypt, but suddenly died on the way. This gave Tirhakah several years to establish his rule. Eventually Assurbanipal, son of Essarhadon, gathered another army, mostly made up of foreign troops. He began a campaign against Egypt, but did not go himself; he merely told his generals to take care of Tirhakah. The Ethiopians were no match for the Assyrian might. The wounded Tirhakah retreated into the Sudan, where he died. His wife Duk-hat-Amun had no son and no suitor, so his nephew Tandamane became king instead.

Meanwhile the twenty kings and governors, appointed by Essarhadon became restive. After the defeat of Tirhakah they were again under Assyrian rule, and they devised means to become independent. They sent messengers to Tirhakah to plot against Assyria, but Assurbanipal became aware of their scheme. They paid the price, except for one. They were deported to Nineveh where nineteen were killed. But Assurbanipal spared Necho, the king of Sais. He needed a trusted ally in Egypt.

The Ramses Dynasty

Necho reigned a year and a few months. Then Tandamane, nephew of Tirhakah, attempted to recapture Egypt, and killed Necho. Heredotus narrates that Necho's son Psammetichos fled to Syria. The Assyrians soon crushed the uprising and placed Psammetichos on his father's throne in Sais. Necho (or Neco) and Psammetichos are Greek names. Father and son called themselves by their Egyptian nomen, Ramses and Seti. It was Seti (the great) who really began the Ramses dynasty. When Assurbanipal "liberated" Egypt, he appointed twelve vice-kings, of whom Seti was the most important. Soon Seti with the help of Ionian (Greek) and Carian mercenaries, deposed all the other vice-kings, and became sole ruler.

Seti/Psammetichos admired Greek civilization. He opened the door to the Greeks and gave his son Necho II/Ramses II a Greek education. Greek pottery and even bones of Greek mercenaries are found among those of the Ramses dynasty. Meanwhile Seti's overlord As-

The Ramessides

surbanipal suddenly found himself surrounded by enemies, which allowed Seti to establish his throne, free from outside interference.

The Assyrians were engaged in a fierce war with Elam (later Persia), and Mesopotamia being more important than Egypt, Assurbanipal used all his resources to defeat Elam. He put a sympathizer on the throne. Then he faced another problem, his own brother. Shortly before his death, Essarhadon decreed that Assurbanipal would be king of Assyria and his younger brother Shamash-shum-ukin king of Babylon. This granted Babylonia a degree of sovereignty. However, after sixteen years Shamash-shum-ukin declared Babylon independent, and schemed a revolt. It took Assurbanipal three years of protracted war to defeat Babylon. His rebellious brother committed suicide. But the king of Elam was in cahoots with Babylon, so another war followed. Elam was destroyed.

Yes, Assyria was at the peak of its power, but the army was exhausted, Babylon lost, Elam ruined and subjected nations filled with an undying hatred. Shortly thereafter Nebopolassar the Chaldean and the Medes began a protracted war against Assyria. Assurbanipal suddenly needed an ally, and he found one in Seti the Egyptian pharaoh. After all, he had pardoned Seti's father Necho. And so Seti/Psammetichos, no more under the heel of Assyria, exercised control over Syria-Palestine, all the way to the Euphrates.

Manetho identified the capitols of the 19th and 26th Dynasties as Tanis and Sais, so they are called the Tanitic and Saitic Dynasties. Sais is supposed to have been to the west, on the Rosetta branch of the Nile. But no ruins have ever been found. However, both Strabo and Heredotus said Tanis was on the Sais branch of the Nile. It follows that the Tanitic (19th) and Saitic (26th) Dynasties were the same. Ramses/Necho lived in the days of the Hebrew kings.

At that time Manasseh, son of Hezekiah was king of Judah. He reigned fifty three years and never got involved in foreign entanglements. For all his moral corruption, he kept Judah out of war, and never challenged Seti on his way through the coastal flat lands. Palestine was in turmoil. Babylon, now occupied by the Chaldeans, instigated local revolts against Assyria and its ally, Egypt. Northern Palestine, the former ten tribes of Israel and Syria were in a state of anarchy. Seti moved into Galilee. He captured Pekanon, or the city of Pekah in the Jezreel valley. Pekah, we recall, was one of the last kings of Israel. Seti also took Beth-Shan, an important city near the Jordan River.

Meanwhile another threat loomed beyond the horizon. The Scythians, Asian hordes from the steppes of Russia, descendants of Ashkenaz, grandson of Japheth, crossed the Caucasus and moved into present-day Armenia. They came to the aid of the Assyrians, battled the Medes and Chaldeans, who were just then attacking Nineveh, and moved into Palestine. (They are referred to in Jeremiah chapters 4-6). At Beth Sham they met the Egyptians. Rather than fight a losing battle, Seti convinced the Scythians that he was on their side; both were allies of Assyria. That satisfied the Scythians, so they desisted from further encroachment. Egypt was spared and so was Judah.

The Scythians remained at Beth-Shan, which was called Scythopia by several ancient writers. Seti went on to capture a number of cities in Syria, and built Riblah on the river Orontes. There he came in contact with the growing might of the Chaldeans, who by that time had made Babylon their Capitol. Their king Nebopolassar was allied with the Medes and the king of Damascus; eventually he persuaded the Scythians to join. The three armies 612 B.C. moved against Nineveh, which fell in a matter of months, as foretold by Nahum. Thus began the Chaldean or Neo (New)-Babylonian Empire.

Following the death of Seti, his son Ramses II became king. At Riblah he had commemorative tablets engraved at the Dog River near Beirut. They were cut in a rock next to a tablet by Essarhadon. The king of Assyria after all had defeated the Ethiopians, and his son Assurbanipal established the Ramesside Dynasty. Ramses supposedly lived six hundred years before Essarhadon, yet their tablets are less than a foot apart. Nor is this unique. Art, such as the famous lion's gate in Anatolia is definitely "Hittite," yet was found immediately above the Assyrian stratum - six hundred years apart. They were not. The "Hittites" were the Neo-Babylonians or Chaldeans who conquered Assyria. Following the fall of Nineveh, Ramses hastened to come to the aid of his fallen ally, but suffered a humiliating defeat instead.

This then is the Ramses Dynasty. It existed at the time of Nebuchadnezzar, not the Judges, during the captivity, and not the exodus. All this happened around the year -600, rather than -1290. Between the end of the Amarna period and the Ramses dynasty centuries passed, rather than decades. The Ramesses were separated from the Thutmose or Theban era by some two hundred years. Egypt had since been suppressed, and exposed to foreign influence, and it showed. Gardiner noted,

> After the recovery from the religious revolution Egypt was a changed world. It is not easy to define the exact nature of the changes, since there are many exceptions; yet it is impossible not to notice the marked deterioration of the art, the literature, and indeed the general culture of the people. The language which they wrote approximates more closely to the vernacular and incorporates many foreign words; the copies of ancient texts are incredibly careless, as if the scribes utterly failed to understand their meaning.[4]

That does make sense, if indeed the world of Ramses II was that of Nebuchadnezzar rather than Moses. But Necho II is not the only one to be mentioned in the scriptures; one of his sons is mentioned as well.

Merneptah

Sometime after the death of Necho, his son Hophra became king. Africanus claims that Psammetichos II reigned six years after Necho, then Pharaoh Hophra, mentioned in the scriptures, became king. The name of the pharaoh who succeeded Ramses II was Merneptah Horphima'e, also spelled Hophrama'e. The Hebrew rendition is Hophra and the Greek Apries. By the time this pharaoh came to power, Israel and Judah had been carried into captivity. Palestine was desolate, its cities ruined. Merneptah is the only pharaoh, believed to have mentioned Israel at all. Following a military victory he had this written on a stele.

> Great joy has come about in Egypt, rejoicing is gone forth in the villages of To-meri. They talk of the victories which Merneptah-Horphima'e has gained in Tjehnu land. How loveable is the victorious ruler, how exalted is the king among the gods, how fortunate is the commanding Lord. Pleasant indeed is it when one sits and chats. One can walk freely upon the road without any fear in the hearts of men. — — The princes are prostrate and cry "Mercy!" Not one lifts his head among the Nine Bows. Tjehnu land is destroyed, Khatti at peace. Canaan plundered with every ill, Ashkelon is taken and Gezer seized. Yeno'am made as though it never had been. Israel is desolate and has no seed. Khor is become a widow for To-meri.[5]

The reference to Israel produced an avalanche of books. It seems so completely out of harmony with what the book of Exodus has to say about the status of Israel at that time. Besides, Israel could have hardly been known as a nation yet. According to the revised version of history presented here, it fits exactly. As we have seen, for breaking their oath and taking their slaves back, God swore that the men of Judah would suffer the consequences. "I will lay waste the towns of Judah so no one can live there." (Jeremiah 34:22). That is exactly what happened. Jeremiah paints a stark picture.

> This is what the Lord Almighty, the God of Israel says: you saw the great disaster I brought on Jerusalem and on all the towns of Judah. Today they lie deserted and in ruins because of the evil they have done. They provoked me to anger by burning incense and by worshiping other gods that neither they nor you nor your fathers ever knew. Again and again I sent my servants the prophets who said "Do not do this detestable thing that I hate." But they did not listen or pay attention, they did not turn from

their wickedness or stop burning incense to other gods. Therefore, my fierce anger was poured out, it raged against the towns of Judah and the streets of Jerusalem and made them the desolate ruins they are today.

Jeremiah 44:2-6

Scripture and Merneptah agree on the status of Israel, the land was desolate. But that also means that Merneptah lived in the days of Jeremiah, and not of Moses. Jeremiah has very interesting things to say. What were the idols the Jews burned incense to? The answer is surprising.

Then all the men who knew that their wives were burning incense to other gods, along with all the women who were present - a large assembly - and all the people living in Lower and Upper Egypt, said to Jeremiah, "We will not listen to the messages you have spoken to us in the name of the Lord. We will certainly do everything we said we would. We will burn incense to the Queen of Heaven and will pour out drink offerings to her as we and our fathers, our kings and our officials did in the towns of Judah and in the streets of Jerusalem. At that time we had plenty of food and were well of and suffered no harm."

Jeremiah 44:15-17

The Queen of Heaven was Ishtar, the goddess of fertility, and the astral form of Ishtar was the planet Venus. Make no mistake about it, Venus was the Queen of Heaven. Its reputation made it supreme among the planets. That is not the end of the story. Just to prove how wrong the Jews were, the Lord gave them this sign.

This will be the sign to you that I will punish you in this place, declares the Lord, so that you will know that my threats of harm against you will surely stand. This is what the Lord says: "I am going to hand Pharaoh Hophra king of Egypt over to his enemies who seek his life, just as I handed Zedekiah king of Judah over to

Nebuchadnezzar king of Babylon, the enemy who was seeking his life."

Jeremiah 44:29, 30

That is exactly what happened to Merneptah Hophrama'e. The inscription on the stele was written at the beginning of a prolonged war with Lybia. Raiding a deserted Palestine was easy, but Lybia was a different matter. The translators of the stele had a big surprise coming. The Lybians received help from Hellenic (Greek) peoples. An invasion of Europeans was certainly unexpected 1200 B.C., but it did happen 600 years later. Greek settlers occupied large tracts of land in eastern Lybia, which got them in trouble with the Egyptians.

Repeated hostilities followed, and the Lybians succeeded in capturing parts of Egypt. Not realizing the strength of the enemy, Merneptah Hophra sent an army against the Lybians and Greeks, which was utterly destroyed. The Egyptian army on the Lybian frontier revolted. Hophra sent a general by the name of Ahmose (Amasis) to take care of the rebels, but he became their king instead.

Amasis fought and defeated the army of Hophra and kept him prisoner in the palace. But the people hated Hophra for atrocities he had committed. He was delivered into the hands of a mob and murdered. The mummy of Merneptah has a hole in the skull. He met a violent death. Ezekiel added a strange detail. He prophesied that both of Pharaoh Hophra's arms would be broken (Ez 30:20-26). As it turns out, both arms of Merneptah were indeed broken. Archaeologists are not sure whether it happened in his life time or maybe grave robbers did it, but broken they are!

Sentence Postponed

There is a controversial issue that must be addressed. It deals with predictions by the prophet Jeremiah that Nebuchadnezzar would invade and devastate Egypt. The problem is that Nebuchadnezzar never did that. This presents an interesting problem. Both Jeremiah and Ezekiel said that Nebuchadnezzar would conquer

Egypt, loot the people, destroy the temples and annihilate the Jews who had fled to Egypt.

> In Tahpanhes the word of the Lord came to Jeremiah: "While the Jews are watching, take some large stones with you and bury them in clay in the brick pavement at the entrance of Pharaoh's palace in Tahpanhes. Then say to them, 'This is what the LORD Almighty, the God of Israel says: I will send for my servant Nebuchadnezzar king of Babylon, and I will set his throne over these stones I have buried here; he will spread his royal canopy above them. He will come and attack Egypt, bringing death to those destined for death, captivity to those destined for captivity, and the sword to those destined for the sword. He will set fire to the temples of the gods of Egypt; he will burn their temples and take their gods captive. As a shepherd wraps his garment around him, so will he wrap Egypt around himself and depart from them unscathed. There in the temple of the sun in Egypt he will demolish the sacred pillars and will burn down the temples of the gods of Egypt."
>
> Jeremiah 43:8-13

Frankly, there is no historical evidence of such a campaign. The only invasion was a friendly one. Nebuchadnezzar visited Egypt when he gave his daughter in marriage to Ramses/Necho as a pledge of the agreement, reached between Egypt and Babylonia. It was on this occasion that Nebuchadnezzar set his throne in Tahpanhes as foretold in Jeremiah 46:8-10. Ramses visited Babylon annually, and since Merneptah-Hophra never fought the Chaldeans, any Babylonian raid must have happened after his death. But Hophra was succeeded by Amasis whose reign was peaceful, and he ruled thirteen years beyond the death of Nebuchadnezzar. Also, Heredotus does not mention a Babylonian campaign during his reign.

Since we deal with prophecy, it should be interesting to see just how exactly these predictions were fulfilled, and how they relate to Egypt and the Chaldeans. Maybe we will find the answer to our question, were the predictions by the prophets fulfilled or did they have it all wrong? Nebuchadnezzar's activities are documented by the prophets Jeremiah, Ezekiel and Daniel. Between the scriptures and what is known from history we should be able to find out.

Necho came to power 610 B.C. In the fifth year of his reign, 605 B.C., he fought and lost the battle of Carchemish. This was the first year of Nebuchadnezzar, who at that time was king of Babylon; later he became king of the Chaldean Empire. That year Jehoiakim, king of Judah, became a vassal of the king of Babylon. Three years later, when Ramses attacked Ashkelon, Judah revolted. Three years after that, 599 B.C., Nebuchadnezzar subdued Jerusalem a second time; Jehoiakim was executed. The Chaldean king returned three months later and took the youthful king Jehoiachin captive; he installed Zedekiah king instead.

In his eighth year, 591 B.C., Zedekiah revolted against Nebuchadnezzar, and the Chaldeans returned to besiege Jerusalem. Then the Egyptian army invaded Palestine, and the Chaldeans retreated from Jerusalem. The Egyptians and Chaldeans agreed to a peace treaty however, which was sealed 588 B.C. That happened in the tenth month of the twenty first year of Ramses II, which was the seventeenth year of Nebuchadnezzar. The Chaldeans returned to Jerusalem to resume their siege 589 B.C. This siege lasted eighteen months, until at last Judah surrendered 587 B.C.

Tyre

Now that Nebuchadnezzar need not worry about possible insurrections in Palestine, and Egypt was a friendly nation, he focused his attention upon the coastal cities of northern Palestine. He was determined to gain control of Tyre and so, two years after the fall of Jerusalem, 585 B.C., the thirteen-year siege of Tyre began. Three years earlier Ezekiel pronounced the word of the Lord.

> I am against you, O Tyre, and I will bring many nations against you, like the sea casting up its waves. They will destroy the walls

The Ramessides

of Tyre and pull down her towers; I will scrape away her rubble and make her a bare rock. Out of the sea she will become a place to spread fish nets, for I have spoken, declares the sovereign Lord. She will become plunder for the nations, and her settlements on the mainland will be ravaged by the sword. Then they will know that I am the Lord. For this is what the Sovereign Lord says: From the north I am going to bring against Tyre Nebuchadnezzar king of Babylon, king of kings, with horses and chariots, with horsemen and a great army. He will ravage your settlements on the mainland with the sword; he will set up siege works against you, build a ramp up to your walls and raise his shields against you. He will direct the blows of his battering rams against your walls and demolish your towers with his weapons, — — They will plunder your wealth and loot your merchandise; they will break down your walls and demolish your fine houses and throw your stones, timber and rubble into the sea. — — I will make you a bare rock, and you will become a place to spread fish nets. You will never be rebuilt, for I the Lord have spoken, declares the Sovereign Lord.

Ezekiel 26:3-14

Nebuchadnezzar besieged Tyre from 585-573 B.C. When at last the Chaldeans broke through the walls they found Tyre deserted. The city on the mainland was destroyed, but the people had moved to an island about half a mile offshore, where they built a fortified city, the new Tyre.

But Ezekiel said that many nations would pound Tyre like successive waves. Nebuchadnezzar did not bother with the island city, but the Greek king Alexander III had reasons to pick up where Nebuchadnezzar left off. After defeating the Persian Darius III in the battle of Issus, 333 B.C., he marched on toward Egypt. To deny the Persians sea ports, he called on the Phoenicians to surrender, but Tyre refused. To reach the island, the Greeks leveled the old Tyre on the main land and with the debris built a two hundred-foot wide land bridge, made up from trees, stones and dirt. The Tyrians countered with fierce counter attacks but Alexander assembled a navy, and the land bridge eventually connected the island with the main land. After a siege of seven months Tyre finally fell. Eight thousand Tyrians were killed and thirty thousand were sold into slavery.

Even though ruined, Tyre was rebuilt and began to recover rapidly. Eighteen years later Antigunus attacked Tyre. After a fifteen-month siege, the city was again destroyed. Though badly crippled, Tyre nonetheless survived and centuries later was captured by the Muslims. The crusaders took it away, and it became an important base. The Muslims succeeded in retaking the city, slaughtered the population and sold it into slavery, after which they leveled the place. It became a bare rock, where to this day fishermen spread their purple nets to dry. It was never rebuilt, even though there is a spring that produces ten thousand gallons of fresh water per day.

Memphis and Thebes

The prophecies of Ezekiel are of great interest because they provide accurate forecast about the nations, including Egypt. Following the campaign against Tyre, the word of the LORD came to Ezekiel.

> Son of man, Nebuchadnezzar king of Babylon drove his army in a hard campaign against Tyre; every head was rubbed bare and every shoulder made raw. Yet he and his army got no reward from the campaign he led against Tyre. Therefore this is what the sovereign Lord says: I am going to give Egypt to Nebuchadnezzar king of Babylon, and he will carry off its wealth. He will loot and plunder the land as pay for his army. I have given him Egypt as a reward for his efforts because he and his army did it for me; declares the sovereign Lord.
>
> Ezekiel 29:18-20

He added considerable details.

This is what the Sovereign Lord says:

> I will put an end to the hordes of Egypt
> by the hand of Nebuchadnezzar king of Babylon.
> He and his army - the most ruthless of nations -
> will be brought in to destroy the land.
> They will draw their swords against Egypt
> and fill the land with the slain.
> I will dry up the streams of the Nile
> and sell the land to evil men,
> by the hand of foreigners.
> I will lay waste the land and everything in it.
> I the Lord have spoken.
> This is what the Sovereign Lord says:
> I will destroy the idols
> and put an end to the images in Memphis.
> No longer will there be a prince in Egypt
> and I will spread fear throughout the land.
> I will lay Pathros waste, set fire to Zoan
> and inflict punishment on Thebes.
> I will pour out my wrath on Pelusium
> the stronghold of Egypt,
> and cut off the hordes of Thebes.
> I will set fire to Egypt,
> Pelusium will be taken by storm,
> Memphis will be in constant distress.
>
> Ezekiel 30:10-16

History records that this prophecy was fulfilled exactly as foretold; only the instrument of God's wrath was not Nebuchadnezzar the Chaldean, but Cambyses the Persian, son of Cyrus the Great. Cyrus captured Babylon 539 B.C., but it was his son Cambyses who conquered Egypt 525 B.C.

Cambyses was a madman. He took Pelusium and proceeded to Memphis where he opened sepulchers, robbed graves, killed women and children, slew Apis, the sacred ox and had every idol burned. He burned all the temples of Egypt and had the idols carried away; in

Thebes he tried to destroy the huge statues. Heredotus relates how Cambyses lined up Pharaoh Psammetich with his nobles to torment them.

> He had the king's daughter dressed as a slave, and sent her out of the city with a pitcher to fetch water, along with other young women, also dressed as slaves, whom Cambyses had selected as being the daughters of the leading men of Egypt. As the young women passed their fathers, they cried out and burst into tears, and all the men who were there responded with cries and tears of their own at the sight of their daughter's humiliation. However, when Psammetichus saw the girls coming and understood what was happening, he bowed his head down to the ground.
>
> Next, after the pitcher carriers had passed them by, Cambyses sent out the king's son, along with two thousand other Egyptians of the same age group, all of whom had ropes toed around their necks and bits in their mouths. — —- When Psammetichus saw the young men passing by and realized that his son was being taken to his death, he did not weep and wail like the rest of the Egyptians who were sitting there with him, but he did the same as he had done in the case of his daughter.[6]

But then he saw an elderly friend who had been robbed of everything and was begging from the army. At the sight of this the king began to cry. His own misfortunes were too great for tears, he said, but the sight of an old nobleman reduced to beggar made him weep. Cambyses was sufficiently impressed to order the king's son execution stopped, but the order came too late.

Memphis, a city filled with idols, was destroyed. It was rebuilt and again attained glory, but with the founding of Cairo it began to decline about the Seventh Century A.D. It has since completely disappeared. Thebes recovered to some extent, but A.D. 92, after a three-year siege, it was leveled. It was broken up into small villages, its population was scattered, its hordes cut off. Memphis is gone, and so are its idols, as decreed by the God who hates idols, and the vile perversions that come with it. (It was a form of demon worship). By contrast, the idols of Thebes still stand in the ruins of the temple walls.

Warnings

Considering the accuracy of these predictions, it is all the more remarkable that both Jeremiah and Ezekiel said Nebuchadnezzar would be the agent of the decreed destruction when they knew about the treaty between Nebuchadnezzar and Necho. Were they wrong? It is evident from the prophets that dire predictions were often conditional. They served as warnings. These prophecies were given to afford the people a chance to repent.

> "Even now," declares the LORD,
> "return to me with all your heart,
> with fasting and weeping and mourning."
> Rend your heart and not your garments.
> Return to the LORD your God,
> for he is gracious and compassionate,
> slow to anger and abounding in love,
> and he relents from sending calamity.
> Who knows but that he may turn and have pity
> and leave behind a blessing-
> grain offerings and drink offerings
> for the LORD your God.
>
> Joel 2:13, 14

In other words, sentence was conditional upon repentance. There are several such statements in Joel, Amos and for that matter throughout the scriptures. We recall the story of Jonah, the reluctant prophet. Rather than obey the Lord he ran away, but the Lord hauled him back to his duty. A great fish swallowed him and after three days vomited him out on the beach. So he went up to Nineveh and cried aloud that forty days hence God would destroy the city, after which he stationed himself on a hill to enjoy the spectacle.

But the prediction did not come true; Nineveh was spared. The reason is given. The people believed Jonah - maybe the miraculous episode with the fish had something to do with it - and they repented. When the king heard about it, (was it the stricken Sennacherib?) he ordered the whole city to dress in sack cloth and ashes, a sign of mourning and repentance. Jonah waited in vain. God was merciful, even with Assyria. He saw that the people of Nineveh repented and did not destroy the city like he said he would. That was the intent of Jeremiah's threat. The people he dealt with were the leftovers of Judah who had not been carried off to Babylon. They were scared to death of the Chaldeans. Jeremiah warned them,

> Therefore this is what the LORD Almighty, the God of Israel says: I am determined to bring disaster on you and to destroy all Judah. I will take away the remnant of Judah who were determined to go to Egypt to settle there. They will all perish in Egypt; they will fall by the sword or from famine. From the least to the greatest they will die by sword or famine. They will become an object of cursing, of condemnation and reproach. I will punish those who live in Egypt with the sword, famine and plague, as I punished Jerusalem. None of the remnant of Judah who have gone to live in Egypt will escape or survive to return to the land of Judah, to which they long to return and live; none will return except a few fugitives.
>
> Jeremiah 44:11-14

Many of the Jews were extradited to Nebuchadnezzar under the terms of the treaty with Ramses/Necho. A great many others had a change of heart. They saw Jeremiah's dire prophecy about Pharaoh Hophra fulfilled and repented. They were not able to return to Judah, so they fled to Elephantine, where they erected a temple to worship Yahweh. It was mixed with the Venus cult, but there was genuine repentance, enough to save them from the sword. They never saw

Judah again, but they escaped with their lives. To give them respite, the LORD ordained that it would be Cambyses, not Nebuchadnezzar, who would carry out the decreed sentence. Their temple was destroyed by furious Egyptians who believed the Jews had collaborated with Cambyses, but then, it should have never been built in the first place. So the prophecy was indeed fulfilled and it served the purpose. The Jews were dealt with mercifully, the Egyptians justly.

Nineveh

Nineveh, the Capitol city of Assyria, had been spared before, but eventually God decreed judgment, and this time there was no turning back. Nahum, who wrote his prophecy shortly after the sack of Thebes, foretold the fall of Nineveh in detail. In vivid, rousing poetry he wrote powerful literature. He said this.

> The LORD is good,
> a refuge in times of trouble.
> He cares for those who trust in him,
> but with an overwhelming flood
> he will make an end of Nineveh;
> he will pursue his foes into darkness.
> Whatever they plot against the Lord
> he will bring to an end;
> trouble will not come a second time.
> They will be entangled among thorns
> and drunk from their wine;
> they will be consumed like dry stubble. 1:7-10

> The LORD has given a command concerning you, Nineveh:
> "You will have no descendants to bear your name.
> I will destroy the carved images and cast idols
> that are in the temple of your gods.
> I will prepare your grave, for you are vile." 1:14

He summons his picked troops,
Yet they stumble on their way.
They dash to the city wall;
The protective shield is put in place.
The river gates are thrown open and the palace collapses
It is decreed that the cities are exiled and carried away.
The slave girls moan like doves and beat upon their breasts.
Nineveh is like a pool, and its water is draining away.
"Stop! Stop!" they cry,
But no one turns back.
Plunder the silver, plunder the gold!
The supply is endless,
The wealth from all its treasures! 2:5-10

You too will become drunk;
you will go into hiding
and seek refuge from the enemy.
All your fortresses are like fig trees
with their first ripe fruit; when they are shaken,
the figs fall into the mouth of the eater.
Look at your troops-they are all women!
The gates of your land are wide open to your enemies;
fire has consumed their bars.
Draw water for the siege, strengthen your defenses!
Work the clay, tread the mortar, repair the brickwork.
There the fire will devour you;
the sword will cut you down
and, like grasshoppers consume you. 3:11-15

Nothing can heal your wound; your injury is fatal.
Everyone who hears the news about you
claps his hands at your fall,
for who has not felt your endless cruelty? 3:19

Nineveh was annihilated because it was vile. Not only was Assyria guilty of unspeakable atrocities, it enslaved and deported peoples and it was a haunt of demonic sorceries and witchcraft.

> Woe to the city of blood,
> full of lies, full of plunder, never without victims!
> The crack of whips, the clatter of wheels,
> Galloping horses and jolting chariots!
> Charging cavalry, flashing swords and glittering spear!
> Many casualties, piles of dead, bodies without number,
> people stumbling over the corpses-
> all because of the wanton lust of a harlot,
> alluring, the mistress of sorceries,
> who enslaved nations by her prostitution
> and peoples by her witchcraft. 3:1-4

What is so amazing about the fall of Nineveh is its sudden and utter collapse. A city under siege would resist for years, even decades; Nineveh fell in three months. That was incredible. The city had formidable defenses. The inner wall of Nineveh was 100 feet high and 50 feet thick. Its towers rose 200 feet high; there were several forts, and the city was surrounded by a 150-foot moat. In addition there were two more ditches and walls. The circumference of the city was seven miles.

Yet Nahum said Nineveh would fall with ease, like figs falling from a tree, which is exactly what happened. A coalition of Chaldeans, Medes and Scythians attacked Nineveh 612 B.C. The king of Assyria unwisely hosted a huge party outside the city walls. He and his soldiers feasted on meat and wine. They had a great time, became stone drunk - and unexpectedly were attacked in a night raid. They suffered severe losses and withdrew within the city walls, only to see another calamity overcome them. After three years of heavy rains the Tigris and other rivers swelled and broke through dykes and sluices (hereby helped by the enemy), and inundated part of the city. The palace was flooded, and the city walls partially collapsed. The king, believing an ancient prophecy came true, ordered the palace burned down. It incinerated in a fiery inferno. The attackers entered the city, killed and exiled the inhabitants and leveled the place. Her injury was fatal.

Nineveh, the crown jewel of the Assyrian Empire, was so thoroughly destroyed that it disappeared from the face of the earth. The very memory of Nineveh and Assyria was lost. Biblical references to the empire were considered mythical, until finally it was unearthed in the 19th Century. These empires were neither the first nor the last to flourish and disappear. Many nations have come and gone since. It inspired Rudyard Kipling to warn the British Empire in his "Recessional."

> Far called, our navies melt away;
> On dune and headland sinks the fire:
> Lo, all our pomp of yesterday
> Is one with Nineveh and Tyre!
> Judge of the nations, spare us yet,
> Lest we forget - lest we forget!

The Assyrian Empire was supplanted by the Neo-Babylonian or Chaldean empire, which in turn lasted less than a century. Babylon fell 539 B.C. Then came the Medo-Persians and the Greeks, and it is with these times that we concern ourselves.

Ramses III

When Egyptologists read the record of Merneptah, they found to their surprise that Europeans had invaded Egypt about 1200 B.C. That fits with the monuments of Ramses III, no relative, who stopped migrating European tribes at the border of Egypt. Roving hordes, called Pereset, probably the Philistines of the Bible, combined with the Sea People in a united assault against Egypt. But Ramses was equal to the task and defeated them in a naval battle.

This feat of arms supposedly happened shortly before Saul became king of Israel, when Samuel was judge. If the prophet ran into migrating hordes, he was strangely silent about it. No such earth shaking event is mentioned in the book of Judges. No tradition of these dramatic events survives. How come? There is, of course, an explanation. The word Pereset appears in the Canopus decree. This decree established the length of the year according to the appearance of two stars. It was written in both Egyptian and Greek, and the word p-r-s-t or Pereset is translated, not as "Philistines," but as "Persians. The 20th Dynasty of Ramses III was actually the 29th / 30th Dynasty which fought and defeated the Persians.

A closer look at Ramses III's murals confirms this. This was not a rag tag outfit. These were trained soldiers, well equipped, in first class uniforms; those of the Persian Empire. They were Persian soldiers; their fluted helmets testify to this, and judging from the murals they fought at first along with the Egyptians. In a later scene the Sea People, actually Greek mercenaries (they look European and distinctly Greek), fought with the Egyptians against the Persians. Finally Persians and Greek sailors battled the Egyptians at the mouth of a branch of the Nile, the Egyptians being victorious in all cases. All this makes sense if we keep in mind that Merneptah was in reality Pharaoh Hophra who fought Greek settlers.

Ramses III obviously was enmeshed in a number of contrary alliances that involved Persians and Greek mercenaries. The monuments he built reflect the art of these civilizations. The ruins of a palace in northern Egypt contain tiles that once were parts of murals. They were colored and glazed, some of them with the seal of Ramses III. The art of these tiles is distinctly Persian. They also have Greek letters in the back, engraved before they were baked. The local cemetery leaves no doubt about the civilization that lived there at that time. The tombs have Greek names; coffins, dating from Greek and Roman times were found with pottery scarabs that had the name of Ramses III inscribed.

The appearance of the Persians and Greeks allows for accurate dating. Persian and Greek soldiers were always bearded, but Darius the Persian about 500 B.C. introduced a change. High-ranking officers could keep their beard, but soldiers had to shave. That way an enemy could not easily grab a beard and dispatch the unfortunate warrior. The Pereset were shaven, except for the officers. The same thing is true of the Greek marines. They are shaven, which was not done until the late Fifth Century. Their weapons are those of Athenian soldiers dating from that time.

Besides palaces, Ramses built temples. They are the only ones to survive intact. That is certainly very strange. When Cambyses the Persian captured Egypt 525 B.C., he destroyed every single temple in Egypt, with the exception of a Jewish temple in Elephantine. Yet here are the temples of Ramses III in all their glory. It follows that they were built after Cambyses ruined Egypt. In a throne relief Darius is depicted sitting on a throne, born by figures symbolizing subject peoples. It was obviously modeled after a similar relief by Ramses III who supposedly lived 600 years earlier.[7] This strains credulity. Rulers are influenced by contemporaries, not ancient kings. Then who was the Pharaoh who is known to us as Ramses III?

Nectanebo

To this day, kings habitually carry a half dozen names. Ramses III had many names as well, and his Horus (throne) name was Nekht-a-neb. The Greek historian Heredotus mentions a pharaoh known as Nectanebo or Nekhtnebef (30th Dynasty), who did everything Ramses III (20th Dynasty) did, with identical results.

Nectanebo came to power 378 B.C., after several Egyptian rulers had made attempts to shake off their Persian overlords. He himself was a general who had been successful against Lybia. In the beginning of his reign he was an ally of the Persians, who probably helped him gain the throne as a puppet ruler. It was in the interest of the Persians to protect the Egyptian border against the expanding power of Carthage. The Lybians were considered a serious threat. A combination of Egyptian and Persian forces helped by Greek marines defeated the Lybians.

The Ramessides

Once he achieved a measure of independence, Nectanebo attempted to get rid of his Persian masters. He was hereby helped by Greek mercenaries who were sympathetic to his cause. The Greek islands were involved in prolonged and confused wars between the city-states of Sparta and Athens. Two years after he mounted the throne, Nectanebo acquired Greek mercenary sailors under Chabrias, an Athenian. The combined Egyptian and Greek forces succeeded in throwing the Persians out.

But Chabrias had acted without the consent of the Athenians who, fearful of bad relations with the Persians, ordered him back. The Persians, unhappy about their reverses in Egypt, demanded that the Athenians provide a navy and marines to help them fight Egypt. The Persians mustered an army of twenty thousand men under Pharnabus and spent several years in preparation for an invasion of Egypt. Iphicrates, a capable commander, came with twenty thousand Greek mercenaries; the armies assembled in Acco, Syria. Ramses noted that "the northerners in their islands were disturbed," and that they had set up camp in Syria.

While Pharnabazus was getting ready all those years, so did Nectanebo. He knew all about enemy intentions and prepared for the naval battle that was sure to come. He had the seven mouths of the Nile fortified and made impassable, particularly the Pelusian entrance. When at last the fleet came, they found the Pelusian mouth impregnable and sailed on to the Mendesian mouth. They managed to land three thousand men and captured the ford in a fierce battle. It became a trap, thanks in part to a disagreement between the cautious Persian Satrap and the Greek commander. Iphicrates requested they sail on to Memphis, before the Egyptian army would be able to defend it. But Pharnabazus was altogether too cautious to go for something that risky. He decided to wait for the Persian army, but the Nile overflowed and to avoid drowning the army left hurriedly. It was an inglorious defeat.

The chronicles of Ramses read, "They were coming, while the flame was prepared before them, forward toward Egypt." Fire ships had been employed in the siege of Tyre and on numerous other occasions. It was believed that this expression, supposed to have been made 1190 B.C., was allegorical. The war of Nectanebo/Ramses III happened 374 B.C., at a time when the use of fire ships was every bit real and not at all allegorical.

There are telltale signs. The ships in Ramses III's murals were open galleys of Greek design, developed around 600 B.C. They have oars, no deck, and a single mast with a longitudinal boom fixed at the top. This design feature allowed the sailors to conveniently raise and lower the sails like Venetian blinds.[8]

The naval battle of Ramses III. The victorious Egyptians carry off their prisoners, who wear Persian uniforms. The galleys are of Greek design.

Conventional history is mistaken. The Pereset were Persians and not Philistines. The Sea People were Greek mercenaries, not European hordes that swept through the Middle East. We are dealing with the inheritance of the Nineteenth Century when well meaning historians for want of known facts had to use their imagination. And that is what we are stuck with, imaginary history.

This much is certain, Ramses III came to power after Egypt had suffered years of foreign oppression. According to Gardiner, the years following the death of Merneptah, son of Ramses II, are

The Ramessides

shrouded in uncertainty. Judging from Egyptian records, evil overcame Egypt. "It is clear that Thebes was going through very troubled times. There are references elsewhere to a 'war' that had occurred during those years."[9] That was the year 525 B.C., when Cambyses raided Egypt and began nearly two centuries of Persian rule.

It comes as no surprise that Ramses III / Nectanebo in summarizing his achievements spoke of foreign oppression, and how he restored peace to Egypt. This is very difficult to fit into the accepted scheme of history; yet Ramses makes it clear that Egypt had been overthrown "from without," and that he liberated his country from anarchy. Egypt had been particularly hurt by a ruler named Arsa, who in exacting tribute plundered the people.

This agrees with what is known of the Persian domination of Egypt, it was brutal. Artaxerxes, after suppressing a revolt in Egypt, appointed a relative named Arsames as Satrap of Egypt. Arsames acquired vast tracts of land and ruthlessly looted his Egyptian serfs. Nectanebo put an end to this, but he was the last to assert an independent reign. The rulers who followed were weak. Ramses III, like Nectanebo, was succeeded by five pharaohs of uncertain ancestry, whose rule was of short duration. Shortly thereafter Egypt was conquered by Alexander the Greek.

All of this raises a disturbing question. Why are these kings totally unknown? We are faced with a perplexing problem. The exploits of the Saise (Ramesse) Dynasty are known rather in detail, mostly from Greek, Assyrian and Biblical sources. Much the same can be said of Nectanebo's heroics. The Greek and Persians have much to say about him. Yet for all their bravery these rulers are barely mentioned in Egyptian records. There is virtually nothing. This is certainly odd, considering that they lived so much closer to our age than the Ramessides; in the case of Nectanebo no less than eight hundred years. With that much information available we should be able to find these kings rather easily. But no, they are virtually missing from the pages of Egyptian history.

Logic dictates that the armaments of the Egyptians under Ramses II must have been identical to that of Necho II. The same holds true of the "Hittites" and the Chaldeans. A strange problem surfaces, nothing is known about the chariotry of Egypt under Necho II, and the same holds true of the Chaldeans. Information from Chaldean sources is strangely missing and as we have seen, precious little is known about Necho II, including armaments.

A straightforward comparison with previous dynasties reveals an echo effect. The voices of late dynasties appear in earlier ones. It is easy to see why. European scholars assigned kings to dynasties long before the Egyptian language was even deciphered. In the absence of a reliable frame of reference, dynastic succession was wholly based upon not-so-educated guess work. Even within the dynasties nobody knows for certain when these pharaohs reigned, or even who. Sometimes kings were assigned to certain dynasties although their regal name appears nowhere in any historical record, as was the case with Ramses III (Nectanebo). It is within this climate that the so-called Dark Age came about.

The Dark Age

Historians inform us that about 1200 B.C., roving hordes of European tribes overran the northern Mediterranean. These people, called Pereset, annihilated the Mycenaean civilization of Greece and the Hittite Empire. Together with the Sea People they invaded Palestine and attacked Egypt. They were repelled by Pharaoh Ramses III. Following that, there is a hiatus in history, a dark age when nothing happened. It is almost as if there is a black hole in history.

This age is not like the middle ages of Europe, when following the fall of the Roman Empire there was a regression in learning. There is nothing at all. From -1200 to about -700, history simply is not accounted for. Of course we know now that the Pereset of 1200 B.C. were not Philistines, but the Persians of 400 B.C. The Sea People were Greek marines and the Hittites were the Chaldeans of 600 B.C.

That should have rung alarm bells, like flashing lights when an operator pushes the wrong button. Something is very wrong. Greek historians of antiquity knew nothing about a gap in history. Archaeology is unable to record anything at all during this phantom age for good reasons. There is no gap. Pharaohs of the Fourth through Seventh Centuries B.C. were mistakenly placed in the time of the judges, when the Hyksos-Amelekites ruled Egypt. The wanderings of whole populations that occurred around 700 B.C. were confused with the battle of Nectanebo and pushed back five centuries, where they became imaginary roving hordes.

There is a glaring conflict between art historians and Egyptologists. The problem is that art is made to fit Egypt's history without regard for archaeological findings such as pottery. Greek, Syrian and Mesopotamian art dating from the 7th Century B.C. was aligned with Egyptian chronology dating five to six centuries earlier. This created an artificial gap that defies reason. The Greek evidently flourished during the 12th Century B.C. during the Mycenaean era (associated with Pharaoh Akhnaton). For reasons unknown they suddenly disappeared and a half a millennium later in the 7th Century during the Archaic period picked up where they left off without any discernable break. Of course there was no break; the Mycenaean era (which was pushed back some five hundred years) flowed into the Archaic period.

The root cause of this incredible error in conventional history is twofold. First of all, historians refuse to even consider the possibility of recent catastrophic events in nature for reasons that are essentially religious and philosophical, and they have rejected the Bible out of hand as a reliable historical document. How then can we account for the wondrous plagues of Egypt, the drastic change in history! Was it because the earth had a near-collision with Venus? The notion is fantastic, but in the light of history the theory cannot be dismissed out of hand. Secondly, events that happened in the days of Hezekiah, king of Judah, point at worldwide migrations. They will be discussed in detail. However, we must consider dating methods.

Sothis

The reigns of the pharaohs to a large extent have been established by the so-called Sothis dating. That is an astronomical computation, derived by Roman astronomers. According to Censorius, the Great Year of the Egyptians begins when the star Sothis, or Sirius, rises on the first day of the month Thot. This is called the Heliacal or morning rising. He said this happened A.D.139. The Egyptians counted the year as consisting of 365 days, instead of 365 1/4. For this reason, four years later Sirius would rise on the second day of Thot. Keep that up and it must have risen on the previous Great Year, the first day of Thot, 365 1/4 x 4 years = 1,461 years earlier. Subtract 139 years and we arrive at -1,322 (or -1321). It is believed that a Pharaoh Menophres ruled that year, and this Pharaoh is identified with Ramses I.

There are serious problems with this. For beginners, there is not a single Egyptian reference to a Sothis year. Also the great astronomer Ptolemy knew nothing about it. Modern research revealed that Sirius that year was nowhere near the celebrated "great" year. Besides, the year 1,321 B.C. simply does not allow the dynasties to fit the allotted time. As a result there is no scholarly agreement at all about historical dating. Besides, in all likelihood it is based upon an erroneous assumption. It is quite possible that "Monophres" refers not to a pharaoh, but to Memphis, the sacred city of the Amon cult. The unpleasant truth is, anyone who relies on the Egyptian dating system is walking on quicksand.

The Canopus Decree

The Egyptian year originally consisted of 360 days, divided into 12 months of 30 days. We find this in the Pentateuch as well. The Law of Moses mentions months of 30 days without allowing for alternate days. At a later time five days were added. Eventually this turned out to be unsatisfactory, because the year was actually six hours longer than that. In the course of four years, the year was off by a whole day. Now if the Egyptians ever had a calendar, it is certainly odd that not one has survived. In all likelihood they merely observed the seasons. Then something disastrous happened, the seasons were displaced. The days and years became longer, the course of the star Venus was off a day every four years. To correct this, a priestly enclave in Canopus decreed that every four years a day should be added, that the feast of the star Isis (Venus) "that follows the seasons," would be in agreement with the fixed stars, such as Sirius. But this reform was considered to be an offense to the god Isis, and so nothing came of it.

It was Julius Caesar who two centuries later established a calendar with a leap year. (Until then the length of the year and even the number of months was a political football.) Meanwhile it would seem strange that an intercalated day was added at so late a date, and that nothing of the kind was mentioned before. A four-year festival on the other hand, such as the Greek Olympics, which began in the Eighth Century B.C., was universal.

> The eight-, later fourth-, year period of the festivals had the same origin in Mexico, in Greece and in Egypt. They were related to a synodical year of Venus, called also "the queen of heaven." The Egyptian calendar of 365 days was tied to Venus so that every eighth year the heliacal rising of that planet fell on the first day of the month Thot: it was the New Year. The shifting of the heliacal rising of Venus after eight years by approximately two days in relation to the seasons can be observed at simultaneous heliacal risings or settings of the planet and of any southern fixed stars. In order to compare the heliacal rising or setting of Venus with the rising or setting of the fixed stars, the brightest among them, Sirius, was chosen. There are symbolic allusions to their functioning as a team, and the Canopus Decree refers expressly to the relative motion of the star of Isis with respect to the star Sothis.[10]

If this is true, the official dating of Egyptian pharaohs, tenuous as it is, has no place in historical records. Something entirely different happened. No doubt this reconstruction of history is revolutionary and controversial, even more so because it involves cosmic catastrophes. Nonetheless, the scriptures describe events that are clearly catastrophic in nature. What was the physical cause of the exodus? Nor is that all. In the final years of Hezekiah, king of Judah, the Assyrian king Sennacherib attacked Judah with the intent to storm Jerusalem and deport the population. Miraculously it was Sennacherib, not Hezekiah, who was butchered. Strange things happened in those tumultuous times. It involved events that changed the course of history. But as with the exodus, is there a single cause that provides a plausible explanation?

Chapter Five

The Assyrian and the Passover

Scoffers

The apostle Peter made a remarkable prediction. He spoke of a time when godless men would ridicule the belief in creation and the second coming of Christ. The world and life itself, according to these men, are the result of gradual change. No global catastrophes happened, least of all a worldwide flood.

> First of all, you must understand that in the last days scoffers will come, scoffing and following their own evil desires. They will say, "Where is this 'coming' he promised? Ever since our fathers died, everything goes on as it has since the beginning of the creation." But they deliberately forget that long ago by God's word the heavens existed and the earth was formed out of water and by water. By the same word the present heavens and earth are reserved for fire, being kept for the Day of Judgment and destruction of ungodly men.
>
> 2 Peter 3:3-7

The notion that the earth and life evolved over eons of time has pervaded the scientific community. For all fact and purpose it is a pseudo science, an atheistic denial of a supernatural beginning. The marvels of creation are discarded in favor of a world view that is mechanical and fatalistic. This is done for a single reason, these men ban God from their lives and necessarily their field of expertise. They try to convince themselves there is no God.

These theories are based upon assumptions that are essentially religious. Since there is no Creator there can be no creation; evolution is sacrosanct, and catastrophic events never happened in recorded history. These things are never proven, they must be accepted by faith. Nor are they based on fact. Yes, evolutionary literature creates the impression that scientist are forced to accept evolution based upon sheer weight of evidence. It is not like that at all, and every scientist knows it. Macro evolution, major changes from one species to another, such as reptiles gradually changing into birds, never happened. The geological record refutes it. So-called micro evolution, changes within the species such as all the varieties of dogs and birds, is a matter of genetics. It could be either breeding or genetic adaptation and isolation, which is what Darwin found on the Galapagos Islands. Genetics is a built-in mechanism that enables species to adapt to changing environments. The best-suited survive. Evolutionists saw changes within the various kinds and *assumed* gradual transformation to higher and ever more complex creatures. Not so! The kinds are fenced in by impassable boundaries. And it flies in the face of the second law of thermodynamics, entropy.

We notice with a certain amusement that evolutionists dismiss evidence from design, which is apparent everywhere, and embrace chance. But random changes in a highly complex system inevitably damage it, and entropy wears it out. Left to themselves things do not get more complicated, they fall apart. Besides, chance has no creative power, just as *Pi* cannot create a circle. These are mathematical concepts that exist in our minds. They are not part of reality. It takes a real being to create something real. This does not bother the faithful. Evolution after all is their creation myth. Some are so convinced of the righteousness of their cause that they consider unbelievers to be evil. They are not exactly paragons of tolerance.

It so happens there is a theory that challenges at least some of these assumptions. Oddly enough, it was a study of ancient civilizations and the records they left that led Velikovsky to the belief that catastrophic events did in fact occur in recent, recorded history. As we have seen, he was convinced Venus was the cause of the exodus and other disastrous events. Eventually Venus ceased to be a problem, only to be replaced by another menace. Mars, hitherto an obscure astral deity, became a feared war god. What happened?

Velikovsky thought Venus had a number of near-collisions with Mars that made both change course. Venus was captured by the sun and became the evening and morning star. Mars on the other hand was deflected from its course and entered into a highly elliptical orbit that regularly brought it close to the orbit of the earth. For about a century it menaced the earth at regular intervals (every fifteen years), until finally it entered its present orbit.

All this happened at a time when Uzziah, Jotham, Ahaz and Hezekiah were kings of Judah. Part of Hebrew history and prophetic literature, in other words, was written against a background of recurring catastrophic events. That certainly sounds odd, but Scripture and ancient records mention a number of things that are unusual to say the least. It happened in the reigns of Uzziah and Hezekiah.

Raash

In the reign of King Uzziah, a disaster struck. The author of Chronicles, who was interested in religious matters, informs us that Uzziah committed an offense, unheard of for a king. He actually entered the temple and burned incense on the altar of incense. This was strictly forbidden by the Law of Moses, so the priests stood up to him. Azariah the High Priest ordered the king to leave, and when Uzziah began to rant and rave, leprosy broke out on his forehead. The dethroned king lived out the rest of his life in seclusion. His son Jotham took over. (2 Chron 26: 16-22)

Jotham is noted for an important project. He "rebuilt the Upper Gate of the temple of the Lord." (2 Chron 27:3) What was wrong with the structure it does not say, but Josephus explains that the temple sustained severe damage. It happened when the priests confronted King Uzziah for burning incense.

> In the meantime, a great earthquake shook the ground, and a rent was made in the temple, and the bright rays of the sun shone through it, and fell upon the king's face, insomuch that the leprosy seized upon him immediately; and before the city at a place called Eroge, half the mountain broke off from the rest on the west, and rolled itself four furlongs, and stood still at the east mountain, till the roads, as well as the king's gardens, were spoiled by the obstruction. [1]

This is referred to in other sources as well. A severe earthquake struck. Centuries later it was said that the quake blocked a valley (Zechariah 14:5). A few years earlier the prophet Amos prophesied "two years before the earthquake," and said the Lord would send fire upon several cities because its peoples committed crime after crime. The Hebrew word *raash*, translated earthquake, also means tumult, commotion. Considering that Amos specifically mentioned the *raash*, it sounds as if it had something to do with his prophecies.

Isaiah

According to rabbinical sources, Isaiah began his ministry the day Uzziah was struck with leprosy and the nation was devastated by the *raash*. Bible scholars often wondered where the first five chapters of Isaiah fit into the life of the prophet. Obviously Judah had just suffered some kind of calamity, and so it is usually assumed that it must have been a military disaster, probably the one 701 B.C., when Sennacherib attacked Judah and left it ruined. But that does not at all fit Isaiah's description of Judah. The nation was rich and militarily strong, and anything but defeated.

> You have abandoned your people,
> the House of Jacob.
> They are full of superstitions from the East;
> they practice divination like the Philistines
> and clasp hands with pagans.
> Their land is full of silver and gold,
> there is no end to their treasures.
> Their land is full of horses;
> there is no end to their chariots.
> Isaiah 2:6-8

That agrees with the picture of 2 Chronicles 26, some fifty years before the Assyrian assault. Uzziah was an arms manufacturer, he had a standing army and the nation prospered. Then what was the nature of the disaster that had obviously struck Judah? Isaiah speaks of cities, burned by fire and fields laid waste. Many people had died in some kind of catastrophe. "Unless the Lord Almighty had left us some survivors, we would have become like Sodom, we would have been like Gomorrah." (Isa 1:9). These cities were totally destroyed. An earthquake struck, with disastrous results. "The mountains shake, and the dead bodies are like refuse in the street." (Isa 5:25)

It sounds very much like a natural, rather than a military disaster. There are indications that these upheavals were not restricted to Palestine, but were of a global nature. Isaiah said humanity would hide in caves for fear of a divine omen. It happened before and it would happen again; the Lord would shake the earth.

> Men will flee to caves in the rocks
> and to holes in the ground
> from dread of the Lord
> and the splendor of his majesty,
> when he rises to shake the earth.
> In that day men will throw away
> to the rodents and bats

their idols of silver and idols of gold,
which they made to worship.
They will flee to caverns in the rocks
and to the overhanging crags
from the dread of the Lord
and the splendor of his majesty
when he rises to shake the earth.
Stop trusting in man,
who has but breath in his nostrils.
On what account is he?
Isaiah 2:19-22

Star Gazers

There are several such predictions that speak of darkness, shaking the earth, a sword in the heavens, and an overwhelming scourge passing by. We should keep in mind however, that we are merely speaking of a situation that may have existed then. What really counts is not the historical background of the message, but the message itself. That message is always true. It speaks of redemption, morals, ethics, the worship of an Almighty God. Regrettably, Velikovsky was blind to these things. He never recognized the noble character of Isaiah, much less the meaning of the message. All he saw was a scheming, calculating star gazer, who came with shrewd guesses which he passed off as the word of the Deity.

It is only human to focus on one aspect of a favorite theory and fail to see the whole picture. It is also tempting to assume things, not in evidence. It happened to Velikovsky. "The seers who prophesied in Judah" he wrote, "were versed in the lore of heavenly motion; they observed the ways of the planetary and cometary bodies and, like the star gazers of Assyria and Babylonia, they were aware of future changes."[2] This is one of those flat statements he never bothers to prove. How do we know this is true, that Isaiah was actually "skilled in the observation of stars," and that he evidently knew that at regular intervals - every fifteen years - a catastrophe occurred? That is an assumption, not a fact. Besides, Isaiah could have hardly been the only one to notice phenomena that were plain for all to see.

Dates

Does the language of Isaiah warrant the belief that every fifteen years a cosmic body, the planet Mars, brushed close past the earth? We could look at the historical facts. Velikovsky thought the first date of record was -747. That year Nabonassar, an otherwise obscure Babylonian king, introduced a new calendar, evidently because the old calendar had become obsolete. If global catastrophes occurred at fifteen-year intervals beginning -747, the dates are -732, -717, -702 and -687. Fortunately four of these dates can be known with certainty, because they synchronize with events in the lives of several Hebrew kings. They are the year of the *raash*, when Uzziah was smitten with leprosy, the year King Ahaz died and the Assyrian campaigns against Judah. Sennecherib attacked Jerusalem not once, but twice. Scholars maintain the second campaign occurred -687. We need to investigate the historical dates for the kings of Judah and Israel

The division of the kingdom into the ten tribes of Israel in the north and Judah (with Benjamin) in the south occurred 930 B.C., when Jeroboam, son of Solomon, foolishly antagonized the population and was left with only two tribes. Now reconstructing the reigns of the kings of Judah and Israel is not quite as easy as it looks, among other things because different dating methods were used. The northern kingdom used a system whereby the year began in the spring of the year, but the southern kingdom it began in the fall. A reign could be counted as beginning in the current regnal year, or the next. Also, reigns often overlapped, for instance with a co-regency. This is the subject of "The Mysterious Numbers of the Hebrew Kings," by Professor Edwin R. Thiele. The accuracy of the scriptural record is nothing short of miraculous. A comparison with Assyrian records enabled Thiele to establish the dates of the Hebrew kings with certainty.

The reign of Azariah, or Uzziah, is of particular importance, not only because it lasted a long time (fifty two years), but also because it establishes the date of the *raash*. Azariah was a popularly elected king. His father Amaziah ascended the throne 796 B.C., when Jehoash was king of Israel. He defeated Edom and stupidly challenged Jehoash. But Jehoash would not hear of it, and warned Amaziah not to try anything foolish. Amaziah would not listen and forced a battle which he lost decisively, and Jehoash took him prisoner. The people of Judah then put his son Azariah (Uzziah) on the vacant throne. Amaziah remained prisoner one year, until the death of Jehoash. He then was released and returned to Jerusalem, and outlived Jehoash another fifteen years, but was not restored to the throne.

Meanwhile Jehoash had already installed his son Jeroboam II as co-regent, so their reigns, like that of the Judean kings, overlapped. Both Uzziah and Jeroboam ruled a long time; Uzziah from -792 until -740 and Jeroboam from -793 until -753. After the death of Jeroboam, serious political factions divided the ten tribes. Zechariah, son of Jeroboam became king -752, which was the 38th year of Uzziah, king of Judah. He lasted six months, then he was assassinated by Shallum, who in turn was himself eliminated one month later by Manehem. Manehem reigned ten years from -752 until -742, and was succeeded by Pekiah, who ruled two years. Meanwhile a rival by the name of Pekah began an independent reign in Gilead, beginning -752, the year Manehem came to power. In his 12th year, -740, Pekah killed Pekiah and ruled all of Israel from Samaria until -732 for a total of twenty years.

In Judah, the reign of Uzziah was long and successful. As we have seen, upon offering incense in the temple, he was stricken with leprosy and lived out his life in seclusion, a leper. This happened -750, in the second year of Pekah. Uzziah's son Jotham became king that year. He ruled sixteen years or fifteen actual years, until -735. There are good reasons to believe he was ousted in a palace coup. A pro-Assyrian faction evidently deposed him and placed his son Ahaz on the throne. Jotham was not killed however; he lived at least another four years. The scriptures refer to foreign problems during his last years, but do not blame him.

This change of command backfired however. The reign of Ahaz could charitably be called a disaster. He was an idolater (he sacrificed his own sons in the fire), and spineless, and his pro-Assyrian position got him in serious trouble with his neighbors. Judah was besieged from every side. From the southeast Edom attacked; from the southwest the Philistines seized Judean territory. From the north the Arameans (Syria) defeated Judah and took many prisoners to Damascus. Pekah, king of Israel, inflicted a serious defeat. Ahaz' son Maasiah was killed, and so were several high-ranking officers. Israel took thousands of prisoners, but then the prophet Oded angrily told Pekah to release the Judeans, which he did. In despair, Ahaz begged Tiglath Pelizer (Pul) for help, bribed him in fact, and the Assyrian king was happy to oblige. He captured Damascus and put Rezin to death. This happened -732, the year Hoshea succeeded Pekah in Israel. Hoshea reigned nine years until -723. Then Shalmanezer captured Samaria and the ten tribes disappeared from the face of the earth. Ahaz ruled fifteen years, and was succeeded by Hezekiah.

Hezekiah

The reign of Hezekiah can be determined, albeit with difficulty. According to 2 Kings 18, Hezekiah began to reign in the third year of Hoshea, king of Israel. Shalmanezer besieged Samaria, the Capitol of Israel, in the fourth year of Hezekiah and captured it three years later. Since Samaria fell 723 B.C., it follows that Hezekiah began his rule seven years earlier, 730 B.C. But that does not at all fit the dates of the Hebrew kings. When Hezekiah began to reign, Hoshea king of Israel was long gone. Thiele thought it was the result of a scribal error; however, it could involve a co-regency between Ahaz and Hezekiah as well.

The reigns of Ahaz and Hezekiah appear to have occurred as follows. Ahaz was born 755 B.C. When he was twenty years old, 735 B.C., he supplanted his father Jotham in a co-regency until the death of Jotham, 732 B.C. That was counted as the first regnal year of Ahaz. Following this he reigned seventeen years or sixteen actual years until his death, 715 B.C. His son Hezekiah was born 740 B.C., when Ahaz was fifteen years old. This was surprisingly common. The Assyrian and Egyptian kings often were mere teenagers. Hezekiah was made co-regent with Ahaz 729 B.C., when he was eleven, approaching the age of maturity, which was twelve. That happened in the third year of Hoshea, king of Israel, and lasted until the death of Ahaz, 715 B.C. Rabinnical source inform us of a strange event. On the day of Ahaz' funeral the sun disappeared at noon and did not return until the next day. The king was buried in pitch darkness.

The first regnal year of Hezekiah therefore was 715 B.C. In his reign two extraordinary events happened. They do not belong together, but are separated by a number of years. Scripture records that Sennacherib attacked Judah, and that Hezekiah agreed to pay tribute. He became deathly ill, but recovered. It was on this occasion that the shadow of the sun moved back the ten steps it had gone down on the stairway of Ahaz. This happened 701 B.C., in the fourteenth year of Hezekiah. A number of years later Sennacherib attacked Judah again in another campaign. When this happened we are not told, but the outcome was disastrous for the aggressor. A hundred-eighty-five-thousand Assyrians were killed in an instant. Bible scholars believe this happened fourteen years later, 687 B.C.

Now that we know the actual dates of the Judean kings, we can have a reality check, and lo and behold, the numbers do not fit the theory. Uzziah fell from grace -750, not -747. Ahaz died -715, not -717, and the invasion of Sennacherib was -701, not -702. That does not necessarily prove the theory of Velikovsky wrong. In fact it fits the circumstances. If a cosmic disturbance affected the rotation and orbit of the earth -750, and as a result the old calendar became obsolete, a new calendar could have hardly been introduced that very year. It would take a year or so before it became sufficiently evident that the months had become disarranged. The second year the king would authorize astronomers to compute the new order, and after checking the numbers to make sure, a new calendar would be introduced the third year, -747. That hardly constitutes irrefutable evidence, we are merely dealing with a possible scenario. However, it is necessary to find out whether or not the dates of the kings of Judah coincide with theoretical oppositions of the planet Mars.

Favorable Opposition

Mars is farther away from the sun than the earth, and for this reason it takes Mars longer to make a full revolution around the sun. The Mars year is 1.881 Earth years, or 687 Earth days. The earth overtakes Mars every 780 days, but because both the earth and Mars move in an elliptical orbit, the distance between both planets between oppositions varies. Every fifteen years they arrive at a point called favorable opposition, when the earth is farthest away from the sun and Mars nearest. Mars then becomes a very bright star, outshining all other stars.

Velikovsky contends that Mars in the beginning of the Eighth Century B.C. after a number of near-collisions with an errant Venus was thrown into a highly elliptical orbit. Mars came much nearer to the earth than it does now, and every fifteen years, during favorable opposition, both planets came disastrously close. This, he maintained, happened 747 B.C., when Uzziah was smitten with leprosy, the year of Ahab's death (unspecified) and again 687 B.C., during Sennacherib's attack on Judah.

Thanks to the accuracy of Scripture and the labors of Professor Thiele, we are able to establish at least three such encounters with precision. The problem is that these dates do not occur at fifteen-year intervals. Yet there is a pattern. Uzziah became a leper -750, Ahab died -715, Sennacherib attacked Judah -701, when Hezekiah was sick, and again -687, with disastrous results. Dating back, these events occurred not at fifteen, but fourteen-year intervals. If catastrophes occurred because Mars and the earth came very close every fourteen years, we must continue this interval and see how it fits the "raash" of Uzziah. Beginning with -715, the year of Ahaz' death, the years would be -729, -743 and -757. But the raash occurred -750. How do we explain this, and how do we account for a fourteen-year cycle?

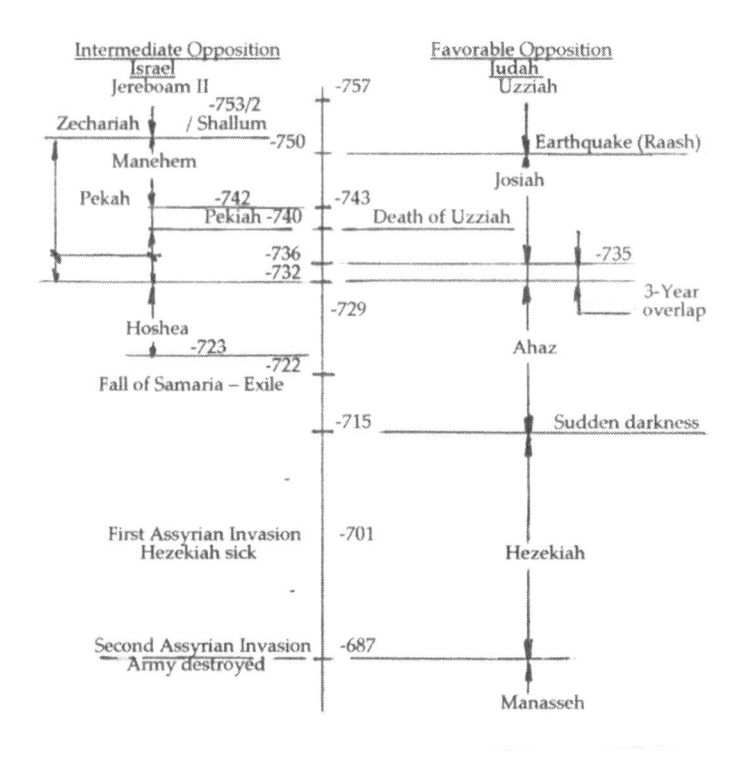

```
              Intermediate Opposition              Favorable Opposition
                     Israel                               Judah
                  Jereboam II          -757              Uzziah
       Zechariah  ↓ -753/2 / Shallum
       ─────────────────── -750                          ↓ Earthquake (Raash)
                 Manehem                                Josiah
         Pekah   ↓  -742        -743
                    Pekiah -740      Death of Uzziah
                           -736
                           -732                                  -735
                                    -729                         ↕ 3-Year
                 Hoshea                                          ─ overlap
                    ↓ -723                Ahaz
                      ─────── -722
              Fall of Samaria – Exile
                                    -715              Sudden darkness
                                                      ─────────────────

              First Assyrian Invasion -701
                 Hezekiah sick                     Hezekiah

              Second Assyrian Invasion -687
                 Army destroyed
                                                      Manasseh
```

There is a solution. According to Kepler's second law of planetary motion, a planet increases speed when its distance to the sun decreases. It involves preservation of energy. If Mars moved in an orbit closer to the sun than it is now, it must have moved faster and the Martian year was necessarily shorter. Favorable opposition could have occurred in fourteen-year cycles. At the present time eight Mars years equal fifteen Earth years. But if eight Mars years equaled roughly fourteen Earth years, the movements of both planets would be more symmetrical. Four Mars years would equal seven Earth years; both planets would again be close. There was an increased threat. 750 B.C. was such a year, halfway between -743 and -757.

Of course there are unanswered questions. Mars is on the far side of the earth. If Mars was the cause of the sudden darkness on the day of Ahaz' funeral, how could it blot out the light of the sun? There is an explanation, but it is drastic. For the time being we will concern ourselves with the theoretical meeting of Mars and Earth.

Animism

Assuming all this actually happened, it follows that the planet Mars must have been clearly visible every seven years, very much so during years of favorable opposition. Since Mars is farther away from the sun than the earth, it must have appeared very bright in the night sky. It is larger than the Moon. Being some distance away, it may have appeared similar in size. As it passed by over a period of weeks it must have been a frightening sight to behold, even more so if the moons of Mars were visible.

Now we would ask of course, if ancient civilizations saw this happen, why did they not report that the planet Mars came near? Maybe in their own way they did. We should keep in mind that these people did not know the true nature of the solar system. The Babylonian astronomers quite likely had a proper understanding of the planets being strung out in outer space, but that was not common knowledge. People on the whole believed in animism, the notion that creation is divine and animated by spiritual powers. This is why they worshiped trees, animals and the planets. Does that sound strange? Read "Cosmos," by Carl Sagan. It still happens. The television series is a perfect example of animism; it is blatantly religious.

What ancient civilizations reported was a fearful prodigy in the sky that they believed to be an astral deity. The Assyrian Nergal, the Greek Ares, the Latin Mars was feared for its violence. It brought unrest and war. The Homeric poems call Ares (Mars) the "blood stained stormer of walls." Judging from the prayers, addressed to the deity, one gets the impression that a fearful sight appeared in the heavens. "Nergal, the almighty among the gods, fear, terror, awe-inspiring splendor,"[3] wrote the Assyrians. "Radiant abode, that beams over the land — who is thy equal?" Mars was feared as the fire god and it became the god of war. The chief deity of Rome, which was founded at that time, was Mars. The prophets of Israel and Judah spoke of signs in the heavens, although not in astral fashion. Which leads us to the question, what did they say and how does that fit history?

Two Campaigns

In the book of Isaiah, we find a major historical interlude. It is remarkable for its detailed description of seemingly insignificant events. The historian who wrote the book of kings (which originally included the two books of Samuel), almost certainly relied on court records, written by the prophets rather than the kings. He repeated much of this story, with additional details. The Chronicler, who came later, did not bother to repeat Isaiah and the historian, but he did add supplementary material. The three books, taken together, pay a great deal of attention to something that would seem to be rather insignificant. Or is it?

The story itself deals with an invasion by the Assyrian king Sennacherib. His officers blasphemed God, and after Hezekiah appealed to God, the angel of the Lord annihilated the Assyrian army. There are two post scripts. King Hezekiah became seriously ill; in fact Isaiah told him he would die. But after Hezekiah prayed for healing, he was given a respite; he would live another fifteen years. He requested and received a sign: the shadow of the clock moved back the ten steps it had gone forward on the stairway of Ahaz. After his recovery, an embassy of the Chaldean king Meredoch-baladan inquired about his health and the strange phenomenon of the shadow moving back.

These events could have hardly happened simultaneously; there are too many differences. In one case Hezekiah submitted, in another he resisted. He was deathly ill and unable to go to the temple, but when he received the blasphemous letter of the Assyrian he hastened there to pray. Isaiah visited him personally to inform him about his health, but sent a messenger regarding the destruction of the Assyrian army. The shadow of the stairway obviously moved back during daylight, but the army of Sennacherib was annihilated at night. The Babylonian embassy, which arrived about 700 B.C., inquired about the miraculous sign of the shadow, but not the defeat of Sennacherib, obviously because it had not happened yet.

We could add that Sennacherib received Hezekiah's tribute in Nineveh, but was ready to personally lead the attack on Jerusalem when his army was destroyed. Besides, the Ethiopian king Tirhakah came out to fight the Assyrians, but in 701 B.C. he was only nine years old, too young to lead an army. That campaign must have happened at a later time.

701 B.C.

All this points at two campaigns, several years apart. The first campaign happened 701 B.C., in the fourteenth year of Hezekiah. 707 B.C., the Assyrian Sargon II conquered Babylon, at that time the Capitol of the Chaldean kingdom, but the Chaldean king Meredoch-baladan escaped and went into hiding. Sargon was killed fighting the Scythians 705 B.C., resulting in a general revolt; subject nations attempted to throw off the Assyrian yoke, Meredoch-baladan among them. Sennacherib, the son and successor of Sargon, having established his throne at home, defeated the rebels. Two years later Sennacherib attacked Egypt and subjugated Judah. "The proud Hezekiah," he reported, "I shut up like a bird in his cage." But he did not capture Jerusalem. Hezekiah submitted and paid Sennacherib tribute; Judah was militarily not strong enough to resist.

It was during this campaign that Hezekiah became seriously ill. Isaiah told him to put his house in order because he would die. Hezekiah earnestly prayed to God, and Isaiah returned with happy news: the Lord had added fifteen years to his life. In three days he would be able to go to the house of the Lord. Hezekiah asked for a sign to prove that this would happen and Isaiah answered,

"This is the Lord's sign to you that the Lord will do what he has promised: Shall the shadow go forward ten steps, or shall it go back ten steps?" "It is a simple matter for the shadow to go forward ten steps," said Hezekiah, "Rather have it go back ten steps." Then the prophet Isaiah called upon the Lord, and the Lord made the shadow go back the ten steps it had gone down on the stairway of Ahaz.

2 Kings 20:9-10

It is certainly very strange that the shadow would "go back the ten steps it had gone down on the stairway of Ahaz." What would cause the shadow to go back? An optical illusion is the usual answer, or a refraction of the light. Yes, but it says the shadow actually moved back. Besides, the Chaldean delegation would hardly be interested in an optical illusion.

There is something else. The very phrasing implies that the retrograde move of the shadow corrected a previous forward move. This is accounted for in a strange natural event that happened fourteen years earlier, 715 B.C., on the day that King Ahaz died. "At the funeral of Ahaz the sun set ten hours before its time, and at Hezekiah's recovery from his illness the sun recovered the lost hours."[4] The sun did not hasten forward; instead the luminary disappeared altogether, to rise the next day at an earlier time. Night fell in the middle of the day. It turned out the sun dial was affected, the shadow moved forward.

The Chaldean Delegation

The mission of the Babylonian or Chaldean delegation is of particular interest. On the surface it was a courtesy call. Hezekiah had been ill, and they came to see how he was doing. Naturally other subjects came up as well. Meredoch-baladan, as we have seen, went into exile following his defeat by Sargon, so it follows that the embassy visited Jerusalem shortly after Hezekiah's illness, probably 700 B.C. The real purpose of this visit was political. The Chaldean king recognized in Hezekiah an ally against Assyria. Nonetheless, there were other reasons.

The Chaldeans were renowned for their astronomical achievements; their astronomers constituted a priestly caste. They were capable of complicated mathematical calculations. The delegation evidently included members of this caste, for they inquired Hezekiah about the "sign" that had occurred in the land. The Hebrew word Erez, "land" can also be translated "world." The expression "in the land" would seem unnecessary. Was not that obvious? But if the retrograde movement of the shadow happened "in the world," this would have certainly been noticed in Babylon. If this phenomenon had been a refraction of the light, only noticed in Jerusalem, no Chaldean astronomer would have paid the slightest attention. In all likelihood they would have never even heard about it. But they did, and they came to Jerusalem to ask about it.

They had good reasons to. Several years earlier, Isaiah made a number of startling predictions that even now are not always appreciated like they should be. Doomsday messages have a way of spreading, and the seers of Israel and Judah were uncannily accurate. The Chaldeans may have very well heard about it, and they came to Jerusalem for instruction. Isaiah's predictions were astounding. They deal with a crucial time in history.

Messiah

The book of Isaiah is divided into three parts. Chapters one through thirty-five deal with Israel and Judah. They lead up to the destruction of the Assyrian army. Then there is the historical interlude. The third part, chapter forty to the end, is truly prophetic, without political underpinnings. It is also controversial. Because of its perspective, a number of scholars maintain it was written by a later prophet, or maybe more than one, who used Isaiah's name to gain acceptance. We will study this later.

When we study Isaiah, and for that matter all of Scripture, we must make sure that nothing is taken out of context, and that Scripture is compared with Scripture. If Isaiah wrote at a time when the planet Mars inflicted repeated disasters, is there any way that we can glean from Scripture what happened? That is not all. Isaiah had a message. Like all the prophets, he spoke of a time when a man would appear who would reconcile God to man.

The Jews had a name for him, or rather a title. When Aaron was initiated as High Priest, Moses employed an interesting ceremony. He did not put his hands on the head of Aaron to ordain him, rather he poured oil over his hair. Aaron, in other words, was anointed with oil. The same thing happened with Saul and David. Samuel poured oil over Saul's head to anoint him king. Significantly, he poured it out of a breakable bottle. Saul's kingdom did not last. Later he did the same thing with David, this time with an unbreakable ram's horn.

It follows that both the priest and the king were anointed, called by God to a high office. The Hebrew word for anointed is "Mashiah," or Messiah. As time went on and God revealed more of himself and his plans for the future, the Jews came to a better understanding of his purposes. They saw that God would send "Messiah." That was not the only title of course; he is also called the servant, the branch, the root, redeemer. "Messiah" is a generic title.

It is necessary to mention this, because Isaiah has much to say about Messiah, and unless we are aware of this, our study would not be intelligible. The Bible after all is not just a book, even a good book; it is a supernatural book. It is the gradual unfolding revelation of God that deals primarily with redemption and that strictly on a need to know base. It was not written to satisfy our curiosity. Having said that, we hasten to add that it is also history. If the history of Scripture is not true, then neither is its message. It is for this reason that we look into this highly unorthodox theory. It may just provide an answer to certain passages in Isaiah and a number of Minor Prophets that are very difficult to explain from a historical point of view.

Exactly because it is controversial, we have to be careful. There are good reasons why we do not accept everything Velikovsky said at face value. He was in many ways mistaken. The reasons are obvious. Nobody questions his sincerity, but he frequently disregarded the historical context of the Old Testament, and placed several events in the wrong time frame. Nor did he get the message. He was sufficiently impressed with the historical data to fit his material into a Biblical frame of reference, but was too focused on his pet project to see the whole picture. This is very much evident in the book of Isaiah.

The Call of Isaiah

Isaiah received his commission in the year that King Uzziah died, which was 740 B.C. He had a vision of the threefold holy Lord, who was seated on a throne, in full command. At the sight of this, Isaiah cried out, "I am a man of unclean lips and I live among a people of unclean lips, and my eyes have seen the King, the Lord Almighty." It was customary for lepers to cry out, "unclean, unclean," and cover their upper lip. When Isaiah saw the Lord, his first reaction was fear. No man can see God and live. He also could see the true problem of human nature, including himself; man is smitten with the leprosy of sin. Only a burning coal could cleanse his lips. Keep in mind that this was a vision.

The Lord said, "Whom shall I send, and who will go before us?" The prophet replied, "Here I am, send me!" He then received orders to proclaim the message of the Lord. It is not at all what we would expect. It could hardly be said that the Almighty was begging the people of Judah to accept him. Rather, he pronounced doom. Isaiah then asked a very strange and seemingly incomplete question: "For how long now, Lord?" One wonders, how long what? Maybe the reply provides the answer.

> Until the cities lie ruined
> and without inhabitant,
> until the houses are left deserted
> and the fields ruined and ravaged,
> until the Lord has sent everyone far away
> and the land is utterly forsaken.

> And though a tenth remains in the land,
> it will again be laid waste.
> But as the terebinth and oak
> leave stumps when they are cut down,
> so the holy seed will be the stump in the land.
>
> Isaiah 6:11-13

The implied question evidently was, "How long must these devastations continue?" The answer is the theme of the book of Isaiah. Through a series of natural and military disasters, the land would be ruined, the people exiled. That was still far away. We should not forget that Isaiah asked this question 740 B.C., when Jotham was king and the failed policies of Ahab in the future. So were the Assyrian campaigns in the days of Hezekiah.

Judah had been hit by natural catastrophes; military disasters were to follow. The prophecy looks forward to the exile to Babylon, and beyond that to the return of a remnant, the symbolic stumps of trees that still contained life. It is, of course, also a message of hope. No matter how badly Israel failed its calling, God would never forsake his people. The life in the trunk was manifest in the Messiah.

Ahaz

Isaiah was now ready to announce the word of God to the nation, which he did by facing King Ahab. Velikovsky interpreted Isaiah's words to mean that the prophet foretold natural disasters. He did this by stringing together a number of quotations cafeteria fashion, pick and choose style. He quotes Isaiah as offering Ahaz a sign "in the height above," after which he skips to the next chapter and in the same breath makes Isaiah face the people: "And they shall look unto the earth; and behold trouble and darkness, dimness of anguish." (8:22) Nevertheless, the dimness would not be as great as on the two former occasions, when "at the first he lightly afflicted the land of Zebulun and the land of Naphtali, and afterward did more grievously afflict her by the way of the sea, beyond Jordan, in Galilee of the nations" (9:11). "He calculated that the next catastrophe would cause less harm than had been caused on previous occasions. But soon thereafter he changed his prognostication and became utterly pessimistic." After which Velikovsky quotes scattered passages from chapters 9, 10 and 11. "Thus, a war of the heavenly host, commanded by the Lord, was proclaimed against the nations of the earth." [5]

Time out. When did Isaiah confront Ahaz and what did he say? Ahaz came to power 735 B.C., five years after the death of Uzziah. The first three years of his reign overlapped with that of Jotham, whom he supplanted. However, his pro-Assyrian policy got him in serious trouble with his neighbors. Israel and Syria (Aram) combined to attack Judah and intended to put a puppet ruler (the son of Tabeel) in charge. This happened 736 B.C., and Isaiah came to encourage Ahaz. The Lord told the king,

> It will not take place, it will not happen,
> for the head of Aram is Damascus,
> and the head of Damascus is only Rezin.
> Within sixty-five years
> Ephraim will be too shattered to be a people.
> The head of Ephraim is Samaria,
> and the head of Samaria is only Remaliah's son.
> If you do not stand firm in your faith,
> you will not stand at all.
> Isaiah 7:7-9

Ephraim, the chief of the ten tribes of Israel, would cease to be an ethnic people in 65 years. Samaria fell twelve years later, 723 B.C., and its people were deported. It was not until 669 B.C. that Assurbanipal began to resettle Israel with foreigners and Ephraim was "too shattered to be a people." Israel ceased to exist.

The Lord spoke again to Ahaz through Isaiah. "Ask the Lord your God for a sign, whether in the deepest depths or in the highest heights." Ahaz refused. "I will not ask, I will not put the Lord to the test."

Then Isaiah said, "Hear now, you house of David! Is it not enough to try the patience of men? Will you try the patience of my God also? Therefore the Lord himself will give you a sign: The virgin will be with child and will give birth to a son, and will call him Immanuel. He will eat curds and honey when he knows enough to reject the wrong and choose the right. But before the boy knows enough to reject the wrong and choose the right, the land of the two kings you dread will be laid waste."

Isaiah 7:13-16

Isaiah went on to say that Assyria and Egypt would invade Palestine with devastating results. Where once vineyards were would be thorns; the land would become a wilderness where cattle would be let loose. They would have curds and honey to eat, but no more. The notion that a sign "in the height above" refers to a cosmic prodigy is absurd. Ahaz received a sign from on high in spite of his refusal. A virgin would conceive and bear a son and call his name *Immanuel*, "God with us." A more literal translation renders it "the God who tabernacles or dwells with us."

Who, we ask, is Immanuel? It could not be Hezekiah, because he had already been born, nor could he be a son of Isaiah, because Isaiah already had a son named Shear-Jashub (a remnant will return, 7:3), so his wife hardly qualifies as a virgin. Now what is so unusual about the birth of a son? That is no "sign." But this was not an ordinary conception. The word "Alma," virgin, is strikingly suggestive; it implies something miraculous. Isaiah indicates as much with the seemingly unnecessary statement that his second son was conceived through natural reprocreation, as distinct from the conception of Immanuel.

Even though Isaiah spoke of the birth of Immanuel as immediate, the implication is that of a messianic prediction. It was understood that this had something to do with the birth of the Messiah; he was to be born of a virgin. About a year later, after the birth of his second son, Isaiah went on to predict the fate of the coalition that threatened Judah. Within a few years, before the boy would eat curds and honey, these nations would come to naught.

The birth of Isaiah's son, whose name meant "quick to the plunder, swift to the spoil," served as a confirmation. Before the boy would be able to say mommy or daddy, "The wealth of Damascus and the plunder of Samaria will be carried off by the king of Assyria." (8:4) As we have seen, Tiglath-pelzer (Pul) captured Damascus 732 B.C., and put Rezin to death. Isaiah spoke of Assyria as the Euphrates River flooding Judah, but the Lord would cause them to be defeated at last.

> Raise the war cry, you nations,
> and be shattered!
> Listen, all you distant lands.
> Prepare for battle, and be shattered!
> Prepare for battle, and be shattered!
> Devise your strategy, but it will be thwarted;
> propose your plan, but it will not stand,
> for God is with us.
>   Isaiah 8:9, 10

The repetition of a word or sentence serves as an exclamation point. It is also significant, in view of what follows, that Isaiah used the expression, "God with us," Immanuel. Clearly Judah failed to put its faith in God, and as a result judgment was decreed; they did not trust the God who was with them, even though Isaiah and his children were signs and symbols from the Lord Almighty. As to the revelation of God, Judah was in the dark. They resorted to divination, but refused to listen to the word. Isaiah's pronouncement was damning. "To the law and the testimony! If they do not speak according to this word, they have no light of dawn." (8:20) The "law and the testimony" was the written revelation of what became known as the law and the prophets. It was the Bible as it existed up to then.

In spite of what Velikovsky believed, Isaiah was not speaking of the darkness of a cosmic disaster. He was speaking of spiritual blindness; those who rejected his words did not have "the light of dawn," they were in the dark about the things of God. Now it is possible, of course, that a literal darkness occurred 750 B.C. with the *raash*, and that Isaiah alluded to it. He spoke of an army that came from the ends of the earth.

> Their arrows are sharp,
> all their bows are strung;
> their horses' hoofs seem like flint,
> their chariot wheels like a whirlwind.
> Their roar is like that of the lion,
> they roar like young lions;
> they growl as they seize their prey
> and carry if off with no one to rescue.
> In that day they will roar over it
> like the roaring of the sea.
> And if one looks at the land,
> he will see darkness and distress;
> even the light will be darkened by the clouds.
>
> Isaiah 5:28-30

But that is not what is meant here, and when Isaiah addressed Ahaz, he did not "face the people" to speak the words of the following chapter. That was said nearly a year later, after the birth of his second son. The darkness of which Isaiah spoke earlier served as a model for the spiritual darkness that gripped the nation. Like its king, Israel refused to consult the Lord. The result was equally devastating.

> Distressed and hungry, they will roam through the land; when they are famished, they will become enraged and, looking upward, will curse their king and their God. Then they will look

toward the earth and see only distress and darkness and fearful gloom, and they will be thrust into utter darkness.

Isaiah 8:21, 22

Certainly this passage has nothing to do with some celestial portent. This becomes even more evident in what follows. The gloom would be lifted in the presence of the messianic child, Immanuel. Zebulun and Naphtali in Galilee had been "humbled" when Tiglath-pelizer during the reign of Pekah deported the population (2 Kings 15:29), but in the future God would "honor Galilee of the Gentiles, by the way of the sea, along the Jordan." (9:2)

> The people walking in darkness
> have seen a great light;
> on those living in the land of the shadow of death
> A light has dawned.
> You have enlarged the nation and increased their joy;
> they rejoice before you as people rejoice at the harvest,
> as men rejoice when dividing the plunder.
> For as in the day of Midian's defeat,
> you have shattered the yoke that burdened them,
> the bar across their shoulders, the rod of their oppressor.
> Every warrior's boot used in battle
> and every garment rolled in blood
> will be destined for burning, will be fuel for fire.
> For to us a child is born, to us a son is given
> and the government will be on his shoulders.
> And he will be called
> Wonderful Counselor, Mighty God.
> Everlasting Father, Prince of Peace.
> Of the increase of his government and peace
> there will be no end.
> He will reign on David's throne and over his kingdom,
> establishing and upholding it
> with justice and righteousness

from that time on and forever.
The zeal of the Lord Almighty will accomplish this.

Isaiah 9:2-7

No doubt much of this is familiar to us from Handel's "Messiah." It speaks of Jesus, the carpenter of Nazareth, who began his ministry by the Sea of Galilee. Through the coastal lands of Palestine, called the *Shepelah*, runs an ancient road, which the Romans called *Via Mara*, the "Way of the Sea." After the Jews returned from the Babylonian captivity, they established a city on that road near the Sea of Galilee, which they called Capernaum, the City of Nahum. Jesus made it his headquarter. He did not establish himself in Jerusalem, that isolated fastness in the Judean mountains, but on the cross road of the ancient world.

The message of Isaiah was about the Messiah, the great teacher who was the Mighty God, the author of eternal life; about the peace and hope he would usher in. It had nothing to do with calamities. That was the promise of the faraway future. As for his own generation, Isaiah pronounced doom upon Israel. Because the nation was ungodly and evil, God would send judgment. The prophet compared wickedness with a forest fire that would consume the nation. It did not involve a conflagration, as Velikovsky thought. Rather Israel provoked God to anger with unjust laws that deprived the poor of their rights and robbed people of justice. God ordained punishment, but it was primarily through the military might of Assyria. The prophecy that follows has serious implications. It speaks of the sovereignty of God - and how the Assyrian army would be annihilated, suddenly and disastrously.

The Assyrian

When Isaiah was commissioned to be a prophet, he learned that the future of his nation was one of punishment and hope. That is the theme of his book. His prophecies are exact; they speak of an Assyrian invasion that would come to a disastrous end. Through it all, the Lord was in command.

> Woe to the Assyrian, the rod of my anger,
> in whose hand is the club of my wrath!
> I send him against a godless nation,
> I dispatch him against a people who anger me,
> to seize loot and snatch plunder,
> and to trample them down like mud in the streets.
>
> But this is not what *he* intends,
> this is not what *he* has in mind,
> *his* purpose is to destroy,
> to put an end to many nations.
> "Are not my commanders all kings", he says,
> "Has not Calno fared like Carchemish,
> Is not Hamath like Arpad, and Samaria like Damascus?
> As my hand seized the kingdoms of the idols,
> kingdoms whose images excelled
> those of Jerusalem and Samaria -
> shall I not deal with Jerusalem and her images
> as I dealt with Samaria and her idols?"
> Isaiah 10:5-11

This may come as a surprise to those who believe in the sovereignty of man, but well, er, God does not need us. He is able to use the intent of men and nations for his purposes, even if that intent is evil. He knows what they think and for that matter what they will think, and holds them responsible. It sheds a rather different light on the character of God. He is not at all the well-meaning but ineffectual grandpa up there that so many people imagine him to be. God is not tame. He is "God the Father, Almighty," not god the sucker, incompetent. He not only has the ability to ordain all things, he also has the power to implement it. He does exactly as he pleases, but it should be understood that his purposes are always righteous and never capricious.

No doubt there are those who object that pagan nations, too, credit their deities with supreme authority. Yes indeed. But which of these gods foretold events with perfect accuracy? They were always credited after the fact. Only the God of Israel revealed his decrees in plain language and what he said, that is what happened. In this case the awful fate of "the Assyrian" is being foretold. Having inflicted punishment upon Judah, the Lord would turn around and wreak havoc upon the instrument of his anger. The reason is given. The unwitting club of God's wrath thought himself borderline divine.

> Does the axe raise itself above him who swings it,
> or the saw boast against him who uses it?
> As if a rod were to wield him who lifts it up,
> or a club brandish him who is not wood!
> Therefore the Lord, the LORD Almighty,
> will send a wasting disease upon his sturdy warriors;
> under his pomp a fire will be kindled like a blazing flame.
> The Light of Israel will become a fire,
> their Holy One a flame;
> in a single day it will burn and consume
> his thorns and his briers.
> The splendor of his forest and fertile fields
> it will completely destroy,
> as when a sick man wastes away.
> And the remaining trees of his forest will be so few
> that a child could write them down.
> Isaiah 10:15-19

The Assyrian army in a single day would receive due punishment; they would die a fiery death. Isaiah compared the army with a forest that would be so utterly ruined that only a few trees would remain. The meaning is clear; only a few Assyrians would survive the onslaught. The Lord told his people not to fear the enemy, although humanly speaking they had every reason to. Assyria was guilty of unspeakable atrocities. They left bas-reliefs that show Assyrian kings sticking hooks through the nose of defenseless prisoners and then gouge their eyes out. A favorite method of execution was smashing prisoners of war through spiked poles. Because of this, the Lord promised to direct his wrath to their destruction.

> The LORD Almighty will lash them with a whip,
> as when he struck down Midian at the rock of Oreb;
> and he will raise his rod over the waters as he did in Egypt.
> In that day their burden will be lifted from your shoulders,
> their yoke from your neck;
> the yoke will be broken
> because you have grown so fat.
> Isaiah 10:26, 27

Obviously this is a word picture that speaks of deliverance. A ruthless oppressor would be annihilated; a burden removed from Judah's shoulders. It definitely does not speak of a natural disaster, as Velikovsky thought. The same thing could be said of his assertion that "He shall shake his hand (sign) against —- the hill of Jerusalem" (10:32) refers to a celestial portent.[6] Rather Isaiah was speaking of a future Assyrian campaign. He said where the army would travel and that they would threaten Jerusalem from a place called Nob, on the Mount of Olives.

> They enter Aiath, they pass through Migron;
> they store supplies at Micmash.
> They go over the pass and say,
> "We will camp overnight at Geba."
> Raman trembles; Gibeah of Saul flees.
> Cry out, O daughter of Gallim!
> Listen O Laishah! Poor Ananoth!
> Madmenah is in flight;
> the people of Gebim take cover.

This day they will halt at Nob;
they will shake their fist
At the mount of the daughter of Zion,
at the hill of Jerusalem.
                    Isaiah 10:28-32

The Stump

Isaiah now uses a wonderful poetic device, similar to that, used in the operas of Richard Wagner. Wagner had a marvelous ability to seamlessly make his music flow into different scenes. Isaiah does the same thing. He previously compared the Assyrian army with a forest that would be cut, which refers to the transcendent vision of the Lord who said, "The holy seed will be the stump in the land." Nations were cut down like forests, but something miraculous would happen to the stump of Judah.

> See, the Lord, the LORD Almighty,
> will lop off the boughs with great power.
> The lofty trees will be felled,
> the tall ones will be brought low.
> He will cut down the forest thickets with an axe;
> Lebanon will fall before the Mighty One.
>
> A shoot will come up from the stump of Jesse;
> from his roots a Branch will bear fruit.
> The Spirit of the LORD will rest on him -
> the Spirit of wisdom and of understanding,
> the Spirit of counsel and of power,
> the Spirit of knowledge and of the fear of the Lord.
>
> He will not judge by what he sees with his eyes,
> or decide by what he hears with his ears;
> but with righteousness
> he will judge the needy,

with justice he will give decisions
for the poor of the earth.
He will strike the earth with the rod of his mouth;
with the breath of his lips he will slay the wicked.
Righteousness will be his belt
and faithfulness the sash around his waist.
Isaiah 10:33, 34, and 11:1-5

The Hebrews thought concrete; they liked to paint graphic word pictures. We can almost see the nation of Israel cut down like a forest. But then the stump of one of the felled trees brought forth a shoot. It was the stump from the tree of Jesse, the father of King David. From his family the real David, the Messianic king would come. We recall how Samuel anointed David with oil from a ram's horn. His kingdom was a lasting kingdom. The Messiah would come from the line of David. He is called the Branch that came from that miraculously revived tree, and is described as a perfect man, endowed with the sevenfold Spirit of God. In the Old Testament, oil was symbolic of the Holy Spirit. God bestowed his Spirit upon the anointed king or priest in some fashion, but the Messiah possessed the Spirit without limit.

The Messianic kingdom he inaugurates is ideal in the sense that it brings men and nations close to God. It ushers in an age where men are at peace with God and themselves. In the context of the vision it is evident that the age Isaiah envisions is one of spiritual blessings, one that is not limited to the nation of Israel. We should keep in mind that the world of the prophets was different from ours. Israel was God's chosen people. Yet here already we see glimpses of an age where that would change. In the Messianic age the gentiles would be part of Israel. The references to dried out seas and rivers have nothing to do with catastrophes. God removed obstacles to gather the new Israel around the banner of the Messiah.

Joshua

When Isaiah spoke of felled trees, a stump, a branch and dried-out rivers, he used metaphors to predict the coming of a real man, the Messiah, who would reconcile God to man. It is only reasonable to ask ourselves, what is literal and what is a metaphor? That depends on the context. In this case it deals with spiritual realities. We can know this for sure from the song of praise that follows.

> In that day you will say:
> "I will praise you, O LORD.
> Although you were angry with me,
> your anger has turned away
> and you have comforted me.
> Surely God is my salvation;
> I will trust and not be afraid.
> The LORD, the LORD
> is my strength and my song;
> he has become my salvation."
> With joy you will draw water
> from the wells of salvation.
> Isaiah 12:1-3

The Hebrew uses a play on words that is most interesting, something we really should know. It involves the expression "my salvation." It goes back to the time of the exodus, when Moses sent out twelve spies to explore the Promised Land. One of these was Hoshea, the son of Nun; but Moses changed his name to Joshua. (Numbers 13:16) Hoshea means "salvation," but Moses made a slight change, he added the name of the Lord, "Yahweh," which rendered his name "Yahweh's salvation." Joshua, or the Aramaic Yeshua, has been translated into the Greek as "Iesus," from which we derive the name "Jesus." We might add that "Isaiah" (Salvation of Yahweh) is a variant of "Joshua." This expression appears more than a hundred times in the Old Testament, always in a Messianic context. This is one of the reasons why we maintain that Jesus is the Messiah. The Greek word for "Messiah" is Kristos, (in Latin, Christus), whence we derive the Anglicized "Christ." Jesus, in other words, is the Messiah, the Kristos, the Christ.

When Isaiah said, "surely, God is my salvation," he was speaking of Joshua - Jesus. The water that is drawn from the wells of salvation is the life giving Holy Spirit. Scripture uses the name of Joshua in fascinating and revealing ways. In the story setting of the conquest of Canaan, it was not Moses who led the people into the Promised Land, but Joshua. Moses received the law on mount Horeb, and that is what he represents, the law. But the law does not save us, it can only show us our failures. Moses was allowed to see the Promised Land. The law does that; it points forward to salvation, just as Moses named Joshua. It is under the leadership of Joshua, Jesus, that we enter the real Promised Land, heaven. There is no other way.

The Nations

In his eagerness to prove recurring disasters, Velikovsky found proof texts with little or no regard for the context. That is a dangerous thing to do. These messages often are not concerned with catastrophic events and actually have a totally different meaning. So far Isaiah addressed himself to Israel, but at this point he looks beyond the borders. The first oracle concerns Babylon, still part of greater Assyria, but later the Capitol of the Chaldeans. This prophecy is highly interesting, because it combines a number of things. It speaks of the ultimate destruction of Babylon by the hands of the Medes, but included is a remarkable prediction that sounds very much like a cosmic catastrophe.

> Raise a banner on a bare hilltop,
> shout to them; beckon to them
> to enter the gates of the nobles.
> I have commanded my holy ones;
> I have summoned my warriors to carry out my wrath -

those who rejoice in my triumph.
Listen, a noise on the mountains,
like that of a great multitude
Listen, an uproar among the kingdoms,
like nations massing together!
The Lord Almighty is mustering an army for war.
They come from faraway lands,
from the ends of the heavens -
the Lord and the weapons of his wrath -
to destroy the whole country.
Isaiah 13:2-5

Considering that this is addressed to Babylon, it certainly means that the faraway Medes, mentioned later, would come to attack the Chaldeans. This happened 539 B.C. On the other hand the "day of the Lord" is described in terms that are clearly universal. It applies to the whole earth. There appears to be a dual application. The Lord summoned "Ariz", the "consecrated ones" to carry out his wrath. Who were they? The Medes, eventually, but considering what follows it could mean something else as well. "Ariz" is variously translated as *Consecrated ones* or *Terrible ones*. "Terror will seize them." (Vs 8) Humanity would be terrified.

See, the day of the Lord is coming -
a cruel day, with wrath and fierce anger -
to make the land desolate
and destroy the sinners within it.
The stars of heaven and their constellations
will not show their light.
The rising sun will be darkened
and the moon will not give its light.
I will punish the world for its evil,
the wicked for their sins.
I will put an end to the arrogance of the haughty
and will humble the pride of the ruthless.

> I will make man scarcer than pure gold,
> more rare than the gold of Ophir.
> Therefore I will make the heavens tremble;
> and the earth will shake from its place
> at the wrath of the Lord Almighty
> in the day of his burning anger.
>
> Isaiah 13:9-13

Near and Far

Certainly, more than the fall of Babylon is involved here. That was two hundred years in the future, and of no immediate concern. But how could anyone be sure this would actually happen? The answer was provided for at the time of the exodus. When God spoke the Ten Commandments, the people were frightened, and they asked Moses to speak for God. Moses was regarded to be the first and the greatest prophet (Deut 5:23-26). But more prophets were to follow and human nature being what it is, false prophets were sure to come.

By what standard would the people be able to judge whether a prophet was from God? There were two conditions. The prophet must give a miraculous sign or a short-term prediction that must come true, and even if that happened, (it could have been a trick or a lucky guess), his message must agree with what had already been revealed, that is with the Law of Moses.

The prophecy about Babylon is such a prediction. Mankind would be terrified by a fearful upheaval of nature. The sun in its forenoon position would be darkened, yet in the premature night the moon and stars would not be visible. The earth would shake and be moved out of its wonted place, and the heavens would be affected. Amos, who prophesied 752 B.C., two years before the "raash," was even more direct. In Judah, the religion of the holy God was a sham, trodden underfoot by a cheating people.

> "Will not the land tremble for this,
> and all who live in it mourn?

The whole land will rise like the Nile;
it will be stirred up and then sink
like the river of Egypt."
"In that day," declares the sovereign Lord,
"I will make the sun go down at noon
and darken the earth in broad daylight.
I will turn your religious feasts into mourning
and all your singing into weeping.
I will make all of you wear sackcloth
and shave your heads.
I will make that time like mourning for an only son
and the end of it like a bitter day."

Amos 8:8-10

There are several references to just such an event. As we have seen, Jewish tradition reports that the sun suddenly disappeared on the day of king Ahaz' burial. "On the day of the dead king's funeral daylight lasted but two hours, and his body had to be interred when the earth was enveloped in darkness." [7] It has all the marks of an eye witness account. Greek authors mentioned something very similar. Zeus "turned midday into night, hiding the light of the dazzling sun, and sore fear came upon men." [8]

Records of strange natural events such as these were recorded in myths and plays. The Stoic Seneca describes it in his tragedy, Thyestes. As the result of a horrendous crime, "unnatural darkness has settled over the world," and the chorus (the people of Mycenae) asks the sun,

> Whither, O father of the lands and skies, before whose rising thick night with all her glories flees, whither dost turn thy course and why dost blot out the day in mid-Olympus? (Mid-day) Why, O Phoebus dost snatch away thy face? Not yet does Vesper, twilight's messenger, summon the fires of night; - the ploughman with oxen yet unwearied stands amazed at his supper-hours quick coming. What has driven thee from the heavenly course?

No stars come out; the heavens gleam not with any fires: no moon dispels the darkness' heavy pall.–
But whatever this may be, would that night were here! Trembling, trembling are our hearts, sore smit with fear, lest all things fall shattered in fatal ruin and once more gods and men be overwhelmed by formless chaos. –
Have we of all mankind been deemed deserving that heaven, its poles uptorn, should overwhelm us? In our time has the last day come? Alas for us, by bitter fate begotten, to misery doomed, whether we have lost the sun or banished it! [9]

This poetry is far too vivid to have come from a fertile imagination. It has the ring of truth. It is an echo of terrifying historical event that left mankind in fear and dread. They thought the world was coming to an end. This was not a solar eclipse, the sun failed to return altogether. It was a global disaster; the stars were displaced. Seneca specifically mentions the Zodiac as being utterly derailed. The language is nearly identical to that of Isaiah; the moon and stars were not visible, and humanity was gripped with fear.

It is fair to say that the short term prediction of Isaiah and the dire warning of Amos were fulfilled the day King Ahaz died, 715 B.C. What would cause the sun to disappear at midday? The luminary did not hasten forward; rather it has all the makings of a solar eclipse. The problem is that the sun did not re-appear.

Then what could have blotted out sunlight instantaneously and that at noon? As we shall have occasion to see, it is possible that Mars once was nearer to the sun than it is now but was forced away, and approached the earth. It came close enough to cause an extended eclipse. Unlike the Moon, which circles the earth, a planet such as Mars would run parallel, which would make an eclipse last much longer. A near-approach like that would tilt the earth's axis, which would account for the sudden displacement of the stars. It certainly would create high tides and earthquakes, and probably result in planetary discharges. Of course sun dials would be affected, as happened to the sun dial of Ahaz. Both planets were wrapped in a plasma sheath, which evidently blocked the light of the moon and stars. The overall effect would be fearful indeed. [10]

Isaiah goes on to mention war and migrations of nations; who would eventually capture Babylon, and what would happen to what until then was the eternal city.

> See, I will stir up against them the Medes,
> who do not care for silver
> and have no delight in gold.
> Their bows will strike down the young men;
> they will have no mercy on infants
> nor will they look with compassion on children.
> Babylon, the jewel of kingdoms,
> the glory of the Chaldean's pride,
> will be overthrown by God like Sodom and Gomorrah.
> She will never be inhabited or lived in
> through all generations;
> no Arab will pitch his tent there,
> no shepherd will rest his flocks there.
> But desert creatures will lie there,
> jackals will fill her houses, there the owls will dwell.
> and there the wild goats will leap about.
> Hyenas will howl in her strongholds,
> jackals in her luxurious palaces.
> Her time is at hand, and her days will not be prolonged.
>
> Isaiah 13:17-22

Meredoch-baladan the Chaldean at that time ruled Babylon and eight hundred cities. Until then it was the religious capitol of the Assyrian empire. The prediction that the Medes, hundreds of miles away, would eventually conquer the Chaldean capitol would seem incredible. Yet that is just what happened. It was Nebopolassar and Nebuchadnezzar who rebuilt Babylon during the end of the Seventh, and the beginning of the Sixth Century B.C. It was taken by the Medo-Persians in 539 B.C., and the decay began. Its doom was sure. Babylon died a slow death; by the time of Christ it had become a desert. Forty-five miles south of Baghdad lie the desolate ruins of Babylon. It is uninhabited, an empty waste. The Bedouins refuse to pitch their tents because they fear evil spirits inhabit the ruins, nor do sheep graze there. The soil does not grow suitable vegetation. Jackals skulk the ruins for food, flocks of owls soar overhead, goats abound and the roar of the lion is heard. It is a dead city, avoided even by tourists. As if that was not enough, Isaiah predicted Babylon would become a swamp.

> "I will turn her into a place for owls
> and into a swampland;
> I will sweep her with the broom of destruction,"
> declares the Lord Almighty.
> Isaiah 14:23

According to the *Encyclopedia Britannica*, "A large part of the old city buried under a deep bed of silt remains to be found, and the Babylon of Hammurabi, of which only the slenderest traces have been detected, now lies beneath the water table." Babylon is a huge swamp. The ancient irrigation canals were neglected and the rivers overflowed, covering the larger part of the city. [11]

One wonders, why this utter devastation? And how could Isaiah predict these things with such accuracy, many centuries before it came true? Babylon, like Thebes and Nineveh, was a temple city, religious places of prostitution. It stood for everything that opposed the One holy God, Yahweh. Its religion was at the core humanism, which believes man to be an exalted animal and treats him accordingly, like an animal. This could not be tolerated by Him who "works out everything for his own ends - even the wicked for a day of disaster" (Proverbs 16:4), and these cities became ruins, never to be inhabited again. It is also a silent testimony to us who before our very eyes see irrefutable evidence of a divine decree carried out to perfection. Prophecy was not intended for Israel and Judah alone. It was also meant to assure those who saw the results, that an Almighty God rules.

Isaiah clearly foresaw the threat of Babylon, long before it ascended to a position of power. But in his time Assyria imperiled Judah, and so he returned to the theme he had sounded before; the Lord would remove the burden from his people. It would happen close to home, on the mountains of Israel, and there is even a hint about the agency involved.

> The Lord Almighty has sworn,
> "Surely, as I have purposed, so it will stand.
> I will crush the Assyrian in my land;
> on my mountains I will trample him down.
> His yoke will be taken from my people,
> and his burden removed from their shoulders."
> This is the plan determined for the whole world;
> this is the hand stretched out over all nations.
> For the Lord Almighty has purposed, and who can thwart him?
> His hand is stretched out, and who can turn it back?
>
> Isaiah 14:24-27

Isaiah's predictions became increasingly detailed. The Assyrian would be wiped out, yes, but where and how? It could have been by an enemy in battle. Not so. It would be on the mountains of Israel, and it involved something that had worldwide implications. The hand of God was stretched out over the nations. The word "Yad," translated hand, can also mean sign. Obviously this is a figure of speech. Either way, the implication is that the nations witnessed something dreadful that could not be thwarted; something that one day would destroy the Assyrian. Velikovsky reasoned that the word "Ariz," the "Terrible ones," may have been adopted by the Greek as "Ares," or the planet Mars. That is possible, but not certain. [12]

Dreams and Visions

We should be careful not to read things into the visions of Isaiah it does not say. This is the case, for instance with the "oracle concerning the Valley of Vision." Jerusalem is surrounded by mountains; it is built on three hills and it has valleys. The "Valley of Vision" therefore is the vision as seen from the valleys of Jerusalem. Isaiah spoke of something that would happen in the future.

> What troubles you now,
> that you have all gone up on the housetops,
> O town full of commotion,
> O city of tumult and revelry?
> Your slain were not killed by the sword,
> nor did they die in battle.
> All your leaders have fled together;
> they have been captured without using the bow.
> All you who were caught were taken prisoner together,
> having fled while the enemy was still far away.
> Isaiah 22:1-4

Velikovsky thought, "Nervous tension grew with the approach of the 'appointed time,' and a rumor sufficed to drive the population of the cities to the housetops." This is on the whole very unlikely. The vision speaks of war and capture, not of a menace in the sky. Besides, it speaks of things to come, not of something that was actually happening.

> The Lord, the Lord Almighty,
> has a day of tumult and trampling and terror
> in the Valley of Vision,
> a day of battering down walls
> and of crying out to the mountains.
> Elam takes up the quiver,
> with her charioteers and horses;
> Kir uncovers the shield.
> Your choicest valleys are full of chariots,
> and horsemen are posted at the city gates;
> the defenses of Judah are stripped away.
> Isaiah 22:5-8

This vision describes the terror of the people of Jerusalem hastening to their house tops only to helplessly see an invincible army arrive. It happened to some extent 701 B.C., when Sennacherib invaded Judah. But the reference to the Persians of Elam and their subject warriors of Kir, points to the siege of Jerusalem 589-587 B.C. The Babylonians starved the city, and when the doors were finally thrown open the leaders had left, only to be captured later. We might add that references in Joel, Micah and Amos to fire and darkness do not necessarily speak of natural catastrophes. A straightforward reading implies the horrors of a military campaign, an exaggeration of speech to emphasize God's power and an allusion to spiritual darkness.

What about the prophecies of Joel? He does have rather unusual things to say. The first chapter without a doubt deals with a plague of locusts that stripped the land bare. The second chapter goes beyond that. It describes something that might be described as an attack of super locusts, only they were not locusts. We shall deal with that later. Following this comes a call for repentance and the promises of healing, and it is in this context that Joel speaks of wonders in the sky and on the earth.

> And afterward,
> I will pour out my Spirit on all people.
> Your sons and daughters will prophesy,
> your old men will dream dreams,
> your young men will see visions.
> Even on my servants, both men and women,
> I will pour out my Spirit in those days.
> I will show wonders in the heavens and on the earth,
> blood and fire and billows of smoke.
> The sun will be turned to darkness
> and the moon to blood
> before the coming of the great and dreadful day of the Lord.
> And everyone who calls on the name of the Lord will be saved;
> for on Mount Zion and in Jerusalem there will be deliverance,

as the Lord has said, among the survivors whom the Lord calls.

Joel 2:28-32

Now we know for a fact that this has nothing to do with a darkening of the sun and the moon in the days of Joel. The prophet specifically said that this would happen later, which it did, when Jesus was crucified and after his resurrection, with Pentecost. When Jesus was hanging on the cross, something very strange happened. About the sixth hour (noon) "darkness came over the whole land until the ninth hour, for the sun stopped shining." (Luke 23:44-45). It could not have been a eclipse, because the timing of the Passover festival renders that impossible, which leaves two options. Either it was something supernatural or a planetary body the size of Mercury moved between the sun and the earth, which would provide and explanation for the earthquakes that struck. Considering that it happened at that time and in that place, this must be considered equally supernatural.

Two months later, when the day of Pentecost came, the followers of a resurrected and ascended Jesus were together when the roar of a tornado-like wind filled their house and tongues of fire dispersed over their heads. The apostle Peter explained what had happened: the prophecy of Joel had been fulfilled (Acts 2), God poured his Spirit upon the believers. How much of Joel's prophecy applies to the crucifixion and how much to Pentecost is a matter, not discussed here.

Time Portal

At this point Velikovsky believed all these prophecies were fulfilled. "Amid the catastrophe Isaiah raised his voice: 'Fear, and the pit and the snare (pitch) are upon thee, O inhabitant of the earth." --- The catastrophe came on the day on which King Ahaz was buried."[13] We recall that on that day the sun disappeared.

Yes, that sounds all very dramatic. Unfortunately it is also very mistaken. The words of Isaiah quoted by Velikovsky were prophetic and not a report of current events. The prophecy is remarkable because it is truly worldwide in scope, and it speaks of a catastrophe that was going to affect the whole earth.

> See, the Lord is going to lay waste the earth
> and devastate it;
> he will ruin its face
> and scatter its inhabitants -
> It will be the same
> for priest as for people,
> for master as for servant,
> for mistress as for maid
> for seller as for buyer,
> for borrower as for lender
> for debtor as for creditor.
> The earth will be completely laid waste
> and totally plundered.
> The Lord has spoken this word.
> Isaiah 24:1-3

There can be no doubt about it; this is a prediction. It speaks of a global catastrophe, something that was about to affect the whole earth and everyone in it, without exception. God would ruin the earth and scatter mankind. There are compelling reasons to believe this happened 701 B.C., although part of what follows points forward to end times. Isaiah saw from afar. When we look at distant mountain ranges they seem to flow into each other, when in reality they are many miles apart. When the prophets of Israel and Judah saw a glimpse of the future, they could not always tell true distance in time.

Isaiah now introduces a very interesting poetic device. Until now he had always said, "In that day you will say," after which he quotes people as speaking. But now he skips this phrase altogether, and speaks as if he sees it happening, in the present tense. It has a three dimensional effect, almost as if he walks through a time portal and finds himself in the future.

> The earth dries up and withers,
> the world languishes and withers,
> the exalted of the earth languish.
> The earth is defiled by its people;
> they have disobeyed the laws, violated the statues
> and broken the everlasting covenant.
> Therefore a curse consumes the earth;
> its people must bear their guilt.
> Therefore earth's inhabitants are burned up,
> and very few are left.
>
> Isaiah 24:4-6

This was not the first time Isaiah spoke out against ecological damage, done to God's creation, but this time it was on a truly global scale. It was no light matter either, for the prophet spoke of cities being devastated.

> The ruined city lies desolate;
> the entrance to every house is barred.
> In the streets they cry out for wine; all joy turns to gloom,
> all gaiety is banished from the earth.
> The city is left in ruins, its gate is battered to pieces.
> So will it be on the earth and among the nations,
> as when an olive tree is beaten,
> or as when gleanings are left after the grape harvest.
>
> Isaiah 24:10-13

If anyone doubts the prophetic nature of this vision, "So will it be on the earth," makes it very clear that this is in the future. It also states quite clearly that a global catastrophe is being forecast. Something terrifying was about to happen, something inescapable.

> Terror and pit and snare await you,
> O people of the earth.
> Whoever flees at the sound of terror will fall into a pit;

whoever climbs out of the pit will be caught in a snare.
The floodgates of the heavens are opened,
the foundations of the earth shake.
The earth is broken up, the earth is split asunder
the earth is thoroughly shaken.
The earth reels like a drunkard, it sways like a hut in the wind;
so heavy upon it is the guilt of its rebellion
that it falls - never to rise again.
Isaiah 24:17-20

Scatter its Inhabitants

It cannot possibly be maintained that this deals exclusively with the end of the world. Isaiah said the Lord would devastate the earth and "scatter its inhabitants." When the world comes to an end there will be no time left for anyone to be scattered. But it did happen about 700 B.C. This is not to deny that the prophecy deals in part with the final judgment. Here, too, we see a blending of faraway horizons, the seeming fusion of distant events. Justice will be served, rebellion put down eventually; but not yet. All the same, disaster loomed.

> In that day the Lord will punish
> the powers in the heavens above
> and the kings on the earth below.
> They will be herded together
> like prisoners bound in a dungeon;
> they will be shut up in prison
> and be punished after many days.
> The moon will be abashed, the sun ashamed;
> for the Lord Almighty will reign
> on Mount Zion and in Jerusalem,
> and before its elders, gloriously.
> Isaiah 24:21-23

The Assyrian and the Passover

Isaiah throughout speaks of an imminent catastrophe that is a model of the judgment day. We can only guess what will happen then, but it would appear to be something similar to what happened in the days of Isaiah. But that also means that dramatic events did happen on a global scale. It is also of considerable interest that Isaiah spoke of "the nations," not merely as the eastern empires, but also the peoples from the west.

This shift in orientation is quite evident in Isaiah, the reason being that western influence was on the rise. Great migrations happened at that time. Humanity was scattered; the populations of devastated nations roamed throughout the earth. The same pattern appears everywhere. Cities were ruined by earthquakes, burned by fire. Populations fled, new nations evolved. The foundations were laid for the Greek and Roman civilizations. It is against this scene of devastation, death and ruin, that Isaiah proclaims the hope of everlasting glory, the resurrection of the dead.

> But your dead will live;
> their bodies will rise.
> You who dwell in the dust,
> wake and shout for joy.
> Your dew is like the dew of the morning;
> the earth will give birth to her dead.
> Go my people, enter your rooms
> and shut the doors behind you;
> hide yourselves for a little while
> until his wrath has passed by.
> See, the Lord is coming out of his dwelling
> to punish the people of the earth for their sins.
> The earth will disclose the blood shed upon her;
> she will conceal her slain no longer.
> Isaiah 26:19-21

There can be no doubt that this deals with eschatology (the doctrine of the last things), and it states explicitly that there will be a resurrection from the dead, just as it says that the Lord "will swallow up death forever" (25:8). Even now death is a beaten enemy. Whatever the meaning of the order to "enter your rooms and shut the doors behind you," it would make a great deal of sense if the potential for doom was present in that generation. It will find its ultimate fulfillment in the last days. Something of the kind is implied in the "woe" to Ephraim that follows. It speaks of Samaria, the Capitol city of Ephraim as if it were the wreath of a drunken mob. Ephraim, the chief of the ten tribes, much more powerful than Judah, would be destroyed.

Invincible

> See, the Lord has one who is powerful and strong.
> Like a hailstorm and a destructive wind,
> like a driving rain and a flooding downpour,
> he will throw it forcefully to the ground.
> That wreath, the pride of Ephraim's drunkards,
> will be trampled underfoot.
> That fading flower, his glorious beauty,
> set on the head of a fertile valley,
> will be like a fig ripe before harvest -
> as soon as someone sees it
> and takes it in his hand,
> he swallows it.
>
> Isaiah 28:2-4

Judging from the history of Samaria, the "one who is powerful and strong," was the Assyrian king Piglath-pelizer, who conquered the city -723. With Samaria gone, the Lord would become the beautiful wreath of the remnant of his people, Judah. Only Jerusalem was equally befuddled with wine. The Hebrew mimics drunken stammering. God himself spoke to a people that believed itself invincible merely because they were in Jerusalem, the city of God. They thought they were safe from any harm and could write their own rules, all of it self-serving. Jeremiah ran into a very similar problem (Ch. 7), and Micah spoke of it as well.

> Her leaders judge for a bribe
> her priests teach for a price,
> and her prophets tell fortunes for money.
> Yet they lean upon the Lord and say,
> "Is not the Lord among us?
> No disaster will come upon us."
> Therefore because of you,
> Zion will be plowed like a field.
> Jerusalem will become a heap of rubble,
> the temple hill a mound overgrown with thickets.
>
> Micah 3:11, 12

The threatened judgment came true A.D. 70, when the Romans under Titus stormed Jerusalem and leveled it. The hill where once stood the temple was overgrown with thickets, and the surrounding area was cultivated as a plowing field.[14] The temple was no magic shield. Those who thought they could get away with evil in the city of God would face judgment.

> You boast, "We have entered into a covenant with death,
> with the grave we have made an agreement.
> When an overwhelming scourge sweeps by,
> it cannot touch us,
> for we have made a lie our refuge
> and falsehood our hiding place."
> So this is what the Sovereign Lord says:
> "See, I lay a stone in Zion, a tested stone,
> a precious cornerstone for a sure foundation;
> the one who trusts will never be dismayed.
> I will make justice the measuring line
> and righteousness the plumb line;
> hail will sweep away your refuge, the lie,
> and water will overflow your hiding place.
> Your covenant with death will be annulled;
> your agreement with the grave will not stand.

> When the overwhelming scourge sweeps by,
> you will be beaten down by it.
> As often as it comes it will carry you away;
> morning after morning,
> by day and by night,
> it will sweep through."
>
> Isaiah 28:15-19

Wishful thinking cannot stand in the face of reality, and self-will vanishes in the presence of the Almighty. God had different ideas. The vain plans of the nation that ignored him notwithstanding, the Lord graciously gave a messianic promise of bedrock certainty. The coming Messiah would be the plumb line of truth and justice. Everything man-made, such as Israel's covenant with death, would be swept away.

In all fairness to the Jews, they were not the only ones to do their own thing. It is a familiar problem. Man has a tendency to reject the objective standard of God, which is external to him. He would much rather go by his own, subjective notions, which are invariably self-serving. I, man, master. The result is anarchy, followed by tyranny, increasing evil, moral and mental disorientation, a society that comes apart at the seams. That is how the ten tribes of Israel lost their religious and national identity, and Judah was not far behind.

Scourge

What must we think of the "overwhelming scourge," that would sweep by? A scourge, according to Webster, is "a grievous affliction, one who or that which inflicts pain, or devastates country." And this one would be overwhelming to boot. A straightforward reading of the text leads one to believe that this scourge was a natural, rather than a military affliction. In fact, it sounds like an atmospheric disturbance of sorts. It would be a recurring disaster that lasted several days. That hardly fits a military incursion or a siege, or even an enemy occupation. That often lasted years, not days. There must have been something highly significant about this prophecy, something that was clearly understood by its audience, something really scary.

> The understanding of this message
> will bring sheer terror.
> The bed is too short to stretch out on,
> the blanket too narrow to wrap around you.
> The Lord will rise up
> as he did at Mount Perazim,
> he will rouse himself
> as in the Valley of Gibeon -
> to do his work, his strange work,
> and perform his task, his alien task
> Now stop your mocking,
> or your chains will become heavier;
> The Lord, the Lord Almighty, has told me
> of the destruction decreed against the whole land.
>
> Isa 28:19-22

Without question, the prospect of this scourge that would sweep by inspired sheer terror. There was no escaping the unpleasant consequences. The references to Perazim and the Valley of Gibeon are instructive. The story of Mount Perazim is related in 2 Samuel 5:17-20. There the Lord "broke out" like a flood against the Philistines who came to battle David. The Lord gave David the victory. In the story that followed he "broke out" against Uzza, who touched the Ark of the Covenant, Uzza being one of the Levites in charge of carrying the Ark.

The implication is that God was about to "break out" again, this time against the scoffers in Jerusalem. What happened in the Valley of Gibeon? It was there that the miracle of Joshua occurred. The sun was arrested in its path and delayed going down by almost a whole day. That was the "strange work" the Lord would perform. It fits an overall pattern, unique to this century. Both historical events and prophetic utterance deal with unusual natural disasters that terrified humanity.

Strange Work

Scripture records in an understated manner that the day was lengthened when Hezekiah was deathly ill, during the Assyrian campaign of -701. It was then that the shadow moved back ten steps on the stairway of Ahaz. Since the shadow is cast by the sun, it follows that the sun made a retrograde move. It must have been a fearful sight to suddenly see the luminary move backward, toward the east, stop after several hours and then move forward again. An extended day like that certainly qualifies as a "strange work." The stoic Seneca, mentioned before, in his play Thyestes speaks of the sun disappearing from the morning sky, and of the fear this inspired. Greece is west of Israel, therefore late morning in Israel would be early morning in Greece; in Greece this event would occur earlier in the day. [15]

According to Velikovsky's theory this happened because the planet Mars had a close brush with the earth. If that was the case, the earth must have overtaken Mars. The visual effect would be that of Mars growing rapidly in size in a matter of weeks. It must have been clearly visible in the night sky, and close enough to see its two moons, small though they are. Homer, in the Iliad, said that Mars had two steeds that drew his chariot. They were known as Phobos (Terror) and Deimos (Rout). Virgil mentioned them as well. The two moons of Mars are called by those names. Jonathan Swift wrote in Gulliver's Travels, "They have likewise discovered two lesser stars, or satellites, which revolve about Mars; whereof the innermost is distant from the centre of the primary planet exactly three of the diameters, and the outermost five; the former revolves in the space of ten hours, and the latter in twenty one and a half."[16] Fifty years later, in 1877, Hall finally discovered the two satellites of Mars. It is unlikely that Swift made a lucky guess; it is more likely that he read about them in ancient manuscripts.

That is not all. Velikovsky theorized that Mars was thrown out of orbit in a near-encounter with Venus. He thought Mars picked up debris from Venus' cometary tail. This is unlikely. Mars may have suffered planetary discharges instead, that threw some of its soil into orbit. It is possible that bands of meteorites, mixed with gases, gravel and dust swarmed around the planet. Seen from the earth, it looked as if troops followed Mars. Others circled the planet, and when Mars approached the earth, these meteorites looked like twisting furies; they terrified the peoples of the earth. [17]

Joel

The book of Joel, mentioned before, is of particular interest. The first chapter speaks of an invasion of locusts, although there are hints of something worse. The language of Joel is in many ways very similar to Isaiah 24. No doubt the nation had been devastated by swarms of locusts, so dense that the sky was darkened. The prophet mentions something else as well.

> To you, O Lord, I call,
> for fire has devoured the open pastures
> and flames have burned up all the trees in the field.
> Even the wild animals pant for you;
> the streams of water have dried up
> and fire has devoured the open pastures.
> Joel 1:19-20

How could locusts cause pastures to be burned and streams to be dried up? Something else is involved here. No doubt there had been a plague of locusts, but worse was to come. Joel called for repentance because "the day of the Lord" was coming: "What a dreadful day! For the day of the Lord is near; it will come like a destruction from the Almighty." (1:15) He then describes the coming devastation.

Blow the trumpet in Zion;
sound the alarm on my holy hill.
let all who live in the land tremble,
for the day of the Lord is coming.
It is close at hand -
a day of darkness and gloom,
a day of clouds and blackness.
Like dawn spreading across the mountains
a large and mighty army comes,
such as never was of old
nor ever will be in ages to come.
                    Joel 2:1-2

It is certain from this and what follows that Joel was not speaking of a human army. No army ever came across the mountains, that was impossible. Armies came from the coastal plains. There had never been an army that large, nor would there ever be anything like it in the future. There have since been armies that dwarf those of Joel's days. But they are no match for what is described here; and they could not possibly be locusts. Joel's language is too powerful for that.

Before them fire devours, behind them a flame blazes.
Before them the land is like the Garden of Eden,
behind them, a desert waste - nothing escapes them.
They have the appearance of horses;
they gallop along like cavalry.
With a noise like that of chariots
they leap over the mountain tops,
like a crackling fire consuming stubble,
like a mighty army drawn up for battle.
At the sight of them, nations are in anguish;
every face turns pale.
They charge like warriors;
they scale walls like soldiers.
They all march in line,
not swerving from their course.

They do not jostle each other;
each marches straight ahead.
They plunge through defenses without breaking ranks.
They rush upon the city;
they run along the wall.
They climb into the houses;
like thieves they enter through the windows.
Before them the earth shakes, the sky trembles,
the sun and moon are darkened,
and the stars no longer shine.
The Lord thunders at the head of his army;
his forces are beyond number,
and mighty are those who obey his command.
The day of the Lord is great; it is dreadful.
Who can endure it?
Joel 2:3-11

The Iliad

Joel was not the first to speak of fields, ravaged by fire. Isaiah said it as well. There is another, unlikely source, that mentions something similar, the Iliad. It is not known when Homer wrote the Iliad. Estimates range from the 12th to the 7th Century B.C., but the world of Homer is that of the 8th to 7th Century B.C. The Iliad is an epic poem, a sort of mythical war novel, filled with gory details of hand to hand combat. It speaks of the battles the Greeks waged against Priam, king of Troy, and of astral deities who resemble comic book characters. They opposed each other according to national deities. Athena was the planet-god Venus, protector of Greece, and necessarily sympathetic. Ares, or Mars, was the patron god of Troy, just as it was the chief god of the Romans.

The role of Ares is relatively minor. He is prominent at the beginning of the war (book 5) and again toward the end (books 20 and 21), but he is much more than merely the antagonist of Athena. Mars is the god of war who threatens mankind. Athena (Venus) was the friend of Hera (Earth). She "caught Ares by the hand and said, 'Ares,

Ares, you mensbane! You bloodthirsty fort-stormer! Why can't we leave Trojans and Achaeans to fight and see which of them Father Zeus will favor?'"

When Athena was gone, Ares joined the Trojans and covered the battle field with darkness. Hera appealed to Zeus: "Father Zeus, have you nothing to say about the violent deeds of Ares?" Whereat Zeus answered, "Go along, do, send Athena on the hunt." Athena, invisible to Ares, battled him and drove a spear through his belly. "Trojans and Achaeans alike trembled to hear the roar of the insatiated war god." Ares complained to Zeus, but Zeus replied, "I hate you more than any other god alive. All you care for is discord and battle and fighting." Hera and Athena returned home, "as soon as they had put an end to the murderous exploits of Ares, the enemy of mankind."

For a people that glorified war, Ares must have stood for something, more than warfare. Ares (Mars) is called "mensbane," meaning the ruin of humanity, a "blood thirsty fort-stormer," the enemy of mankind. That is how Homer regarded Mars, and commentators have often wondered why he would mention the planets the way he did. In the Homeric poems he said that Ares was one of the planets.[18]

The Iliad reflects Greek thinking. The Greek regarded the affairs of man as a shadow of the real thing in heaven, of no concern to the gods. In this case, things on earth may have involved intervention of planet-gods. Around the year -700, give or take a decade, the Phrygians came from southern Russia, and were in turn dispossessed by the Cimmerians. The Archaeans, Mycenaean Greeks, fearful of an invasion of their homeland, attacked Troy to prevent a possible assault by the invaders. Although at first successful, their fleet was wrecked in natural upheavals that also ruined Troy. Who knows, the Trojan War could have occurred at a time when Mars posed a real threat to mankind, and Homer wove it together in myth and poetry.

Ares joined the Trojans in the final battle, and the gods took sides. "The father of men and gods thundered terribly from on high. Poseidon made the solid earth quake beneath, and the tall summits of the hills. Mount Ida shook from head to foot, and the citadel of Iliod trembled, and the Achaean ships. Fear seized Aidoneus the

Lord of the world below." The heavens roared and earthquakes shook the ground.

Earthquakes did destroy Troy in the days of king Priam. This is established by archaeology. Troy is the present day village of Hassilik in Turkey. Claude Scheaffer, who excavated Ras Shamra, noticed that the devastation of Troy was identical and synchronous with that of Ras Shamra in Syria. Violent earth shocks, followed by widespread conflagrations destroyed Troy and civilizations all over the Middle East.

In the 21st book we find striking parallels with the prophecy of Joel. Scamandros, the god of the river, wanted to protect Troy and drown Achilles, because he was a ruthless killer. But Hapshaistos, the god of fire, raised a conflagration that burned the plains and everything around the river. The river began to boil and stopped running. This was followed by great turmoil between the planet-gods. Granted, this is mythology, but it is part of a real war, and the repeated allusions to planetary deities suggest that the planets, particularly Mars, posed an actual threat. [19]

Fire

Joel mentioned something very similar, without mythology. He spoke of fields, pastures and trees being burned by a fire, so intense that even the streams dried up. Where did that fire come from? Both Joel and the Iliad continue with a description of a most unusual battle. It may provide an explanation. According to Joel, the army that came across the mountains was accompanied by a fire that burned everything in its path. It was not limited to Israel; nations were in anguish. The Babylonians were terrified by raging demons that accompanied Nergal (Mars). The Vedic hymns mention the "Maruts" or terrible ones, in language, very similar to that of Joel. Isaiah, as we have seen, foretold the day when God would devastate the earth (Ch 24).

We could explain these phenomena, mentioned by Isaiah, Joel and the Iliad as the result of an encounter with Mars. The dust, gravel, gases and meteorites that accompanied the planet terrified the people of the earth. The sky was darkened; a rain of gravel and meteorites showered the earth. They entered the atmosphere with a roaring din, and flew into defenseless cities and houses. Gases, mixed with gravel, could have caused fires to erupt, although it could have involved planetary discharges as well. Another thing to be considered is the effect of a disturbance in the rotation of the earth. If the earth was arrested in its motion, the outer crust would slip over the core; magma erupted and the surface of the earth was heated. We shall see later that there is considerable evidence this actually happened. And historical records mention Mars as the feared agent. Houses and cities collapsed in earthquakes, meteorites and gravel bombarded the earth; all this made Mars the "bloodstained stormer of cities," "bane of men," the enemy of mankind. [20]

Joel makes it quite clear however, that the threat was not carried out. He called for repentance and the people responded. "Let the priests, who minister before the Lord, weep between the temple porch and the altar." (2:17) The people repented at least to some extent, and for this reason the Lord relented; Judah was spared

Ariel

It is evident from the description of the scourge that repeatedly swept by, that this happened over an extended period of time, presumably because Mars gradually approached and then disappeared. This is altogether different from the instantaneous blast that was to come. The events of 701 B.C. were accompanied by visible and long lasting effects. But now Isaiah speaks of an assault on Jerusalem that would end in a sudden, catastrophic defeat for the aggressor. This happened fourteen years later, 687 B.C., when Sennacherib attacked Judah a second time. Isaiah picks up on something he mentioned in chapter 10. God was going to send the Assyrians against a godless nation to inflict due punishment, and having done that punish the proud Assyrian king.

> Woe to you, Ariel, Ariel,
> the city where David settled!

The Assyrian and the Passover

> Add year to year
> and let your cycle of festivals go on.
> Yet I will besiege Ariel;
> she will mourn and lament,
> she will be to me like an altar hearth.
> I will encamp against you all around;
> I will encircle you with towers
> and set up my siege works against you.
> Brought low, you will speak from the ground;
> your speech will mumble out of the dust.
> Your voice will come ghostlike from the earth;
> out of the dust your speech will whisper.
> Isaiah 29:1-4

The word "Ariel" sounds very much like the Hebrw word for "altar." The city of David is, of course, Jerusalem, and it is compared with an altar hearth, where sacrificial animals were burned. The fire of God would burn against an unrepentant nation. The enemy would come to besiege Jerusalem; the people in their distress would humble themselves and appeal to God with their faces in the dust. Isaiah assured the people that their prayer would be heard in a miraculous way.

> But your many enemies will become like fine dust,
> the ruthless hordes like blown chaff.
> Suddenly, in an instant,
> the Lord Almighty will come
> with thunder and earthquake and great noise,
> with windstorm and tempest
> and flames of a devouring fire.
> Then the hordes of all the nations that fight against Ariel,
> that attack her and her fortress and besiege her,
> will be as it is with a dream,
> with a vision in the night -
> Isaiah 29:5-7

In his cavalier fashion, Velikovsky thought the land would be invaded with "small dust" and with "the multitude of terrible ones," and linked this with similar language in the following chapter. Of course, it does not say the nation would be invaded with small dust, rather the enemy would "become like fine dust." In the parallelism of Hebrew poetry, this is followed with a similar statement, "the ruthless hordes like blown chaff." The meaning is that the enemy would crumble like dust; disappear like chaff, blown away by the wind. This is a generic prediction of the fate that awaited the Assyrian. Isaiah now becomes very specific. He describes in detail the phenomena that would accompany the destruction of the Assyrian hordes.

There can be no doubt about it; it would be instantaneous. Yahweh Sebaoth, the LORD Almighty, would come and providentially intervene with an upheaval in nature. It involved atmospheric disturbances, a searing flame, thunder, great noise, wind storm and earthquake; the assorted hordes of the Assyrian army would be wiped out in a single moment. Their dreams of easy victory would fade away, their thirst for conquest would be unquenched.

Not that Judah understood the vision. It was like giving a book to someone who cannot read and then say, "Read it." They just did not get it. The Lord made it clear that he did this to shake the people out of their spiritual lethargy. The same thing was true in the days of Jesus. In the parable of the sower he said the prophecy was ultimately fulfilled in him. (Mark 13:1-17). Isaiah went on to proclaim a prophecy, so exact that it must be quoted in full.

> See, the Name of the Lord comes from afar,
> with burning anger and dense clouds of smoke;
> his lips are full of wrath,
> and his tongue is a consuming fire.
> His breath is like a rushing torrent, rising up to the neck.
> He shakes the nations in the sieve of destruction;
> he places in the jaws of the peoples
> a bit that leads them astray.

> And you will sing
> as on the night you celebrate a holy festival;
> your hearts will rejoice
> as when people go up with flutes
> to the mountain of the LORD,
> to the Rock of Israel.
> The LORD will cause men to hear his majestic voice
> and will make them see his arm coming down
> with raging anger and consuming fire,
> with cloudburst, thunderstorms and hail.
> The voice of the LORD will shatter Assyria;
> with his scepter he will strike them down.
> Every stroke the LORD lays on them with his punishing rod
> will be to the music of tambourines and harps,
> as he fights them in battle with the blows of his arm.
> Topheth has long been prepared;
> it has been made ready for the king.
> Its fire pit has been made deep and wide,
> with an abundance of fire and wood;
> the breath of the LORD,
> like a stream of burning sulfur, sets it ablaze.
> Isaiah 30:27-33

This is very similar to what was said before. The Name of the LORD in Hebrew thinking was identical with the Presence of the LORD. Yahweh would intervene on behalf of his people and "shake the nations in the sieve of destruction." So far this is universal, but now Isaiah speaks of a very specific time, and a specific nation. Judah would sing on the night that they would celebrate a holy festival. There is only one Hebrew festival that is celebrated at night, and that is the Passover. It was then, when the people were singing and making music, that the Lord would shatter Assyria. Isaiah again speaks of lightning and thunder, but this time he emphasizes the actual agent of destruction. The Assyrians would die a fiery death, comparable with the immolation sacrifices of Topheth.

Topheth was to the southwest of Jerusalem in the valley of Hinnom, where the people sacrificed to the Moloch. A furnace had been built to throw very young children alive into the fire. Its modern equivalent is the abortion clinic, another shrine of human sacrifice which, although equally barbaric, is far more cruel. Something to think about, considering how the Almighty dealt with nations who did these things. The destruction of the Assyrian army having been decreed, Isaiah now adds very interesting details. The Lord said,

> "As a lion growls, a great lion over his prey -
> and though the whole band of shepherds
> is called together against him,
> he is not frightened by their shouts
> or disturbed by their clamor -
> so the LORD Almighty will come down
> to do battle on Mount Zion and on its heights.
> Like a bird hovering overhead,
> the LORD Almighty will shield Jerusalem;
> he will shield it and deliver it,
> he will "pass over" it and will rescue it"
> Isaiah 31:4, 5

Isaiah speaks again of divine intervention. Intimidating though Assyria certainly was to the people of Jerusalem, the Lord was like a lion who simply ignored the shouts of shepherds. The Assyrians to him were of no consequence whatsoever. There is a hint of a portent on high, the picture of a bird hovering overhead, and a not-so-subtle prediction of the occasion. The Lord would "pass over" Jerusalem, just as he had done with Israel at the time of the exodus. The Hebrew word used here is "Pascha," meaning Passover. For all fact and purpose, this amounted to a second Passover, for it was during the Passover that the nation would again be rescued in supernatural fashion. A fascinating hint of the agency involved in executing the divine decree follows.

"Assyria will fall by a sword that is not of man;
a sword, not of mortals, will devour them.
They will fall before the sword
and their young men will be put to forced labor.
Their stronghold will fall
because of terror;
at sight of the battle standard
their commanders will panic,"
declares the Lord,
whose fire is in Zion,
whose furnace is in Jerusalem.
                    Isaiah 31:8, 9

A Sword

The repeated references to a sword "not of man" are intriguing. Assyria would be defeated, yes, but not by a human army. The instrument of God's wrath resembled a sword that appeared in the sky. How could that be? Velikovsky had an interesting explanation. "In one of its great conjunctions, Mars' atmosphere was stretched so that it appeared like a sword." That is not as fantastic as it may sound. The Babylonians called Nergal (Mars) "Great sword god —- horrible, raging fire god." The Romans had similar traditions about Mars. [21]

Rome was founded about 750 B.C., at a time when great disturbances in nature took place. Thunder roared, darkness prevailed, the sun disappeared. The Romans connected these events with their national deity, Mars. Roman origins are shrouded in the mist of mythology, but it is definitely associated with Mars. The earliest Roman rulers according to Augustine lived during the reign of Hezekiah. The Romans were a war-like people, and Mars, hitherto an obscure deity, became their great war god. It was shown as having a sword. Mars is often associated with a wolf. The Romans called Mars "Lapius Martius," and Mars is often referred to as the Wolf Star. The atmosphere of Mars may have taken the shape of a wolf or coyote. Mars became the god of war because it appeared like a sword in the heavens. It frightened the nations; they thought the world was coming to an end, which explains why Isaiah had so much to say about the judgment day. Velikovsky noted that this led to great unrest.

> The fear of the Judgment Day not only did not pacify the nations, but on the contrary, uprooted them, impelling them to migration and war. The Scythians came down from the plains of the Dnieper and Volga and moved southward. The Greeks left their home in Mycenae and on the islands of the Aegean and carried on the siege of Troy through years of cosmic disturbances. Assyrian kings waged war in Elam, Palestine, Egypt and beyond the Caucasus.
>
> The trembling earth, the displacement of the poles, the change in the climate, the frightening prodigies in the sky, caused great movements of peoples. The Aztecs changed their homeland —-. In India the patron of the invading Aryan race was Indra, the god of war, the Hindu Mars. The Ionians and Dorians spread to the islands; the Latins were pressed by newcomers to the Apennine Peninsula, the Cimmerians wandered from Europe across the Bosporus into Asia Minor. [22]

That these events were worldwide in scope is evident from Isaiah. Following the reference to a sword that would devour the Assyrian, he spoke of the Messianic king who would reign in righteousness, and the coming of the Holy Spirit, poured down from on high.(ch 32) There can be no doubt that he is speaking of the Messianic Age, and that the reign of the Messiah is worldwide. Isaiah throughout speaks of a world system that is opposed to "Zion" (the site of the temple). That was not the Jerusalem of his day of course; he blasted the sins of the people of Jerusalem, their indifference to God and man. No, the real Zion was the community of true believers. In days to come this was to be fully realized in the Messianic Age.

Edom

Meanwhile Isaiah proclaimed judgment. "The LORD is angry with all nations, his wrath is upon all their armies." (34:2) The doom, announced by Isaiah to some extent applies to the last days, but in the context of what was going on then, it is certain that he spoke of thing that happened in his days. He focused his attention on Edom and foretold its awful fate. Velikovsky quoted scattered passages to "prove" that a global catastrophe would burn the earth. A straightforward reading leads the unbiased reader to a rather different conclusion.

> My sword has drunk its fill in the heavens;
> see, it descends in judgment on Edom,
> the people I have totally destroyed.
> The sword of the LORD is bathed in blood,
> it is covered with fat - the blood of lambs and goats,
> fat from the kidneys of rams.
> For the LORD has a sacrifice in Bozrah
> and a great slaughter in Edom.
> And the wild oxen will fall with them,
> the bull calves and the great bulls.
> Their land will be drenched with blood,
> and the dust will be soaked with fat.
> For the LORD has a day of vengeance,
> a year of retribution, to uphold Zion's cause.
> Edom's streams will be turned into pitch,
> her dust into burning sulfur;
> her land will become blazing pitch!
> It will not be quenched night and day;
> its smoke will rise forever.
> From generation to generation it will lie desolate;
> no one will ever pass through it again.
> The desert owl and screech owl will possess it;
> the great owl and the raven will nest there.
> God will stretch out over Edom

the measuring line of chaos
and the plumb line of desolation.
Her nobles will have nothing there to be called a kingdom.
All her princes will vanish away.
Thorns will overrun her citadels,
nettles and brambles her strongholds.
She will become a haunt for jackals,
a home for owls.

Isaiah 34:5-13

Isaiah's prophecy obviously deals with Edom, not the world. However, he employs an interesting play on words. Edom was the inheritance of Esau, the twin brother of Jacob (Israel). "Edom" means *red*. The word-picture Isaiah paints leaves the distinct impression that a phenomenon appeared in the sky that looked like a sword, "bathed in blood." In other words it looked as if it was blood-stained, red. That corresponds with "Edom" (red) and definitely agrees with the dominant color of Mars, the red planet. Isaiah warned that a blood-stained sword (was it the war planet Mars?) was stretched over Edom, and that it served as a symbol of judgment. The implication was that Edom would have a bloody history, which it did. Ezekiel (and Jeremiah as well) made similar predictions. Edom was a close and often hostile neighbor of Israel and Judah.

> This is what the Sovereign LORD says: "Because Edom took revenge on the house of Judah and became very guilty by doing so, therefore this is what the Sovereign LORD says: I will stretch out my hand against Edom and kill its men and their animals. I will lay it waste, and from Teman to Dedan they will fall by the sword. I will take vengeance on Edom by the hand of my people Israel, and they will deal with Edom in accordance with my anger and my wrath; they will know my vengeance, declares the Sovereign LORD."
>
> Ezekiel 25:12-14

The Assyrian and the Passover

The word of the LORD came to me: "Son of man, set your face against Mount Seir; prophesy against it and say: 'This is what the Sovereign LORD says: I am against you, Mount Seir, and I will stretch out my hand against you and make you a desolate waste. I will turn your towns into ruins and you will be desolate. Then you will know that I am the LORD.

Because you harbored an ancient hostility and delivered the Israelites over to the sword at the time of their calamity, the time their punishment reached its climax, therefore as surely as I live, declares the Sovereign LORD, I will give you over to bloodshed and it will pursue you. Since you did not hate bloodshed, bloodshed will pursue you. I will make Mount Seir a desolate waste and cut off from it all who come and go. I will fill your mountains with the slain; those killed by the sword will fall on your hills and in your valleys and in all your ravines. I will make you desolate forever; your towns will not be inhabited. Then you will know that I am the LORD."

Ezekiel 35:1-9

Following the death of Saul, the first king of Israel, David battled Syria to the north. Edom took this opportunity to invade Judah in the south, but David returned in time and inflicted a serious defeat, killing some eighteen thousand Edomites. Edom remained subservient to Judah until the reign of Jehoram, about 850 B.C. However, Amaziah (Uzziah) invaded Edom and captured its capital Sela, also called Petra, meaning rock. The stronghold was literally hewn out of the mountains. More bondage followed under Assyria and the Chaldean Empire.

Then the Nubians (probably the "children of the east," mentioned in Jeremiah 25:4), who also conquered Moab-Ammon, in the sixth century B.C. expelled the Edomites from Petra, its rock fortress. The Jews under the Maccabeans consequently captured Edom, killing forty thousand Edomites. In Roman times it was incorporated into the Jewish nation; the province became known as Idumea. At the time of Christ, Petra was prosperous. It was the terminus of a great commercial rout into Asia, and a market for spice and frankincense.

Shortly before Titus attacked Jerusalem A.D. 70, twenty thousand Idumeans (Edomites) were admitted into the stronghold "which they filled with robbery and bloodshed." Edom ceased to be a people, and Petra over the centuries declined. By the time of the Islamic invasion of the 7th Century A.D. it was reduced to nothing. The crusaders built a castle there in the 12th Century, after which it disappeared from the scene. Nobody even knew it existed until 1812, when it was rediscovered. Amazed Europeans found the ruins of a fastness that literally was cut out of beautiful red-rose stone. A single entrance through a narrow canyon rendered it virtually impregnable.

But there it was, utterly ruined and deserted. Arabs avoid the city because of the scorpions; eagles and owls soar overhead. Large herds of goats roam through the mountains and desert; jackals howl, lions and leopards are seen in the city and the surrounding desert, nettles and thistles abound, and snakes are everywhere. By contrast Teman or Maan, the only surviving city in that deserted land, prospers. No one could have foreseen that, but the Hebrew prophets did. [23]

The Assyrian Assault

So far Isaiah had always been a prophet in the true sense of the word, but all of a sudden he becomes a historian. It is surprising to find in his writings an extended account of an assault on Jerusalem. A casual reading would lead one to believe that there was but one invasion, which is known to have occurred 701 B.C. A comparison with the second book of Chronicles on the other hand makes it clear this attack happened later. The first campaign was disastrous for Judah. Sennacherib who, as we have seen, was on his way to Egypt, deported more than two hundred thousand people, and Hezekiah was forced to sue for peace. He did not surrender, but paid a hefty tribute. Sennacherib left without bothering to capture Jerusalem.

Meanwhile Hezekiah had learned a lesson. He did not enter into an alliance with foreign nations, such as Egypt, but relied on the Lord. He built up his defenses and encouraged the people. It was quite common for foreign overlords to allow subdued nations a measure of independence, but Sennacherib eventually felt that Hezekiah had gone too far. So he came again, ready for another attack on Egypt, and this time he intended to capture Jerusalem rather than to by-pass it. This happened 687 B.C., and it is with this campaign that Isaiah concerns himself.

Sennacherib used tactics, identical with those he had used previously against Babylon. He sent envoys to talk the people into submission. It was war propaganda. They urged the people in Hebrew to surrender rather than fight. No god had ever delivered any of the conquered nations. What made them think the Lord could help them? Hezekiah, familiar with these tactics, issued orders to say nothing in reply; the Assyrians heard a deafening silence. When the king heard about the summons, he mourned and sent some men to Isaiah to "pray for the remnant that still survives."

Isaiah assured Hezekiah that evil would befall Sennacherib, who at the time was fighting against Libnah. According to Jewish sources, Sennacherib came himself to lead the assault on Jerusalem. He arrived at the appointed time. Armies as a rule begin their campaigns in the spring because of favorable weather. One commentator made an interesting comment; he showed that the assault occurred late March or early April.[24] That was the time of the Jewish spring festival, the Passover. Isaiah said the enemy hordes would be wiped out during the Passover celebration, in preparation of an attack on Jerusalem and there they were, right on schedule.

There are good reasons why Isaiah recorded these events in such detail: his prophecies were being suddenly and dramatically fulfilled. The Assyrians with their allies were caught up in the execution of a divine decree that presently was to lead to their utter destruction. They were assembled at the place of execution: the mountains of Israel. After his arrival, Sennacherib was informed that Tirhakah the Ethiopian pharaoh was coming out for battle. That did not deter Sennacherib. He made preparations for a siege assault on Jerusalem and tried to intimidate Hezekiah with a threatening letter. With the Egyptian threat on his flank, it would be advantageous if Jerusalem were taken without a battle; if not, he would have to take it by storm. His letter was more than threatening; it was blasphemous.

Say to Hezekiah king of Judah: Do not let the god you depend on deceive you when he says, 'Jerusalem will not be handed over to the king of Assyria'. Surely you have heard what the kings of Assyria have done to all the countries, destroying them completely. And will you be delivered? Did the gods of the nations that were destroyed by my forefathers deliver them - the gods of Gozan, Haran, Rezeph and the people of Eden who were in Tel Assar? Where is the king of Hamath, the king of Arpad, the king of the city of Sepharvaim, or of Hena or Ivvah?

Isaiah 37:10-13

Unbeknown to Sennacherib, the God of Hezekiah whom he disdained had read his thought from afar. Forty years earlier, Isaiah recorded what "the Assyrian" would think, and the price he would have to pay for his pride.

'Are not my commanders all kings' he says.
'Has not Calno fared like Carchemish?
Is not Hamath like Arpad,
and Samaria like Damascus?
As my hand seized the kingdoms of the idols,
kingdoms whose images excelled those of Jerusalem and Samaria -
shall I not deal with Jerusalem and her images
as I dealt with Samaria and her idols?'
Isaiah 10:9-11

Sennacherib never knew he walked his army into a death trap. If he thought Hezekiah would surrender, he was mistaken. Hezekiah put his trust in the Lord, not in Egypt. In tears he went to the temple, where he laid the blasphemous letter before the One to whom it was addressed, and prayed for deliverance. A messenger came. The prophet Isaiah sent him to let Hezekiah know that God had heard his prayer and would deliver the city.

The Assyrian and the Passover

By that time Sennacherib arrived. The day before the planned assault, he took a look at Jerusalem from a place called Nob, on the Mount of Olives, something foretold by Isaiah several years earlier (10:32). He was amazed at the small size of the temple city. His astronomers advised him against attacking the following day. "When Rabshekah heard the singing of the Hallel he counseled Sennacherib to withdraw from Jerusalem, as on this night - the first night of Passover - many miracles were wrought for Israel."[25] The soldiers in fear asked their king not to wait, but to attack at once. Sennacherib chose to ignore this advice.

> His journey having lasted but one day instead of ten, as he had expected, he rested at Nob. A raised platform was there erected for Sennacherib, whence he could view Jerusalem. On first beholding the Judean capital, the Assyrian king exclaimed : "What! Is this Jerusalem, the city for whose sake I gathered together my whole army, for whose sake I first conquered all other lands? Is it not smaller and weaker than all the cities of the nations I subdued with my strong hand?" He stretched himself and shook his head, and waved his hand contemptuously at the Temple mound and the sanctuary crowning it. [26]

The Blast

Exactly what happened that night has been the object of long debates, none of them satisfactory. Scripture gives a bone-dry account:

> Then the angel of the LORD went out and put to death a hundred and eighty-five-thousand men in the Assyrian camp. When the people got up the next morning - there were all the dead bodies! So Sennacherib king of Assyria broke camp and withdrew. He returned to Nineveh and stayed there.
>
> Isaiah 37:36, 37

What is meant with "the angel of the LORD"? An angel obviously is a person, and the angel of the LORD is a very special person. He is mentioned frequently in the Old Testament, and is always represented as Deity. Isaiah said the LORD would come, and the angel of the LORD executed the judgment of God. How that was done is another matter. We must not think that an angel with wings, dressed in shiny white garments, walked through the Assyrian camp and dispatched 185,000 soldiers with a magic sword. It involved some kind of natural phenomenon; everyone agrees about that. But what could have possibly annihilated a whole army overnight? There can be no doubt that it was instantaneous.

Several solutions have been suggested. A simoom, a cyclonic sand storm has been suggested, but that theory has been discarded. Such desert storms, deadly as they are, occur only in the summer. Perhaps it was a sudden fever, but there is no good evidence for that either. The most popular assumption is the plague, but that cannot account for a sudden annihilation; the plague takes a mounting toll, often lasting weeks. Besides, if that were the case, the Hebrews would have avoided the camp, well, like the plague.

This raises a question that has never been asked. Is it possible that the sudden destruction of the Assyrian army involved a meteor? A sizable meteor would explode high in the atmosphere and depending on its size would create a huge fire ball. That happened in 1908 in Siberia, when a 200 ft meteor struck with devastating results. That is the problem with this theory, the impact of a meteor would have been too great. How could it affect the Assyrians but not the nearby Judeans? Besides, it does not explain the world wide phenomena that accompanied these events.

Josephus assumed it involved the plague because of the story by Heredotus, who said mice gnawed the bow strings of the Assyrians. One commentary relates this story with a highly interesting twist. According to Heredotus, Sennacherib attacked Egypt and its king, Sethos, prayed to his god Ptah for help.

The Assyrian and the Passover

In the night the god Ptah sent hosts of field mice, which gnawed the quivers, bow strings and shield straps of the Assyrians, who consequently fled and were massacred. An image of the priest-king with a mouse in his hand stood in the temple of Ptah, and on its pedestal the inscription, which might also point the moral of the Biblical narrative, " — —- let him who looks on me be pious." The mouse in the hand of the statue probably originated the detail of the legend; but according to Horapollion it was the hieroglyphic sign of destruction by plague. Bahr says that it was also the symbol of Mars.[27]

There is a statue of this god in Letopolis, in northern Egypt, and it speaks of a fire that was celebrated: "the flame before the wind to the end of heaven and the end of earth," which "devoured the enemy." Since an Egyptian army was near, we would expect the memory of the event to survive in Egyptian records. But is it accurate?

The most reliable source would seem to be the record of the surviving witnesses, the people of Jerusalem. Jewish sources unanimously claim the Assyrian army was destroyed by a blast from heaven. As Hezekiah and the people were singing the hallels (songs of praise) in the temple during the first night of the Passover, the Assyrian camp was struck by something that resembled lightning. "Hezekiah and Isaiah were in the Temple when the host of the Assyrians approached Jerusalem; a fire arose from amidst them, which burned Sennacherib and consumed his host."[28] It was accompanied by a tremendous roar, "so terrific that the Assyrians gave up their ghosts."[29] Hezekiah wisely waited until the following day, and when the expected assault did not materialize he sent scouts.

They witnessed a scene of death and destruction. Men and horses had died instantaneously. By the time the Hebrews arrived the few survivors had left hurriedly, including Sennacherib. Rabbinical sources say he was badly burned. What killed the army? The Assyrians evidently had been exposed to a flash fire that choked them to death; but their clothing was merely scorched. "Their souls were burnt, though their garments remained intact."[30]

Velikovsky was not quite sure about the exact nature of the "blast" that smote the Assyrian army. He thought that "gaseous masses reaching the atmosphere could asphyxiate all breath in certain areas." [31] Maybe it could, but it is wholly inadequate to account for the reports of the phenomena that accompanied the disaster. History and the testimony of scripture call for a far more radical explanation. If Mars did indeed approach the earth, it still was very far away - too far for its thin atmosphere to affect the earth at all, least of all to choke the life out of an army. But if an electrical discharge took place between the two globes, everything would fall into place. It could have happened through a plasma discharge. Donald E. Scott explains how.

> Each planet is an intruder in the plasma. As far as we can tell from our space probes, each planet is surrounded by its own cell of plasma, called its plasmasphere. A double layer (DL) separates the plasmasphere from the plasma. It should be noted that Venus has little if any magnetic field, but it does have a large plasmasphere. This is an example of why the words *magnetosphere* and *plasmasphere* are not interchangeable. [32]

What would happen if the plasmaspheres of earth and Mars were to clash?

> When a double-layer sheath surrounds a planet, it is protected from direct electrostatic interaction with any outside body. Two planets, each surrounded by an intact plasma sheath, can have no electrical effect on each other. However, if a body having a different electrical potential (voltage) penetrates the double layer boundary and moves into the plasmasphere surrounding a planet, charges will flow to try to cancel the voltage difference. Electrical discharges will occur. Thus, if any other body, such as a large meteor, asteroid or comet should come close enough to Earth to penetrate our plasma sheath, violent electrical discharges would occur between the two bodies. It would, of course, be un-

fortunate to be standing on Earth surface at the point of origin (or reception) of such a mega-lightning discharge. But the massive discharge itself might either deflect the intruding body of break it up and thus protect Earth from a collision. [33]

Assuming Mars was indeed near, something of the kind could have happened. An interplanetary spark is bound to be enormous. Since it would jump through the vacuum of outer space, it would probably involve a plasma bolt. The earth being larger than Mars and its voltage much higher, a spark like that would probably jump from the earth to Mars. If it erupted in the Assyrian camp, the electrical potential alone would be enough to fry the army. Add to this that the intense heat of the spark would not only scorch the soldiers to death, it would also leave a vacuum that asphyxiated them. It is consistent with reports of a fire erupting in the Assyrian camp, accompanied by a tremendous noise. The effect would be similar to that of a nuclear explosion without the fallout. In such a conflagration, the greatest damage is done by air rushing into the vacuum. All this fits the prophecy of Isaiah:

> Suddenly, in an instant,
> the LORD Almighty will come
> with thunder and earthquake and great noise,
> with windstorm and tempest
> and flames of a devouring fire.
> Isa 29:5, 6

That agrees with a later oracle, which speaks of a consuming fire and of Topheth, the fiery pit, prepared for this occasion (30:27-33). Air rushed into the vacuum with an unbelievable roar and created hurricane force winds. Brief though it was, it would certainly be destructive. Something of the kind is mentioned in Psalm 46

> God is our refuge and strength,
> we will not fear, though the earth give way

and the mountains fall in the heart of the sea,
though its waters roar and foam
and the mountains quake with their surging.
There is a river whose streams make glad the city of God,
the holy place where the Most High dwells.
God is within her, she will not fall;
God will help her at break of day.
Nations are in uproar, kingdoms fall;
he lifts his voice, the earth melts.
The LORD Almighty is with us;
the God of Jacob is our fortress.
Come and see the works of the LORD,
the desolations he has brought on the earth.
He makes wars cease to the ends of the earth;
he breaks the bow and shatters the spear,
he burns the shields with fire.
Be still, and know that I am God;
I will be exalted among the nations,
I will be exalted in the earth.
The LORD Almighty is with us;
the God of Jacob is our fortress.

This psalm inspired Martin Luther to compose "A mighty fortress is our God." It has served as a source of inspiration every time calamities strike, particularly earthquakes. It is easy to see why; this psalm was inspired by an upheaval in nature that providentially delivered God's people from a deadly menace. It was catastrophic. A major earthquake struck. Mountains sank into the sea, tidal waves irrupted, molted rock poured out of the earth. The psalmist uses language, similar to Isaiah. Both speak of divine intervention, of the voice of God causing a great disaster, accompanied by fire.

God was very much present, not far away, and he made his abode in the holy city, Jerusalem. The river that gladdens God's people is the gentle stream of Shiloah, mentioned by Isaiah (8:6). It cannot be said that the psalmist was merely speaking of a weather disturbance,

The Assyrian and the Passover

rather this was a global disaster; the nations were in anguish. The psalmist was impressed with the evidence of divine intervention: "Be still and know that I am God." Psalms 76 and 97 deal with the same subjects, but relate more to man's awe of God's power. Although not specific, they do mention a number of details.

That this happened 687 B.C. and not 701 B.C. can be known from a number of sources. Isaiah said explicitly that Sennacherib returned to Nineveh and stayed there. While worshiping his god Nisroch[34] he was assassinated a few years later by two of his sons. He never came out to fight again, probably because he had been badly burned. That could only be true 687 B.C., not earlier. Also Tirhakah, the Ethiopian pharaoh who came out to meet Sennacherib, came to power 688 B.C., which renders 701 B.C. impossible.

We know now that the disaster of 687 B.C. happened during the first night of the Passover. Thanks to Chinese sources, the exact day is known as well. Velikovsky found this entry in an old book by the Frenchman Edouard Biot. "The year 687 B.C., in the summer, in the fourth moon, in the day of sin Mao (23rd of March), during the night, the fixed stars did not appear, though the night was clear (cloudless). In the middle of the night stars fell like rain." Biot based his calculation on sources, ascribed to Confucius. [35] The Bamboo books mention something similar without however giving an exact date. "The five planets went out of their courses. In the night, stars fell like rain. The earth shook." So much for the exact day. What about the evidence for the catastrophic events, described in the Scriptures?

Crete

Arguably the best book, written by Velikovsky, is "Earth in Upheaval." It is required reading in major universities, like it certainly should be. "Earth in Upheaval" deals with the geological evidence for catastrophes that repeatedly shook the globe. Velikovsky paid a great deal of attention to the Minoan civilization on the island of Crete. The Middle Minoan II civilization perished at the time of the exodus. It was overwhelmed again fifty years later, when the sun delayed going down for about a whole day during the miracle of Joshua.

Much later, toward the end of the Late Minoan I period, the palace of Knossos was destroyed, along with great mansions and whole cities. A great earth shock struck, and a tidal wave that came from the north swept across the island. Volcanic ash fell. Not much later came the end.

> Then came the destruction of Late Minoan II. The sudden catastrophe interrupted all activity; but there are indications also that, though the upheaval was instantaneous, some preparations had been made in an effort to appease the deity for fear of the impending event. Evans writes: "It would seem that preparations were on foot for some anointing ceremony .. But the initial task was never destined to reach its fulfillment." Beneath a covering mass of earth and rubble lies the "Room of the Throne" with alabaster oil vessels. "The sudden breaking off of tasks begun - so conspicuous .. surely point to an instantaneous cause." It was "another of those dread shocks that had again and again caused a break in the Palace history." The earthquake was accompanied by fire. The actual overthrow was greatly aggravated by "a wide spread conflagration," and the catastrophe attained "special disastrous dimensions owing to a furious wind then blowing." Evans assigns the final destruction of the building to the month of March. [36]

The utter destruction of these structures evoked the wonder of historians. Was its cause a natural disaster or military action? Nobody really knows. The Minoans knew it was coming. It could have been visible in the sky. Nobody can foresee an earthquake, but a menace in the heavens would inspire believers in astral religion to appease the angry deity. It also confirms Isaiah's prediction. A great windstorm accompanied the destruction. Isaiah spoke of fire that would burn like sulfur, and Psalm 46, in poetic fashion, says that the voice of the Lord made the earth melt. There is considerable evidence

The Assyrian and the Passover

that this actually happened. When liquefied rock reaches a temperature of 580 degrees Celsius, it acquires a magnetic orientation which, after solidifying, it never loses. This is the science of paleomagnetism. It was found that rock formations all over the earth have reversed polarization, often much stronger than that of the earth's magnetic field.

When a magnet is struck by lightning, its polarity is reversed. The earth is a large magnet, and if it were struck by a bolt from space, its magnetic poles would be reversed. If Mars came sufficiently close to the earth, its magnetic field would create electrical currents in the earth's crust and induct enough heat to melt rocks. Subterranean water would heat up with explosive results; the sudden change from water into steam would cause great earthquakes. Depending upon the conductivity of metallic layers, heat would be transferred deep into the earth. Upon cooling, the rock would acquire the polarization of that magnetic field. The earth having been struck by an interplanetary spark, its polarity was reversed. The last time that happened was in the Eighth Century B.C. Greek and Etruscan vases, fired in kilns at that time, had a magnetic orientation, opposite to that of our day. It was found that the magnetic poles were reversed shortly after the beginning of the Eighth Century B.C.

When the Chaldean delegation visited Hezekiah 700 B.C., they were eager to find out about the phenomenon of the sun reversing its course. It turns out they had good reasons to. A study of astronomical tablets, found in Babylon, revealed that the length of the day at summer solstice points at latitude, about 2½ degrees farther north than it is now. In other words, Babylon moved 180 miles to the south. It follows the countries on the other side of the northern hemisphere moved that much farther north. It is certain that northern Europe suffered severe climatic changes, and as a result was greatly impoverished. It became much colder. There is evidence of an extended winter that virtually destroyed the flora. It happened suddenly, around 700 B.C.

The Catastrophe

In his scholarly work, "The End of the Bronze Age," Professor Robert Drews maintains that the Bronze Age in its various forms came to a catastrophic end about 1200 B.C. It was an all-encompassing disaster which he simply calls "the catastrophe," that ended the Bronze Age civilization. Although acknowledging that earthquakes did happen at that time, he nonetheless believes that the real cause was a new form of warfare: displaced peoples coming from Europe and Asia used the chariot, the tank of that day, to loot and burn cities. He adopts this position because the evidence points at widespread and intense fires, something not normally associated with earthquakes.

If we adjust the year -1200 by eliminating the 450 ghost years of the Dark Age, we theoretically arrive at the year -750, generally the end of the Eighth Century B.C. The displacement of whole nations that marks these years was confused with the wars of Nectanebo/Ramses III, whose murals picture a sea battle. Drews maintains there is no historical evidence for the "Sea Peoples." It is all conjecture.

> The thesis that a great "migration of the Sea Peoples" occurred ca 1200 B.C. is supposedly based on Egyptian inscriptions, one from the reign of Merneptah and another from the reign of Ramesses III. Yet in the inscriptions themselves such a migration nowhere appears. After reviewing what the Egyptian texts have to say about "the Sea Peoples," one Egyptologist recently remarked that although some things are unclear, "Einst ist es aber sicher, nach den aegiptishen Texten haben wir es nicht mit einem 'Voelkerwanderung' zu tun." (*One thing is certain, according to the Egyptian texts we are not dealing with a "migration of peoples."*) Thus the migration hypothesis is based not on the inscriptions themselves but on their interpretation. [37]

He goes on to explain that the origin of the migration thesis was wholly based upon an intelligent guess.

Current beliefs that vast migrations were partly or wholly responsible for the ruin of Bronze Age civilization do not in fact rest on documentary evidence. They are instead the residue of a radical and imaginative conjecture that was launched late in the nineteenth century. The migration thesis is largely the creation of Gaston Maspero, who developed his thesis in the 1870's and promoted in his popular *Histoire encienne des peuples de l'orient classique.* — —-

What Maspero intended his thesis to explain, then, was not the Catastrophe, whose occurrence had not yet been perceived, but the unsuccessful assault upon Egypt in the reign of Merneptah and Ramses III. [38]

Without denying Professor Drew's excellent study of chariot warfare, it is necessary to see these historical events in an altogether different light. Among other things, Ramses III, who was identical with Pharaoh Nectanebo, had nothing to do with the catastrophic events of the Eighth Century B.C. He was dragged into it because well-meaning historians confused the sea battle of Nectanebo with the mass migrations of the late Eighth Century B.C. and mistakenly assigned these events to -1200.

Like so many historians and archaeologists, Professor Drew finds himself on the horns of a dilemma. Once there was a global catastrophe, evidently of a seismic nature, that involved all-consuming fires. Earthquakes are rarely accompanied by fires, much less so in the ancient world, where no fuel was readily available. What was the cause of these fires? A logical assumption is that armies destroyed and burned these cities. If that is the case we are faced with the perplexing question where these armies came from, and how could they be so powerful! Drew thought it was a new form of warfare with improved chariots.

There is another explanation. During the Eighth Century B.C. there were repeated violent earthquakes, accompanied by blazing fires and violent windstorms that devastated the world and left cities in ruins. Whatever the cause, it resulted in widespread migrations of whole nations, looking for new habitat. According to one fantastic explanation this was the result of encounters between the earth and the planet Mars. Interplanetary discharges burned forests and dried out rivers. Enormous electrical sparks burrowed into the earth with explosive results. Earthquakes ruined whole cities. No reasonable person expects historians to accept this hypothesis at face value. However, it does provide a format, an alternative, to fit known historical facts. Could historians at least give it some thought?

Times and Seasons

The prophet Daniel had a dream that revealed a mystery. He praised God and said, "He changes times and seasons" (2:21). This sentence has a curious meaning. Daniel did not say, "He brings about the change of seasons," rather the "appointed times," were themselves changed and the seasons disrupted. Unbelievable though it may sound, the year was not always 365 1/4 days long. Between the exodus and early 8th Century B.C., the year lasted 360 days. Calendars all over the world mention a lunar year of 12 months, each lasting 30 days. The Old Testament mentions months lasting 30 days; in Biblical interpretation the prophetic year is assumed to consist of 360 days.

During the 7th Century B.C., the months became disarranged. For a while, the months consisted of four weeks, lasting nine days each, which made for a year of ten months. That was the Roman calendar during the late 7th Century. This system survives to some extent in our reckoning, which is based on the Roman calendar. The Romans numbered the last four months of the year: September (7), October (8), November (9), and December (10), although they actually are 9, 10, 11 and 12. Sometime later a different order was introduced. Five days were added to the year; also the months of January and February were added.

The astronomers of Nineveh and Babylon repeatedly adjusted the calendar. They knew three different systems whereby they reckoned time, but only the last one is identical with our own. The sun, in other words, did not always follow the path that it travels now. This is evident from the foundations of ancient temples. Temples doubled as observatories. There were, after all, no clocks, and the only way to establish the summer and winter solstices was to point the door of the temple toward the East, where the sun rose. Earlier temples were not oriented to that point where the sun rises now. They are all offset in the same direction. Eventually the correct length of the year was settled. Numa, who was a contemporary of Hezekiah, adjusted the Roman calendar. But it was Thales, a Greek astronomer, who first divided the year into 365 days, and predicted solar eclipses.

It is certainly very odd that the actual length of the year was not known until the middle of the 7th Century B.C. In the ancient world, astronomers were members of a special priesthood (they still are), and they were capable of advanced mathematical calculations. They were not stupid. Why then, did they report a year of 360 days? It appears that following the events of -687, there were no more global threats, presumably because Mars in the course of a century or so moved to its present orbit. That did not happen overnight. Judging from the scriptures there must have been a terrifying sight in the sky. The Lord told Jeremiah,

> Do not learn the ways of the nations
> or be terrified by signs in the sky
> though the nations are terrified by them
> Jeremiah 10:2

No doubt some would argue that this must have involved signs in the Zodiac, since pagan nations lived by these superstitions, much as modern pagans do. But the language of Jeremiah does not warrant that at all. People may very well look for signs where there are none, but the whole world is not terrified by that. Nebonassar the Chaldean, father of Nebuchadnezzar, still counted Nergal (Mars) as the most terrifying of all astral deities. It is therefore quite possible that Mars gradually receded, but for a long time was plainly visible in the night sky, and the nations lived in fear that the red planet would again threaten the earth. It didn't, and eventually it circled the sun in the path where it is now, faraway and out of mind.

Meanwhile the prophets of Judah proclaimed their message, most important among them Isaiah. The prince of the prophets lived a very long life. It reached from Uzziah to Manasseh, the son of Hezekiah. Even at that we are not really prepared for the kind of literature he produced in his final years, it is quite controversial.

Second Isaiah

Following the historical interlude in the book of Isaiah, a very different kind of prophetic literature appears. It is in many ways puzzling and controversial. In a number of cases, the author (or authors), describes events that occurred at least a century after the death of Isaiah. The Persian king Cyrus is mentioned by name, although he was the one who ended the Babylonian captivity. Of course, Isaiah could have never known that. The same thing could be said of passages where the author encourages the Jews who were leaving Babylon. The temple is mentioned as having been destroyed, and Jerusalem is remembered as a ruin. So what follows naturally? These parts could have never been written by Isaiah. Rather they were attached to that book by a later prophet, or maybe more than one, who though he would gain acceptance that way.

If that is true, and on the surface this would appear to be the case, honesty compels us to arrive at unpleasant conclusions. This part of the book of Isaiah is a fraud. A pious fraud no doubt, but a fraud all the same. Men of good character cannot in good conscience accept as authentic or authoritative "deutero" Isaiah. Matter of fact, it casts a shadow of doubt upon other Scriptures as well. Who knows, maybe "prophecy" was written after the fact and then passed off as genuine. Sort of like Joseph Smith, the Mormon prophet, who changed his "revelations" to make it appear his priesthood had been restored from on high in the latter days, when in fact it evolved haphazardly.

Yes, that is what they teach in seminaries. But is it true? Maybe the problem is more perceived than real. Who, we ask, was the literary giant who wrote in Babylon during the captivity? Jewish tradition knows nothing about a second Isaiah, and the New Testament knows of only one prophet by that name. Besides, the Quamram (Dead Sea) scrolls, which date from before the time of Christ, preserve the book of Isaiah in its entirety. It includes so-called second Isaiah.

This may seem a silly question, but consistency demands we ask it: who wrote that part of second Isaiah that speaks of Jesus, the Messiah? One of the most famous passages in prophetic literature speaks of events as if they had just happened. This is the case with the Servant Song. It is clear from the context that different speakers are involved, and they discuss the life and suffering of the mysterious Servant of the Lord.

> God: See, my servant will act wisely;
> he will be raised and lifted up and highly exalted.
> Just as there were many who were appalled at him -
> his appearance was so disfigured
> beyond that of any man
> and his form marred beyond human likeness -
> so will he sprinkle many nations,
> and kings will shut their mouths because of him.
> For what they were not told, they will see,
> and what they have not heard, they will understand.
>
> God's
> people: Who has believed our message
> and to whom has the arm of the LORD been revealed?
> He grew up before him like a tender shoot,
> and like a root out of dry ground.
> He had no beauty or majesty to attract us to him,
> nothing in his appearance that we should desire him.
> He was despised and rejected by men,
> a man of sorrows, and familiar with suffering.
> Like one from whom men hide their faces
> he was despised and we esteemed him not.

Surely he took up our infirmities
and carried our sorrows,
yet we considered him stricken by God,
smitten by him and afflicted.
But he was pierced for our transgressions,
he was crushed for our iniquities;
the punishment that brought us peace was upon him,
and by his wounds we are healed.
We all, like sheep, have gone astray,
each of us has turned our own way;
and the LORD has laid on him
the iniquity of us all.

God: He was oppressed and afflicted
yet he did not open his mouth;
he was led like a sheep to the slaughter,
and as a sheep before her shearers is silent,
so he did not open his mouth.
By oppression and judgment, he was taken away.
And who can speak of his descendants?
For he was cut off from the land of the living;
for the transgression of my people he was stricken.
He was assigned a grave with the wicked,
and with the rich in his death,
though he had done no violence,
nor was any deceit found in his mouth.

God's
people: Yet it was the LORD's will to crush him
and cause him to suffer,
and though the LORD makes his life a guilt offering,
he will see his offspring and prolong his days,
and the will of the LORD will prosper in his hand.

God: After the suffering of his soul,
he will see the light of life and be satisfied;

> by his knowledge my righteous servant
> will justify many,
> and he will bear their iniquities.
> Therefore I will give him a portion among the great,
> and he will divide the spoils with the strong,
> because he poured out his life unto death,
> and was numbered with the transgressors.
> For he bore the sin of many,
> and made intercession for the transgressors.
>
> Isaiah 52:13-15, Ch 53

Third Isaiah

We should have no trouble establishing the time when this was written. After all, it speaks of events past, present and future. A straightforward reading of the gospels provides the answer; it was written shortly after the crucifixion of Jesus. During his lifetime, Jesus was constantly confronted with sorrow and suffering; he healed hurting people. Yet he was rejected. The reasons are apparent; he was not at all the Messiah the Jews expected. They looked for a knight in shining armor who would throw the Romans out. It is understandable enough. There are all kinds of Christians who expect him to do something similar when he comes back. Jesus was not at all like that. He spoke of the Messianic era as "the Kingdom of God," meaning the rule of God in the hearts of men, which he represented. His kingdom was not of this world.

This is very much evident from the reasons, given for the suffering of the Servant. It is all couched in Old Testament language by someone who was familiar with the sacrificial system of the temple ceremony. The Servant, the Messiah, was the Passover lamb, the guilt offering. He was scourged and crucified; he suffered unbearable agony, and died a violent death. Make no mistake about it, the Hebrew expression to be "cut off" means to be executed. This is all the more remarkable because it says that he "would see the light of life." People who are dead as a rule stay dead. The Messiah defeated that rule; he rose from the dead and lives forevermore. Death is a beaten enemy. Prophecy testifies to this. Psalm 30 is the song of the risen Christ.

Jesus was crucified because God willed it. He was the empath who took upon himself the iniquity of God's people. Anyone can come to him, and anyone who comes is graciously saved from the penalty for his sins. On the cross, Jesus paid in full. Those who come and believe are justified by faith and declared righteous. Not because of anything they have done, but because the righteousness of Christ is credited to their account. That is the message of the gospel, and that is what Isaiah said.

We can now establish with certainty that point in time when this was written. Jesus had "poured out his life unto death." It was not taken from him; he gave it up himself. The question has been raised, who killed Jesus? Jesus was not killed. He was crucified and he died, but he was not killed. Death is the penalty for sin. Jesus never sinned, therefore death could not take him; instead he gave up his life to pay the penalty for sin. Joseph of Arimathea, a rich man, took the body from the cross and laid it in his tomb. The author of this prophecy stands at the stone, rolled in front of this tomb, and reflects upon what had just happened. One chapter was closed; another was about to open. The Messiah was going to be raised from the dead to a glorious future. This is what the risen Christ told his disciples and the two men on the road to Emmaus.

Obviously Isaiah, who lived seven centuries before the fact, could have never given this eye witness account. There must have been a third Isaiah. Does not logic demand that we ascribe this passage to an unknown prophet who lived at the time of Christ? But we know from irrefutable evidence that Isaiah 53 existed centuries before Jesus was born. The riddle is solved when we see that it was not really Isaiah who witnessed these things, but rather the Spirit of God speaking through him. Once this is seen it becomes understandable why shortsighted critics are so convinced someone other than Isaiah wrote these hotly debated chapters.

The prophet, prince and statesman spent the last years of his long life in exile. In the shimmering heat of the Judean desert, phantasmagorical visions appeared; a gate to the future opened, and he saw glimpses of things to come. He was privileged above all others to see flashes of the life of the Servant of the LORD, the Messiah. Almost dreamlike he saw a life passing before him. The man of destiny lived a life like no other; he was admired, betrayed and cruelly executed, but for a purpose. By his death and suffering he accomplished the redemption of his people and rose from the dead to seal their future. The Spirit of the LORD guided the hand of the prophet as he recorded his vision and gave it its spiritual content.

The Time Traveler

Isaiah was, in a sense, a time traveler. In the apocalyptic passage of Ch 24 already, he spoke as if he had been transported in time, and reported seeing things that were yet in the future. That is the prophetic style of the mature master, with a unique variant. The prophet walks, as if it were, through a time portal, and at various points in history reports his visions: it is the Lord, engaging his people in a debate.

It is this, the instantaneous shift in time, the apparent reality of God the Lord talking to a future people as if they were present that has bedeviled so many scholars. No doubt several of these are well meaning folks. Yet there is no excuse. The hand writing of Isaiah is all over these chapters. It says outright that the Assyrian campaign had only recently occurred. "At first my people went down to Egypt to live; lately, Assyria has oppressed them." (52:4). The Lord reminds his people that prophecies had been fulfilled as foretold, abrupt and sudden. It proved beyond a doubt that Isaiah was a true prophet.

Dramatic as they were, even more spectacular prophecies were to come. Isaiah speaks of the greatness of God, his sovereignty and power. All who rely on him renew their strength. It is in this context that God speaks to a world that had recently been exhausted by recurring disasters. "Let the nations renew their strength" (41:1). The

Lord repeatedly challenges the nations and Judah to find anyone who foretold events, to find any idol that is capable of doing that. But no, they cannot, they are worthless. By contrast, the Lord introduces the Messiah, who had just been baptized. (Mark 1:9-11)

> "Here is my servant, whom I uphold,
> my chosen one in whom I delight;
> I will put my spirit on him
> and he will bring justice to the nations.
> He will not shout or cry out,
> or raise his voice in the streets.
> A bruised reed he will not break,
> and a smoldering wick he will not snuff out.
> In faithfulness he will bring forth justice;
> he will not falter or be discouraged
> till he establishes justice on the earth.
> In his law the Island will put their hope."
>
> This is what God the LORD says-
> he who created the heavens and stretched them out,
> who spread out the earth and all that comes out of it,
> who gives breath to its people,
> and life to those who walk on it:
> "I, the LORD, have called you in righteousness;
> I will take hold of your hand.
> I will keep you and will make you
> to be a covenant for the people
> and a light for the Gentiles,
> to open eyes that are blind,
> to free captives from prison
> and to release from the dungeon those who sit in darkness.
> I am the LORD; that is my name!
> I will not give my glory to another
> or my praise to idols.
> See, the former things have taken place,

and new things I declare;
before they spring into being
I announce them to you."
                                Isaiah 42:1-9

We merely need to read the gospels to see what the Messiah did. This is Jesus, all the way. It is he who helped the distressed, gave sight to the blind and delivered men from the dark prison of sin. He also became a light to the Gentiles, at first those of "the Islands," that is toward the Mediterranean, and eventually of the whole world. Clearly, this prophecy is universal in scope. The former things that took place had been predicted; other things were to happen. Soon the Lord would give specific predictions. He reminded the people that they had been witnesses to fulfilled prophecy. That could only be said of the generation that saw the predictions of Isaiah come true.

Cyrus

The coming of the Messianic Servant was still far away, and Judah did need more assurance of its ultimate reality. This is one reason why we find a highly unusual example of someone being called by name long before he was born. That was that case with Cyrus, the king of Persia. Another reason is stated; Cyrus is called to restore Israel. It even mentions the manner in which Cyrus captured Babylon. That was done in an original way, over the dry bed of the river that ran through Babylon.

> I am the LORD,
> who has made all things,
> who alone stretched out the heavens,
> who spread out the earth by myself,
> who foils the signs of false prophets
> and makes fools of diviners,
> who overthrows the learning of the wise
> and turns it into nonsense,
> who carries out the words of his servants

> and fulfills the predictions of his messengers.
> who says of Jerusalem, "It shall be inhabited,"
> of the towns of Judah, "They shall be built,"
> and of their ruins, "I will restore them,"
> who says to the watery deep,
> "Be dry, and I will dry up your streams,"
> who says of Cyrus, "He is my shepherd
> and will accomplish all that I please;
> he will say of Jerusalem, 'Let it be rebuilt,'
> and of the temple, "Let its foundations be laid."
> This is what the LORD says to his anointed,
> to Cyrus, whose right hand I take hold of
>
> — —
>
> For the sake of Jacob my servant,
> of Israel my chosen, I call you by name
> and bestow on you a title of honor,
> though you do not acknowledge me.
>
> Isaiah 44:24-28; 45:1, 4

According to legend, Cyrus was raised a shepherd. Once he became king of the Medes and Persians, he led the assault on Babylon, at first without much success. Then two disgruntled defectors informed him about a weakness in the Babylonian defense: he had the river diverted, so the river bed ran dry, and entered the city underneath the walls. He captured Babylon intact, and magnanimously granted the Babylonians a measure of autonomy. They welcomed him as a liberator. He did not destroy the city. When Cyrus, according to Josephus, read the prophecy of Isaiah, "an earnest desire and ambition seized upon him to fulfill what was so written," so he ordered Jerusalem and the temple rebuilt. [39]

It is easy to see why some people believe this part of Isaiah was written later, by someone else. Yet this does not wash. Isaiah assumes all along that the things of which he speaks are in the future. Nor can it be said that he was ignorant of things to come. As we have seen, he foretold the fate of Babylon in detail. After Hezekiah welcomed the Chaldean delegation and showed them all his treasures, Isaiah said that the day would come when the Babylonians would plunder the palace. Hezekiah's descendants would be abducted, mistreated and carried off to Babylon (Ch 39). Besides, what is so unusual about Cyrus being called by name? If that was written when he was living, big deal! There is nothing impressive about that. But if this was written long before Cyrus was born, yes, that would be astonishing indeed.

We might add that the poetry in the historical interlude is identical with that of "second Isaiah." For that matter, there are many words and expressions that appear throughout the book of Isaiah. Isaiah 14:1, 2 is the message of "Second Isaiah" in a nut shell. The references to the "ruins of Jerusalem" are prophetic. The temple was still standing when these prophecies were written. "I will disgrace the dignitaries of your temple" (43:28). Chapter 66 mentions sacrifices as if they were still being made, and Jerusalem was still occupied.

> Hear that uproar from the city,
> hear that noise from the temple!
> It is the sound of the LORD
> repaying his enemies all they deserve.
> Isaiah 66:6

According to Rabbinical sources Isaiah, after the death of Hezekiah, fled to the desert to escape the wrath of Manasseh. He wrote these prophecies in the seclusion of the desert. That explains why these writings fail to mention any personal contact at all with anyone, so utterly unlike the first part of the book. That is true of the other major prophets as well. Jeremiah has all kinds of trouble with his contemporaries. Ezekiel and Daniel lived in Babylon, and they always dealt with the people among whom they lived on a very personal level. They also spoke of the canals and flat lands of Babylon, unlike Isaiah, who saw mountains, hills, the world of the desert. There, in the wide open spaces, the prophet saw from afar. There the Spirit of God spoke through him.

> Remember this, fix it in mind,
> take it to heart, you rebels.
> Remember the former things, those of long ago;
> I am God, and there is no other;
> I am God, and there is none like me.
> I make known the end from the beginning,
> from ancient times, what is still to come.
> I say, My purpose will stand,
> and I will do all that I please.
> From the east I summon a bird of prey;
> from a far-off land,
> a man to fulfill my purpose.
> What I have said, that will I bring about;
> what I have planned, that will I do.
> Isaiah 46:8-11

What makes the Judeo-Christian religion so different from any other on the face of the earth is its concept of a God who transcends time and space. This Almighty, Eternal God is distinct from the space/time continuum he created. Just as God is distinct from his works, so the creation is distinct from the Creator. In a way that is beyond our power to imagine, God ordains all things from beginning to the end, yet in such a way that the volitions of human beings are not violated.

Augustine figured there is nothing strange about the idea that God knows everything past, present and future, because he created time, and necessarily all things connected with it. It is also important to realize that this God is not a watch maker who wound up the clock and walked away, leaving man to his own devices. That is where Benjamin Franklin got the notion that "God helps those who help themselves." Not so. God is very much concerned with the crown of his creation, man. So much in fact, that "he gave his only Son, that whosoever believes in him should not perish, but have everlasting life." (John 3:4)

The Assyrian and the Passover

Second Beethoven

In the annals of art, there are interesting cases of masters who for a while rested, and suddenly came with creations that astounded the world. It happened with Ludwig van Beethoven, perhaps the greatest composer ever. Now imagine that after a thousand years the music of Beethoven survived, but nothing was known about his personal life. It would not take the experts long to realize there were two Beethovens, or maybe three. His later piano sonatas and the ninth symphony are all together different from his previous compositions. Also the first two symphonies along with the first four piano concertos lack the depth of his later works.

Of course, we know better. It was all written by the same man, but the circumstances were different. Beethoven was a great composer from the very beginning, but when he became deaf, his music intensified. Then there was a ten-year hiatus, when he was absorbed with personal problems and composed nothing at all. His last works were those of the mature master. There are also tell tale signs. The ninth symphony is rooted in everything that came before. It incorporates a theme of the second, the mysterious opening of the fourth, the strong rhythm of the seventh, and so on. The hand of the same genius is written all over these works, not only in details, but in style as well.

Is not this what we find in the book of Isaiah? It was written by the same man, but the circumstances were different. The first part of Isaiah was written in the royal courts of Jerusalem; Isaiah addressed the people of Judah and Jerusalem. Not so in the latter part. It is addressed to a people far away; not only in Judah, but also in the future. Yet the theme that runs throughout Isaiah is the same. There is also a recurring reminder that God had acted on behalf of his people, sudden and as foretold. He had dealt with the Assyrians, now the Babylonians were on the horizon.

A Sudden Act

Isaiah has much to say about Babylon. He foretold its fate long before Nebuchadnezzar made it one of the wonders of the world. Isaiah now addresses the "daughter of Babylon," the queen of kingdoms. God gave his people into the hands of the Babylonians, but that did not make Babylon just. They were merciless. The Babylonian mentality was that of atheistic humanism. "I am, and there is none beside me." They believed themselves divine. Nothing could harm them; no one could call them to account for their cruelty. Because of this, the God of Israel would make an end of their satanic sorceries, no matter how potent their spells. "Let your astrologers come forward, those stargazers who make predictions month by month, let them save you from what is coming upon you" (47:13).

To be sure, Israel was far from perfect, but in spite of their rebellion, God had not rejected them. They were, after all, his people. In the context of Isaiah's oracles, we again run into a seemingly conflicting time frame. Isaiah speaks of Babylon as if it had already oppressed Israel, but following this he addresses the stubborn people of Judah who obviously still lived in the holy city, Jerusalem. This was the generation of Hezekiah that had witnessed prophecy being fulfilled, sudden and dramatic. Because of that, God held them accountable.

> Listen to this, O house of Jacob,
> you who are called by the name of Israel
> and come from the line of Judah,
> you who take oaths in the name of the LORD
> and invoke the God of Israel-
> but not in truth or righteousness-
> you who call yourselves citizens of the holy city
> and rely on the God of Israel-
> the LORD Almighty is his name:
> I foretold the former things long ago,
> my mouth announced them
> and I made them known;

then suddenly I acted, and they came to pass.
For I knew how stubborn you were;
the sinews of your neck were iron,
your forehead was bronze.
Therefore I told you these things long ago;
before they happened I announced them to you
so that you could not say,
"My idols did them;
my wooden image and metal god ordained them."
You have heard these things;
look at them all.
Will you not admit them?
From now on I will tell you of new things,
of hidden things unknown to you.
They are created now, and not long ago;
you have not heard of them before today.
So you cannot say,
"Yes, I knew of them."
                              Isaiah 48:1-7

There can be no doubt that the event predicted had been fulfilled in an instant. This refers to the sudden annihilation of the army of Sennacherib, 687 B.C. Isaiah reminds the people they were eye witnesses of the fact. New prophecies were to come, many of them profoundly messianic. The style of these prophecies is "Babylonian," as if they were written at a particular time.

We find an example of that in the gospel of Luke. Jesus was baptized by John, after which the Holy Spirit descended upon him. Filled with the Spirit he returned to Galilee. He went to Nazareth, where he had been raised, and on the Sabbath went to the synagogue, the local church. The synagogue had scrolls of the prophetic writings, and it so happened that "the scroll of the prophet Isaiah was handed to him." It was opened at a most appropriate place:

The Spirit of the Sovereign LORD is on me,

> because the LORD has anointed me
> to preach good news to the poor.
> He has sent me to bind up the brokenhearted,
> to proclaim freedom for the captives
> and release for the prisoners,
> to proclaim the year of the LORD's favor
> and the day of vengeance of our God.
> Isaiah 61:1-3

Jesus sat down and told his spellbound audience, "Today this Scripture is fulfilled in your hearing." They were stunned. Jesus, a relative, claimed he was the Messiah. The prophecy fit the circumstances exactly. He had been anointed with the Holy Spirit, which made him indeed "Messiah," anointed, and he was at the beginning of his ministry. The year of the LORD's favor was the year of Jubilee, when all debts were canceled. Jesus came to proclaim the Lord's favor - and the vengeance of God.

In the synagogue of Nazareth he did both. Familiarity breeds contempt, and he was not at all the Messiah they expected. Nazareth had an interesting beginning. Following the Babylonian captivity, some four or five families of David's line settled in Galilee. They reasoned that maybe the promised Messiah would come through one of their families. The prophets called Messiah the "root" and "branch" of David, and so they dubbed their settlement Nazareth, after the Hebrew word *Nezer*, meaning "root." Of course these families intermarried, which is why the lines of Mary and Joseph occasionally crossed. They were related.

Yes, the Messiah came from "Rootville", but the Galileans unwittingly fulfilled another prophecy, the root grew in dry ground. (Isaiah 53:2) This was a violent people that rightfully earned a bad reputation. It showed when Jesus made his Messianic claim. When he reprimanded them for their unbelief they dragged him out of the synagogue and hauled him to the top of a hill to throw him down the cliff. As if to prove who he was, he walked right through their ranks.

He could have used his powers to annihilate them, but that was not why he came. It was, after all, the day of grace.

Fake Isaiah

There is one question that must be asked. How could a fake Isaiah in Babylon get away with the things he said? What must the Jews think when they read this.

> But you - come here, you sons of a sorceress,
> you offspring of adulterers and prostitutes!
> Whom are you mocking?
> At whom do you sneer and stick out your tongue?
> Are you not a brood of rebels, the offspring of liars?
> You burn with lust among the oaks
> and under every spreading tree;
> you sacrifice your children in the ravines
> and under the overhanging crags.
> The idols among the smooth stones
> of the ravines are your portion; they, they are your lot.
> Yes, to them you have poured out drink offerings
> and offered grain offerings.
> In the light of this, should I relent?
> Isaiah 57:3-6

They probably would not take very kindly to the author. They would also point out to him that nothing he said made sense. Spreading trees, oaks, ravines, crags? These things are found in Palestine, yes, but not in Babylon. And offerings? That is what the apostate Judeans did; no offerings of any kind were made in Babylon. What would they do if they found out that this gentleman was about to attach these writings to the scroll of Isaiah? They would expose him for what he was, a fraud. There is no way that a fake could write literature with such high morals, spoken by Almighty God, and pass it off as the genuine article. Only a contemporary, a man of impeccable character could say these things.

It does not stop here; this part of Isaiah is full of denunciation. What complicates the matter is the constant walking through a time portal from the present to the future and back, and the recurring themes of divine wrath and grace. Which raises the question, if an unknown author wrote this near the end of the Babylonian captivity, why would he present the Lord as still angry? Certainly, by that time Israel had paid the penalty in full. But if Isaiah wrote this near the end of his life in the Judean desert, during the depraved reign of Manasseh, these writings make perfect sense. It explains the constant mood swings. God's anger at what was going on in Judah is at once followed by assurances of mercy; this pattern repeats itself almost like a roller coaster, back and forth. In the final days of Isaiah the Lord had every reason to be angry. His people had utterly forsaken him. The deliverance of the remnant, even though reported as present, was still in the future. Isaiah was a true prophet, and it is he who wrote this book, all of it.

The Tents of Shem

Jesus was born in a world where the Greek culture and language were dominant, and the Roman Empire the great power. The Eastern or Hamitic empires had disappeared from the scene, instead Western civilization was on the rise, and Christianity moved in that direction, toward Europe. When the apostle Paul tried to spread the gospel in Asia, he was prevented from doing so (Acts 16:6-10).

It is of particular interest that the Servant Songs of Isaiah frequently mention a gentile audience, and without exception this audience is that of the emerging western civilizations. This is very odd, considering that the dominant powers always had been the Eastern Empires. In his day the Chaldeans and Medo-Persians were still to come.

The world wide devastations of the late Eighth Century had serious effects. Populations fled ruined homelands and migrated to faraway places. New nations emerged, most notably Greece and Rome. Indo-European tribes invaded Greece; they were the Achaeans of the Iliad. Rome was founded after the sudden decline of the Etruscan civilization. At the time of Christ, Greek was the common language, and Rome provided several generations of relative peace, combined with good roads and the beginnings of a postal system. Also the Jews established synagogues throughout the Roman Empire; they had a considerable following among the gentiles. All this contributed to the rise of Christianity and the civilization that was based upon it.

The prophecy of Noah had come true: "May God extend the territory of Japheth, may Japheth live in the tents of Shem" (Gen 9:27). The descendants of Japheth were generally the European nations. As we know, Shem was the father of the Messianic line. Yes, everything fell into place. But that also means that none of this was happenstance. It was all ordained. And the most dramatic sequence of events happened in the days of Isaiah, when a new world order was founded. Against all odds, the Servant who spoke in Isaiah addressed himself primarily to the west, not the east. That is where the early Church began; after that the word spread throughout the world.

Coincidence?

Velikovsky was not inclined to regard the prophecies of Isaiah as something supernatural. He was an agnostic, someone who believes that God, if he exists, has not revealed himself. He thought the so-called miracles of the Bible were merely unusual natural events that were foreseen by the prophets.

This is wishful thinking. It is futile to believe, as Velikovsky did, that Isaiah at the time of the Assyrian invasion of 687 B.C. "reckoned with the possibility of a disaster in the year of the opposition of Mars, and thus built his hope on the intervention of the forces of nature."[40] It is begging the question how Isaiah could possibly know that the Assyrians would be affected at all. It would have to happen at the right time, in the right place, and on top of that nearby Jerusalem had to escape unscathed. Besides, the predictions of Isaiah were far more exact than Velikovsky was willing to admit. The prophet said exactly when and where these things would happen.

The supernatural character of Biblical events often is not so much in the nature of these events as in their providential timing. Crucifixion was a common method of execution in Roman times. The crucifixion of Jesus was in that sense ordinary. Yet strange things happened. The place of execution was suddenly plunged into deep darkness that lasted three hours. There are several historical accounts that refer to a sudden darkness in that general area. Events that had been foretold centuries earlier were literally fulfilled at the appointed hour. From arrest to resurrection, everything happened as had been ordained. In a matter of days, scores of prophecies came true. From the symbolism of the sacrificial system, to the Messianic Psalms, the prophecies of Isaiah and the exact dating of Daniel, everything fell into place. It proves that Jesus was exactly who he said he was, God's Messiah; God the Son, the Creator, who became man.

Mars

In an attempt to find a solution to strange historical circumstances, we came across an explanation that defies belief. Is it really possible that the planet Mars in the course of about a century at regular intervals menaced the earth? Difficult though this is to accept, the evidence nonetheless is there. If it did happen, Mars must have still been a considerable distance away. The planets carry a negative charge, therefore they will repel each other.

Still, the thought of one of the planets appearing perhaps the size of the moon is so contrary to human experience that the thought is virtually unacceptable. Yet we should not reject the theory out of hand. Those who think the approved thought never achieve anything truly novel. History is, after all, to a large extend based upon assumption and speculation. The theory does have this great advantage: it is the single simple premise that explains everything. The devastations that mark the latter part of the 8th Century B.C., the

The Assyrian and the Passover

sudden large scale movements of nations, the strange phenomena mentioned in the scriptures that defy any other explanation.

Quite understandably there are those, particularly astronomers and historians, who dismiss the whole thing as unscientific and impossible. There is for instance the matter of planetary energy dispersal. Planets do not of their own accord enter into a different orbit. Since there does not appear to be a plausible cause for such a thing it could have never happened. Perhaps. We could counter however, that scientists often accept assumptions for which there is no basis of proof whatsoever.

Where is the vaunted black matter? It has never been observed. The famous Dutch astronomer Jan Oort calculated there must be a large band of gas, dust and comets outside the solar system. That is very well possible, and who am I to question a mind that great? But the fact remains, it still remains to be found. It has never been seen, yet it is believed to be there.

Astronomy is a fascinating subject, and it takes excellent brains to understand it all, but it is only human to embrace theory as fact. Planets could never suffer catastrophic collisions; but then Jupiter was hit by a string of meteors, each of which could have wiped out the earth. Let's not be too hasty in our pronouncements.

The theory of an electric universe and an electrically charged solar system provides a theoretical answer to several legitimate questions. The powerful magnetic attraction of the sun would affect the planets depending on their size and electrical potential and the distance from the sun. Mercury is small, lacks electrical potential and consequently has a highly eccentric orbit. Venus has a high electrical potential and is greatly affected by the solar magnet. It has the most nearly circular orbit of all the planets. The earth is farther away, is larger but has lower potential, and therefore is more elliptical. Mars is farther still, is small and has a very low potential, and is therefore no surprise that it has a highly elliptical orbit. The gas giants are too far away to be greatly influenced. Since the magnetic field of the sun affects the solar system, it could indeed restore wayward planets.

There is more. What about the ancestor worship that cripples the study of the past? Ancient history is believed to be fool proof, yet it is riddled with problems. How can there possibly be a five hundred-year gap in history, particularly when ancient historians know nothing about a glaring black hole like that? The Mycenaean age of Greece was not separated from the Archaic period by five or more centuries, it flowed into it without any interlude whatsoever. It was the faulty historical construction of Egyptology that placed pharaohs and whole dynasties in places where they do not belong, and it dislocated all of ancient history. Historians may not necessarily agree with the solution proposed here, but something definitely is very wrong.

Then there is the planet Mars, reported to have come close to the earth and suffered multiple electrical discharges in the process. If that is true, the surface of Mars must show signs of a catastrophic past. It does. That does not necessarily prove it happened during the 8th Century B.C., but there is unmistakable evidence of planetary disasters. Mars is a ruined planet with an enormous scar (the canyon Valles Marineris) running along the equator. It is more than 2,500 miles long, 30 to 70 miles wide and five miles deep, the result of electrical scarring: tons of debris was thrown into space. Some of it fell back on the planet (rocks are strewn everywhere), but much remained in the form of meteors. Martian rocks have been found on earth. Permit stupid man to ask dumb question. How did they get here? The only mechanism powerful enough to blast rocks into outer space is an electrical discharge, a lightning bolt between two planets in close proximity. The surface of Mars has lightning scars, sinuous riles typical of lightning machining, which also accounts for terraced craters that abound.

It has often been noted that the length of the day and the axial inclination of Mars are very similar to that of the earth. Is it just possible that Mars once came close enough to the earth to be gripped in a gravitational/magnetic vice that forced the red planet into an earth-like configuration?

Strange though it may sound, there is a great deal of water on Mars, most of it trapped in surface rocks. Actually that is merely the

The Assyrian and the Passover

remnant of what was once a water planet. Astronomers found evidence of a flood "of biblical proportions." One wonders if the two were related. It is even possible that Mars once was a water planet, covered by a single ocean. It means that Mars once had an atmosphere not unlike the earth. That is difficult to believe, but the evidence is unmistakable. How is this possible, considering the frigid conditions on Mars? The average temperature on Mars is -55F, and drops below -200F, worse than the South Pole. Even with an earth-like atmosphere the planet should have been ice covered. The solution is as radical as it is simple: Mars once was much closer to the sun than it is now; it had dense atmosphere, warm enough for water to run freely. But how could Mars so drastically change place?

There are additional problems that must be addressed. Bode's law postulates that the planets are separated by ever increasing distances from the sun. If, as Velikovsky maintained, Venus is a recent addition to the solar system, and if the asteroid belt is the remnant of an exploded planet, how could the planets rotate in their present orbit? Besides, with Venus missing, the earth must have been dangerously close to the sun. Another problem is the theory mentioned before, that Mars was the cause of a prolonged night, and on top of that shifted the axis of the earth enough for sun dials to be affected. That would seem to be impossible in its present orbit.

There is a theoretical solution, but a radical one. Velikovsky and others reasoned that Mars once was nearer to the sun than the earth, which explains a water planet. It had a benign climate. Then Venus with its high electrical potential entered an elliptical orbit around the sun and encountered Mars. This resulted in devastating electrical discharges from Venus to Mars. Venus lost much of it electrical potential. Although ruined, Mars briefly became more highly charged and was repelled by the sun's magnetosphere. Eventually it came close to the earth, resulting in a number of encounters described before. This explains the fourteen-year cycles: being closer to the sun, it took Mars less time to make a full orbit. Electrical discharges from the earth to Mars resulted in Mars receiving another charge; it was pushed farther away from the sun into the orbit where it is now. [41]

Venus lost much of its potential and entered into a near-circular orbit. The earth and moon were affected as well, temporarily resulting in abnormal months. This is a radical theory indeed; it solves some problems, but not all. How does it fit into Bode's law? However, it does solve the Mars riddle. Mars once was a water planet because it was nearer to the sun. How could that ever be in its present location? That is a mystery waiting to be solved. This is one answer.

End Times

It is not the purpose of this book to prove that the planets were the cause of catastrophes. The evidence is circumstantial, and all we can say is that it may have happened. Certainly these things are not necessary for our understanding of the scriptures. Nonetheless, there is one more reason why we should not disregard this theory. I wonder if Christ spoke of the end of the world in terms of a cosmic catastrophe. His prediction is intriguing.

> There will be signs in the sun, moon and stars. On the earth, nations will be in anguish and perplexity at the roaring and tossing of the sea. Men will faint from terror, apprehensive of what is coming on the world, for the heavenly bodies will be shaken.
> Luke 21:25, 26

If the planets at times left their wonted orbit, could that happen again? Who knows. We could make a case. It would seem, does it not, that Christ pointed at outer space. When he mentioned "the sun, the moon and the stars," he spoke of the solar system. The "stars'" are the wondering stars, the planets, the heavenly bodies. Men will be terrified by what they can see coming, but what could that be?

It could be a comet, or perhaps several such rocks. Or it could be something much more dramatic. The planets could leave their orbits or a large planet, hitherto undiscovered, could enter the solar system. That would create quite an impression. Imagine the huge ball being drawn into the ecliptic, the plane where the planets travel. It is attracted to Jupiter, an electrically charged giant. They exchange electrical discharges; strangely shaped plasma bolts. The planetary newcomer disentangles itself from Jupiter and rapidly moves toward the inner planets. Now plainly visible, it meets Mars which disintegrates. We can about imagine the horror this inspires. A terrified humanity knows the hellish end is near. Men scream in terror as the immense globe fills the horizon; they can see the end coming, and the nations are powerless.

Magnetic interference interrupts communications. Traffic comes to a halt, supplies dwindle, terror reigns. The earth, arrested in its motion, shudders in a series of global earthquakes. Tsunami waves irrupt. The earth's crust, gripped in the gravitational vise of the nearby planet stops, but the core keeps going. Magma erupts from the earth. The continents burn, the waters of the ocean basins begin to boil. Air and water, due to inertia, rush over the face of the earth. Mountain high waves of boiling water pour over land, aggravated by hurricane force winds.

We can only guess how men would react to this scenario, but quite likely despair and anarchy would reign. Someone might object, if that were to happen, would not this result in mass conversions? Certainly people would turn to God. That's the beauty of it. There is a simple scientific explanation. There is an equal chance that belief in God would not be appreciated. Now of course, this is just a not-so educated guess, and hopefully this is not going to frighten unstable people. But on the whole it fits prophecy fairly well. How does this fit into the second coming? That is not for me to judge. Maybe the pan-millennial theory applies: it will all pan out in the end.

The controversial aspects of this study should not obscure the message of the Scriptures. After all, we are merely dealing with events that may have happened. We could consider it an alternate version of history which we can either accept or reject. No matter how controversial, it is not to be compared with the revelation of God in Christ. Beyond doubt, the importance of that revelation far outweighs historical theories, no matter how intriguing.

To the extent that Velikovsky tried to explain the scriptures as something less-than-divine, he defaulted to the naturalist position that monotheism evolved from astral religion. Many of his followers, although often disenchanted, nonetheless follow this line of reasoning, and that renders his work misleading at best. He denied the divine origin of the Bible altogether and reduced it to something manmade, the result of human genius. There is nothing in the scriptures to suggest such a thing. To the contrary, it condemns astral religions and the perverse practices that came with it. However, it is only fitting that those who are interested should be informed about the teachings of Scripture. So far more questions have been raised than answered. I owe my readers an explanation. Be prepared, it is controversial.

Chapter Six

The Covenant

Illusion

My appreciation for art is a mixed bag at best. I like music with a nice melody, both popular and classical, a good story and paintings that make sense. It does not have to be realistic. Visitors of the Walter Anderson Museum in Ocean Springs, Ms are invariably impressed with the art of "the American Picasso." His pottery and paintings are the work of a truly great artist. They show Indians, birds, fish and the Barrier Island as the artist saw it. His art is wonderfully dynamic. It is a far cry from the silly trends that are here today and gone tomorrow.

The same holds true for music. Great composers of all ages have created real classics. On the other hand, what experts call great music, both ancient and modern, to me often sound like a wailing cat walking over a piano keyboard. These composers are musically impaired. Real art stirs our ability to create mental images. It makes us see with our imagination, and takes a wondrous hold of us.

I have a confession to make. I am a Star Trek fan, a trekker. It began with the original TV series, then the movies, the "Next Generation," and several spinoffs. Like most people, I have thought of plots. We could send Captain Kirk and Mr. Spock to an alternate universe where they emerge as Captain Jerk and Mr. Spook. Who knows, in

The Covenant

"The Next Generation" Lieutenant Barkley could fantasize on the holodeck and transform Mr. Data and Commander Ryker into Laurel and Hardy.

It is doubtful if this would go over very well. The characters are too strong to allow that. Let's face it, the world of illusion can take a powerful hold; almost as if it is real. It happened in one cliffhanger episode (The best of both worlds), the one where Captain Picard was kidnapped by the Borg, an alien race, who changed him into a Borg. Commander Ryker was promoted to captain of the Star Ship Enterprise. He rescued Picard and defeated the Borg. Captain Picard was reinstated to his rank, and Ryker chose to go back to being "number one," First Officer. The personality of Commander Ryker was so strong that I actually believed there were two captains on the Enterprise.

Yes, it all feels real. As a matter of fact it becomes real to the actors, and it carries over to the viewers. The problem is, it is not. William Shatner, who plays Captain Kirk, sometimes tries to tell his audience, "Get real folks, it is all an illusion." (Get a life). It is not appreciated, perhaps because people like to escape the doldrums of everyday existence. They live another life in the galaxy. This is not limited to Star Trek. No doubt soap opera viewers can relate to it. Years ago, Batman fans were furious because the TV series was a comedy. (What else could it be?) They wept and wailed in the letters to the editors of the Batman magazine. The editors wept with them - all the way to the bank.

Historians

All this is the result of good or at least convincing art. Much the same applies to history. There can be no doubt that historians are dedicated people with a high regard for accuracy. How the facts fit priory assumptions is an altogether different matter. Historical reconstruction is often a matter of speculation. That works reasonably well with recent history; with the remote past that is not so easy. Nobody accuses historians of deliberate deception. It is however quite natural that their notions of the dynamics of the past should be governed by personal beliefs, most notably their religious convictions, or lack thereof.

That is why the history of Egypt is a shambles. Historians refused to take the Bible seriously. The present construction of ancient history, which is based upon Egyptology, is something art has made. It is convincing because it entered the main streams of learning. History books tell only one story, mistaken though it is, and professors and Bible commentators accept it as factual.

These things take on a life of their own. Historians and scientists are human. It is, after all, asking quite a lot to admit that a life time of study was wasted. It is much safer to take refuge in popular opinion: theories are true because everybody says so, not because of irrefutable evidence. One escapes a herd mentality at the risk of being overrun by the herd. Yet the herd frequently runs in the wrong direction. Take for instance "Primitive man." It is largely conjecture, much of it wishful thinking and in a number of cases, such as "Piltdown man," an outright fraud. "Neanderthal man" turned out to be modern, and "Lucy" a monkey. In the Scopes trial, the prosecution managed to reconstruct "Nebraska man" from a single tooth. An enterprising magazine even pictured an entire Nebraska man family. The tooth turned out to be that of an extinct pig. So much for scientific fact.

Reformed

There is no trap as dangerous as the one you put up for yourself. How do you know your belief-system is true? We must ask that of Christianity as well. It is by far the most radical of all religions, and the most despised. How do we know it is not an illusion? Is there a God at all, and is the Bible actually true? The usual answer is, "Oh well, you just have to believe it." That will not do. Biblical Christianity is not the result of wishful thinking. To the contrary, it says all kinds of unpleasant things about man. For the time being let's just say that the Bible has all the internal evidence of divine inspiration.

The true God speaks through his word. Can we interpret the Bible as we see fit? No. Scripture has a message all its own.

Now imagine if someone were to put all the teachings of Scripture in a comprehensive system of thought; a philosophy of life that measures the depth of God's wisdom, even though that cannot be measured. Anyone who looks into that sooner or later discovers that this has been done. Calvin did it. There are four truly great theologians who stand out in history. They are Augustine, Aquinas, Luther and Calvin. Of these, Calvin is the most influential; not merely because he was a brilliant scholar, although that is true enough. Calvin gave his heart to the Lord; he always saw God enthroned in glory. It governed everything he stood for.

Calvin admired Luther, but he went far beyond the great Reformer. Luther's world was that of the Middle Ages, whereas Calvin was a Renaissance man. Luther discovered the great doctrine of justification by faith, and he did not go much beyond that. Lutheranism on the whole remained limited to Germany and Scandinavia. Not so Calvin; he went all the way. He did not come with new doctrines and he never emphasized anything, rather he attempted to apply the whole counsel of God to life. His theology is God-centered. It was the guiding light for his spiritual children, and it had a profound influence upon civilization. It shaped the histories of Europe and the United States.

Calvinism, commonly known as the Reformed faith, sees God as the ultimate sovereign. We do not put our trust in man or the institutions established among men for their good. There is a place for the individual, the family, the church and the state, but no one has the right to play God. These realms have their assigned place in the overall scheme of things. They do not merge, they are distinct, yet often overlap. And God's dominion rules over all. In no way does he depend on the creatures of his hand; he alone is supreme, and he does as he pleases in heaven and on earth. Is not this what the Scriptures teach from Genesis to Revelation?

Supremacy

Those who study the Bible sooner or later are faced with a baffling mystery. How can the future be described with such accuracy? If events are foreknown with certainty, does that mean they have been ordained? There can be only one answer, YES! All things are ordained according to the perfect will of an Almighty God. We have problems with that. If that is true, is their room for human liberty? The usual reasoning is: if God ordains everything, it does not matter what you do. It does matter, but more about that later.

Another reason is more basic. We like to think of ourselves as gods in our own little universe. We instinctively resent that Great Intruder who barges in and pushes us off our exalted throne. That is the real reason why atheists hate this God with a passion. It is amazing how much they hate the God who does not exist. Quite likely there are ill-informed believers who do not grasp that. Maybe they were never told or they did not bother finding this out for themselves. Nonetheless, it is there for all to see.

If anyone has notions of human supremacy, throw these ideas in the garbage can. God alone is supreme. He does not need us at all; rather we need him for everything. Human liberty and Divine sovereignty overlap. God's attitude seems to be: "Go ahead, it is your ball game, do as you please, but it is going to happen my way." We have seen this in his dealing with the Assyrian. This is the reason these things have been recorded. This is the God we deal with, and this is why we must take the history of the Scriptures seriously.

Feel Good?

No doubt there are those who wonder why anyone would be interested in historical controversies, such as the one mentioned in this book. Why should we not merely praise the Lord and feel good? Because we are called to do more than that. Because that is self-centered. Christianity is joyous, but there will be problems. Unlike Hinduism or its derivative, New Age religion, we are not interested in warm, fuzzy feelings, much less in getting spaced out. God never said we will feel good, far from it. Rather he demands obedience, and he asks of us that we trust him. How can we obey unless we know what he has commanded? How can we trust him unless we know that he has always kept his promise? How can we believe the record of his acts in the past unless we know these things really happened?

Faith is not wishful thinking; it is based on facts, not feelings. Our hope of the future and of the world to come is based on the promises of Him who is faithful and true. It is not the empty promise of an imaginary world beyond the grave. It deals with the realities of this world. We have seen that the history of salvation is based on real events, not fanciful tales.

The Judeo-Christian religion takes life seriously. There is no room for mysticism, much less an escapist mentality. We live in a very real, often harsh present; not in a timeless, unreal shadow world. Life, the world, time and history are real because God is real. We cannot withdraw into a mental monastery, like spiritual hermits and let the world go to the dogs. Christianity is rooted in history, and by that we mean the reality of everyday life. It proclaims that history is but the unfolding of God's purposes for the ages. That also means that life has a purpose, though much of it may be hidden from our view.

Give credit where it is due, atheists often see this more clearly than many a Christian, or at least those who claim to be Christian. This is why they aim their attacks at the historical claims of Christianity, particularly the book of beginnings, Genesis. Some of these men proclaim their opinions loud and clear, and so at least we know where they stand. More insidious are the practical atheists, those who would rather betray their Master with a kiss. They come disguised as man of the cloth. They are seminary professors, ministers or priests. These men deny left and right the historical accuracy of Scripture. According to them it was all a late fabrication that cannot be taken seriously. But is that true?

We found evidence that the exodus actually happened, that the history of Israel matches that of Egypt, and that certain unusual events can be explained, albeit by unorthodox means. We found evidence of something else as well: perplexing proof that all things are ordained by a God who is truly all-mighty and all-knowing. So far we merely touched upon the subject; the time has come to take a closer look. It deals largely with revelation.

Revelation

God has revealed himself in two ways. His power, majesty and greatness are manifest in the book of nature, where evidence of design abounds. Those who have eyes to see can only be utterly amazed at the infinite complexity of creation. God reveals something about himself in the book of nature. Common sense tells us that life comes from life and design from a designer. However, since we cannot know from creation what the Creator is like, God has chosen to reveal himself in a special revelation, his Word. The Scriptures are at the same time human and divine; the human authors were infallibly led by the Author on High, the Holy Spirit. They function like eye glasses that correct our blurred vision. Calvin put it this way.

> Suppose we ponder how slippery is the fall of the human mind into forgetfulness of God, how great the tendency to every kind of error, how great the lust to fashion constantly new and artificial religions. Then we may perceive how necessary was such written proof of the heavenly doctrine, that it should neither perish through forgetfulness nor vanish through error nor be corrupted by the audacity of men. It is therefore clear that God has provided the assistance of the Word for the sake of all those to whom he has been pleased to give useful instruction, because he foresaw that the likeness imprinted upon the most beautiful form of the universe would be insufficiently effective. Hence we must strive onward by this straight path if we seriously aspire to the pure contemplation of God. We must come, I say, to the Word, where God is truly and vividly described to us from his works,

while these very works are appraised not by our depraved judgment, but by the rule of eternal truth.[1]

Strange as it may sound, the Bible is the only book that *claims* to be divinely inspired. Neither the Book of Mormon nor the Koran says that. To its credit, the Koran inspired an interest in literature, and the Mormons have always been interested in education. However, the human origins of both are all too obvious. The first three verses of the Book of Mormon mention no less than sixteen times the words I, my and myself. Compare that with the opening of Scripture: "In the beginning God — —." It is God-centered. We have already seen compelling evidence that it is indeed the written word of God. It speaks with authority: "Thus says the LORD!" Scripture derives its authority, not from the church, but from its divine author: God the Holy Spirit. It is the standard for objective truth exactly because it comes from a Higher Authority, external to us.

But is it not so difficult to understand that only a select elite is able to interpret it correctly and explain it to the lesser endowed? It is plain enough for the mentally retarded to understand. This is an attempt to deny personal responsibility. Moses already called the people to live by the word as it had been revealed from on high.

> Now what I am commanding you today is not too difficult for you or beyond your reach. It is not up in heaven, so that you have to ask, "Who will ascend into heaven to get it and proclaim it to us so we may obey it?" Nor is it beyond the sea, so that you have to ask, "Who will cross the sea to get it and proclaim it to us so we may obey it?" No, the word is very near you; it is in your mouth and in your heart so you may obey it.
>
> Deuteronomy 30:11-14

Naturally we ask, how can we know that the Bible is divinely inspired and to what extent? The evidence is written all over Scripture. We have already seen undeniably evidence of prophetic accuracy. Then there is the wonderfully convincing style of writing that says so much in so few words without trying. It is the work of a Supreme Mind, original in thought and word. Its ideas are the opposite of what we are inclined to think. It has inspired men to great deeds because of its divine origin. The Spirit of God speaks to our spirit. An example from the world of music comes to mind.

It was known that the French composer Hector Berlioz wrote an early work called "Messe Solennelle," a solemn mass. He was only twenty years old, and he had one year of formal musical education. It was performed in 1824 and again in 1827. A few years later the mature Berlioz was so unhappy with it that he destroyed the score. In 1991 a copy of the original manuscript was found, and two years later the Mass was again performed. Anyone who has heard it must agree with Berlioz's music teacher; only a genius could have written that. Whatever the composer's misgivings, this music stirs the soul. It speaks to our spirit. Great art does that. The Bible is in many ways an inspired work of art; it is in every way the inspired word of God. It speaks to our soul. Only God could have created that.

When we study the Bible, we should be careful to refrain from private interpretation. Do not read things into it that it does not say. We are under the word and not above it. God has revealed what he wants to be known and that touches things beyond our understanding, such as freedom. How can finite man be free if he is under the absolute control of an Almighty God? Who is the ultimate authority, God or man? Every Christian instinctively knows the answer, God alone is Supreme. This does not mean that everyone has thought out the implications, or even whether some actually accept it intellectually. It is, after all, humiliating to eat humble pie.

Sovereignty

Those who bother to read the Bible soon discover it is a very different book from what it is often believed to be. There is something about God that disturbs us. It involved authority. There rings throughout the Bible a note of divine sovereignty: the unlimited power and dominion of an Almighty God who "— works out everything in conformity with the purpose of his will."(Eph 1:11) It follows that he does not need us at all; he does however, hold us accountable. Considering that we live in a troubled world, this raises all kinds of uneasy questions. If God is good, just and righteous, and he can do anything, why does he allow evil? Maybe he doesn't, and the power to rule is in the hands of the Evil One, Satan! Then who needs God?

The Moscow Symphonic Orchestra once played Tchaikovsky's sixth symphony. Just as they started the last movement a brownout struck, and the lights went out. These were real professionals, so they kept playing in the dark until they came to the end of this difficult piece. As they played the last strains the lights came back on, and they finished with a standing ovation from the audience. The players congratulated each other with this remarkable feat, but then they realized that the conductor sat there, crying. It dawned on them that he had good reasons to. He was not needed; they had done very well without him swaying his baton. That is how many person regard God. Who needs him, and who is in control anyway? Is God in control, is he able to deal with the evils of this world and does he rule over the affairs of man?

Here comes the shocker. God is perfectly able to deal with evil; in fact he ordains it. No, God is not the author of sin, that is impossible. Sin and evil go together, but they are not the same. Sin is rebellion that produces evil, but God is in full control regardless. This is not an opinion; God said so.

> I am the LORD, and there is no other.
> I form the light and create darkness,
> I bring prosperity and create disaster,
> I, the LORD, do all these things.
> $\qquad\qquad\qquad$ Isaiah 45:6, 7

We have seen ample evidence that he has done just that. Does that make God evil? Why, no, of course not. It is not necessarily wrong to inflict evil. Punishment falls in that category. Anyone in authority will occasionally use disciplinary measures. Parents do it.

My Sergeant did it, too. That does not make them evil. (Sarge may have been an exception). A judge may very well sentence a criminal to death, but that does not make him a killer; he merely exercises justice. Those in authority take corrective action for the common good.

Does not the Judge of all the earth have the right to punish and discipline as he sees fit? We can be sure it is always done for a righteous purpose. This is not mere speculation; he has said that he does it. We have seen numerous cases where God metes out punishment on people, armies and nations. He even destroyed the whole earth through a flood. These things usually involve an agency; either predatory nations or upheavals in nature. Through it all, God is in control. He does whatever pleases him. That may not be what we expect him to do. His ways are inscrutable.

The Will of God

Fulfilled prophecy proves the point. Unpleasant things happened just as foretold. We saw this in the Servant song. God did not merely foresee what would happen to his Messiah, nor did he "allow" it. The crucifixion was no happenstance; God planned it. "It was the will of the LORD to crush him and cause him to suffer. (Isa 53:10) The New Testament affirms this throughout. Christ came to die. "He was chosen before the foundation of the world." (1 Peter 1:20). The meaning is that the whole thing was decided before the world was even created.

Across Jerusalem is the Mount of Olives, and on that mountain was a *getsemaneh*, an olive press. This is where Jesus faced the terrible ordeal of the crucifixion; he felt as if he was being crushed to a point where he sweat blood. He prayed, "Father, if you are willing, take this cup from me; yet not my will but yours be done." (Luke 22:42). Jesus was human. He feared the hell he was called to go through, yet he was obedient to God unto a ghastly death. The point is, there was no way out. God willed that this should happen because it was the only way to redeem man, and Jesus submitted. Jesus was a good soldier. He was called to a duty and he did it. Then did the Pharisees do God's will? The apostles Peter and John spoke of it when they prayed to God.

> "Sovereign Lord," they said, "you made heaven and earth and the sea and everything in them. You spoke by the Holy Spirit through the mouth of your servant, our father David.
> *Why do the nations rage?*
> *And the peoples plot in vain?*
> *The kings of the earth take their stand*
> *and the rulers gather together against the Lord*
> *And against his anointed one. (Ps 2)*
> Indeed Herod and Pontius Pilate met together with the Gentiles and the people of Israel in this city to conspire against your holy servant Jesus, whom you anointed. They did what your power and will be had decided beforehand should happen."
>
> Acts 4:24-38

The "will of God" is twofold. His plan for our lives is hidden in his secret counsel, which we can never know or penetrate, but he has given us rules to live by. This is based on Deuteronomy 29:29.

> The secret things belong to the LORD our God, but the things revealed belong to us and to our children forever, that we may follow all the words of this law.

There are numerous cases where God clearly revealed how he wanted his people to live. When they failed to live up to these expectations, he dealt with them as their deeds deserved, which frequently resulted in comments that on the surface would seem contradictory. A case in point is the idolatry that resulted in human sacrifice. They offered their children to the Moloch, which angered God no end.

> The people of Judah have done evil in my eyes, declared the LORD. They have set up their detestable idols in the house that

bears my Name and have defiled it. They have built the high places of Topheth in the Valley of Ben Hinnom to burn their sons and daughters in the fire - something I did not command, nor did it enter my mind.
>> Jeremiah 7:30, 31

That is certainly true. These practices were specifically forbidden in the Law of Moses. However, God was not exactly defeated; whatever the intent of the apostate Jews, God in his secret counsel punished them by the very idols they worshiped.

I also gave them over to statutes that were not good and laws they could not live by; I let them become defiled through their gifts - the sacrifice of every first born - that I might fill them with horror so they would know that I am the LORD.
>> Ezekiel 20:25, 26

Nowhere do we find orders to sacrifice the firstborn. To the contrary. However, Israel deliberately violated God's revealed will, so he "gave them over" to evil pagan laws, the very statutes they were supposed to fight. Contradictory? No way. Both Jeremiah and Ezekiel truthfully reported God's will, both revealed and hidden. The Lord has told us how he wants us to live our lives, for instance in the Ten Commandments. This is his revealed will. He has told us what we should do, and knows what we will do. The Pharisees knew the commandment, "You shall not kill," and they certainly knew that this refers to murder. Contrary to the commandment, they plotted to kill Jesus anyway, God knew the intent of their hearts, and ordained events in such a way that they carried out their schemes according to his purposes. He did this in accordance with his hidden will, which is his eternal counsel that is unknown to us. It is in that sense that he ordains everything that happens. In an evil world that includes evil. All the same, the spiritual leaders of Israel were responsible for their actions. The Apostles did not see a conflict in this; they hinged everything squarely upon the sovereignty of God.

Providence

With providence we do not mean God himself, but rather "something that is affected by God's foresight." (Webster). This goes beyond foreknowledge. The Westminster Confession defines providence as follows.

> God, the great Creator of all things, does uphold, direct, dispose and govern all creatures, actions and things, from the greatest even to the least, by his most wise and holy providence, according to his infallible foreknowledge, and the free and immutable counsel of his will, to the praise of the glory of his wisdom, power, justice, goodness and mercy. Although in relation to the foreknowledge and decree of God, the first cause, all things come to pass immutably and infallibly, yet by the same providence, he orders them to fall out according to the nature of second causes, either necessarily, freely or contingently.

It is true that God foresees all things. It is also true that he ordains all things accordingly. But he does not helplessly observe events as they happen, unable to do a thing about it. God does not live in a faraway heaven. Rather he "inhabits eternity." He exists in an eternal present and he rules over all.

> I make known the end from the beginning,
> from ancient times what is still to be.
> I say, My purpose will stand,
> and I will do all that I please.
> From the east I summon a bird of prey;
> from a far-off land, a man to fulfill my purpose.
> What I have said, that will I bring about;
> What I have planned, that will I do.
> Isaiah 46:10

God's providence includes all. He holds the keys of life and death. Whatever he purposes, that is what happens, including bad things. "When disaster comes to a city, has not the LORD caused it?" (Amos 3:6) This is not at all what we expect, but it makes perfect sense. If God is in control of all things, as he must be, then nothing escapes his decree. God does not inspire sin, that is against his nature, rather he implements evil for his purposes, which in the very nature of the case are altogether righteous and good. If tragedies befall us or disaster strikes, it is God who ultimately directs these things for a high purpose. He does it in a way that baffles our understanding.

> The LORD foils the plans of the nations,
> he thwarts the purposes of the peoples.
> But the plans of the LORD stand firm forever.
> The purposes of his heart through all generations.
>
> Psalm 33:10, 11

Joseph

We could cite several examples. The patriarch Jacob had twelve sons by two wives and two concubines. It was a divided family and it showed, for Jacob had a favorite. That was Joseph, the first son of Rachel. His brothers hated him so much that they sold him into slavery; then they told their father a lion had killed his son. Joseph ended up in Egypt, in the home of Potiphar, pharaoh's Chief of the Treasury. There he did so well that he was put in charge of the house. This did not last; he spent years in jail on false charges. While in jail, he interpreted the dreams of two of pharaoh's officials, a baker and a cup bearer, that came true as foretold. The baker was hanged, the cup bearer survived, but he did nothing for Joseph.

Then pharaoh had troublesome dreams; seven fat cows came up out of the Nile, but were devoured by seven skinny cows, which remained skinny. Then in his dream he saw that seven good heads of grain were swallowed by seven skinny heads of grain. This greatly bothered pharaoh. The cup bearer informed him of Joseph's unusual abilities. Joseph came, and explained that seven good years were to come, followed by seven lean years. He advised pharaoh to store up for the bad years. Pharaoh was so impressed that he put Joseph in charge. He became second in command after pharaoh. The years of plenty came, followed by persistent drought. Canaan, too, was affected, and so Jacob told his sons to buy grain in Egypt. They never knew who welcomed them. Joseph wanted to find out if they had changed at all, and when he was satisfied that they had indeed mended their ways, he revealed his identity. Jacob and his clan moved to Egypt, where they were given pasture land in Goshen. They escaped not only the famine, but also the perverse life style of Canaan.

After the death of Jacob, his sons feared that maybe Joseph would take revenge on them for their misdeed. After all, they had caused him years of grief. Joseph was sad when his brothers came to him, and he assured them, "Don't be afraid. Am I in the place of God? You intended to harm me, but God intended it for good to accomplish what is now being done, the saving of many lives." (Gen 50:19, 20) Joseph saw God's hand in his life and that of his brothers. God works in ways that are beyond our understanding. His is a timeless providence.

Judah and Tamar

The Almighty is perfectly able to use the intent of men for his own purposes. He is also in full control of nature. He causes plenty and want; he appoints these things from eternity. What he ordains now was already active in the past, just as everything is being readied for the future. Nothing is insignificant in his sight. His sovereignty includes all things. He does not forget the birds; every hair on our head is counted. (Luke 12:6, 7) We are that important to him.

Another evidence of providence comes from an unexpected source: the sordid story of Judah and Tamar, found in Genesis 38.

This is one of those things we would never expect to find in scripture; it would be far more interesting to find details about Joseph's life in Egypt. Instead we are surprised by a strange and sad story, a story of incest and betrayal.

Judah married a Canaanite woman and had three sons by her. Tamar was the wife of his oldest son Er, but Er was evil and God took his life. In accordance with local law Onan, the younger son, must marry Tamar to continue the line of Er. But Onan resented that and resorted to birth control methods, he "spilled his semen on the ground." What he did was evil in God's sight, and Onan died as well. Judah had lost his two oldest sons, and told Tamar to wait until the youngest grew up. After all that, Judah's wife died.

When Tamar saw that Judah was not about to give his youngest son to her, she resorted to trickery. She disguised herself as a temple prostitute and seduced her father-in-law, who did not recognize her. When Tamar was found to be pregnant, she faced the death sentence. Then she provided evidence that Judah was the father; he rose to the occasion and blamed himself. In all his grief he ultimately proved himself a man of honor. Tamar gave birth to a son whom she called Perez who, it turned out, was an ancestor of King David.

Why, we ask, was this lurid story recorded in such detail? Oh well, it provides the line of King David. Yes, but what king likes to have that kind of skeleton in his family closet? The real reason is far more important. King David was the ancestor of the Messiah, and this story was recorded to dispel the notion that God needs nice people to achieve his purposes. The Messianic line continued through the depth of human depravity.

Far more charming and romantic is the story of Ruth and Boaz, the "kinsman-redeemer," a Messianic type. Ruth and Boaz, too, were in the Messianic line, for Ruth was the great-grandmother of King David. Ruth was a Moabite; she was not born into the covenant nation. But Israel was an open society, being readied for the Messiah who was to redeem his people. Ever so slowly the nation matured, and more was being revealed. Particularly the Book of Psalms reflects the religious experience of God's people. These Psalms are alive. They speak to us exactly because they were drawn from delight and despair. That is why the prophetic voice of this poetry is so personal.

Crucifixion

An example of that is found in a profound Messianic prophecy. When Jesus was hanging on the cross, he cried out, "My God, my God, why have you forsaken me?" He said this for a reason; it involves prophetic utterance. The spectators realized he was quoting Psalm 22, a Messianic prophecy. What must Jesus have thought when he was dying a slow and terrible death on that torture rack? We know it in detail; this Psalm provides a window into the mind of Christ. It describes not only the crucifixion but also the terrors the suffering Servant endured while hanging on a cross, his hands and feet pierced by nails, enduring inhuman suffering. He was in hellish pain.

> My God, my God, why have you forsaken me?
> Why are you so far from saving me,
> so far from the words of my groaning?
> O my God, I cry out by day, but you do not answer,
> by night, and am not silent.
> Yet you are enthroned as the Holy One;
> you are the praise of Israel.
> In you our fathers put their trust,
> they trusted and you delivered them.
> They cried to you and were saved;
> in you they trusted and were not disappointed.
> But I am a worm and not a man,
> scorned by men and despised by the people.
> All who see me mock me;
> they hurl insults, shaking their heads:
> "He trusts in the LORD;
> let the LORD rescue him.

Let him deliver him
Since he delights in him."
Yet you brought me out of the womb;
you made me trust in you
even at my mother's breast.
From birth I was cast upon you;
from my mother's womb you have been my God.
Do not be far from me, for trouble is near,
and there is none to help.
Many bulls surround me;
strong bulls of Bashan encircle me.
Roaring lions tearing their prey
open their mouths wide against me.
I am poured out like water,
and all my bones are out of joint.
My heart has turned to wax;
it has melted away within me.
My strength is dried up like a potsherd,
and my tongue sticks to the roof of my mouth;
you lay me in the dust of death.
Dogs have surrounded me;
a band of evil men has encircled me,
they have pierced my hands and my feet.
I can count all my bones;
people stare and gloat over me.
They divide my garments among them
and cast lots for my clothing.
But you, O LORD, be not far off;
O my strength, come quickly to help me.
Deliver my life from the sword,
my precious life from the power of the dogs.
Rescue me from the mouth of the lions;
save me from the horns of the wild oxen.

Psalm 22:1-21

This is a description of death by crucifixion. We see Jesus hanging on the cross. His bones were twisted out of joint, his wrists and feet pierced by nails, resulting in excruciating pain. His back was torn by the merciless flogging of the Roman soldiers; he was seriously weakened. His heart was affected, and he was dying of thirst. To add to the shame, he was hanging there naked. The Roman executioners divided his belongings between them. When they found that his garment was woven out of one piece they did not tear it up but gambled over it instead. (John 19:23, 24)

Meanwhile the priests and elders hurled insults at him. Shaking their heads they said, "He trusts in God. Let God rescue him now if he wants him, for he said, 'I am the Son of God.'" (Matthew 27:43) This mocking stopped when daylight suddenly was swallowed up by pitch darkness (the day and night mentioned in Ps 22). The sun hid her face in shame. The spectators finally realized what they had done; they left weeping and beating their breast.

Trust

The gospels are based on eye witness accounts. They describe the events surrounding the crucifixion in a very restrained style, and for this reason they do not relate what Jesus was thinking when he was hanging on the cross. Frankly there is no need to, it is revealed in Psalm 22. The prophetic voice gives us wonderful insight in the character of Christ. In the worst possible circumstances he trusted in God. In his humanity he may have known all the reasons for his plight, but God was still his God.

As we have seen, the repetition of a phrase served as an exclamation mark. What really got Jesus was not the terrible pain or even the inhuman taunting of his enemies. Rather, he was literally in a God-forsaken place. On the cross Christ became sin, and God poured out the full measure of divine wrath on that accursed human who was hanging there, rejected by heaven and earth. Even then, when God did not answer, Christ still placed his full trust in God, and that is why the Father answered him and delivered him.

Naturally the question arises, if Jesus was indeed God incarnate, how could he die? God is immortal. It is more complicated than that. Why do we die? Because we are sinful. Death is the penalty for sin. But Jesus did not sin. It follows that he never was under the curse of death. Not only in his divinity, but in his humanity as well, he was immortal. Nothing could kill him. He endured suffering that would have killed anyone else. It is certain however that his divine nature empowered him to lay down the life of his human nature. He himself said so. He "poured out his life unto death." He could die at will, yet he endured his hellish suffering in the ultimate act of perfect obedience to the will of the Father. Only when his redeeming work was accomplished did he give up his spirit. Tempting though it certainly was, he endured the cross until the ransom was paid in full.

In the interest of sound interpretation, we should point out that some things were fulfilled figuratively. The prophecy says that Messiah was surrounded by bulls, dogs and lions. Obviously this refers to the terrors he endured. Here too, the details are exact, and this is all the more remarkable when we realize that crucifixion was invented by the Phoenicians, about 500 B.C. The Romans adapted and refined this method of death by torture.

It is certain that Psalm 22 was written much earlier. David composed this psalm a thousand years before, probably when he fled from his son Absolom. Upon leaving Jerusalem he crossed the Kidron valley to the Mount of Olives, the very place where a millennium later Jesus agonized in the face of the crucifixion. (2 Samuel 15:23, John 18:1) Considering the circumstances, it was the perfect spot for David to pour out his heart before the Lord. It was a vehicle for the Holy Spirit to render it a prophetic prayer.

It is beyond our power to understand how the very thoughts of Christ were known so far off. So were the words and actions of the religious leaders. This goes to prove that God determines all things according to an eternal decree, yet no violence is done to the will of the creature. He carried out his purposes not only in the crucifixion and the actions of those involved, but also in the crowning of his redemptive plans, the resurrection.

The Covenant

Beginning with verse 22 of this Psalm, we find a song of praise and triumph. The Messiah trusted in God and God heard his prayer. He rose from the dead. It was the same hope beyond hope that made Hezekiah trust the Lord when Sennacherib threatened to take Jerusalem by storm. When everything was lost, deliverance came in miraculous fashion. God's wonderful purposes would be known throughout all the earth, and in all ages.

> All the ends of the earth
> Will remember and turn to the LORD,
> and all the families of the nations
> will bow down before him,
> for dominion belongs to the LORD
> and he rules over the nations.
>
> Psalm 22:27, 28

This involves something we need to know. God has a plan. This plan was conceived in eternity, and it is certain to come true. When Adam transgressed in the Garden of Eden, God was not caught by surprise, nor did he shift to an alternate plan. It was all foreseen and ordained accordingly, which rendered the event certain. The Almighty has never given us a formal explanation why it happened that way, other than that it involves his glory. We can however hazard a guess.

All things are created for the manifestation of God's glory. That is why we live. God did not take the easy way out. Rather he chose a path that would exhibit not only his majesty, but also his justice and severity, his love and mercy. How this was done is another matter, it involves a Covenant. The Lord agreed within himself, so to speak, to enter into a triune compact. It is certain from the Scriptures that the God who is One is also Three.

The Knowledge of God

It should be clearly understood that the doctrines or teachings of which we speak are not personal opinions. The Word has a message all its own. We do not pick and choose our way through the Bible cafeteria style. It is all or nothing. What the Scriptures in our modest opinion should say and what they actually do say are often two very different things. When we speak of divine truth we do not come with guesses. These things have been revealed. In our search for the truth of God we have a single guide, the Word of God. What then does that Word say about the Lord God Almighty?

It is only human to think of God as a sort of exalted Superman. There are cults that do just that. They make God human and man divine. God is not human and he is not physical. The commandment not to bow down before any image at all testifies to that. God cannot be represented in any fashion because he is not limited in space. That belongs to the realm of creation. This is the otherness of God. The Creator transcends his creation. The material world in the very nature of the case has its limitations. God the Creator does not. He is a pure Spirit, infinite in every way, and cannot be discerned by the physical senses.

Christ told the Samaritan woman, "God is Spirit." Clearly the meaning is that God is not in any way physical. We should make it clear that God is not a force or power that energizes everything. God is personal. He is self-conscious and has, what Thomas Aquinas called, "necessity of being." He is a self-determining Being. Now there have always been false prophets who deny this and come with fake visions. This happened already in the days of Jeremiah.

"Am I only a God nearby,"
declares the LORD
"and not a God far away?
"Can anyone hide in secret places
so that I cannot see him?" declares the LORD.
"Do I not fill heaven and earth?" declares the LORD.

"I have heard what the prophets say who prophesy lies in my name. They say, 'I have had a dream, a dream!' How long will this continue in the hearts of these lying prophets, who prophesy the delusions of their own minds?"

Jeremiah 23:23-26

God fills heaven and earth; he is omnipresent. It is folly to ascribe physical attributes to God merely because it speaks of his eyes, hands and arms. Psalm 91 speaks of his wings and feathers. Obviously this has nothing to do with appearance. Scripture employs physical language because we can relate to that. Imagine if God was limited by a physical body, then how could he know what goes on throughout the world at any time anywhere, and what could he do about it? He could not possibly be there when we need him. We can pray to God because he is ever present; he is always there, and he is personal.

He is also unique. There is only one God, the Creator of all that is, and he has no equal. There is none like him. He alone is eternal and immortal, perfect in purity. Where did God come from? He always existed. He never had a beginning and he will have no end. He is the Great I AM.

Trinity

In our study of ancient history we came across several flat statements: there is One and only One God. There is no other. Naturally that makes us wonder, if God is all by himself, isn't he lonesome? That must be, shall we say, unpleasant, with no one to talk to. Well, that is not quite true. God is solitary in the sense that he is unlike any one else, but he is not lonesome. He has perfect happiness within himself. This involves a mystery; the being of God is three in one. He is Triune. It is evident throughout the Scriptures.

There is something unusual about God. He is spoken of in the singular, but also in the plural. Both the Old and New Testament speak of persons within the Deity. The Hebrew word El means God.

Elohim is a plural word, but it is always used in the singular; something like "United States." The famous "Shemah," spoken daily by devout Jews in their prayers, employs it that way. "Shemah, Yisrael, Yahweh Elohenu, Yahweh echod." (In deference to the Name of God the Jews always say Adonai) "Hear O Israel, the LORD our God, the LORD is one." (Deuteronomy 6:4).

The word Elohenu literally means "our gods." In the context of the sentence its meaning is that of a plurality within the Deity. It means Godhead. "Echod" does not mean one in the sense of a single being; this word is used in Genesis 2:24, where it is said that a man and his wife shall be "one" flesh. It indicates a union. The Old Testament already speaks of distinct persons within the Godhead, as in Psalm 2.

> Why do the nations rage
> and the peoples plot in vain?
> The kings of the earth take their stand
> and the rulers gather together against the LORD
> and against his Anointed One.
> "Let us break their chains," they say,
> "and throw off their fetters."
> The One enthroned in heaven laughs,
> The LORD scoffs at them.
> Then he rebukes them in his anger
> and terrifies them in his wrath, saying,
> "I have installed my King
> on Zion, my holy hill."
> I will proclaim the decree of the LORD:
> He said to me, "You are my son;
> today I have become your Father.
> Ask of me and I will make the nations your inheritance,
> the ends of the earth your possession.
> You will rule them with a iron scepter;
> you will dash them to pieces like pottery."
> Therefore, you kings, be wise;

> be warned, you rulers of the earth.
> Serve the LORD with fear
> and rejoice with trembling.
> Kiss the Son, lest he be angry
> and you be destroyed on the way,
> for his wrath can flare up in a moment.
> Blessed are all who take refuge in him.

As we have seen, the apostles said this came true when the gentiles and the priests crucified Jesus, the Lord's Messiah. To some extent this is always true. Humanity is in rebellion against the Lord; men always try to get rid of God and Christ. Obviously the relationship between the Lord and his Anointed One, the Messiah, is very close indeed. The Lord says he is the Father who begets the Son. "Today I have become your Father," or its equivalent, "Today I have begotten you," implies this is an ongoing thing. The Father generates the Son from all eternity.

Also the Spirit of God is frequently spoken of as a person; never as a mere force. Of course, we deal with a mystery no one can fathom. If we do not even understand ourselves, how much less the being of the Almighty! We could however, draw an analogy with our make-up. This is valid because we are, after all, created in the image of God, and the Scriptures often do just that. Since we resemble God to some extent, we could make a comparison.

Character

Hebrews is among the most fascinating of all the books in the New Testament. It is rooted in the Old Testament, and it establishes the preeminence of Christ over all things. He is the Supreme Revelation.

> In the past God spoke to our forefathers through the prophets at many times and in various ways, but in these the last days he has spoken to us by his Son, whom he appointed heir of all things,

and through whom he made the universe. The Son is the radiance of God's glory and the exact representation of his being, sustaining all things through his powerful word.

Hebrews 1:1-3

The author of Hebrews speaks of "the Son" in terms that very much resemble character and personality. We can see this in ourselves, or at least in some people. Occasionally we run into people (they are few) with a powerful personality. They are always good communicators. The moment these people express themselves, we know we are dealing with great character. For better or for worse, we cannot forget them; they have made a strong impression, their presence is being felt.

Well now, the personality of God is that way. The character of God is eternal and immense. It involves a personality of infinite perfection. This, the effulgence of God's splendor that reflects his glory, is a person. Perhaps this is so because only a person, himself divine, can fully reflect the glory of God. The first person of the Godhead is God the Father. Humanly speaking, the first person is God proper. The second person is God the Son; the image of God's being. He is his personality, his presence, his character personified.

The scriptures speak of these persons in terms of a Father/Son relationship. The Father generates the Son, as a person generates personality, and the sun generates light. The Father and the Son are both fully divine, just as a person and his (or her) personality are both fully human. The Son is also called the Word of God. So is the Bible, but there is a difference. The Son is the personal Word of God, the Bible the written Word. Both are at the same time human and divine; the Son however is the Logos, the Word, because he is the full expression of God. He is the final revelation, the reason being that God himself appeared. Luther spoke of the Son as "the eternal wisdom, residing in the Father." It is generally believed that the Wisdom referred to in Proverbs 8 and 9 speaks of the eternal Son.

There is more. The person and the personality are not isolated. There exists between them a bond, a spirit that proceeds from both, like an arc, and unites them. Scripture speaks of God in similar terms. The Father and the Son are united in their One-ness in a Spirit of Love. This is the Holy Spirit. It is certain that the Holy Spirit is not merely a force or a power; he is a person. What is true of the Son is equally true of the Spirit. The infinity of God's love is so immense and so perfect that the Spirit who proceeds from the Father and the Son is a person. The Spirit alone is able to probe and understand the depth, the infinity of God, because he is himself God, the Lord and Giver of life. Only God has life in himself.

Economy

There are people with advanced mathematical skills who insist that one plus one plus one adds up to three. It follows that there must be three gods (or maybe more), or that there can be no Trinity. Others object that this word is nowhere mentioned in the Bible. That is certainly true, but we have the authority to create words that fit a concept, and the concept of a Triune God is written all over the Scriptures. All this is defective reasoning. It is certain there are three persons. They are not

one *plus* one *plus* one equals one, but

one *times* one *times* one equals one.

The three persons of the Godhead are coequal; they are fully divine and share the same glory. They understand each other perfectly. Concord exists between them; they are always in perfect agreement. This implies something that goes to the heart of the gospel: God in his very nature is a Covenant God. He has entered into a Triune Covenant.

Between the persons of the Godhead there is an order of authority, and related to that an economy of labor. The Father is the Planner. It is he who ordains all things according to the counsel of his will. He is in all things supreme; among the persons of the Trinity he is the first among equals.

The Son executes the will of the Father. He is the King of Glory; God's right-hand man, so to speak, the Supreme Executive. The Spirit is the One who empowers and enlightens; he is the giver of life. Since God is One, the works of the persons of the Trinity are the same. To elevate the work of one person above the other is heresy.

The Spirit sheds light upon the works of the Father and the Son. It is he who leads believers to the Son. Keep in mind that the Son is called the Word of God, and the Spirit the Breath of God. When we speak, our breath vibrates and produces articulate sounds, the word. That is how close the Son and the Spirit are. We could think of the Spirit in other ways. A game played at night is lit up by bright lights. We do not come to watch the lights, we come to watch the game. That is what the lights are for. That is what the Spirit does; he sheds light upon the Son.

Yahweh and Allah

There are those who believe that all religions are the same, and that it does not matter what you believe, just so you are sincere. I have known Nazis who were sincere about their notions, but that did not make it right. All religions are not the same. As a Christian I have this conviction that there is a Being higher than I. I am also convinced that this Being is personal and that I can communicate with him.

This is the great, the insuperable difference between Christianity and Islam. Mohammed borrowed many of his ideas from Judaism and Christianity, but Allah (originally a desert god), unlike Yahweh, is impersonal. Yahweh and Allah are not at all the same. A Triune God by his very nature communicates; a God who is a single being never does. Allah is a single person, absolutely supreme, who is entirely unapproachable; he is too exalted to communicate with man. He is the God without a heart, the God of fate who does not care. Allah's unity is such that he is altogether divorced from creation.

Naturally if God is altogether unapproachable, it makes no sense to pray to him. Muslim prayers are learned by rote; they are mechanical and never implore the deity for aid or mercy. For much the same reason Muslims have a very different understanding of sin. It has nothing to do with a broken relationship between God and man (there is no such thing), it is a matter of transgressing the law or sinning against the majesty of Allah. Man is not by nature sinful, he must earn his way to heaven. It is legalistic. Islam is just as dry as the desert it came from. Christianity is the very opposite. It deals with God and man, the broken relationship between them, and what God did about it. God is not remote and he wants us to be close to him. That is why he created us in his image.

In Islam, entrance into paradise has nothing to do with justice. Righteousness and justice are not at all the foundation of Allah's throne. The Muslim hopes that his good deeds outweigh the bad, but in the end it all depends upon the whims of an unpredictable deity, the wholly unapproachable Allah. It defines Islamic culture. Without a revealed standard for truth there is no justice, no mercy, only fatalistic acceptance. Whatever the family, the Muslim cleric or dictator pronounces, that is the will of Allah.

To the Muslim life is *Jihad*, a continual struggle. Do the best you can to enter paradise. There is no guarantee that the believer will achieve this feat. The more fanatical factions convince their adherents that taking the lives of infidels does just that. Islam historically has resorted to the sword. It spread by violence and war. And where Islam is the state religion, it is dangerous to say the least to convert to Christianity. Parents have killed their children for becoming Christians. Yes, there have been fringe "Christian" movements that are violent as well, but they are the exception to the rule. Christianity proper is a religion of peace.

Now of course, these are extreme cases. Historically Christians and Muslims have been able to live together in peace. It is possible now. Muslim neighbors are hospitable and willing to discuss Christianity. There is tolerance and hope.

The Image of God

What makes human beings what they are - human, superior over the animal kingdom? The answer lies in the creation account. Physically a mammal, man is a spiritual being as well, endowed with moral and ethical values. He is a spiritual amphibian, so to speak; a link between heaven and earth. Animals are programmed, but man is among the highest of created beings, made "in the image of God." We resemble God in a number of ways.

It behooves us to ignore the fantastic nonsense penned by Zachariah Sitchin, and to refute the errors of Mormonism, whose gods are human. There is no need to go into detail, but like so many religions, they fail to explain why we cry for justice, why we are offended at ruthless acts of oppression and terrorism, and why we look for answers that seem so elusive. Yet the reason is given, man has certain faculties that reflect the nature of God.

Man is neither divine nor a god, rather the divine imprint is stamped on his being. This has profound and far reaching implications. If we harm the image of God, we offend God, therefore human life is precious. Unborn children are human from the moment of conception; from day one they are human beings in the making.

In the Roe vs. Wade case, the U.S. Supreme Court noted that Christianity, unlike paganism, historically always protected the unborn. Roman Christians rescued abandoned infants from the garbage dump. However, the court was being manipulated and the justices, unwittingly perhaps, resorted to pagan ways. The unborn were left at the mercy of pagans, and paganism has no mercy. As a general rule, religions outside the Judeo-Christian tradition have little or no regard for human life.

Criminal law is based upon this very doctrine. We are allowed to kill animals (but not cruelly so). To kill a human being is an altogether different matter. Granted there are unusual circumstances, such as war and crime fighting, but even then there are restraints. To kill a human being deliberately and with malice aforethought is murder, and demands retribution. This sense of justice is not accidental, it is part of our make-up. God, who is perfectly just, made us that way.

Ultimately it leads us back to the One from whom these things came. Animals cannot be held responsible for their conduct. Although they have a soul, they were not created in the image of God, and when they die their life goes back to the great pool from which it came. Not so man. He is a moral agent and his sense of justice will ultimately be satisfied. When the Supreme Judge settles all accounts, all will be brought to light; sentence will be proclaimed, final destiny established. Some will cry out, "The harvest is past, the summer has ended, and we are not saved." (Jer 8:20). For the day of salvation is now, not at the Day of Judgment, when it is forever too late.

God and Man

The story of the Bible is the story of redemption, and the story of redemption is the story of representation. When God created man and angels, he did not make them robots. They were capable of obedience if they chose to do so. They could also go their own way and rebel, which is what happened. There is ample evidence that a rebellion took place in heaven, just as it did on earth. The outcome was in many ways very different, however. Simply stated, no redemption was provided for the fallen angels, but God did provide redemption for man. How come?

The reason lies in the way man and angels were made. The heavenly beings called angels were created individually. God called the heavenly host into being, myriads of them, all at once. Their number is fixed; it can be neither diminished nor added to. They were not born and they will not die; they are spirit beings. The angels who did not sin, or perhaps were prevented from doing so, are forever blessed. The angels who rebelled on the other hand are forever cursed. Their nature is fixed; they have become utterly evil and will not change. Because of this, they are doomed.

Man was created more complicated than that. Humanity did not come into being all at once; man multiplies through reprocreation. In a real sense, when God saw Adam he saw the federal head of the human race. Mankind after all is not merely a collection of individuals. All were represented in Adam; whatever he did affected them. The kernel of humanity was present. Something like that happens at the moment of conception. A union occurs whereby God creates a human being in the making. Everything that makes us what we are is there, in the genetic code.

The same thing was true of the first couple. Everything that made mankind was there, under extremely favorable conditions. Adam chose to rebel; a representative failed, and that made all the difference. The angels rebelled as individuals; no one could take their place. For man on the other hand, redemption was possible. Another representative could step in and right things. However, there is a catch. God's rule is just. Righteousness and justice are the foundation of his throne. (Ps 89:14). Man's rebellion could not be overlooked; it was high treason and carried the death penalty. The righteousness of God is based upon infinite justice, and that justice demands that the penalty for rebellion be paid in full. How can finite man do that? It cannot be done. To make matters worse, man's stained nature only adds to his guilt.

Who, we ask, can satisfy the demands of God's justice? Only God himself, obviously. It follows that the perfect representative must be human, and a perfect, sinless human at that. God can accept nothing less. Assuming such a person exists, can he pay the penalty for the collective and personal sins of man? Only if he is fully divine. The Redeemer must be both God and man. Man must suffer, but only God can pay. Since no human being is divine, something drastic must occur, which is exactly what happened. God intervened.

Redemption

Mankind is afflicted with original sin. Original sin is not the first sin that Adam committed, rather it is a personal bias that causes us to rebel against God. We want to do our own thing. Man is totally depraved. This is not something people love to hear, but it is the truth. That does not mean man is totally evil, or even as bad as he could be. Even Hitler liked his dog. Man's reasoning is darkened, but there is a glimmer of light; nor has the image of God been erased. That image is like a shattered mirror; the refection is distorted but still visible.

The Covenant

The problem of humanity is this: God entered into a covenant with Adam, and the condition of that covenant was perfect obedience. Adam could have done that, had he chosen to do so. He had the ability. When he transgressed, he lost that ability; human nature became corrupt, and Adam being a representative, that corruption was passed on to his posterity. Man is not born neutral, he is born corrupt. That seals his fate. In Eden God demanded perfect obedience, and he never lowered his standard. That demand still stands. Situation: hopeless. Well, not exactly. When the Lord confronted Adam, he announced a promise of redemption - and a declaration of war. He told the tempter,

> I will put enmity
> between you and the woman,
> and between your offspring and hers;
> he will crush your head,
> and you will strike his heel.
> Genesis 3:15

The world is a spiritual battle ground in a war that will not cease, as long as the earth endures. The seed of the woman and the seed of the serpent stand for diametrically opposed values. The latter is obviously headed by Satan, even though those who belong in that camp do not necessarily think of it that way. The seed of the woman is a person, a man, who is the head of all true believers. He would "crush the head" of Satan, meaning he would give him the death blow. He himself would be crippled in the process.

There is already a hint of a bloody sacrifice. After the fall, Adam and Eve covered themselves with fig leaves; mankind still does that. That was not good enough. "The LORD God made garments of skin for Adam and his wife and clothed them." (Gen. 3:21) It is quite clear that an animal was killed for the purpose. Not only was blood shed to cover Adam and Eve, God provided the sacrifice, and he clothed them with appropriate garments. This is the primeval promise of redemption; God would send a redeemer who would shed his own blood and clothe his people with righteousness.

Who is this redeemer? The "seed of the woman" obviously is human, and he is a man. There is an implication of a human sacrifice in the story of Abraham, who was about to sacrifice his only son Isaac. It is the picture of a father, willing to sacrifice his own son; a son who carries the wood of his sacrifice to the place of execution and submits to the will of the father. It was a test of faith; Abraham obeyed God. At the last moment the Lord called from heaven and told Abraham not to harm his son. The Lord does not want human sacrifice. Abraham saw a ram, caught by his horns in the thicket, and he sacrificed it instead as a burnt offering, that is an offering totally burned as a complete sacrifice to God. "So Abraham called that place 'The LORD will provide.' And to this day it is said, 'On the mountain of the LORD it will be provided.'" (Gen 22:14) Solomon built a temple on that mountain, and a thousand years after that the great sacrifice was made; a divine sacrifice.

The Hebrew prophets spoke of the redeemer; they called him God's anointed, his Messiah. As the Jewish people came to a better understanding of the Messiah, a puzzling problem arose. The Messiah would come, and he would be a man; an ideal man. On the other hand, he is also spoken of as a divine person. For all fact and purpose, he is God himself. Psalm 110 comes to mind. There is a counsel within the Godhead. Yahweh, the Great I AM, is reported as speaking to Adonai, my Lord. There is a mysterious reference to his eternal origin.

> The LORD says to my Lord:
> "Sit at my right hand
> until I make your enemies
> a footstool for your feet."

> The LORD will extend your mighty scepter from Zion
> you will rule in the midst of your enemies.
> Your troops will be willing on the day of your battle.

Arrayed in holy majesty,
from the womb of the dawn
you will receive the dew of your youth.
The Lord has sworn
and will not change his mind:
"You are a priest forever,
in the order of Melchizedek."

The Lord is at your right hand:
he will crush kings on the day of his wrath.
He will judge the nations heaping up the dead
and crushing the rulers of the whole earth.
He will drink from a brook beside the way;
therefore he will lift up his head.

Yahweh and Adonai are names for God. This Psalm is often quoted in the New Testament. It says that the Messiah is the Supreme King and Priest. It speaks of his ultimate victory; it is done in the language of that day. This is how kings recorded their victories.

It was only natural for the Jewish people to look forward to the Messiah as a national liberator, but from the beginning this was not the case. Adam was not a Jew; he was the federal head of the human race. Israel was chosen by God to be his people; the whole world would be blessed through them. The Messiah came to redeem. His kingdom was spiritual, not political. The Israel he redeemed is made up of all believers throughout the ages. Racial and national boundaries vanish in that kingdom. But how can we know that the Messiah was indeed both God and man?

The Angel of the LORD

There appears throughout the Old Testament a person who is referred to as "Yahweh Malachi," the angel or messenger of the LORD. This "angel" is most unusual. He appears as a man who turns out to be God himself. In a number of cases it involves some kind of unusual phenomenon in nature. This is called a theophany, a divine manifestation. Some theologians maintain the appearances of the angel of the LORD are sacramental, meaning it involves the presence of God in a special way. Already in Genesis it says the LORD walked in the Garden of Eden. Although it does not expressly say that this was the angel of the LORD, it is nonetheless significant that it involves a divine presence. The Creator appeared to man in human form. There is evidence that this happened after the fall as well.

Hagar

The first to meet the angel of the LORD was Hagar, the slave girl of Abraham and Sarah. Sarah had no children. The Lord promised she would have a son, but Sarah figured the Lord needed help, so she resorted to local custom. She gave her slave girl Hagar to Abraham as wife. Legally the offspring of Hagar and Abraham would be her child. This backfired. Hagar became pregnant and despised Sarah, who mistreated her in turn. Hagar ran away and rested near a spring in the desert, at a loss what to do.

The Angel of the LORD appeared in person and reminded her of her position. "Go back to your mistress and submit to her," the angel told her. Then he said something very strange: "I will so increase your descendants that they will be too numerous to count." It dawned on Hagar who this mysterious man was. Only God can do that. "She gave this name to the LORD who spoke to her: 'You are the God who sees Me'" (Gen 16:9) She reasoned that this strange encounter must have been a vision of God. The angel who spoke to Hagar was God himself.

Abraham

Something similar happened to Abraham when he welcomed three visitors who turned out to be angels. One of these angels was Yahweh, the LORD. We must not think of angels as humanoids with wings in white shining garments. That is how they are seen in visions, to denote purity and holiness. They are spirit-beings who are able to appear as men. Abraham came to this belated conclusion when he provided them with a meal. Visions do not eat steak.

No doubt Abraham was close to God. He had talked with the Lord, and he knew that God had appeared to Hagar in human form. It should come as no surprise that he talked rather freely with the angel who appeared like a man and was Yahweh. His knowledge of God was limited. Later generations became increasingly aware of the greatness of God; his holiness and his power. We know much more about God than Abraham ever did. To Abraham anyway, the man who was Yahweh was not intimidating.

The Lord told him that Sodom and Gomorrah were about to be destroyed, but upon Abraham's intercession agreed that the destruction would not happen if ten righteous men were found there. There was only one righteous man, Abraham's nephew Lot, who gradually drifted toward Sodom and eventually settled there. As it turned out, he was something less than perfect. He also was seriously mistaken about the moral character of his daughters.

Sodom and Gomorrah were destroyed in a cataclysm that turned the lush valley into a burning pit. "Then the LORD rained down burning sulfur on Sodom and Gomorrah - from the LORD out of heaven." (Gen 19:24). Salt and sulfur shot out of the fractured rift high into the sky and poured down on the doomed valley. Scripture makes it quite clear that the angel who judged those cities was Yahweh. Yahweh on earth rained down sulfur from Yahweh out of heaven.

After the birth of Isaac, Sarah saw Ishmael mistreat Isaac, and insisted that Hagar and her son Ishmael be dismissed. Abraham was very sad, but when God told to him do so, he sent Hagar and his son away. The angel of the Lord provided for them when they were near death. He did not appear in person, but spoke to her from heaven. Scripture presents the angel as God who was speaking. The angel said he would make Ishmael into a great nation, something only God can do. The role of the angel, whose home was in heaven, appears to be that of a mediator. When God dealt with people, the angel of the Lord appeared as an intercessor.

The same thing happened when God tested Abraham and told him to sacrifice his son Isaac. It was the angel of the Lord who stopped Abraham and gave the Messianic promise: "Through you all the nations on earth will be blessed." (Gen 22:18)

Jacob

Abraham's grandson Jacob had a vision of God when he fled from his brother Esau, whom he had cheated out of his birth right. His parents told him to leave for Aram, where they had relatives. In a dream he saw a ladder that reached to heaven, with angels going up and down. Above it stood the Lord, and he told Jacob, "I am the LORD, the God of your father Abraham and the God of Isaac." He would give Jacob the land on which he was lying, and bring him back to that land. All the nations would be blessed through the offspring of Jacob. When Jacob awoke he was afraid because the Lord had been at that place. He called it Bethel, House of God.

By that time Jacob was at least seventy years old, but he still had much to learn. He came from a family where cheating was the order of the day; he had callously deceived his blind father. True to form, Jacob and his uncle Laban swindled each other back and forth. Jacob fell in love with Laban's youngest daughter Rachel, an empty-headed beauty. Laban pretended to give her to Jacob, who discovered too late he had married Rachel's older sister Leah instead. He married Rachel as well. That was tragic, because Leah loved Jacob. To his credit, Jacob eventually came to see that. On his deathbed he requested that he be buried with Leah. The Messianic line was continued through Leah's son Judah.

Meanwhile, he resorted to trickery to shortchange his miserly father-in-law. He asked that spotted lambs, born in his flock, would belong to him for his wages. Laban agreed, removed all the spotted sheep and made sure his flocks were far away. Jacob tried to help

The Covenant

himself by placing stripped rods of poplar in the trough before the sheep. Sure enough, spotted sheep were born in abundance, and Jacob became rich. That did not improve friendship with Laban, so Jacob ran away with his wives, children and herds. Rachel and Leah approved, and then Jacob confided something. The angel of God had shown him in a dream that the flocks would produce speckled sheep. The angel added, "I am the God of Bethel, where you anointed a pillar and where you made a vow to me. Now leave this land at once and go back to your native land." (Gen 31:10-13)

Jacob had fooled Laban for nothing. Those poplar sticks had not done the trick; it was genetics, but he did not know that. The rams had dominant genes for speckled offspring. As is often the case, Jacob thought the Lord needed help, even if that meant cheating, and as always, that backfired. His cheating was fast catching up with him. First he had to face Laban, then he would have to deal with his twin brother Esau in Canaan. For all he knew Esau was ready to kill him.

God warned Laban not to harm Jacob. Laban said farewell to Jacob and his daughters, but Esau was a different matter. Jacob tried a bribe, but that did not guarantee anything. When they arrived in Canaan, he moved everything and everyone across the stream of Jabbok, but remained by himself all night. There a mysterious stranger attacked him.

> So Jacob was left alone, and a man wrestled with him till daybreak. When the man saw that he could not overpower him, he touched the socket of Jacob's hip so that his hip was wrenched as he wrestled with the man. Then the man said, "Let me go, for it is daybreak." But Jacob replied, "I will not let you go unless you bless me." The man asked him, "What is your name?" "Jacob," he answered. Then the man said, "Your name will no longer be Jacob, but Israel, because you have struggled with God and with man and have overcome." Jacob said, "Please tell me your name." But he replied, "why do you ask my name?" Then he blessed him there. So Jacob called that place Peniel (face of God),

saying, "It is because I saw God face to face and yet my life was spared."

Genesis 32:22-30

Jacob never knew whom he was fighting. Only when the man miraculously crippled him did he realize that he was dealing with deity. He wrestled with someone who was at the same time God and man. When daylight came, the man said, "What is your name?" That was the very questions his father Isaac asked him. The name Jacob was not flattering. It meant something like "Heel," a cheat. The man changed his name to Israel, meaning "He strives with God." Israel was at odds with him who is at the same time God and man. It was prophetic of the nation that was born there.

It turned out Jacob's fear for his twin brother Esau was unfounded. Sympathetic as always, Esau had long since forgotten about Jacob's cheating. He was doing fine, and he never cared about the blessing anyway. So they parted in peace. Esau never gave God another thought, but Jacob did. God after all does not need sympathetic characters to accomplish his purposes; he molds failed men. For all his faults, Jacob had a heart for God. He never forgot his encounter with that strange man who turned out to be God himself.

The man refused to give his name, but in changing Jacob's name to Israel left no doubt about his identity. He blessed Jacob. By that time Jacob had come to a better understanding of the nature of God; more so than Abraham. He could not understand how he could be face to face with the Almighty and yet live. That is indeed a mystery, but evidently it was possible for God to conceal his glory and somehow appear as a man. On his deathbed Jacob spoke of the God before whom his father had walked, and he identified him with the angel who delivered him from all harm. (Gen 48:15, 16) He also spoke prophetic words about his children and grand children, from whom the twelve tribes of Israel came. Most prominent of these was his son Judah, a man with a noble character.

Judah, your brothers will praise you;

> your hand will be on the neck of your enemies;
> your father's sons will bow down to you.
> You are a lion's cub, O Judah;
> you return from the prey, my son.
> Like a lion he crouches and lies down,
> like a lioness - who dare to rouse him?
> The scepter will not depart from Judah,
> nor the ruler's staff from between his feet,
> until he comes to whom it belongs
> and the obedience of the nations will be his.
>
> Genesis 49:8-10

This is a Messianic promise. The regnal power would be vested in Judah until the arrival of "Shiloh," meaning "he to whom it belongs." Shiloh has always been believed to be the Messiah. The implication is that the Messianic ruler would come at a time when the scepter, the power to rule, had been taken away - far away in the future. Yet the nations world wide would be obedient to him.

Moses

Time passed, and the Hebrews were enslaved by Egypt. Strangely enough, one of the princes in Pharaoh's court was a Hebrew, Moses, the Egyptian pharaoh Merkaure (Mycerinus). He was very popular with the Egyptians. When he was forty, he took the law in his own hand when he killed an Egyptian. As we have seen, he fled to Midian, where he married the daughter of Jethro the priest.

Forty years later he led his flock of sheep to mount Horeb. He saw something very strange. A bush was ablaze in a roaring fire without being consumed; it kept burning. Moses walked toward the bush to find out what was going on, when he heard a voice. The angel of the Lord appeared to him in the burning bush.

> When the LORD saw that he had come over to look, God called to him from within the bush, "Moses, Moses."

And Moses said, "Here I am."

"Do not come any closer," God said. "Take off your sandals for the place where you are standing is holy ground." Then he said, "I am the God of Abraham, the God of Isaac and the God of Jacob." At this, Moses hid his face, because he was afraid to look at God.

Exodus 3:4, 5

There can be no doubt about it, the angel of the LORD and God are the same. It was a theophany, a divine manifestation. God talked to Moses, and he revealed the sacred name, Yahweh, the great I AM. It is quite possible that the divine name was known, but the special meaning was now being revealed. Yahweh is the name for God that reveals something about his Being. He is a self-determining God; what the Greek called the "Unmoved Mover." He is the First Cause who ordains what shall come to pass and by what means. The name relates to Israel in a special way. Yahweh is the Covenant God who binds himself to his people.

This is why the Scripture relates the strange story where the Lord was ready to kill Moses. The reason is given, his son had not been circumcised. Circumcision was the sign of the Covenant that God had initiated, and the LORD was dead serious about it. If the leader of the nation did not bother with the sign of the Covenant, how could he bring the nation to God?

The story of the exodus speaks of a series of upheavals in nature. The plagues that devastated Egypt were unusual natural events. There is nothing mystical about it. Scripture does not portray Moses as a Warlock with a magic wand, rather he spoke for the Lord; that was his prophetic office. His staff was a prop that he used to prove his word carried weight. It was God's doing.

The Presence

Moses has always been highly regarded by the Jewish people: he spoke face to face with God. (Ex 33:11) Yet he never saw God in any physical fashion. The angel of the Lord appeared to him as well, but not in human form; always through a phenomenon in nature. It says the angel of the Lord went before Israel during the exodus, and he is often associated with a cloud. Perhaps this was done to avoid the notion of a human image that might be associated with God. He is presented as Israel's guardian angel, but in a way that carries a profound meaning.

> See, I am sending an angel ahead of you to guard you along the way and to bring you to the place I have prepared. Pay attention to him and listen to what he says. Do not rebel against him; he will not forgive your rebellion, since my Name is in him.
>
> Exodus 23:20, 21

The angel was able to forgive rebellion or sin, a divine prerogative. He could do that because the Name of God, Yahweh, was in him. That was tantamount to saying the angel was Yahweh himself. The mystery deepens with the promise of the Presence. That happened when Moses was called to lead Israel to the Promised Land, but found himself unequal to the task. When he went up to mount Horeb to receive the law from God, he was gone a long time. In his absence the people became restive and after nearly six weeks they fell back to their pagan ways; they made themselves a golden calf and worshiped that. This was the god who had brought them out of Egypt, they said.

The Lord was ready to annihilate them. Only the intercession of Moses saved them from destruction, yet many people died. The Lord told Moses, "Now go, lead the people to the place I spoke of, and my angel will go before you." (Ex 33:34) The angel would drive out the nations of Canaan, but for their own good the Lord would not go with them, "because you are a stiff-necked people, and I might destroy you on the way." (Ex 33:2) This left Moses in a serious predicament. He was called to lead the people to the Promised Land, but he needed divine help, and the Lord was not going to do that. He implored Yahweh for help.

> Moses said to the LORD, "You have been telling me, 'Lead these people,' but you have not let me know whom you will send with me. You have said, 'I know you by name and you have found favor with me.' If I have found favor in your eyes, teach me your ways so I may know you and continue to find favor with you. Remember that this nation is your people."
> The LORD replied, "My Presence will go with you, and I will give you rest." Then Moses said to him, "If your Presence does not go with us, do not send us up from here. How will anyone know that you are pleased with me and with your people unless you go with us? What else will distinguish me and your people from all the other people on the face of the earth?"
> Exodus 33:12-16

The Presence is spoken of in terms that closely resemble God's personality. The tabernacle was called the tent of the Presence. That is where God's Shekinah glory dwelt. The Presence is identified with the angel of the Lord. Isaiah referred to it: "In all their distress he too was distressed and the angel of his presence saved them." (Isa 63:9) For their own safety, God himself would not go with them. That was too dangerous; the holy God was too pure to tolerate sin. He was liable to destroy them. Instead his Presence would lead them, as if it were, as an intermediary.

What must we think of the punishment that came? Thousands of people were killed or died of a plague. That would seem to be not only severe, but arbitrary. It was a very serious matter. Israel's desertion of the true God amounted to high treason. What about the unfortunates who died? The answer lies in God's sovereign decree. "I will have mercy on whom I will have mercy, and I will have compassion on whom I will have compassion." (Ex 33:19) Even though many people died, God was still gracious. Thanks to the intercession

The Covenant

of Moses, the LORD did no annihilate the whole nation, like he very well could have done. The people evidently needed an intermediary, someone who stood between them and the Almighty. God provided the mediator. God the Son, the second person of the Trinity, was the manifestation of God's presence. It was he who appeared as the angel of the LORD.

We recognize this in the symbolism of the Ark of the Covenant. The ark contained the two tablets of the law, engraved with the finger of God. The law reflects God's purity and holiness. That absolute law, to which we are subject, kills whatever fails to live up to its demands. For this reason it was covered by the mercy seat, symbolic of Christ. His sacrifice covers our sins, and we are no more subject to the demands of the law. Once we are in Christ, our file in heaven is stamped, "Paid in Full." Those who take these things lightly are in trouble. During the ministry of Samuel, a number of Israelites removed the cover of the Ark of the Covenant to look inside. They gazed upon the two tablets of the law, and died. (1 Sam 6:19)

The split rock at Mount Horeb

The presence is often mentioned in connection with Mount Horeb. The Lord appeared to Moses in a number of different ways. Then there is the very physical reality of a huge boulder, split right down the middle. When God told Moses to take a number of elders to Mount Horeb to provide water for Israel, why did he choose a sixty-foot rock? It would have made more sense to hit his staff on the ground. God did the impossible; he provided water from a rock. It has definite Messianic implications. It is symbolic of Christ, stricken, yet providing the water of salvation and the life-giving Holy Spirit. Christ is often spoken of as a rock, and the Old Testament proclaims the praise of "the rock or our salvation."

Balaam

After forty years in the desert, the children of Israel were sufficiently toughened to begin the conquest of the Promised Land. They approached Canaan from the east, away from Egypt, and at once ran into trouble. Unbeknown to them Balak, king of Moab, summoned a diviner by the name of Baalam. He promised great riches, just so Balaam would curse Israel.

Balaam is an enigmatic character. He was an Arameans. Aram, later Syria, was the home of the original believers. Abraham was an Aramean. Isaac and Jacob had Aramean wives because they would not intermarry with the pagan Canaanite women. Aramean eventually became the international language of the East. This lasted well into Roman times.

Balaam's knowledge of El Shaddai, God Almighty, such as it was, suffered from centuries of corruption. He was a clairvoyant who knew that God was supreme, but not much more. For all we know, he may have been somewhat of a prophet outside the Covenant. All the same, his heart was crooked. It showed when Balak's emissaries knocked at his door. He would have liked to go, but was prohibited from doing so. When a second delegation came, richer than the one before, the LORD allowed him to go. That did not mean he *wanted* him to go. The extended story of Balaam, recorded in Numbers 22-24, reports how the angel of the LORD met him. Balaam never saw the angel, but his donkey did. What must Balaam's companions think when their "savior" turned out to be dumber than his beast of burden? The angel of the LORD made the animal speak, and it was wiser than its master.

Balaam's freedom of speech was equal to that of his donkey. The Lord made him say things that were beyond his comprehension. Three times his attempted curses came out as blessings. All the time the angel of the LORD is represented as God the LORD who put words in Balaam's mouth. This story adds considerable insight into the nature of God's being. It speaks of God, the angel of the LORD who is himself God, and the Spirit of the LORD, the One who inspires and reveals. He does all these things as he sees fit.

Within the story setting we discover things about God and man we would never expect. Those who insist that God cannot violate man's free will are sadly mistaken. Balaam's will was not free any more than ours; it was governed by greed. He was free to sin, and he did. On top of that, God imposed his will upon the diviner. He did not Balaam's permission any more than that of his donkey.

The Commander

All this happened in accordance with God's promise that his angel would go before Israel and protect them. So far that merely involved Israel's enemies; soon that would change. God's people would meet him as well. It began when Joshua was ready to attack Jericho, and ran into a stranger.

> Now when Joshua was near Jericho, he looked up and saw a man standing in front of him with a drawn sword in his hand. Joshua went up to him and asked, "Are you for us or for our enemies?"
> "Neither," the man replied, "but as commander of the army of the LORD I have now come." Then Joshua fell face down to the ground in reverence and asked him, "What message does my

Lord have for his servants?" The commander of the LORD's army replied, "Take off your sandals, for the place where you are standing is holy." And Joshua did so. Joshua 5:13-15

There can be no doubt about the identity of this man. The "commander of the LORD's army" was Yahweh C'baoth, the LORD of Hosts. He told Joshua the same thing he said to Moses in the theophany of the burning bush. The ground on which Joshua stood was holy. He was in the presence of Deity. The man demanded worship and he received it. It is together fitting that he would not take sides. Never pray that God is on our side; pray that we are on his side.

Bokim

After the death of Joshua, Israel settled in the Promised Land. It was a slow struggle, and they failed to deal with the Canaanites as they had been told. Something strange happened. The angel of the LORD appeared in person. He spoke to the people, and they recognized him for whom he was.

> The angel of the LORD went up from Gilgal to Bokim and said, "I brought you up out of Egypt and led you into the land that I swore to give to your forefathers. I said, 'I will never break my covenant with you, and you shall not make a covenant with the people of this land, but you shall break down their altars.' Yet you have disobeyed me. Why have you done this? Now therefore I tell you that I will not drive them out before you; they will be thorns in your sides and their gods will be a snare to you. When the angel of the LORD had spoken these things to all the Israelites, the people wept aloud, and they called that place Bokim. There they offered sacrifices to the LORD.
>
> Judges 2:1-4

The angel of the LORD quoted words that were spoken by Yahweh. He said outright that he was the God who had spoken to Moses. The people evidently accepted him as such, for they offered sacrifices to him, again an act of worship. The memory of this event obviously lingered. It was another step in the gradual unfolding of God's revelation. It is even more apparent in two stories that deal with the man who appeared to unsuspecting people - and turned out to be God himself.

Gideon

The history of Israel is in many ways unique. Following the exodus, a nation emerged on Canaanite soil that was unlike any other. The Law of Moses, the Constitution of Israel, vested civil authority in the elders, which made for a representative form of government. A federation of twelve autonomous tribes formed a primitive republic, and God was the federal head. It was a theocracy.

That was a far cry from the despotic kingdoms that surrounded them. Religion was the glue that bonded civilizations. Common loyalty guaranteed stability, so quite naturally the head of state was also the high priest (or close to him), and was even believed to be deity personified. These "gods" in the very nature of the case possessed dictatorial power. Nothing of the kind existed in Israel; God himself was the king. When Israel fell into one of those cyclic apostasies, he sent local rulers to restore his people. These people were called judges (some rabbis call them elders), and they came from all walks of life. Some of them definitely were highly unqualified candidates.

One of these was Gideon, a young man from the tribe of Manasseh. His family by his own admission was the weakest in his tribe, and he was the least in his family. He was threshing wheat in a winepress, away from spying eyes, when he saw a stranger sitting under an oak tree. "The LORD is with you, mighty warrior," the man said. That must have sounded somewhat ironic, and Gideon was defensive. Why had the LORD forsaken them and given them over the

Midianites? Scripture leaves no doubt about the identity of the man. "The LORD turned to him and said, 'Go in the strength you have and save Israel out of Midian's hand. Am I not sending you?'" (Judges 6:14) Gideon began to have an inkling whom he was talking to. He was no hero, and this challenge did not at all appeal to him. How could he, of all people, save Israel? But he dealt with the One who inspired men to great deeds.

> The LORD answered, "I will be with you, and you will strike down the Midianites as if they were but one man." Gideon replied, "If now I have found favor in your eyes, give me a sign that it is really you talking to me. Please do not go away until I come back and bring my offering and set it before you." And the LORD said, "I will wait until you return."
> Gideon went in, prepared a young goat, and from an ephah of flour he made bread without yeast. Putting the meat in a basket and its broth in a pot, he brought them out and offered them to him under the oak. The angel of God said to him, "Take the meat and the unleavened bread, place them on this rock, and pour out the broth." And Gideon did so. With the tip of the staff that was in his hand, the angel of the LORD touched the meat and the unleavened bread. Fire flared from the rock, consuming the meat and the bread. And the angel of the LORD disappeared. When Gideon realized that it was the angel of the LORD, he exclaimed, "Ah, sovereign LORD! I have seen the angel of the LORD face to face!" But the LORD said to him, "Peace! Do not be afraid. You are not going to die."
> So Gideon built an altar to the LORD there and called it, "the LORD is Peace." To this day it stands in Ophrah of the Abiezrites.
> Judges 6:14-24

We can imagine Gideon's feeling of dread and wonder when he realized who this man was. This changed to certainty when he prepared a sacrifice that was summarily accepted in miraculous fashion. The angel of the LORD demonstrated that he was able to accept worship. He disappeared; he went back to heaven. Gideon was afraid he would die because he had seen God. This did not happen. Somehow it was possible for God to conceal his glory and appear as a man.

The effect on Gideon was remarkable, not because he was so outstanding, but because of the character building it involved. The Lord step by step led him to higher ground, until eventually he became a leader of men. He had the bearing of a prince. The people even wanted to make him king, but he declined the honor. That was wise, among other things because God never authorized him to do that. Besides, Gideon was far from perfect. It served as a warning for Israel of the potential dangers of hereditary kings.

Samson

A century later, the angel of the LORD visited a childless couple of the tribe of Dan. He appeared to the woman, and told her she would have a son who was called to be a Nazirite. That was someone who was set apart in the service of God. A Nazirite would not take fermented drinks, eat or touch nothing unclean, such as a dead body, and never cut his hair.

The woman told her husband, "A man of God came to me. He looked like an angel of God, very awesome." And she told him the details. Her husband, whose name was Menoah, prayed to the Lord, "O LORD, I beg you, let the man of God you sent to us come again to teach us how to bring up the boy who is to be born." (Judges 13:1-8) God heard Menoah's prayer, and the angel of God again appeared to the woman. She at once ran for her husband and told him, "He's here! The man who appeared to me the other day!"

> Menoah got up and followed his wife. When he came to the man, he said, "Are you the one who talked to my wife?" "I am," he said. So Menoah asked him, "When your words are fulfilled, what is to be the rule for the boy's life and work?" The angel of the LORD answered, "Your wife must do all that I have told her. She must not eat anything that comes from the grape vine, nor

drink any wine or any other fermented drink nor eat anything unclean. She must do everything I have commanded her."
Menoah said to the angel of the LORD, "We would like you to stay until we prepare a young goat for you." The angel of the LORD replied, "Even though you detain me, I will not eat any of your food. But if you prepare a burnt offering, offer it to the LORD." (Menoah did not realize it was the angel of the LORD). Then Menoah inquired of the angel of the LORD, "What is your name, so that we may honor you when your word comes true?" He replied, "Why do you ask my name? It is beyond understanding."
Then Menoah took a young goat, together with the grain offering, and sacrificed it on a rock to the LORD. And the LORD did an amazing thing while Menoah and his wife were watching. As the flame blazed up from the altar toward heaven, the angel of the LORD, ascended in the flame. Seeing this, Menoah and his wife fell with their faces to the ground. When the angel of the LORD did not show himself again to Menoah and his wife, Menoah realized it was the angel of the LORD. "We are doomed to die," he said to his wife. "We have seen God." But his wife answered, "If the LORD had meant to kill us, he would not have accepted a burnt offering and grain offering from our hands, nor shown us all these things or now told us this."
The woman gave birth to a boy and named him Samson. He grew and the LORD blessed him and the Spirit of the LORD began to stir him while he was in Mahaneh Dan, between Zorah and Eshtaol.

Judges 13:9-24

Scripture is the gradually unfolding revelation of God. If we compare this story with the account of Gideon, we discover several additional details. There is the conspicuous reply of the angel of the LORD, "I am." That is the name of God, Yahweh. The reaction of the woman is intriguing. With female intuition she at once sensed something extraordinary about this man. Menoah, although courteous and respectful, did not.

The man did not speak as a prophet, sent by God on an errant. He did not speak for God, rather he spoke as if he was God. He gave orders to be obeyed. All the same, Menoah did not have the slightest notion that this man was God himself. He appeared to be a perfectly normal human being. As if to prove that he was more than that, the angel of the LORD refused to have a meal with them. Instead he directed them to make a sacrifice, which he summarily accepted. He ascended to heaven in the flame of the fire. He accepted the worship, due to God alone.

The reaction of Menoah was identical to that of Gideon. He had seen God face to face; he was certain that he would die. But his wife applied cool logic. It was certainly not the intent of God to kill them; otherwise he would not have done the things he did or given them instructions. So the woman gave birth to Samson. We see something of the threefold nature of God. The story speaks of the LORD, the angel or messenger of the LORD, who gave the Word of God, and the Spirit of the LORD, the One who inspired and stirred Samson.

The story is worthy of our attention, among other things because the angel of the LORD never again appeared to anyone in human form. He is mentioned in connection with divine manifestations in nature, such as the one mentioned earlier, when the army of Sennacherib was annihilated. As we have seen, Isaiah said the LORD would come to wipe out the hordes that attacked Jerusalem, and the angel of the LORD was the one who put to death one-hundred-eighty-thousand soldiers. No doubt it involved an upheaval in nature, but all the same, it was God's doing.

Zechariah

After the fall of Jerusalem 587 B.C., the Jews were carried off to Babylon. They spent seventy years in captivity, then a remnant returned to Palestine. These were difficult times. Unfriendly neighbors did everything they could to prevent the building of the temple, and

Nehemiah, the governor, had problems with his own people. The rich enslaved the poor, just as they had done before the fall of Jerusalem. Nehemiah resorted to high-handed methods to correct them.

Meanwhile a number of prophets arose. Of these, the prophet Zechariah is of particular interest: his visions deal with the angel of the LORD. These visions provided words of comfort to the Jews, and increasingly detailed promises of the coming redeemer. They report the angel of the LORD as promising restoration and renewal. What makes his message so fascinating is the way he speaks of himself. He is Yahweh, yet is also sent by Yahweh.

> "Shout and be glad, O daughter of Zion. For I am coming and I will live among you," declares the LORD. "Many nations will be joined with the LORD in that day and will become my people. I will live among you and you will know that the LORD Almighty has sent me to you. The LORD will inherit Judah as his portion in the holy land and will again choose Jerusalem. Be still before the LORD, all mankind, because he has roused himself from his holy dwelling."
>
> Zechariah 2:10-12

Obviously this relates to the prophecy of Isaiah. The Messiah was the divine "Immanuel," God with us, and Zechariah identifies him with the angel of the LORD. Make no mistake about it, God would come. How that would happen and what was involved is foretold in visions that speak of things to come. In these visions, Joshua the High Priest plays a major role. He is central, the focus of attention.

Joshua stood before the angel of the LORD, who rebuked Satan because he accused Joshua. For good reasons no doubt, because Joshua was dressed in filthy clothes. But the angel of the LORD would not hear of it. He ordered the dirty clothes removed and rich garments put on. The dirty clothes stood for Joshua's sins. They were removed. Instead he was dressed in robes of righteousness. The angel of the LORD said this.

The Covenant

"Listen, O high priest Joshua and your associates seated before you, who are men symbolic of things to come. I am going to bring my servant, the Branch. See, the stone I have set in front of Joshua. There are seven eyes on that one stone, and I will engrave an inscription on it," says the LORD Almighty, "and I will remove the sin of this land in a single day. In that day each of you will invite his neighbor to sit under his vine and fig tree," declares the LORD Almighty.

Zechariah 3:8-10

Joshua was a symbol of things to come. Keep in mind that the name Joshua is a variant of Jesus. It means Savior (Salvation of Yahweh). This vision speaks of cleansing and renewal. The Branch is another name for the Servant of Isaiah; it has always been understood that the Messiah is meant. Joshua represented the Branch. The promise is unmistakable. In a single day the LORD would wipe out sin, and as a result men would live in peace.

Zechariah now develops an interesting relationship between Joshua and Zerubbabel, the son of Shaltiel. The prophet does not say it (everybody knew it), but Zerubbabel was a descendant of King David. He belonged to the royal family, and as it turned out, was an ancestor of the Messiah. (Luke 3:27) The Jews who returned from Babylon looked at him for past and future glory. The Lord praised him for his leadership in building the temple of the Lord, but warned against a power grab. "'Not by might nor by power, but by my Spirit,' says the LORD Almighty." (Zechariah 4:6) The kingdom God had in mind was spiritual.

This is evident from a remarkable vision that speaks of a priest-king. In God's kingdom the power to rule was assigned, not to Zerubbabel, but to Joshua the high priest. These visions speak of the priesthood and the temple. In a highly unusual maneuver they are linked with royalty. Zechariah spoke of a priest who, like the enigmatic Melchizedek, was a king as well.

The word of the LORD came to me: "Take silver and gold from the exiles Heldai, Tobiah and Jediah, who have arrived from Babylon. Go the same day to the house of Josiah son of Zephaniah. Take the silver and gold and make a crown, and set it on the head of the high priest, Joshua son of Jehozadak. Tell him this is what the LORD Almighty says. 'Here is the man whose name is the Branch, and he will branch out from his place and build the temple of the LORD. It is he who will build the temple of the LORD, and he will be clothed with majesty and will sit and rule on his throne. And he will be a priest on his throne. And there will be harmony between the two.' The crown will be given to Heldai, Tobiah, Jediah and Hen son of Zephaniah as a memorial in the temple of the LORD. Those who are far away will come and help build the temple of the LORD, and you will know that the LORD Almighty has sent me to you. This will happen if you diligently obey the LORD your God."

Zechariah 6:9-15

This is unprecedented. The coronation of a priest, that was against the law. The office of priest and king were distinct. They did not mix. When King Uzziah overstepped that boundary line, he was smitten with leprosy. Now we realize of course, that this is a vision and not a historical fact. It speaks of things to come. The Messianic kingdom was not one of war and military might, such as represented by Zerubbabel. Rather it was a kingdom of sacrifice and service. This vision deals with a royal priesthood. The apostle Peter spoke of it.

As you come to him, the living Stone - rejected by men but chosen by God and precious to him - you also, like living stones, are being built into a spiritual house to be a holy priesthood, offering spiritual sacrifices acceptable to God through Jesus Christ. — — — - But you are a chosen people, a royal priesthood, a holy nation, a people belonging to God, that you may declare the praises of him who called you out of darkness into his wonderful light. Once

The Covenant

you were not a people, but now you are the people of God; once you had not received mercy, but now you have received mercy.

1 Peter 2:4, 5,9,10

Joshua was symbolic of the Branch, the Messiah. These things are fully explained in the book of Hebrews. The Messiah Joshua (Christ Jesus) was both priest and king. Of course, he was not a political king. That was never the intent. The priesthood of Jesus was "in the order of Melchizedek," the priest-king of Salem, mentioned in Genesis 14 and Psalm 110. The temple he built was not a physical monument. The first temple was built by Solomon, the second by Herod; it was destroyed A.D. 70.

Josephus informs us that every single Aaronic priest was killed in that holocaust. The empty shell of the Old Covenant was crushed; the Old Testament priesthood and the system of sacrifices it administered disappeared. No priest offered any more sacrifices, no high priest made annual atonement. A new temple arose, a royal priesthood was inaugurated, a priesthood of all believers. Every Christian is a priest before God. The third temple is the New Testament Church.

Malachi

The last book of the Old Testament is in many ways mysterious. For beginners, the author of this book is unknown. "Malachi," meaning "messenger," is a pen name. It does not say that Malachi was a prophet, nor is any genealogical record given which is very unusual. Then who wrote it? We could make a good case for Haggai. Chapter 2:13 of that book identifies Haggai as the LORD's messenger, that is his Malachi, and the message of both books is very similar. There is a mystery surrounding this book, much like the New Testament book of Hebrews; both deal with the mysterious origin of the Messiah.

Malachi is the book of and about the messenger or angel of the LORD. The prophecy is very specific; it says that the LORD, the angel of the Covenant would come. His coming would be heralded by Elijah the prophet, or someone like him.

> "See, I will send my messenger, who will prepare the way before me. Then suddenly the LORD you are seeking will come to his temple; the messenger of the covenant, whom you desire, will come," says the LORD Almighty.
>
> Malachi 3:1

This is an echo of Isaiah 40:3. "In the desert prepare the way for the LORD." It involves two messengers. First the Herald would come who prepared the way of the LORD, then the LORD himself would appear in his temple, suddenly and unexpectedly. There can be no doubt about it, the LORD and the messenger or angel of the Covenant were the same. Considering that the angel of the LORD appeared in human form, he could arrive in a way no one expected. But why is he called the angel of the Covenant, and who is the Herald?

It is obvious by now that the Angel of the Covenant, mentioned by Malachi, is identical with the Angel of the Lord. God the Son, the second person of the Trinity was "incarnate," meaning he actually became a human being, yet remained fully divine. "The word became flesh, and dwelt among us." (John 1:14) The herald was John the Baptist, a man who closely resembled the prophet Elijah. He was not Elijah himself, reincarnate or come back in some fashion, rather he was another Elijah who prepared the nation for the coming Messiah.

The sudden appearance of the Lord, identical with the Angel of the Covenant, came at the exact right time and for a purpose. It involved the fulfillment of the Eternal Covenant God made before the world was even created. The covenants, mentioned in the Old Testament were part of that greater Covenant. The coming of the Messiah involved the consummation, so to speak, of all the covenants that came before. When that would happen and how it would be accomplished was revealed by Daniel.

Daniel

It is obvious from the Gospels that Jesus lived at a time of high expectations. There was a general belief, not limited to the Jews, that a new age was dawning, the Messianic age. How come? The prophecies of Daniel, that is the answer. Daniel gave several very specific prophecies. It was known that many of these had come true as predicted. This was known not only to the Jews, but also to the gentiles. Daniel did not prophecy in hiding, he was a statesman of international stature. Besides, the scriptures by that time had been translated into Greek and were widely known.

The Jews, scattered all over the Roman Empire, attracted many gentiles to their synagogues. They knew not only *that* the Messiah was coming, but even when. Daniel said so. It happened when Daniel, at the end of the seventy-year Babylonian captivity, prayed to God for his people and the temple in Jerusalem. While he was praying, the angel Gabriel came and said this.

> Seventy "sevens" are decreed for your people and your holy city to finish transgression, to put an end to sin, to atone for wickedness, to bring in everlasting righteousness, to seal up vision and prophecy and to anoint the most holy.
> Know and understand this: From the issuing of the decree to restore and rebuild Jerusalem until the Anointed One, the ruler, comes, there will be seven "sevens" and sixty-two "sevens." It will be rebuilt with streets and a trench, but in times of trouble. After the sixty-two "sevens," the Anointed one will be cut off and will have nothing. The people of the ruler who will come will destroy the sanctuary. The end will come like a flood: war will continue to the end, and desolations have been decreed. He will confirm a covenant with many for one "seven," but in the middle of the "seven" he will put an end to sacrifice and offering. And one who causes desolation will place abominations on a wing of the temple, until the end that is decreed is poured out on him.
>
> Daniel 9:24-27

These "sevens" are sabbatical weeks of years, seven-year cycles, mentioned in the Law of Moses (Lev 25:8). Daniel prayed after the seventy years of captivity predicted by Jeremiah had run their course, so seventy cycles of seven years (week-years) or 490 years were ordained for Daniel's people and his holy city, Jerusalem. At that time a number of things would happen, all of them spiritual in nature. The coming of the anointed one, the Messiah, involved divine redemption. He would usher in an era of righteousness, pay the penalty for sin, and reveal God in a final manner. Vision and prophecy would be sealed; the supreme revelation would reveal all that must be known. There would be no more divine revelation after that.

So much for the general tenor. Detailed predictions followed. The decree to restore and rebuild Jerusalem evidently was the one of Artaxerxes in the seventh year of his reign, 457 B.C. (Ezra 7:12-26) The city and the temple were rebuilt over a fifty-year period, with great difficulty. After 7+62=69 weeks of years (483 years), the Messiah would appear. 483-457=26. The exact year is difficult to calculate, but it must have been about A.D. 26 - 30. [2] He would be "cut off," that is executed, in the middle of the following "week," that is three and a half years later.

The prophecy speaks of the Messiah and of the prince or ruler to come. The Messiah would confirm the covenant with many during the last "week," but would put an end to the sacrificial system in the middle of that seven-year period. In other words, after a ministry of 3½ years, he would make the Old Testament Covenant obsolete. He did that when he, the Supreme High Priest, gave his own life as a sacrifice for many. Afterwards the prince of a foreign nation would come and destroy the city and the sanctuary. That happened A.D. 70, when the Romans under Titus utterly destroyed Jerusalem.

The dire prediction of Jesus that not one stone would be left standing upon the other came true in dramatic fashion. Titus gave orders to spare Herod's magnificent temple, but the furious Roman soldiers fired burning arrows into the sacred stronghold. The temple caught fire; the golden ornaments melted in the inferno and poured into the foundation. The Romans afterwards leveled the charred ruin and tore up all the stones to get to the gold.

Micah

The Jews, in other words, had every reason to be apprehensive. They knew the time was near, and they looked for any candidate who might qualify as Messiah. The choice was limited. The Messiah must come from the lineage of David; also he must be born in Bethlehem. The prophet Micah said so in the days of Hezekiah, king of Judah.

> Marshall your troops, O city of troops,
> for a siege is laid against us.
> They will strike Israel's ruler
> on the cheek with a rod.
> But you, Bethlehem Ephrathah,
> though you are small among the clans of Judah,
> out of you will come for me
> one who will be the ruler over Israel,
> whose origins are from old,
> from ancient times.
> Therefore Israel will be abandoned
> until the time when she who is in labor gives birth
> and the rest of his brothers return
> to join the Israelites.
> He will stand and shepherd his flock
> in the strength of the LORD,
> in the majesty of the name of the LORD his God.
> For then his greatness will reach
> to the ends of the earth.
> And he will be their peace.
>
> Micah 5:1, 2

The people of Micah's days could relate to a city under siege. It happened to Samaria, which was ultimately captured and destroyed, and also to Jerusalem. In Micah's time it was besieged twice. The promise of the Messianic ruler speaks of the abuse he would endure, and of the place of his birth. He would be born in Bethlehem, Ephrathah, in Judah. (There was another Bethlehem further north). Israel would be abandoned, carried into captivity. The Messiah would appear after Israel returned to the Holy Land. He would be their peace, and his kingdom would encompass the whole earth. Jesus did not come to establish a Jewish kingdom; his kingdom was about salvation, not politics, and it included the gentiles. The author of Hebrews commended Old Testament saints for their faith, though they often suffered persecution. "They were all commended for their faith, yet none of them received what had been promised. God had planned something better for us so that only together with us would they be made perfect." (11:39, 40) It follows that the Old and New Testament are essentially the same.

We know from the Christmas story that the wise men (probably Chaldeans), came to Jerusalem to find out where the newborn king of the Jews was. They had seen his star. According to an informed source, this was probably a nova. Herod, much alarmed, asked the Jewish leaders, and they told him this prophecy. Bethlehem is a suburb of Jerusalem, and it did not take the wise men long to find the right place.

The implication is that the coming of the Messiah was anticipated, not only by the Jews, but by the gentiles as well. They had the sacred writings in their possession; they knew the prophecies of Daniel and Micah. The wise men not only presented the child with royal gifts, they worshiped him as well. This indicates knowledge of his nature. His origins were "from of old, from ancient times." The meaning is that he came from all eternity. It says he was divine and the gentiles, knowing the prophecy, believed the child to be deity. They recognized him as their king.

Jesus, who are you?

The appointed time arrived and a man appeared who talked and acted as if he was God. "What is so strange about that," you will say. "More people have done that." Yes, but Jesus was a Jew! None of Abraham's descendants ever said that. For a Jew to say he was Deity was unthinkable - the thought would never enter his head. The most depraved of Israel's kings never hinted at that, although every pagan ruler from Pharaoh to Caesar, proclaimed himself divine. Yet here was a man, a devout Jew, who openly said he was the Son of God, which in the eastern mind set meant that he claimed to be equal with God.

All that sounds familiar, does it not? It happened before that a man appeared who turned out to be God himself. These theophanies - divine manifestations - were meant to teach God's people that God was not way out there, far away. He could appear in human form if he chose to do so. Furthermore, even though no man can see God and live, there is something about God that enables him to conceal his glory and come to us on the human level. In the incarnation he became part of the human race. One who is both God and man restores the broken relationship between God and man. He bridges the gap. That was the hope, promised in the Old Testament. The New Testament writers saw him as the promised Messiah who fulfilled the Covenant promises of the Old. He was the great and final prophet, priest and king. We see this, for instance, in the book of Hebrews.

> In the past God spoke to our forefathers through the prophets at many times and in various ways, but in these the last days, he has spoken to us by his Son, whom he appointed heir of all things, and through whom he made the universe. The Son is the radiance of God's glory and the exact representation of his being, sustaining all things be his powerful word. After he had provided purification for sins, he sat down at the right hand of the Majesty in heaven.
>
> Hebrews 1:1-3

The church fathers already realized that the author is speaking of the threefold office of Christ. He was at the same time prophet, priest and king. Clearly, Jesus is the supreme revelation, the Prophet whose word is final. Daniel said that prophecy would be sealed. Jesus did it. Christ reveals God like no one else can because he is himself God. Prophecy is fulfilled in him, all we need to know is revealed through him. He also is the great High Priest, who made full and final atonement for sin, and when he was seated at the right hand of God, he was coronated King of Kings and Lord of Lords.

Something similar is portrayed in the first chapter of Revelation, where he is the High Priest in the setting of the heavenly temple. The sword that came from his mouth not only speaks of the King of glory, but also his prophetic office: the sword is the Word.

The Perfect Man

Jesus leaves us no choice. Either he was a lunatic or he was who he said he was, God incarnate. There is something about Jesus that makes him a class all by himself. That is all the more remarkable because he never apologized to anyone, the reason being that he was always right. And he always had the right answer. He never had to think about a proper response, he always knew. A wise ruler realizes he does not know it all, so he has advisors. Jesus never did. He never solicited advice, and when on occasion well-meaning folks told him what to do, he had his own itinerary. Who will counsel God? He acted as if he was royalty; his subjects had no right to question him, such as happened when he stood before the Sanhedrin, the Jewish council, following his arrest. Clearly he alone was the King of Kings, the long expected Messiah who was more than man. He told the Jewish leaders he had seen Abraham. Naturally they laughed: "You are not yet fifty years old and you have seen Abraham?" And then Jesus spoke those mysterious words: "Before Abraham was, I Am." (John 8:58). They knew exactly what he meant. Jesus said he was the "I Am," Yahweh, who appeared to Abraham.

Yet he never overreached. Unlike Moses, he did not assume the role of judge and executioner. Nor did he seek revenge when his honor was insulted. David was ready to maim and kill when he was mortally insulted, but Jesus did nothing of the kind, he kept his cool. He also was patient and forgiving, and restored people's dignity. It is quite fascinating to study prophecy with respect to his Messianic character. Jesus was so exactly the Messiah the prophets envisioned. He dealt mercifully with the downtrodden. "A bruised reed he will not break, and a smoldering wick he will not snuff out." (Isa 42:3)

What strikes us more than anything is his sinless nature. It explains the very unusual circumstances regarding his birth. Isaiah prophesied that *Immanuel*, "God with us," would be born of a virgin. This is all-important. God the Son received his humanity from Mary; a sinless humanity, because he was not begotten of an earthly father, but through a creative act of the Holy Spirit. A cat begets a cat, a dog a dog, and a sinful nature a sinful nature. Jesus origin was divine, without sin, therefore he was sinless.

It is evident throughout his ministry. Every time he talked about sin or man's sinful nature, he excluded himself. He would say things like, "You who are evil," not complementary, even more so because it implied he was not. He was the only one to say that everything he did pleased God, and he openly challenged the Pharisees, "Which of you convicts me of any sin?" When they tried to find any fault in him they found nothing; they sentenced him to death on a charge of blasphemy, he said he was "the Son of God," meaning God himself. In the eastern mindset that was the same. This is no light matter. Jesus was the spotless lamb, without a single flaw, who gave himself as a perfect substitute for sinful man.

The Regnal Line

The virgin birth solves an interesting problem. The Messianic line must come from David through his son Solomon. Then something happened that derailed Solomon's line. One of his descendants, the

Judean king Jehoiachin, was cursed for all the evil he committed. Jeremiah pronounced doom.

> Is this man Jehoiachin a despised, broken pot,
> an object no one wants?
> Why will he and his children be hurled out,
> cast into a land they do not know?
> O land, land, land,
> hear the word of the LORD!
> This is what the LORD says:
> "Record this man as if childless,
> a man who will not prosper in his lifetime,
> for none of his offspring will prosper,
> none will sit on the throne of David
> or rule anymore in Judah."
> Jeremiah 22:28-30

Jehoiachin was the reigning king. By divine decree the regnal line of Solomon would never again have a king on a throne, and it never did. How then, could the Messianic king be seated on David's throne? The virgin birth solves the problem. Since Jesus was conceived by the Holy Spirit, he did not come from the cursed line of Jehoiachin. He received his royal status through Mary, a descendant of David's son Nathan, as recorded in Luke, chapter 3. Luke, the historian, received his information from Mary, the focus in the early chapters of his gospel.

Joseph on the other hand came from the executive line of Solomon and Jehoiachin, as recorded in the gospel of Matthew. Since Matthew addressed himself to the Jews, he throughout provided proof that Jesus was indeed the promised Messiah. (He called Jesus *Nezer*, a word meaning "root," and related to *Nazirite*, because Nazareth, as we have seen, means "Rootville.") He concerned himself with the line of Joseph because that was the crucial regnal line. That is where Jesus received the authority to reign.

Although Joseph was not his real father, Jesus nonetheless was the rightful heir. In the Jewish culture of that day, marriage was two-tiered. A betrothal was legally a defacto marriage; a year or so later the marriage was formalized and consummated. Joseph and Mary were in the first stage of marriage, which made Joseph the legal father of Jesus. Jesus was born of a virgin, but Joseph by law was his legal father. Providentially, Jesus was the last man able to claim David's throne. Following the sack of Jerusalem A.D. 70, all genealogical records were lost. The royal line of David vanished. The curse on Jehoiachin was a fire wall that obstructed any would-be Messiah. The real Messiah must have the right credentials, and Jesus certainly did.

Salvation

All these things speak of the salvation he achieved for his people: those who put their faith in him. He did that when he suffered hell on the cross; he took upon himself the sins of the world. By doing so he *became* sin. God saw sin hanging on that cross and he poured the full measure of his anger over it, without mercy. Jesus suffered utter and complete separation from God, torture, and public mocking at his terrible plight. His suffering was physical, mental and spiritual. Let no one think it was easier for him to bear all that because he was after all the Son of God. Jesus was a man. When they slammed those spikes through his wrists and his feet, he was screaming in pain. We could even make a case that he was more sensitive, and in any event, he refused to take any kind of sedative.

There are, of course, legitimate questions. If Jesus was divine, how could he die? After all, God is immortal. It is more complicated than that. The man Jesus was sinless. Death is the penalty for sin, but since Jesus never sinned, he would never die. He was immortal. That makes his suffering so horrible. When the Roman soldiers scourged him with lead-laden whips they tore his back apart. He received blows that would have killed any other man. But since he was immortal, nothing could kill him. He died because his divine nature had the power to lay down his human life on the altar of salvation. In other words, when he was hanging on that cross, subject to inhuman suffering, he could have stopped it anytime. Not until the penalty for sin was paid in full did he command his spirit into the hands of God. It was an act of ultimate obedience. He came to do the will of God and he did it.

Quite understandably the objection has been raised that God could hardly leave Christ if he is omnipresent. But this was not something physical. It happens to us, does it not, that we are face to face with people, yet miles apart. Maybe the wrong thing was said, or we are alienated. That is what happened between God the Father and God the Son, deliberately so. We recall the vision of Isaiah who saw God enthroned in glory. It is believed that the dialogue between Isaiah and the Lord was an echo of a divine council, made before the world was created. Knowing that man would fall, God decided upon a plan of redemption whereby an intermediate would save mankind. This is referred to in many parts of the scriptures. The Father said, "Whom shall I send, and who will go before us?" And the Son replied, "Here am I, send me."

The Bible as a whole is a witness to salvation. The covenants of the Old Testament accrued until finally they were consumed in the New. A covenant after all by law is irrevocable. There is and always was, only one way of salvation, by grace. From the very beginning, God saved his people by his great mercy. It is erroneous to say, as some do, that the Bible is divided in "dispensations," all of them failed attempts to achieve salvation through different means. It makes God a failure, and chops scripture in totally unrelated bits and pieces. It not only destroys the unity of the Bible, it renders the Old Testament, three quarters of the Bible, obsolete. We cannot pit the Old Testament against the New; they are reciprocal, they belong together. The New is founded on the Old.

In the context of Covenant theology, salvation is applied to those who place their trust in Christ, and that applies to the Old Testament saints just as much as it does to us. It was done in a different context, under the symbols of the great sacrifice to come. The blood of bulls and goats never saved anyone; no ritual does. It was the faith of the believers that justified them in the sight of God. Yet even that faith is a gift. God is in all things Supreme, including salvation, and God being absolutely perfect, the sacrifice of Christ was perfect and all-sufficient. It is he who saves us to the utmost. We did not find him, he found us. It was true in the Old Covenant. Israel was chosen by God. This is called divine election.

It is only human to think ourselves capable of finding and accepting salvation. "God has done his part, but brother, now it is all up to you." But when we consult scripture, we find ourselves in an altogether different world. The Bible proclaims that we are objects of mercy. We are saved because God mercifully gave us a heart to accept him. That is all very confusing, like flying in a thick fog and having to make an instrument landing. We have the instrument, it is a tulip.

Tulip

In the 17th Century, a controversy arose in the Reformed churches of the Netherlands. The Remonstrants, followers of Jacobus Armyn, (who Latinized his name to Arminius) presented five points of doctrine which denied the Reformed teachings that were proclaimed in the churches. Politically it was a potentially dangerous situation, for the nation was fighting a protracted war of independence against Spain. The Remonstrants championed government supervision over the church, which the Calvinists strenuously opposed. To them civil and religious liberty were all the same.

The civil magistrates interfered in the matter, appointed ministers to their liking and persecuted dissidents until Maurice, the prince of Orange, angrily ordered them to stop harassing believers. The province of Holland refused to go along, and threatened to secede from the Republic. After a near-civil war order was restored, and the churches were allowed to gather in a Synod or general meeting.

They dealt with the matter in the city of Dordtrecht in 1618/19. The great "Synod of Dordt" restated the doctrines under five headings, since known as the Canons (rules) of Dordt. In a slightly altered order, these Canons became known as the Five Points of Calvinism, although Calvin had nothing to do with it. It could have just as well been called the Five Aspects of Salvation; they constitute a pattern that is evident throughout the scriptures. These five points are easily remembered by the acronym *TULIP*.

*T*otal Depravity
*U*nconditional Election
*L*imited Atonement
*I*rresistible Grace
*P*erseverance

We will never understand ourselves unless we first look at the One who made us, and whom we resemble. God alone is supreme, holy, righteous, good and totally free. There is no limit to his understanding, wisdom and power. The scriptures abound with praise to his holy name, and proclaim with one voice why he called the existing order into being: all things are created for the manifestation of his glory. That is why we live; it is the reason for our being. Unfortunately we make a shambles of our high calling. Man is just as much able and willing to follow God as the dead are capable of living. It is the result of his condition, he is totally depraved.

1. Total Depravity

Several years ago, a politician plastered his smiling face all over bill boards. "Ready, Willing, Able," the eye sore read. Then one morning we noticed a definite improvement, a midnight artist had made subtle alterations. A red van Dyke beard and mustache, and eye brows similarly amended rendered the would-be senator a grinning old devil, which was much closer to the truth. Maybe that is why he lost. The gentleman in all likelihood did not appreciate the humor, much as we do not appreciate the picture of ourselves we find in the scriptures. Ready? Willing? Able? What about rebellious, self-willed, dead? The apostle Paul reminded believers what they once were like, and he included himself.

> As for you, you were dead in your trespasses and sins in which you used to live when you followed the way of this world and of the rulers of the kingdom of the air, the spirit who is now at work in those who are disobedient. All of us also lived among them at one time, gratifying the cravings of our sinful nature and following its desires and thoughts. Like the rest, we were by nature objects of wrath.
> Ephesians 2:1-3

We will never understand such doctrines as predestination and divine election unless we see ourselves for what by nature we truly are, spiritual dead. Not sick or crippled, no, dead. There are cemeteries everywhere. No matter how logical and persuasive you are, the dead will never reply. They cannot. And that, ladies and gentlemen, is the natural man. Are you one of them?

Now of course, an author is not supposed to say that. It does not sell books. But Christianity is not a religion of fuzzy feelings. It deals with unpleasant realities. Humanity has a problem, and we must find out what it is. Beginning in Eden, where God told the first man he must not rebel on penalty of death, humanity was corrupted at the root. Physical death was postponed, spiritual death instantaneous. When Adam rebelled, something in him died; the band with God was broken. The scriptures are replete with comments about man's true nature, it is corrupt. After the flood, God said, "Never again will I curse the ground because of man, even though every inclination of his heart is evil from childhood." (Gen 8:21) It is all-pervasive. We are not, as Palagius would have it, born neutral, affected by our environment; no, humanity was corrupted at the root. Are there any who are capable of any good? Fortunately we have the exact number.

The fool says in his heart,

"There is no God."
They are corrupt, and their deeds are vile;
there is no one who does good.

The LORD looks down from heaven
on the sons of men
to see if there are any who understand,
any who seek God.
All have turned aside,
they have together become corrupt;
there is no one who does good,
not even one.

Psalm 14:1-3

The exact number of willing, good, able people has been revealed, it is zero. Even our presumed goodness is failed. The good we are capable of doing, however noble, falls far short of the righteousness that God requires. We may think of ourselves as basically good, possessed of free will and capable of finding God, but the Scriptures teach the very opposite.

The heart is deceitful above all things
and beyond cure.
Who can understand it?
"I, the LORD search the heart
and examine the mind,
to reward the sons of man according to his conduct,
according to what his deeds deserve."

Jeremiah 17:9, 10

An incurably deceitful heart is not likely to seek the God of truth, much less find him. It stands condemned. The natural man has no inclination whatsoever to find God. To him it is all sheer nonsense and superstition, and any rational explanation must be found elsewhere. The apostle Paul makes no bones about it, the unbeliever despises the things of God.

> The man without the Spirit does not accept the things that come from the Spirit of God, for they are foolishness to him, and he cannot understand them, because they are spiritually discerned.
> 1 Corinthians 2:14

That is merely a realistic observation. Far worse are the consequences of man's corruption. It leads to moral decline, sex perversions and ultimate damnation.

> The wrath of God is being revealed from heaven against all the godlessness and wickedness of men who suppress the truth by their wickedness, since what may be known about God is plain to them. For since the creation of the world God's invisible qualities - his eternal power and divine nature - have been clearly seen, being understood from what has been made, so that men are without excuse. For although they knew God, they neither glorified him as God nor gave thanks to him, but their thinking became futile and their foolish hearts were darkened. Although they claimed to be wise, they became fools and changed the glory of the immortal God for images made to look like mortal man and birds and animals and reptiles. Therefore God gave them over in the sinful desires of their hearts to sexual impurity for the degrading of their bodies with one another. They exchanged the truth of God for a lie, and worshiped and served created things rather than the Creator - who is blessed forever. Amen
> Romans 1:18-25

It is not a pleasant picture. Man has a craving for sin with an insatiable appetite for more. He is not at all basically good, rather he is a sin addict, hopelessly in love with himself, and inclined to all evil; not because he has to, but because he wants to. I am not a sinner because I sin, I sin because I am a sinner. Now that does not mean that man is totally evil, or even as bad as he could be. His depravity is total, but not absolute, like demons. It affects all his faculties, which leaves all his doings sinful. Yet this evil is curtailed. Man is capable of hatred, but that does not mean he will commit murder. Demons do. The good we see in man is relative. He is still capable of noble things, but they are always flawed. It is never that perfect goodness that God requires of us. The truth is, man's depraved nature leads him to do what is evil in the sight of God. He is forever on the slippery slope to ever degrading sins. In other words, a world like that is bound to go wrong, and that is the world in which we find ourselves. There is evil in the world, and it is in us. Christ once remarked that what makes a man "unclean" is not a dirty skin, but a dirty heart.

> What comes out of a man is what makes him "unclean." For from within, out of a man's heart come evil thoughts, sexual immorality, theft, murder, adultery, greed, malice, deceit, lewdness, envy, slander, arrogance and folly. All these evils come from inside and make a man "unclean."
>
> Mark 7:20-23

Sin being an addictive force, we are inevitably afflicted with some sort of evil addiction. It comes in many forms and often catches us by surprise, and having been trapped we always find good reasons to justify it. Most often it involves sex perversions. It could be pornography, prostitution, homosexuality and the like. It could also be alcoholism, gambling and even eating or work. Sometimes it involves things that are neither good nor bad, but sinful neglect makes it evil. We simply have to realize that there is such a thing as evil, and that it must be defeated.

Man's total depravity manifests itself in his total inability to follow God's ways. It is not that he tries and fails, rather he has a total disregard for the things of God. Why is it that so many scientists with their brilliant minds fail to see the handiwork of the Supreme Scientist? They cannot see because they are dead. They have the perception of man's best friend. Point at something and tell your dog, "look, look!" Guaranteed, he will look at your hand - not what it points at.

The Covenant

That is the problem of the unregenerate. They focus on the hand, creation, oblivious to what it points at, the Creator. Of course, we still argue the point, if only because others will not be led astray, and assuredly because we wish to honor the Creator.

But what about man's free will, his decision? Since when is the will free, as if it were divorced from every other faculty? Would parents gladly allow a child molester to babysit? The man has, after all, a free will. He has a perverted will! Courts order restraints for a reason. Nobody in his right mind acts on the assumption that someone will act totally different from his normal behavior because he has a free will. This is contrary to common understanding.

When men speak of *free* will they really mean a *capable* will. But man "wills" according to his nature and the circumstances. An evil man will do evil things, a decent man decent things. Yes, Adam and Eve had a free will, but when they transgressed they lost it. In Martin Luther's words, "A lost free will in my book is no will at all." Man's will proceeds from his nature, and since human nature is sinful, his will is sinful. In this sense freedom of the will is merely freedom to sin. As Luther told Erasmus, "What you call free will is really self will." Man's "free" will is that of an alcoholic in a liquor store. Freedom to him is a matter of choosing his favorite booze. People act in character. For this reason conversion is like falling in love, and never a "decision." The notion is alien to the scriptures and human experience.

Of course, we have choices, but the doctrine of "decision" appears nowhere in the scriptures. The word *decision* appears only once in the New Testament, (NIV) in a context that has nothing to do with salvation. The one word we do see everywhere is *obey*, and its derivatives. The Lord wants us to be obedient to his revealed will. As we will see, man's salvation is rooted, not in his own decision, but in God's mercy: he makes us willing. We see this everywhere. When Lydia was converted, she "decided to accept to Jesus Christ as her Lord and Savior," did she not? Well, not exactly. "The Lord opened her heart to respond to Paul's message." (Acts 16:14) It is God's mercy, not man's decision that makes us come to him.

Of course, it helps when we understand what man is really like. The founding fathers did; they mistrusted human nature and shackled the government with the chains of the Constitution. The whole system of checks and balances is based upon just that fear. It also provides an argument for justifiable war. There is evil in this world; sometimes we deal with demonic forces that are out to destroy, in which case war is the final resource. The fact of the matter is, the doctrine agrees with human experience. We see it all around us and for that matter in ourselves.

Fallen man is caught in a vortex that spirals him into ever deeper sins. It manifests itself in what Rushdoony dubbed "secular humanism," a religion that makes man his own god. It comes under different names, but it is at the core a religion that makes man supreme. It is a blue print for disaster. If there is no God then neither are there absolutes, least of all moral absolutes. In this mind set there is no truth, no right or wrong, meaning that everybody is right. It creates mindless zombies, willing to accept any belief no matter how contradictory as equal, except of course objective truth. Tolerance means acceptance and in inverted intolerance, dissent is suppressed. "Truth has perished, it has vanished from their lips." (Jer.7:28) They believe themselves free to do anything they please.

However, the heart of man being "deceitful above all things and desperately wicked," their depraved natures draw them into increasing sins that only add to their guilt and damnation. It has a devastating effect on society. A humanistic culture is a death culture: life has no value, other than what man says it has. Historically governments have conveniently declared the unwanted subhuman, and pursued them with the sword. How much blood has been shed because men despised the powerless?

It is against this background that we discover a God, Almighty, Supreme, who in unconditional love reaches out and saves those whom he is pleased to save. He does this freely and touches them in a way that uplifts them and gives their lives purpose. Salvation is much more than saving souls, it directly affects the lives of believers and necessarily society.

In matters of salvation, total depravity is the first step in our appreciation of divine redemption. If man is dead in his sins, he cannot possibly save himself. There is nothing in man that makes him in any way qualified for heaven, nor is he inclined to seek God, to the contrary, and that is why God in sovereign mercy chooses some, but not all, to everlasting life, as he sees fit. And there are no conditions attached.

2. Unconditional Election

There is a generally held belief that divine election is based upon God's foreknowledge. Being all-knowing, God chose those whom he foresaw would put their faith in him. After all, are there not numerous passages in the scriptures that presume ability? A case in point is Moses' exhortation in Deuteronomy 30:15, 16

> See, I set before you today life and prosperity, death and destruction. For I command you today to love the LORD your God, to walk in his ways, and to keep his commands, decrees and laws; then you will live and increase, and the LORD your God will bless you in the land you are entering to possess.

And then there is the invitation by Christ himself: "Come to me, all you who are weary and burdened, and I will give you rest." (Matt. 11:28) We could cite more, but the conclusion is the same: man is capable of accepting God's call, otherwise it would not say that, and if man is incapable of that he cannot be held accountable.

Is that true? Traffic signals presume that drivers are capable of following the law. Is a drunk driver capable? The law presumes he is, but his condition renders him incapacitated. This is not to hurt people whose lives have forever been changed by the carnage caused by DUI drivers. Must these traffic criminals be held unaccountable because they were, after all, incapable of keeping the law? Ask the family of the victims! The courts keep him accountable; in fact even more so.

When God created man, he held him accountable (the so called Covenant of Work) and he never lowered his standard. His demands stand, even if man is drunk with sin. This is very much evident if we continue to read Deuteronomy. The LORD predicted this.

> Then the LORD appeared at the Tent in a pillar of cloud, and the cloud stood over the entrance to the Tent. And the LORD said to Moses: "You are going to rest with your fathers, and these people will soon prostitute themselves to the foreign gods of the land they are entering. They will forsake me and break the covenant I made with them. On that day I will become angry with them and forsake them; I will hide my face from them, and they will be destroyed. Many disasters and difficulties will come upon them, and on that day they will ask, 'Have not these disasters come upon us because our God is not with us?' And I will certainly hide my face on that day because of all their wickedness in turning to other gods."
>
> Deuteronomy 31:15-18

Man is not able, merely because he is held accountable. And Jesus' words take on a very different meaning if we read his tidings in the context of the whole message. His disciples just returned from a missionary trip and he praised God for his sovereign decree.

> At that time Jesus said, "I praise you, Father, Lord of heaven and earth, because you have hidden these things from the wise and learned, and revealed them to little children. Yes, Father, for this was your good pleasure. All things have been committed to me by my Father. No one knows the Son except the Father, and no one knows the Father except the Son and those whom the Son chooses to reveal him.
> Come to *me*, all you who are weary and burdened, and *I* will give you rest. Take my yoke upon you and you will find rest for your souls. For my yoke is easy and my burden is light."
>
> Matthew 11:25-29

Mysterious though these words may sound, in light of the absolute supremacy of an Almighty God they make perfect sense. God is not exactly begging the creatures of his hand to please accept him. He hides and reveals things as he sees fit since he deals with human beings who never care to begin with. They do not know him because they are spiritually dead. "No one knows the Father except the Son *and those whom the Son chooses to reveal him.*" Surely, the choice is in God, not man. Election is not based upon foreseen faith; there is none. When God looked down the corridors of time he foresaw that no one would come to him, not until he mercifully would give them a heart to follow him. Jesus made this very clear. "No one can come to me unless the Father who sent me draws him." (John 6:44)

Jesus always spoke of salvation in terms of divine election. Although he mentioned hell more than anyone else, he never tried to scare anyone into accepting him; that was not his style. Instead he spoke with the full assurance that his people would come to him, certain and sure, and they would come willingly. To say that it all depends on man would seem to be somewhat lacking in humility, to put it mildly.

It is quite remarkable that scripture speaks of conversion in terms that have nothing to do with human volitions. Jesus told Nicodemus, "You must be born again." How do you do that? Take out the word "again." You must be born. How do you do that? You don't "do" anything. God placed you in this world without asking your permission, now live your life. It is something that happens to you. Jesus spoke in very similar terms, but used the metaphor of a spiritual resurrection instead.

> For just as the Father raises the dead and gives them life, even so the Son gives life *to whom he is pleased to give it*. Moreover the Father judges no one, but has entrusted all judgment to the Son, that all may honor the Son just as they honor the Father. He who does not honor the Son does not honor the Father who sent him. I tell you the truth, whoever hears my words and believes him

who sent me has eternal life and will not be condemned; he has crossed over from death to life. I tell you the truth, a time is coming and has now come when the dead will hear the voice of the Son of God and those who hear will live. For as the Father has life in himself, so he has granted the Son to have life in himself. And he has given him authority to judge because his is the Son of Man.

John 5:20-25

It ties in with the doctrine of total depravity. God gives life to whom he is pleased to give it, and he does so unconditionally. How can you demand conditions from the dead? Salvation is offered freely. There is no need to look at the bait and worry about the hook. God being Almighty and perfectly free to give life to whom is pleased, his grace applies to hopeless cases, people sunk in the pits of depravity. It is freely available to them.

On the surface it would seem odd that the dead will hear the voice of Christ and that those who hear will come to life. How can they hear when they are dead? These words were spoken primarily as an assurance to those who believe in him that they are indeed alive. Jesus gave a visible demonstration of this when he raised his friend Lazarus from the dead. This happened shortly before the crucifixion. How could Lazarus hear Christ if he was dead? Because the voice of the Savior kindled life in him, and he responded. We do not always think of this, but this miracle was limited to one man. He did not raise all in that cemetery. The same thing is true of those who are raised to spiritual life; it is not given to all.

3. Limited Atonement

When Christ hung on the cross, he endured the agonies of hell. Hell was not merely the excruciating pain that seared through every part of his body. Far worse was the utter and complete separation from God the Father. Add to that the inhuman mockery of his enemies and the outer darkness that enveloped the cross, and we have an accurate picture of hell. Hell is pain and loneliness. Why did he endure the agonizing horrors that seemed to last forever? He made a complete atonement that fully satisfied the furious anger of God. The payment was such that all mankind could have been saved, had God chosen to do so.

Why didn't he? For the same reason he allowed sin to enter creation: he is perfectly free to do as he pleases. He could choose some or all, a few or many. These things are up to him who alone acquits the guilty, and man must be silent in his presence. Who shall judge the Lord? Certainly not fallen man! Grace by definition is a free gift. Since when does God (or for that matter anyone) owe a free gift, particularly when the recipients deserve just punishment? Is it just possible that God did not save all so we would see the ravages of sin? Things always work out according to their nature, and in a sinful world we know as otherwise we would have never known, what sin is like. In any event, creation is the theater of God's grace and justice, and he is perfect in both. Knowing human nature one wonders why God saved anyone at all. He did not have to! Paul gave the reason, it was love.

> Praise be to the God and Father of our Lord Jesus Christ, who has blessed us in the heavenly realms with every spiritual blessing in Christ. For he chose us in him before the creation of the world to be holy and blameless in his sight. In love he predestined us to be adopted as his sons through Jesus Christ, in accordance with his pleasure and will - to the praise of his glorious grace, which he has freely given us in the One he loves.
> Ephesians 1:3-6

In his great mercy God found a way to destine some to eternal life. Since he did so from an eternal perspective, before he created anything at all, he predestined, and from this eternal perspective he determined who would be the recipient of his undeserved favor and who would not. Not everybody is a Christian. Some have never even heard of Christ, and those who have do not all put their faith in him.

It is foolish to think, as Universalists do, that all are saved regardless. Yes, ideally God desires an orderly society where all can come to a saving faith (1 Tim 2:1-7), but the fact is, that never happens. Christ and the Apostles made it crystal clear; Christ is the great High Priest who is the way to God. The only way. God the Son paid the penalty for man's sin, and God the Father does not recognize any other method of payment. Atonement is limited, not in value, but in application. We already saw that Christ clearly said the choice was his, not ours. "For just as the Father raises the dead and gives them life, even so the Son gives life to whom *he* is pleased to give it." The apostle Paul said it from a different perspective, that of man in awe of God's sovereign choice.

Not only that, but Rebekah's children had one and the same father, our father Isaac. Yet before the twins were born or had done anything good or bad - in order that God's purpose in election might stand: not by works but by him who calls - and was told, "The older will serve the younger." Just as it is written, "Jacob I loved, but Esau I hated."

What shall we say? Is God unjust? Not at all. For he says to Moses,

I will have mercy on whom I have mercy
and I will have compassion on whom I have compassion.

It does not, therefore, depend on man's desire or effort, but on God's mercy. For the scripture says to Pharaoh, "I raised you up for this very purpose, that I might display my power in you and that my name might be proclaimed in all the earth." Therefore God has mercy on whom he wants to have mercy, and he hardens whom he wants to harden.
One of you will say to me, "Then why does God blame us? For who resists his will?" But who are you, O man, to talk back to

God? Shall what is formed say to him who formed it, 'Why did you make me like that?' Does not the potter have the right to make out of the same lump of clay some pottery for noble purposes, and some for common use?

Romans 9:10-21

That goes hand in hand with the words of Jesus quoted above, "I praise you, Father, Lord of heaven and earth, because you have hidden these things from the wise and learned and revealed them to little children. Yes, Father, for such was your good pleasure." (Matt. 11:25) In other words, both Paul and Christ squarely hinged election upon the sovereignty of God. It cuts both ways. If God chooses some, but not all, to eternal life, it follows that the rest by default are left to eternal punishment.

We must not think that well meaning people come to God and he callously pushes them away, far from it. Rather he merely leaves them alone, and in their dead state of mind they never come to him. For this they stand condemned. Calvin mentioned it, and he shuddered. Yet Christ said so unequivocally when he proclaimed that he had come to save the world. "Whoever believes in him is not condemned, but whoever does not believe stands condemned already because he has not believed in the name of God's one and only son." (John 3:18)

Hopefully they had a change of heart (the apostle Paul did), but the fact remains, mankind stands condemned. Nor can it be said that Christ desperately tried and failed to convince all. The very reason why he spoke in parables proves the point. When he drove out demons, the Pharisees claimed he did it by the power of Satan. Jesus at once exposed the fallacy. "How can Satan drive out Satan? If a kingdom is divided against itself, that kingdom cannot stand." (Mark 3:23, 24) Then he pronounced doom: "—whoever blasphemes against the Holy Spirit will never be forgiven, he is guilty of an eternal sin." (Mark 3:29) They were guilty of the ultimate sin, utter and callous disregard for the power of God. Blasphemy against the Holy Spirit is contempt of the divine court. No court permits contempt, least of all the court of the Judge of all the earth.

Now it is possible that someone hastily says something uncouth about the Holy Spirit (John Bunyan did it as a youth and it bothered him no end), but that is not the ultimate sin. It is borne out by Bunyan's regret. One who willingly and deliberately blasphemes the Holy Spirit will never repent, nor will he feel any regret. He has been found guilty. Judgment has been decreed, no repentance is possible. He will never change, his doom is sure. It goes to prove that the Holy Spirit is a person, not merely a force. Gravity is a force, and it can never be insulted.

More to the point, Jesus from then on presented his message in parables. He had good reasons to. People came, not to hear his message, but to see him perform miracles. His ministry was fast changing into a three-ring circus. Then came the Pharisees with their blasphemous charges. So he told a story about a sower, something they saw happen as he told it. His disciples and other believers afterwards asked him what he meant with these stories. So what did Jesus say, "Thank God, a few good men?" No, they had been chosen, the others were shut out.

> He told them, "The secret of the kingdom of God has been given to you. But to those on the outside everything is said in parables so
>
> *They may be ever seeing but never perceiving and ever hearing but never understanding, otherwise they might turn and be forgiven."*
>
> Mark 4:11, 12

What was true in the days of Isaiah (Ch 8:16) was true in the days of Christ. Hardened sinners reject God's salvation; they want nothing to do with it, and for this God judges them. Lest anyone construe this to be anti-Semitic, the scriptures make it very clear that this is a human problem. It was true of the Jews, yes, but it was equally true of gentiles. However, there were those who believed, and it is abundantly clear that this faith is given (Christ's words). How this is done is another matter, it comes from the council of the Triune God.

4. Irresistible Grace

Salvation is a matter of sovereign grace, based upon love. God issued a divine pardon to those whom he was pleased to give it, and they come to him gratefully and willingly. The scriptures abound with explicit declarations about God's mercy.

> Like the rest we were by nature objects of wrath. But because of his great love for us, God, who is rich in mercy, made us alive with Christ even when we were dead in transgressions - it is by grace you have been saved. And God raised us up with Christ and seated us with him in the heavenly realms in Christ Jesus, in order that in the coming ages he might show the incomparable riches of his grace, expressed in his kindness to us in Christ Jesus. For it is by grace you have been saved, through faith - and this not from yourselves, it is the gift of God - not by works, so that no one can boast. For we are God's workmanship, created in Christ Jesus to do good works, which God prepared in advance for us to do.
>
> Ephesians 2:3-10

It is only human to believe salvation is a matter of cooperation between God and man. There is a fundamental problem with that, the scriptures tell us something totally different: it is all God's doing. God does something for man that man cannot do for himself. Man being spiritually dead God does not meet man halfway, he saves him all the way. Salvation is not a wide bridge that reaches halfway the great chasm, it is a narrow bridge that spans all the way across.

The creed of humanism in all it varied forms is nonetheless alike: "By works are you saved through sweat, and it is all your own doing that we may boast. For we are the masters of our own fate and we do not need God." Then there are those who would rather avoid extremes and settle somewhere in the middle. It is our choice of course, but God has to help us. This is based upon the proposition that God saves those who save themselves. In this paradigm Christ effectively saved no one, he merely provided an opportunity for man to save himself. It is a form of self-salvation. Without question it denies the plain teachings of God's word: "— this is not from your-selves - it is the gift of God." Just as it says elsewhere that salvation is not a matter of man's desire or effort, but of God's mercy. (Romans 9:16)

Why then do some willingly embrace salvation and others are either totally indifferent or outright hostile? Because God kindled the light of life in those whom he is pleased to save, and all of a sudden they become aware of their plight. They realize they have a problem and look to God for an answer. They are in no way coerced; they come willingly and gladly, just as foretold in that famous Messianic prophecy: "Your people shall be willing on the day of your power." (Ps 110:3)

The idea is that of a willing sacrifice. When the disciples asked Jesus why he used parables he told them, "The secret of the kingdom of God has been given to you." Unlike the others, they wanted to know what Christ meant with these stories. Not because they were better or smarter, but because God gave them the ability. Unless God so works in men's hearts, they will never come to him. They are incapable of it, it makes no sense whatsoever. The more educated among them study scripture only to deny it.

The grace of God is irresistible in the sense that it is real and effective. It is like falling in love. You may have met all kinds of girls, but all of a sudden you run into the one that steals your heart. You cannot imagine your life without her; in fact, she is your life. And what if you meet the one man who means everything to you. When he gets down on his knee and asks you to be his wife, what do you say? "I have decided to accept you as my husband?" No way! That is the one thing you want him to ask, and you say, "Oh yes, I do." This is life. "My beloved said 'Come,' and I came." Scripture and human experience teach us what all men will and will not do. Jesus said it when he spoke of God's sovereign choice.

> All that the Father gives me *will* come to me, and whoever comes to me I will never drive away. For I have come down from heaven not to do my own will but to do the will of him who sent me.
>
> John 6:37, 38

Jesus made it clear that he was not self-willed. He would not "do his own thing," so to speak, nor would he accept anyone grudgingly. All whom the Father has given to him will come to him, and he embraces them. This goes to the heart of election. Divine election is not absolute in the sense that the Father chose whom he would save and the Son obeyed. It is clear from the words of Christ that the choice was his. When God met in Divine Council to deal with salvation, the Son volunteered to be the great substitute who would pay the penalty for man's rebellion. Although this sacrifice was sufficient to save all men, God decreed to save some, but not all. The Son purposed to die for his people and no one else. It was the Son, not the Father, who chose whom he would save, and he asked the Father to grant salvation to his chosen people. And so, within the Triune Council it was agreed that the Father would grant salvation, the Son would pay the price, and the Holy Spirit would give life to those the Father and the Son sealed unto salvation.

It makes sense that the Son would make the choice. After all, he paid. Still, salvation involved sacrifice for all three persons of the Trinity. The Father made a terrible sacrifice when he gave his only Son, and the work of the Holy Spirit was that of self-sacrifice. Although he is the one who applies that undying life, he remains in the background. The Holy Spirit avoids the lime light, the reason being that he *is* the lime light. He sheds light upon the Son.

The doctrine refutes a popular notion. According to some, people go to heaven or hell against their wishes. Laura wanted to go to heaven but she was not elect, so entrance was refused. Tony could not care less, but because he was elect he was dragged kicking and screaming into heaven. This is a silly misrepresentation, presumably based upon ignorance. There are those to whom Classical music is plain boring. I personally cannot stand Country, although others live by it. To each his own. Truth is, I am dead to that kind of art. So are those who despise Classical. We go wherever our taste leads us.

The same thing is true of salvation. Those whom God has left alone will never come to him; they are spiritually dead. But those whom he raised from spiritual death want to worship him because they are alive to him. Is not this the experience of the true believer? Those who are truly converted to Christ suddenly find themselves awake; they see him for who he actually is and they worship him. Jesus illustrated this when he spoke of the good shepherd.

> The man who enters by the gate is the shepherd of the sheep. The watchman opens the gate for him, and the sheep listen to his voice. He calls his own sheep by name and leads them out. When he has brought out all his own he goes on ahead of them, and his sheep follow him because they know his voice. But they will never follow a stranger; in fact they will run away from him because they do not recognize a stranger's voice.
> I am the good shepherd; I know my sheep and my sheep know me - just as the Father knows me and I know the Father - and I lay down my life for the sheep. I have other sheep that are not of this sheep pen. I must bring them also. They too will listen to my voice, and they shall be one flock and one shepherd.
>
> John 10:2-5, 14-16

American Indians often place the sheep of different shepherds in the same corral. In the morning the shepherds return to retrieve their sheep. How is that possible with all those sheep that look alike in the same pen? No problem. The shepherds simply call their sheep, who know the voice of their shepherd and gather around him. Jesus used this example to illustrate divine election. He called himself the good shepherd; interesting, considering that David said, "The Lord is my shepherd." He calls his sheep and unfailingly they flock to him. He added that there was another sheep pen, that of the gentiles, that was to be opened in the future. The Jews and the Gentiles then would be one flock, the church, with one head, Christ. The book of Acts often mentions it.

The doctrine of divine election therefore credits Christ with the honor that is due to him; in mercy he laid down his life for the people of his choice. It avoids a dangerous pitfall. If salvation is something conjured by man from an internal effort, theology necessarily becomes subjective. It makes man supreme. In a subjective mind set where God himself must wait for man's sovereign decision, any appreciation of the Word of God will be equally subjective. So men pick and choose as they see fit and ignore what they do not like. It is a self-centered mind set where ego is on the throne. It also leads to subjective judgment. How do you know if someone is truly saved? That is often obvious, but you don't always know. In cases like that it is not for us to judge. Unless a professing believer proclaims heretical doctrines or acts like an unbeliever, leave these things to God. Let's not go on a witch hunt.

Then will those who are elect remain saved, or are they capable of falling away and be lost in the end? After all, many have come to some sort of commitment and made a shipwreck of their faith. That makes for a life on anxiety. If that is true, the best thing that can happen to you is to die; at the right time of course, when you feel close to God. Imagine if you happen to harbor a bad thought and get run over by a car! Fortunately Christ himself addressed that problem: once God gives you everlasting life, that life will never be extinguished. It is, after all, everlasting and not temporary.

5. Perseverance

Imagine if God based election upon foreseen faith. God being all-knowing he would know for certain who would choose him and who would not. Man's ultimate destiny would be known to God, just as surely as if he had predestined them. The problem is that this makes God a helpless bystander who merely observes what the creatures of his hand do. He also would know who would persevere and who would not, but leave them in the dark about their final destiny.

That is bound to result in persistent fear. Salvation leads to sanctification. If redemption ultimately is man's doing, then so is sanctification. If that is how you are going to *be* saved, then that is how you are going to *stay* saved. Hence revival meetings, re-dedications, altar calls and religious excitement, all of it emotion-driven. But as a black Baptist preacher once put it, "You are not saved just because you go to a cowboy-yippyayay church." It is not what you feel, it is what you believe, and that faith had better be based on fact. And the fact is, God guarantees our salvation.

It is important that we know this. When I told my children their mother had just died, the first thing I said was, "We will stay together as a family. You will never go to relatives." And God in his own unfathomable way provided another wife and mother. What if the threat of separation always hung over their heads? It would have made their lives impossible. For these very reasons God has made it clear that he will never let us slip away. If we live our lives in constant fear of ultimate damnation, we cannot live life like we should, to the glory of God. We would be too preoccupied with our own presumed problem. It was exactly to prevent such self-inflicted wounds that Christ spoke of God's faithfulness to the end. When the Jews asked him if he was the Messiah he answered,

> I did tell you, but you do not believe. The miracles I do in my Father's name speak for me, but you do not believe because you are not my sheep. My sheep listen to my voice; I know them, and they follow me. I give them eternal life, and they shall never perish; no one can snatch them out of my hand. My Father, who has given them to me is greater than all; no one can snatch them out of my Father's hand. I and the Father are one.
>
> John 10:25-30

He made it very clear who would listen to him and who would not, and why. The Jewish religious leaders saw what he did, but in the face of his miraculous deeds they refused to believe him. He just was not the sort of Messiah they expected, a great man who would

The Covenant

restore the Jewish kingdom. And here came this strange man who appeared to be the promised Messiah, but acted as if he was much more than a great man, he said he was the "Son of God," that is to say God himself. This they would not accept.

Jesus made it clear why, they did not belong to his flock. They were unbelievers who would never understand him. But there were also those who did believe him. They were his chosen, his sheep, and he guaranteed them eternal life. Not one would be lost.

> And this is the will of him who sent me, that I shall loose none of all that he has given me, but raise them up at the last day. For my Father's will is that everyone who looks to the Son and believes in him shall have eternal life, and I will raise him up at the last day.
>
> John 6:39, 40

This agrees with the words of the Apostle Paul, that nothing can separate us from the love of God which is in Christ. (Romans 8:38, 39) Now of course there will always be fakes and those who claim to be Christian but they are not. It is only a matter of time before they are found out, either by their lives or corrupt doctrines. The Apostle Peter had unkind things to say about them.

> These men are springs without water and mists driven by a storm. Blackest darkness is reserved for them. For they mouth empty, boastful words and, by appealing to the lustful desires of sinful human nature, they entice people who are just escaping from those who live in error. They promise them freedom, while they themselves are slaves of depravity - for a man is a slave to whatsoever has mastered him. If they have escaped the corruption of the world by Christ and are again entangled in it and overcome, they are worse off at the end than they were at the beginning. It would have been better for them not to have known the way of righteousness than to have known it and then to turn their backs on the sacred command that was passed on to them.

Of them the proverbs are true: "A dog returns to its vomit" and, "A sow that is washed goes back to her wallowing in the mud."
2 Peter 2:17-22

Their true colors show. All the time they pretended to be something they were not, believers. They may have very well known all the right doctrines, said all the right things, been properly baptized and even spoken in tongues, but their hearts were far from God. They defaulted, so to speak, to their real selves. America's jails are filled with "born again" prisoners. It is, after all, the best way to get out of the slammer. That is what they say, but that is not what they believe. Once they are pardoned, they at once go back to their old ways. It was all pretense. The apostle John said much the same: "They went out from us, but they did not really belong to us. For if they had belonged to us, they would have remained with us; but their going showed that none of them belonged to us." (1 John 2:19)

Through it all we should remember that we are human and necessarily prone to stumble. Christians are not perfect, they are merely forgiven. They also have a heart to follow God. God's promise assures them that although sinful, they cannot fall away from grace. This is entirely different from the unbeliever who likes to sin, and will never turn to grace. However, sin in the believer is restrained. He can never "sin unto death," that is deliberately and willingly try to disobey God, the reason being that his heart is turned toward God. Now he will frequently fail. The spirit is willing, but the flesh is weak. For this reason the scriptures abound with warnings against falling away, wake-up calls against complacency.

For perseverance was meant to give us that peace of mind that enables us to live in obedience to God's word, not to take it easy. It does not give us a license to do our own thing, as some suggest. These doctrines have a quieting effect. They produce people who are deeply grateful for what God has done. They are steadfast. To those who trust in man or their own abilities, these things seem absurd at best and demonic at worst. The problem is, this is what the scriptures teach. Men may not like it, but to deny these things is to deny the word of God. The apostle Peter showed another angle, it gives us gratitude, certainty and hope.

> Praise be to the God and Father of our Lord Jesus Christ. In his great mercy he has given us new birth into a living hope through the resurrection of Jesus Christ from the dead, and into an inheritance that can never perish, spoil or fade - kept in heaven for you, who through faith are shielded by God's power until the coming of the salvation that is ready to be revealed in the last time.
>
> 1 Peter 1:3-5

These doctrines put fire in the hearts of men. There is something else. Now that we know what human nature is like, there is no need to look for evil in people; we already know it is there. It is in all of us. It follows that nobody has bragging rights. Instead look for good in others and for that matter think of others as better than yourself. Furthermore if we are saved by sheer grace and nothing else, we should be gracious to others. If God forgave us so much, should we not be willing to forgive others? These things are forcefully taught in scripture.

This is not a fuzzy good-feeling doctrine, and it is understandable that men would be offended, which is exactly what happened to Christ. When he spoke plainly about divine election, people turned against him. "This is a hard teaching," they said. "Who can accept it?" (John 6:60) Yes, this is a hard doctrine, just as hard as the spikes that nailed Christ to a cross.

Do we dare face reality? Drugs, cults, New Age religion are merely escapist devices that lead to unreality and eventually the very unpleasant reality of hell. We must mention this, but would rather not dwell on it. We prefer to speak of salvation. Of course, we have only scratched the surface; there is much to be studied and discussed. However, all that would still be useless if we did not know for sure that Jesus was indeed the promised Messiah. Fortunately we do know. His resurrection proved who he really is.

The Resurrection

The resurrection of Jesus Christ defines Christianity. It proves that Jesus was who he said he was, God incarnate. If Jesus did not physically rise from the dead, Christianity must be discarded as a cruel hoax. A number of atheists realized that, and set out to prove the fraud. Surprise, after years of investigation they came back, utterly convinced that the resurrection is a historical fact. The evidence is everywhere. As we have seen, the resurrection was predicted in the Servant Song, (Isa 53) and the Crucifixion Psalm (22). Psalm 16, quoted by the apostle Peter on the day of Pentecost, is even more explicit. (Acts 2)

> I have set the LORD always before me.
> Because he is at my right hand,
> I will not be shaken.
> Therefore my heart is glad
> and my tongue rejoices;
> my body also will rest secure.
> Because you will not abandon me to the grave,
> nor will you let you Holy One see decay.
> You have made known to me the pathway of life;
> you will fill me with joy in your presence,
> with eternal pleasures at your right hand.
> Psalm 16:8-11

Peter explained that David was not speaking of himself, but of the Messiah, the Holy One. David was not raised from the dead, and he did not physically ascend into heaven, as Christ did. His skeleton remains proved it. What is more, the dead body of the Messiah would not suffer the fate that is common to all men, it would not decay. That is very strange, yet it fits the overall pattern. Death and decay are the result of sin. But the Messiah was sinless. Jesus was crucified and he died, but he was not killed. His life was not taken from him. He did not succumb to death, rather he "poured out his life unto death," (Isa 53:12) as a perfect sin offering, and arose to defeat death. Death had no power over his body. He did not suffer the penalty for sin because he never sinned. For that very reason his body, while resting in the tomb, did not decay.

The circumstances of his death are attested. Jesus was not stabbed in a back alley, he died in full view of the public, executed by professsionals who made sure he was really dead. His frightened followers were nowhere near, and they refused to believe reports that he had risen from the dead. The Pharisees tried to stop these tales with a version of their own. While the guards were sleeping, Jesus' disciples stole the body. This is almost humorous. Armies do not take kindly to sentries sleeping while on guard duty, least of all the Roman army; and if they were sleeping, how could they know who stole the body? They must have really been snoring while scared men, at the risk being crucified upside down, tried to roll away a two-ton sealed stone.

This much is certain, the body was gone. Christianity began downtown Jerusalem in the face of determined opposition. The apostles loudly proclaimed that their crucified master was the long-awaited Messiah, and that he had been raised from the dead. It should have been very easy for the Pharisees to prove them wrong. All they had to do was produce the body, and they never did.

The question has been raised, why did Jesus appear to his followers but never to unbelievers? Jesus did appear to unbelievers. The apostle Paul is a case in point, and so is James, the brother of Jesus, a leading man in the early church. Then there is the remarkable change in the lives of the apostles. How could these men change from ignorant followers of the master to death defying evangelists! The vast majority sealed their testimony with their blood. No conspiracy survives persecution. They knew Jesus was God, and they gave their lives as a testimony to the resurrection.

There are striking parallels between the Old Testament appearances of the Angel of the LORD and the resurrected Christ. The disciples knew of course that Jesus was unlike anyone else, just as the Old Testament people who dealt with the Angel of the LORD soon realized this was not just anyone. But after Christ rose from the dead there suddenly was a distance. Now they knew who he really was, and there was a distinct sense of fear and awe. We find much the same attitude in the reaction of Gideon and the parents of Samson. This strange person, like Christ, disappeared in miraculous fashion. The conclusion is inevitable, Christ and the Angel of the LORD were the same person, in different fashion.

Then there is the change of the day of rest from the last day of the week to the first. From time immemorial Saturday was the Sabbath, a word meaning "rest." Christianity changed that, the reason being that Christ rose on a Sunday, the first day of the week. Christians assembled on that day in celebration of the resurrection. The change was highly significant, and could have only been based upon a real event.

There is something more intangible, but nonetheless real, and that is the effect on believers. It is the effect of standing at the grave of your parents, your wife, your grandson, and knowing this is not the end. It is knowing you will die, but that death is a beaten enemy. It is knowing that the suffering of this world will once end, and the Savior awaits us, the same Jesus who was faithful unto death. It makes for a life, free from fear. No, the resurrection is not hypothetical; it opens the way to heaven, and that makes all the difference.

Justification by Faith

There are those who sincerely believe that we are saved by faith. That is true to the extent that we place our faith in Christ. Technically it is in error. We are not saved by faith (what if you put your faith in money), we are saved by grace. It is all God's doing. Faith accomplishes something altogether different, by it we are justified in the sight of God. Yes, we have been saved by grace, but when we stand before a perfectly just, righteous God, what do we have to show for?

Our righteous acts are like filthy rags. (Isa64:4) If we are nothing but unrighteousness, how can we possibly gain entrance into heaven? In our own strength, no! But the Messiah lived a perfect life, just and righteous in every way, a life in which God was well pleased. That life is credited to our account, and that life alone enables us to enter God's glory. In the Apostle Paul's words, "—and those he predestined, he also called, those he called he also justified, those he justified he also glorified." (Rom. 8:30) It was exactly on this point that the Reformers broke with Rome.

The medieval church believed salvation was collective, corporate. Rome has a corporate structure. Baptism acquired salvation through the corporation (the church) with its mystic rituals. The faithful were saved as long as they remained true to the corporation. Justification which ultimately leads to glorification, was a matter of good works, penance and the like, that supplemented the perfect life of Christ administered by management, the priesthood.

The problem is that scripture does not allow for that. It is the perfect life of Christ alone. Appeals to the epistle of James will not do. When the apostle truthfully assured his audience that "faith without works is dead," he was talking about fake "believers" who talk like Christians and act like pagans. Such hypocrites will always be with us, like bad weather. Good works prove a man's faith, just as the works of money grabbing television "evangelists" ensure their own damnation.

Faith ultimately is of God. Because the believer puts his faith in Christ and what he has done for him, he is judicially declared righteous. He does not have that righteousness in himself, rather the perfect righteousness of Christ is credited to his account, and God stamps that account "Paid in full." That is not a license to sin, rather the works we perform are rooted in gratitude for what God has done. These works do not contribute to either our salvation or our righteousness, they prove our loyalty.

In light of man's total depravity it is clear that whatever righteousness he has is utterly insufficient in the sight of God. The Law of Moses is the measuring stick for the righteousness God requires; the problem is, it is altogether too good. We cannot keep it. To say we can is utter folly and mere legalism. We are not just in God's sight, nor are we justified by keeping the law. The apostle Paul made this very clear in his letter to the Romans. Yes, we are justified, but not by keeping the law.

> But now a righteousness from God apart from law, has been made known, to which the Law and the Prophets (*the Old Testament*) testify. This righteousness from God comes through faith in Jesus Christ to all who believe. There is no difference, for all have sinned and fall short of the glory of God, and are justified freely by his grace, through the redemption that came by Christ Jesus. God presented him as a sacrifice of atonement, through faith in his blood.
>
> Romans 3:21-25

The sacrificial system of the Old Testament law foreshadowed the great and final sacrifice of the Messiah. The tabernacle was symbolic of the incarnation; it was the tent of the presence, that is the presence of God himself. The law presumed that Israel was a sinful community, and for this reason a system of provisional sacrifices was provided. The book of Hebrews makes it quite clear that the blood of animal sacrifices did not remove sins, they merely reminded people of their sins. Perfunctory observance of the law saved no one, nor did it make them just. The perfect sacrifice of Christ does. It does not make believers perfect in this life, and the only reason why they are "just" is because the divine court judiciously declared them so.

Now that we are saved by grace and justified by faith, how shall we live? Paul addressed it. "Work out your salvation with fear and trembling," he said, "for it is God who works in you to will and to act according to his good purpose. (Philippians 2:12, 13) He did not say "work *for* your salvation," he said work it out. When a teacher gives a math problem, he works it in. It is up to his students to work it out. In the same way God works redemption in us, now live up to so great a salvation. We recall that Paul mentioned it in the letter to the

Ephesians as well. "We are God's workmanship, created in Christ Jesus to do good works, which God prepared in advance for us to do." (Eph 2:10) It avoids a dangerous pitfall many well meaning folks fall into, the problem of legalism. Perfunctory observance of rules and regulations may give the appearance of faith, but it is nothing of the kind. Legalism not only kills joy, it chokes real love and a true relationship. That is what Paul's letter to the Galatians is all about.

The upshot is that we work hard for a living, not salvation. It is a terrible thing to live in fear, and God removed that fear. Now that our hearts are set free from all anxiety about salvation and damnation, we can fully apply ourselves to the divine mandate to subdue the earth. Put the raw materials to good use without ruining God's creation. Christians are called to influence society for the good. That should be in politics, whatever your orientation, business, education, the arts. Besides, since God ordains all things it follows that life has a purpose. There is no need to conjure that "wonderful plan" God made for us. That is impossible because it lies hidden in the secret will of God which cannot be discovered or looked into. Live your life by what has been revealed; a life of obedience will do.

The Law

When God gave Israel the Ten Commandments, he established a nation based upon law. This was followed by extensive legislation, consisting of ceremonial (religious) law, civil law and laws dealing with diets and hygiene. The ceremonial law was Messianic: it pictured the Messiah. This involved a system of sacrifices, many bloody, some monetary, connected with redemption. This is recorded in Exodus and Leviticus.

The civil law established liberty and proprietary rights, and even equal rights for women. The people had rights as well as obligations, among them the right of private property, kept in the family. There were also bankruptcy laws, aimed at restoration, and laws intended to phase out slavery, at least among Hebrews. Hygienic laws were remarkably advanced for their day, something recognized by the scientific community.

Then there is Deuteronomy, the second giving of the law. That is the farewell address of Moses, and could just as well be called the secondary law. It is not a straightforward repetition of what had been revealed before, (what good would that do?) rather Moses the wise law giver realized that the nation was far from perfect. He allowed for instance for divorce, without encouraging it. Deuteronomy unlike the other books of the law does not claim it was dictated by God. It certainly received divine sanction, but to the extent that it allows for human failure it falls short of that standard of divine perfection that marks the other books.

Deuteronomy is important in many ways. Christ quoted Deuteronomy at length, and it had a profound effect on western civilization. The U.S. constitution derives many of its ideas from Deuteronomy. The founding fathers were largely lawyers, and they knew it by heart. The principle of representation, the system of lower and higher courts, the republican form of government, it is all there. Constitutional law is the cornerstone of American civilization. Jefferson insisted that the government must be restrained with the chains of the constitution. The notion of a "living constitution" is a euphoric way of bypassing the law of the land.

The question that plagues many Christians is the place of the law in the church. Is there a place for it at all? If we are saved by grace and not by keeping the law, why have a law at all? But that never was the intent of the law. It was meant to make us aware of our sinful nature, how far we fall short of what is required. It also gives us a standard to live by.

Granted the tough penalties for violating the law are done with, but the law does give us a fairly good idea what God likes and what he abhors. The Ten Commandments for instance make it quite clear that the Lord alone is God and he does not take kindly to idolatry of any kind. It provides an anchor for our lives. To do away with the law altogether makes for a lawless society, a world of anarchy. No, the law does not save us, but it does give us a standard for living, a plumb line for truth.

Sacraments

Under the Old Covenant, Israel performed two divine conventions, circumcision and the Passover. The former was instituted with the patriarch Abraham, the latter at the time of the exodus. Both were bloody. Circumcision was the visible sign of the covenant that symbolized a number of things. It was common practice at that time, but as instituted by the Lord it meant getting rid of sin, and dedication to God. It included infant children (boys), for scripture does not see humanity as a gathering of individuals. The children were part of the covenant because they belonged to the family of God. To the Israelites to be circumcised meant to be part of the covenant community. It was a religious symbol.

The Passover, as we have seen, was instituted at the time of the exodus. It was symbolic of salvation. It involved the killing of an innocent lamb and escaping death by the blood of the victim. After a miraculous escape from slavery the people wondered a life time in the wilderness until they finally entered the Promised Land. The reality of the exodus was seriously questioned, but as shown earlier it did happen exactly as recorded. It was real, just as real as the sacrifice it symbolizes.

The word sacrament obviously has to do with sacred, a synonym for holy or set apart. Roman soldiers employed it to swear allegiance to their commander. The New Testament knows two such divine institutions, carried over from the Old, non-bloody signs of a very bloody sacrifice. They are baptism, the New Testament equivalent of circumcision, and Communion or the Lord's Supper, transformed from the Passover by Christ the night before he died. Now we all know that Rome has seven sacraments, but five of these are not valid, the reason being that the scriptures either know nothing about it or do not raise them to that status, and the remaining two have been given a meaning they never had. Taken together they are devices that give the clergy cradle to the grave control over the lives of the laity. It is a police church that has always produced a police state.

But is not Rome the original church? Do its offices resemble that of the New Testament? It declares the doctrine of salvation by grace "anathema," cursed. Rome is the continuation of the church of the middle Ages, the medieval church, part and parcel of the ancient Holy Roman Empire. Over the centuries, Greek philosophy and humanism blended with Christianity to create a hybrid. And like most hybrids, Rome proved hardy. The church was the only institution, able to maintain civil order, so she became very much political. In a world where people were largely ignorant of the scriptures, the church was seen as the ark of salvation. Only the ark lost her buoyancy, she was weighed down by barnacles. Gradually foreign doctrines crept in, which by the way is a common problem.

It happened in the world of opera. In the 19th Century, the performers considered the music and libretto a guide, subject to their own whims. So they added thrills and swirls to a point where the music never even resembled the original score. One soprano once asked Rossini what he thought of her performance in one of his operas. "You did fine," Rossini said bitingly. "Who was the composer?" Something like that happened to Rome. The Reformers eventually broke with this hybrid and attempted to restore the full truth of the Word of God. As it turned out, it was of the greatest importance to define the sacraments. The Anabaptists thought adult baptism all important but downplayed communion, which they merely regarded as a memorial meal. Luther and Calvin however could see that it involved more than that. In fact Calvin thought his work on communion his greatest contribution. And both differed from the Anabaptists regarding baptism.

Baptism

Baptism and its Old Testament equivalent circumcision are signs and seals of the Covenant. Both signify the elimination of sin, either by the removal of the foreskin or washing. The Old Covenant was temporary, the New lasting, the reason being that the former was administered amid human frailty, the latter firmly established on the rock of Christ. Yet it is the same covenant of old, established in the triune council of God before the world was made. In the words of Augustine, the New is in the Old concealed, the Old in the New revealed. Paul said that circumcision and baptism were essentially the same.

> For in Christ all the fullness of the Deity lives in bodily form, and you have been given fullness in Christ, who is the head over every power and authority. In him you were also circumcised in the putting off of the sinful nature, not with a circumcision done by the hands of men but with the circumcision done by Christ, having been buried with him in baptism, and raised with him through your faith in the power of God, who raised him from the dead.
>
> Colossians 2:9-12

The Old and New Testament are seen to converge. The rituals of the Old Testament were meant to teach the believers something, they symbolized spiritual realities. Circumcision had a messianic character, it was the equivalent of baptism. It involves the removal of sin, the death of the old, sinful nature and the beginning of a new life in Christ. The practice of baptism arose when gentiles converted to Judaism. Gentiles were considered unclean, so the Jews initiated a cleaning ceremony, baptism, derived from the cleansing rituals of the Mosaic Law. John the Baptist applied it to the Jewish nation as well, in preparation of the coming Messiah and the Kingdom of God. Christian baptism took on the meaning of the removal of sin.

From the beginning the question arose, is baptism necessary for salvation? No. Certainly the thief on the cross was not baptized, yet Jesus said he was saved. Nor has baptism inherent power. As in communion, there is no such thing as ritual magic. Both merely symbolize something, and we must distinguish the symbol from what it symbolizes. However, it is agreed that not anyone can administer it. It is, after all, a divine ordinance, not to be taken lightly. For this reason it is done by ordained men, people set apart for the ministry of the gospel.

Then how is it done, and who should or should not be baptized? Frankly, there never was a problem with that until the Reformation. The Reformers soon realized they were not the only ones to leave Rome, others departed with them. The Reformation was to a large extent an Augustinian revolt. However, the followers of Palagius, delivered from the iron fist of Rome, now came out of hiding. The orders within the Catholic Church are just as varied as Protestant denominations. The Franciscan order, followers of Francis of Asissi and semi-Palagians, produced a Franciscan lay movement, the Anabaptists. Rome and the Anabaptists were the opposite poles of Palagianism. The one was corporate, the other individualistic, and both were humanistic, man-centered.

They were very independent, so much so that they renounced the civil ruler. It was in many ways a violent phenomenon, the result of an irrational belief in direct inspiration that allowed them to do as they pleased. In the early Fifteen Hundreds they led insurrections against the magistrate and even took over a number of cities, resulting in bloody repressions. Appalled by this anarchy, others went the opposite way; they became pacifists and withdrew in spiritual communities, among them the Mennonites. These people believed the Reformers with their all-inclusive state churches contaminated the faith; believers were mixed up with unbelievers. They insisted that true believers must be rebaptized. That is why they were called Rebaptizers or Anabaptists. They also believed that children, being unable to make a decision for Christ should not be baptized, and that the only proper mode of baptism was by immersion. They sought a "pure" church for the regenerate only, which they enforced with strict discipline. This bothered Calvin. Much though he agreed with church discipline, he thought the Anabaptists were too harsh. Soon their individualistic beliefs caused innumerable quarrels and the movement fell apart. By and large they are the spiritual ancestors of the Baptists. Their legacy is religious tolerance.

Without going into detail, it should be said that the Baptist denial of infant baptism is based upon an argument from silence: it says nowhere that children must be baptized. But an argument from silence can prove anything. Grass must be good for your eyes; I have never seen a cow with glasses! And it cuts both ways: it says nowhere that children must be excluded from baptism, nor does it say they must be dedicated instead. (It is essentially a dry baptism, and why dedicate at all?) We could go on. It says nowhere that women can participate in communion, that the day of rest must be changed from the last day of the week to the first. Words such as Trinity and sacrament appear nowhere in the Bible. Yet these things have always been practiced and believed, for good reasons.

Scriptural silence about infant baptism is highly significant, exactly because under the Old Covenant children were included. With the onset of the New Covenant the rituals of the Old Covenant became obsolete, so circumcision was abolished. It caused an uproar, which is understandable enough; circumcision was a way of life. Now imagine if Jewish parents presented their child for baptism, only to be told that children were not eligible. At the very least they would be upset and demand a formal explanation. But no, the subject was never raised. To the contrary. On the day of Pentecost the apostle Peter told his audience,

> "Repent and be baptized, every one of you, in the name of Jesus Christ for the forgiveness of sins. And you will receive the gift of the Holy Spirit. The promise is to you *and to your children* and for all who are far off - for all whom the Lord our God will call."
>
> Acts 2:38, 39

Clearly the apostle included children in the covenant promise. It anticipated the debate about a formal profession of faith. We should not forget that Christianity entered virgin territory. No one had been baptized yet, therefore baptism was to a large extent the seal of a formal profession, an initiation ceremony for the first generation of newly converted believers. How should it be done? It does not matter how. Immersion, sprinkling, pouring, all of it will do fine. In Acts chapter two, which deals with outpouring of the Holy Spirit on Pentecost, the apostle Peter said that the prophecy of Joel 2:28 had come true. "I will pour my Spirit upon mankind." It is agreed that this is the baptism of the Holy Spirit. Yet it involved pouring, not immersion.

The Greek word "baptismo" means dipping. In the scriptures it is used in a wider sense; it is a generic word associated with cleansing. For instance the water, changed to wine at the wedding of Cana was meant for *baptismo*, that is cleansing ceremonies. To insist that certain ceremonies must be performed a certain way is contrary to the spirit of the New Testament. A narrow mind set like that is likely to spill over into other areas. Paul could have easily laid down the rule what was proper to eat and what was not. Instead he called for tolerance and respect. The only guide line for formal worship is that it must be done "decently and in order."

We appreciate the wide latitude. Widely divergent cultures in the course of millennia could proclaim salvation in a language their own and baptize according to customs their own. Immersion may be preferable at certain times in certain places, but it cannot be done in a waste desert such as the Sahara. Pity the Eskimo. In some cultures it is not done because it is considered embarrassing. My mother was baptized when she was in her forties. She was a hunchback. Must it be demanded of her that she be immersed in some sort of bathing suit before an audience? What about the bedridden, the dying? We could go on. In the scriptural record, baptism was performed in places where immersion was practically impossible, such as the temple in Jerusalem and the house of the Philippian jailer. Besides, it was not a strictly individual matter.

The book of Acts mentions several cases where not merely professing individuals, but whole households were baptized. Children are considered holy when a single parent is a believer. (I Cor. 7:14) Christianity is not a religion of prescribed ritual or formal liturgy.

These things are to be commended, but we cannot insist that it must be done a certain way. It is divisive. The same is true of speaking in tongues. If you have it, fine. If you don't, fine. Just do not disparage others, and do not make up your own doctrines. To say that a "second baptism" is necessary for salvation is tantamount to saying the sacrifice of Christ was not all-sufficient; something else is needed as well, and that renders these teachings heretical.

Finally, it is wrong to speak of "baptizing babies." We do not baptize babies, we baptize our children, children of believers. They, too, have the covenant promise, and they are not left out. They are part of Christ's church.

Communion

On the night before he was betrayed, Jesus celebrated the Passover with his disciples. That was altogether fitting, since it culminated his ministry. It was at this, the last night of his earthly life that he told his disciples who he really was and why he had come. They must have been stunned when he told them, "Take and eat, this is my body." (Matthew 26:26) The implication was undeniable; he said in essence, "The Passover is all about me. I am the Passover lamb."

More than fifteen centuries had passed since Moses instituted the Passover at that dramatic time, when Israel hastened to leave the land of slavery. Jesus was the Messiah, the real Passover lamb, unblemished, sinless and pure. From the triumphant entry in Jerusalem to the hour he was condemned four days passed, the days that the Paschal lamb was inspected. Christ was inspected - and found without fault.

After his arrest the Sanhedrin, the Jewish authorities, looked for any violation to charge him with, and they found nothing. The longer they looked, the less they found. They condemned him on charges of blasphemy because he said he was "the Son of God." In the eastern mindset that meant equality with God himself. Pilate said outright there was no guilt in him. Rome, the judicial State, declared him righteous. The Lamb of God was sacrificed for a full and complete atonement that opened heaven's gates. We now can cross over to the Promised Land just as surely as Israel crossed that foreordained road across the Strait of Tiran toward freedom.

Then what does communion represent? Oh well, it is commemorative. Jesus said so. The Passover looked forward to the ultimate sacrifice, Communion looks back. We remember what God did for us. Yet much more is involved, we commune with Christ. That is why it is called Communion. Christ is spiritually present. It is like dining together and have a heart to heart talk. We are after all spiritual and physical beings, and the physical elements of the Lord's Supper awaken us to the reality of it all.

The question naturally arises, what do the bread and wine symbolize? The bread is a direct transition of the Passover. It stands for the broken body of the Lamb of God, a sacrifice for sin. The book of Hebrews makes it clear that it was a once-for-all sacrifice, never to be repeated. The wine stands for the blood of the Covenant. It goes back to the blood of the Passover lamb, applied to the doorpost of the house at the time of the exodus. Why these bloody ceremonies? They foreshadow the very real and very bloody sacrifice on the cross, all-sufficient, that saves us from the angel of eternal death. The wording however is that of a formal engagement ceremony. These words were spoken by the groom when he proposed to his wife-to-be. It was Jesus' way of asking his bride, the church, "Will you marry me?" The book of Revelation speaks of the wedding of the lamb and his bride, the Church. Heaven is a place where the believers are one with Christ, a place where no unbeliever wants to be.

What are we to think of Rome's doctrine of trans-substantiation, the notion that the bread and wine literally turn into the body and blood of Christ? If that is true there must have been two bodies of Christ in the upper room. What is more, Christ held his own body in his hands. That would seem somewhat illogical. John the Baptist introduced Jesus as "The lamb of God," but that does not mean Jesus actually was a lamb. These things are symbolic. The doctrine is really part of a larger whole. It grew over the centuries, something that sneaked up on people without realizing it. Something of the kind happens in Protestant churches as well. The Communion meal is always carefully covered with a beautiful cloth; it is almost a sacred vestment. That is a far cry from the original purpose, it was meant to keep the flies away. The meal sacred, the vestment not.

In the Mass Christ is not remembered, he is constantly being sacrificed, and without that there is no salvation. The method by which it is administered speaks volumes; the believer does not even take the bread, it is put in his mouth. The message is clear: the thinking has been done, the Church takes the place of God, now swallow. It runs throughout the sacramental system. Strictly speaking, it is an easy religion; everything has been taken care of. There is no need for the believer to personally appeal to God for forgiveness of sins. Confession to a priest result in prescribed repetitions of the Rosary and that takes care of it. It does not make for a high sense of morals. For all fact and purpose Rome does not see Christ as the King of Glory, he is the victim. The crucifix pictures an ever dying Christ. The dead Jesus is always in the arms of his deified mother, which never was the case by the way. The last time Mary saw Jesus when from the cross he told the apostle John to take care of her. John took her to his house, and she never came back.

The sacerdotal system that evolved chokes personal responsibility and makes its adherents depend wholly upon the church rather than upon God, who becomes a rather distant deity. As a result Roman Catholicism historically behaved in a manner, very similar to Islam. Many of its adherents were indifferent, but the church tended to be intolerant, which all too often resulted in a violent society. Both Roman Catholicism and Islam were inclined to spread their religion with the sword. Granted, no church is perfect. It is well known that Calvin supervised the execution of Servetus, that unfortunate genius, who was sentenced to death by fire for blasphemy. Both Luther and Melanchton wholeheartedly agreed. Yet for all their failures, the Reformers aimed at greater tolerance.

Now of course, this does not mean that every Catholic is hell bound, any more than membership of a church is a ticket to heaven. The Lord knows who are his. There are fine people in the Catholic

Church, and Rome has always championed sound scholarship, particularly in the area of ethics. We merely object to the manifest errors that value tradition over the clear teachings of the New Testament. It is obvious from the gospels that the Jews did the exact same thing, and it angered Christ no end. Roman Catholicism is tradition bound. It has its roots in the medieval church. While embracing Augustine's doctrine of church supremacy, the Papacy rejected that of sovereign grace. Instead Pelagius' belief in human ability prevailed. Cornelius van Til put it this way.

> The Roman Catholic Church attempted to synthesize the worship of God and the worship of man. The genius of the Romanist position is that it combines an interpretation of man and his world as given by the method of the Greek philosophers, especially Aristotle, with an interpretation of man and his world as given by Christ in the Scriptures. In the nature-grace scheme of Rome the Aristotelian view of human autonomy and the biblical view of divine sovereignty are supposedly cooperating peacefully with one another for the welfare of man and for the glory of God.
>
> In the Roman scheme of things the natural man is not told that he is, because of his fall in Adam, a slave to sin and that only the grace of God in Christ applied to him by the regeneration of the Holy Spirit can set him free. The natural man is rather told that, although he is naturally free, he may have a greater degree of freedom though Christ. Through grace man may be lifted in the scale of being toward participation in the being of God. This largely metaphysical lifting in the scale of being is a gradual process. The church is therefore, in effect, a continuation of the incarnation of Jesus Christ. The mass is a non-bloody continuation of the sacrifice of Christ. The faithful who partake of it are, hopefully, moving onward and upward toward the vision of and participation in the being of God. [3]

In all fairness to Rome, they are not the only ones to assume a place where they do not belong; numerous Protestant churches do the same thing. Only it is the individual, not the church, who arrogates himself an honor that belongs to God. If Rome believes itself above the Bible, so do fundamentalist churches, mostly in the charismatic camp. As a matter of fact, many of its adherents have a definite aversion toward scripture. After all, a hot line with the Almighty renders the Word redundant. They believe themselves supreme. It is the people who shout the loudest "Praise the Lord, "who never believe a word of what he said. A comparison with the Mary cult of Rome proves the point. When the angel visited Mary to announce the birth of the promised Messiah, Mary supposedly said, "Fiat," meaning "granted." Of course she didn't, but that is beside the point. By it the church now has autonomy over salvation.

Now what is the difference if it is not Mary, but the individual who answers God's offer of salvation with "granted!" Either way, God is denied the honor due to his Holy Name. It makes either man or the church supreme. No Protestant would ever say, "Hail Mary." But how many say, "Hail me!"

The One and the Many

We are obviously dealing with fundamental presuppositions. What is more important, the one or the many? It is the age old question of particulars and universals. Is the corporate body more important than the individual or is it the other way around? Is the church all-important or is the believer? It is the choice between despotism and anarchy. In some societies the state has complete control over the individual, in others the individual is given control over the state. We find the same thing in churches. Rome as we have seen is corporate. It has a hierarchical setup that dictates everything from above; it is monarchical form of government. Congregational churches such as Baptists on the other hand are strictly individualistic and necessarily highly independent.

However, the world where the individual is supreme is a world of isolation, alienation and consequent separation, a world of all Chiefs and no Indians. There is a distinct tendency to withdraw from everything and everyone, including the world and the state. Rome tends to breed statism (dictatorships). Baptist churches are ruled by deacons, although several ministers, appealing to scripture, claim to be elders (presbyters). The problem is that the congregational form of government (a democracy) almost always leads to chaos. The individual is supreme. Baptist churches, temples, tabernacles and independent congregations abound. They stick tether like dry sand.

The Reformed tradition, thanks to its God-centered Covenant Theology, has taken a consistently different track, it looked to the model of the Trinity for an answer. God is personal, so we can communicate with him. Yet God is not strictly one, he is three-in-one. The one-ness of God is not the same as his three-ness; the being of God is not uniform. The three Persons of the Trinity are One God, and so it follows that the one and the many are equally ultimate in God. Since man is created in the image of God, the one and the many are equally ultimate in humanity as well, something demonstrated in the family, an institution established by God himself.

In the family the interests of the corporate whole and the individual are equally guarded. It is a balance between the one and the many. God sees the family as a genuine corporation, within the sphere of his Covenant of grace, and therefore the whole family is part of his church. For this reason the Reformed and Presbyterian churches baptize whole families. Individually the members of the family are still responsible before God. Of course Catholics and Arminians believe in the Trinity and the family as well, only they have not always considered the implications.

The Reformed form of government is representative; the elders are chosen by the congregation to represent the people. The New Testament mentions ruling elders and teaching elders, also called bishops or overseers (the ministers) and deacons, but not a select priesthood: all believers are priests. The representative system is evident throughout the scriptures. Adam was a representative, as was

Christ. The same applies to the churches, they constitute a federation with higher and lower courts. As a result Calvinists have always been inclined to look at the republic as the best form of government. It avoids extremes, and opposes both the unlimited power of the state and unbridled individualism.

Calvin sought to reform not only the church, but the state as well. He instructed believers to submit to the authorities, and in case of oppression appeal to the lesser magistrate. Calvinists have always been interested in state craft, and they resisted tyranny, witness the Scottish Presbyterians and the American Revolution. The British called the War for Independence the "Scottish-Irish," that is Presbyterian rebellion. The framers of the Constitution consciously rejected Democracy, and opted for a Republic instead. It is a form of government that protects both the one and the many, and provides liberty under the rule of law.

Justice

In this world, justice is imperfect. Much as the judiciary would like to arrive at the right verdict and pronounce correct sentence, nobody knows every motivation or even who did what. How many criminals literally got away with murder? And that is assuming courts and juries really want to do justice. That is not always so. Think of all the deliberate injustices, the horrors of tyrannies, the persecution of the innocent. Where, we ask, is the God of Justice? He is where he was when his own innocent Son was crucified, enthroned in Glory. He allows these things to happen because he has ordained a day of reckoning. The Judge of all the earth one day will meet out perfect justice.

Some atheists reason there can be no God because a Being that is perfectly righteous must necessarily eliminate evil. If God can do everything and he is perfectly holy he will always stop everything that is contrary to his holy will. Since we see evil everywhere there can be no God. This is self-defeating logic. Where did we get the knowledge of good and evil? It could have only come from on high.

And it defies common sense. There are things God cannot do. He cannot swear by anything greater than himself, he cannot lie, he cannot make anything greater than himself, he cannot drill a square hole and he cannot eliminate himself. God is always true to his Being.

Evil did not first appear when God's creatures rebelled. Before anything was created, it existed as a concept in the mind of God. The question was how to deal with it. One of God's perfections is his freedom to act as he pleases, which is always right. Of all the options available, he chose the one that deals with evil in a final manner; he allowed it to happen and determined to judge the perpetrators. However, he also chose to be merciful, so he provided a way out. Sin is finite because it involves failure on the part of man, therefore a finite man must make full payment. He must be infinite as well, because it involves the wrath of an infinite God. The redeemer must be human and divine, both God and man.

Yet on the cross we also see something that bothers and frightens us. It is the severity of God. God showed his love when he gave his only son, yes, but it certainly was a severe love. This is no light matter, and it is the great stumbling stone for Atheists. They hate the God who does not exist for just that reason.

It strikes a chord in all of us. Surely a good God would never send anyone to everlasting damnation! But a God who is good is necessarily just. The cross therefore is the great exhibition of God's righteousness and justice: he demands full satisfaction. An analogy is that of the family of a murder victim who want to see the killer fried. Justice demands that he pay for his crime.

In the same way divine justice demands that man pay for his rebellion, which is part of an evil, greater than we can fathom. The cross is a vivid picture of hell. Granted it is a worst-case scenario, but the reality of it is too awful to comprehend. This fills us with wonder. How great was God's love for us that he would send his only Son through hell to pay for our sins! Christ is the way; the only way. There is no other.

Yes, there is a way out and justice will prevail. The righteousness of God demands it; so does the sense of justice in all of us, created in his image. The Judge of all the earth demands full satisfaction. The day will come when all will appear before the High Court of no appeal, a court that knows everything and will pronounce perfect sentence, just, hard and without mercy. The only way out is Christ: throw yourself on the mercy of a merciful court, only do not wait until it is forever too late. The day of salvation is now, not tomorrow.

> For God will bring every deed into judgment,
> including every hidden thing,
> whether it is good or evil.
>
> Ecclesiastes 12:14

Hope and a Future

In an age of uncertainty and confusion, a world where evil men plot murder and innocent people die, the future seems bleak to say the least. Yet God has planned a hope and a future.

> "For I know the plans I have for you"
> declares the LORD,
> "plans to prosper you and not to harm you,
> plans to give you hope and a future."
>
> Jeremiah 29:11

God has a vision and a plan of action. It was conceived in eternity and is being executed in the present. It is one of God's perfections that it is the best possible plan. Unlike army Generals who make up a plan of battle and back it up with several alternate plans in case something goes wrong (which is always the case in war), there is only one plan. It only makes sense that God began Creation with a plan in mind. Christ asked his hearers, "Suppose one of you wants to build a tower. Will he not first sit down and estimate the cost to see if he has enough money to complete it?" (Luke 14:28) If men have enough brains to first count the cost and plan ahead, how much more an all-knowing God? He does it in a way that is beyond our power to imagine.

> "For my thoughts are not your thoughts,
> neither are your ways my ways,"
> declares the LORD.
> "As the heavens are higher than the earth,
> so are my ways higher than your ways,
> and my thoughts than your thoughts."
>
> Isaiah 55:8, 9

Logic dictates that an omniscient God knows what will happen, and that he orders the affairs of his creation with a plan in mind. It would have been the height of irresponsibility indeed to start a universe, unaware of the potential dangers, not knowing where it would lead and in ignorance see humanity plunge itself into despair. Of course, nothing of the kind happened. God chose this particular plan of action because it was the best possible way to deal with sin. By doing so he demonstrated both his justice and his mercy. He also gives us a reason for living.

From the very beginning it was God's intent to communicate with man, the crown of his creation. In the Garden of Eden already, God the Son appeared in human form, enjoying his creation. He desired to be with humanity, the link between Heaven and earth. When the first man plunged the human race into destruction, God did not abandon us. Over the centuries he would appear as the Angel of the Lord or he would speak through the Hebrew prophets. In the man Jesus we see God who is fully human, such as he never was before. In his life, death and resurrection we see the love, mercy, justice and severity of an Almighty God who cares. Life suddenly has meaning. Ultimately our focus is on the holy, righteous, just God who made us for unending glory and happiness.

It is an empty life indeed, to exist for no reason, other than gratifying the urge of the moment. Man is not a cosmic accident, he was designed to adore and worship. The natural man adores and worships himself, which is a prescription for disaster, and God has set out to correct that. His intent is basically that of restoration. He wants to restore the broken communion that once existed, and he paid a terrible price to do it. His plan is meant for our good, to give us a hope and a future, meaning and a life worth living. Christianity is a religion of hope; not the wishful kind that leads nowhere, but that of certainty and assurance. There are those who maintain that all roads lead to God. Granted; but when you get there, where will he send you? Hell is life in prison, a life that will never end, but has no future. It is a life of loneliness, agony and never ending punishment. There are those who live a life much like that here and now.

Throughout the ages empires have come and gone, but there is an age to come when the Empire of the Son will shine in all its glory. The kingdom of God will have no end, a kingdom of righteousness and peace, where God rules in the hearts of men. The hope and future that God promises comes through Christ, and no one else. The world may offer glitter and passing pleasures, but they vanish and in the end are nothing but fool's gold. We may be engrossed in fascinating subjects, for instance historical events such as discussed on these pages, but in the end, what good does it do?

Who knows, maybe the planets did veer off their course and maybe they did cause catastrophes, but that does not change human nature. It is a mistake to assume, as well meaning folks do, that realizing our catastrophic past will heal the psychological scars of humanity. Just as mistaken as those who believe that gradual evolution inevitable will lead to ever higher planes and ultimate divinity.

Is this the solution that will lead us to Nirvana? It does not. The real vision for humanity is that of an ugly, blood stained cross, where a perfect man died to pay the penalty for our sins. That man, it turned out, was God the Son. If we look up to the heavens, look beyond planets, stars and galaxies, look for the heaven of heavens, for there is the solution for earth's problems.

Planets, Ages and Empires

References

Chapter One
Israel and Egypt

1. Rashi, The Torah, with Rashi's Commentary translated, annotated and elucidated. The Saperstein Edition, p.119.
2. William Kelly Simpson, The Literature of Ancient Egypt, The Maxims of Ptahhotep. p.137, 138.
3. Peter A. Clayton, Chronicle of the Pharaohs, pages 30-31, 42, 50, 53, 68-69. Similar information is available on the World Wide Web.
4. It is so identified in the Reader's Digest World Wide Atlas, 1984, p.105.
5. See "The Times Atlas of the World," Seventh Comprehensive Edition, published in 1992, p.86. "Magha'ir'shu'ayb" means "caves of shu'ayb." (Jethro)
6. Sir Alan Gardiner, Egypt of the Pharaohs, p.46, 47.
7. Cosmos Without Gravitation. Synopsis by Immanuel Velikovsky.
8. Gardiner, op.cit, p.109.
9. William Kelly Simpson, The Literature of Ancient Egypt p. 210, "The Admonitions of an Egyptian Sage" appears on pages 211-233. It was translated by R.O. Faulkner. All quotations are from these pages. © 1973 by Yale University Press
10. John J. Davis, Moses and the Gods of Egypt, p. 99, 100.
11. Ibid, p.111
12. Heredotus, the Histories. A new translation by Robin Waterfield, p. 109, 110. Book 2,37
13. Stuart Flexner with Doris Flexner, The Pessimist Guide to History, p.95
14. Davis, op.cit, p.122.

15. Ibid, p.124.
16. Expositors Bible.
17. Louis Ginzberg, Legends of the Bible, p.338.
18. Davis, op.cit, p.126.
19. Ginzberg, op.cit, p. 339, 340.
20. Quoted from Immanuel Velikovsky, Worlds in Collision, p.79.
21. R.S.Bray, Armies of Pestilence. The Impact of Disease on History, p.154.
22. The Oxford history of ancient Egypt, edited by Ian Shaw, p.190. Manfred Bietak was an Austrian excavator.
23. Josephus, Against Apion, p.610.
24. Gardiner, op.cit, p.156.
25. A reprint of Griffith and Goyon's translations can be found on the web site.
26. Peter A.Clayton, Chronicle of the Pharaohs, p.91
27. Cyril Aldred, The Egyptians, Third Edition, Thames & Hudson p.143.
28. Ian Shaw, op.cit, p.188.
29. Cyril Aldred, op.cit, p.143.
30. George Steindorff and Keith C. Seele. When Egypt Ruled the East, p.26.
31. A. Rosalie David, The Egyptian Kingdoms, p. 20.
32. The Literature of Ancient Egypt, The Prophecies of Neferti, translated by R.O.Faulkner, p.236, 237.
33. Ibid, p.236,238
34. Pliny, Natural History, Vol. I, p.235.
35. Velikovsky, op.cit, p.97
36. Ibid, p.97
37. Ibid, p.87
38. Larry Williams and Bob Cornuke discovered Mount Sinai in 1988. Their exploits are recorded in "The Gold of Exodus," by Howard Blum. However, at least half of the book is fictional. Bob Cornuke established the "BASE Institute." The web site is www.baseinstitute.org. Jim and Penny Caldwell, who

lived ten years in Saudi Arabia, visited the sacred mountain several times. They took numerous pictures and videos. See www.SplitRockResearch.com. Pictures used with their kind permission. I was privileged to see artifacts dating from Israel's stay at Mt Horeb, such as weapons, arrows and a portable mill stone in a bowl.

39. Velikovsky, op.cit. P.111
40. Owusu, Symbols of Egypt, p.147.
41. Ibid, p.149. For a good illustration of Egyptian priests carrying a naos on a sacred bark, see John Romer: People of the Nile. Everyday life in Egypt. P.146-147.
42. Ginzberg, op.cit, p.372, 373
43. There is evidence that humans before the flood were taller than modern man. For reason that are obscure, there also were "Nephilim" giants, at least ten feet tall. A strain of giantism evidently survived. These "sons of Anak" giants are mentioned a number of times, Goliath among them.
44. For a good study on this subject see "Synchronized Chronology," by Roger Henry. The author aligns dynasties and kingdoms with archaeological data and pottery in the reconstructed version of history.
45. Owusu, Ibid, p.57.

Chapter Two
Venus

1. Immanuel Velikovsky, Worlds in Collision, p.386, 387.
2. Notes by Wallace Thornhill.
3. Wallace Thornhill, The Electric Universe. Slide presentation & notes.
4. Eric J. Lerner, The Big Bang Never Happened, p.193, 195, 196.
5. Donald E. Scott, The Electric Sky. A Challenge to the Myths of Modern Astronomy, P.144, 145
6. Wallace Thornhill, Planet, Stars and Plasma Physics, Thoth, a catastrophic newspaper, Vol 1, No. I, p.8.
7. Kuiper in *Sky and Telescope*, March 1959, p. 259.
8. Ancient peoples celebrated a seven-day festival of lights, in honor on Saturn. Roman Christians observed the birth of Christ during the Saturnalia festivities, the feast of lights. Rabinnical literature connects it with the seven days in the ark before the flood came. Isaiah 30:26 may refer to this.
9. Heinsohn wrote his findings in German in "Die Sumerer gab es nicht." (There were no Sumerians). An abridged English version appears in "Aeon, a Symposium on Myth and Science," Vol. 1, No 2, p.17-51. It is available on the World Wide Web under www.kronia.com.
10. Strabo, Geography, 11.13.5

Chapter Three
The Thutmose Dynasty

1. Immanuel Velikovsky, Ages in Chaos, p.51, 52, citing W.M. Petrie.
2. Josephus, Antiquities of the Jews, Book 8, p.513.
3. In "The Literature of Ancient Egypt," in a footnote to "The Victorious King," R.O.Faulkner identifies Punt as "applied to a region in or adjoining Syria, perhaps Transjordan is meant." (P.286).
4. Louis Ginzberg, Legends of the Bible, p.562.
5. Sir Alan Gardiner, Egypt of the Pharaohs, p.185
6. The Oxford History of Ancient Egypt, edited by Ian Shaw, p.241.
7. They were reproduced by Velikovsky in "Ages in Chaos," also by Roger Henry in "Synchronized Chronology," p.65.
8. Seindorf and Seele, When Egypt Ruled the East, p.47.
9. The Legend of King Keret. www.maravot.com Hittite treaties. A translation by H.L. Ginzberg appears in "Bulletin of the American Schools of Oriental research. Supplementary studies Nos. 2-3. The legend of King Keret, a Canaanite epic of the Bronze Age," 1946. "The pre-biblican narrative tradition" by Simon B.Parker gives interesting insight in the poetic structure of the poem, but does not record the poem itself.
10. The Literature of Ancient Egypt, p.190, 191. W.K.Simpson translator.
11. Ibid, p.242-265. WKS
12. Ibid, p.297-326. WKS

Chapter Four
The Ramessides

1. Sir Alan Gardiner, Egypt of the Pharaohs, p.262.
2. Heredotus, The Histories, p.159, 160, 248.
3. Josh McDowell, Prophecy Fact or Fiction, p.56.
4. Gardiner, op.cit, p.247
5. Ibid, p.273.
6. Heredotus, op.cit, p.174.
7. The Persians, by Jim Hicks and the Editors of Time Life Books, p.32.
8. See "The ancient mariners," by Lionel Casson. See p. 39 and 40. Also plate 40, the photograph of a reconstructed ship.
9. Gardiner, op.cit, p.276, 277.
10. Immanuel Velikovsky, Peoples of the Sea, p.241, 242.

Chapter Five
The Assyrian and the Passover

1. The works of Josephus, Antiquity of the Jews, p.20.
2. Immanuel Velikovsky, Worlds in Collision, p.215.
3. Ibid, p.248.
4. This is mentioned in the Talmud. See also Ginzberg, Legends of the Jews, Vol VI, p.367, note 81.
5. Velikovsky, op.cit, p.220, 221.
6. Ibid, p.221.
7. Louis Ginzberg, The Legends of the Jews, Vo. IV, p.266.
8. A fragment of Archilochus, known primarily from other writers.
9. Seneca, Tragedies II, Thyestes, p.157-161.
10. Thoth, a catastrophic newspaper, Vol. III, No. 2, p.3 quoting Babylonian omens: "If the Sun goes down (by a darkness/eclipse) and Mars stands in its place, there will be an Usurper."
11. See Josh McDowell, Evidence That Demands a Verdict, p.287-293.
12. Velikovsky, op.cit, p.293.
13. Ibid, p.223.
14. Ethan Smith, the View of the Hebrews, p.41. "The Talmud and Mamonides relate that the foundation of the temple was so removed that the site was ploughed by Terentius Rufus."
15. Velikovsky, op.cit, p.224.
16. Jonathan Swift, Gulliver's Travels, p.162.
17. Velikovsky, op.cit, p.284-293, quite correctly, quotes several ancient sources. They are mentioned in Homer, by the Babylonians and in the Vedic Hymns.
18. Homer, The Iliad, translated by Samuel Butler, p.77-87.
19. Ibid, p.239, 340.
20. Ibid, p.77.
21. Velikovsky, op.cit, p.266, 270

22. Ibid, p.270.
23. See Josh McDowell, Evidence that demands a verdict, p.287-293.
24. The NIV study Bible, commentary on 2Kings 19:21.
25. Louis Ginzberg, the Legends of the Jews, Vol VI, p.362, note 54.
26. Ginzberg, op.cit, Vol. IV, p.268.
27. W. Roberson Nicoll, The Expositor's Bible, Vol. II, p.425, article by Frederick W.Rarrar.
28. Ginzberg, op.cit, Vol VI, p.363, note 55.
29. Ibid, note 58.
30. Ginzberg, op.cit, Vol. IV, p.268, 269.
31. Velikovsky, op.cit, p.240.
32. Donald E. Scott, The Electric Sky, p. 129.
33. Op. cit. p.137.
34. Nisroch was a human idol with an eagle face. It was a fire god connected with agriculture, generally considered to be beneficial. Nisroch is not associated with any planet.
35. This is mentioned by Velikovsky, op.cit, p.240-242.
36. Immanuel Velikovsky, Earth in Upheaval, p.172, 173, quoting Evans, The Palace of Minoa, Vol IV, pt 2, p.942.
37. Robert Drews, The End of the Bronze Age, p. 48. Translation from the German in italics mine.
38. Ibid, p.53, 54.
39. The works of Josephus, Antiquities of the Jews, p.228.
40. Velikovsky, op.cit, p.271.
41. See: The Cataclysm: A Monthly Symposium on Myth and Science, January 1988. Vol. 1, No. 1. Article by Charles Genenthal, The Electro-gravitic Theory of Celestial Motion, p. 24. Assuming there was an encounter between Mars and Earth 715 B.C. when Mars was inside the orbit of the earth, (the day Ahaz was buried), it affected the axial inclination of the earth. If fourteen years later, 701 B.C., Mars moved outside the earth's orbit, did this counter the previous change? This of course would be noticed on sun dials.

Chapter Six
The Covenant

1. John Calvin, The Institutes of the Christian Religion, Book 1, p. 72, 73.
2. Rejecting the odd interpretation of certain scholars and a number of Rabbis, which would make Cyrus the Anointed. This does not fit the prophecy at all. If indeed the "times and seasons" were actually changed, it is nearly impossible to give the exact year when the Messiah would appear. There is considerable debate about the decree to restore Jerusalem. Four such decrees are mentioned in scripture. Here it is assumed that it is the one, recorded in Ezra 26. It is the only one to be recorded in detail.
3. Crisis in the Reformed Churches. Peter Y. De Jong, Editor. Cornelius Van Til, The Significance of Dordt for Today, p.181, 182.

Bibliography

Aldred, Cyril. The Egyptians. Third Edition. Revised and updated by Aidan Dodson. Thames & Hudson. 1998

Allen, D.S and J.B.Delair, Cataclysm. Compelling Evidence of a Cosmic Catastrophe in 9500 B.C. Bear & Company, Santa Fe, New Mexico, 1995

Arp, Halton. Seeing Red. Redshifts, Cosmology and Academic Science. Apeiron, Montreal, Quebec, Canada. 1998
http://redshift.vif.com

Blum, Howard. The Gold of Exodus. Pocket Books, New York, London, Toronto, Sidney, Singapore. 1998

Bray. R.S. Armies of Pestilence. The Impact of Disease on History. Barnes & Noble Books. New York. By arrangement with James Clarke & Co Ltd. 1996

Breasted, James Henry. Ancient Records of Egypt, Vol 1 The First through the Seventeenth Dynasties. University of Illinois Press. Urbana and Chicago. 2001

Calvin, John. The Institutes of the Christian Religion, edited by John T. McNeill, translated and indexed by Ford Lewis Battles. Philadelphia, The Westminster Press Copyright © MCMLX W. L. Jenkins. Seventh Printing, 1975

Casson, Lionel. The Ancient Mariners. Seafarers and Sea fighters of the Mediterranean in ancient times. Princeton University Press, Princeton, New Jersey.

Clayton, Peter A. Chronicle of the Pharaohs. The Reign-by-Reign Record of the Rulers and Dynasties of Ancient Egypt. Thames & Hudson. 1994

David, A. Rosalie. The Egyptian Kingdoms. Peter Bedrick Books, New York.

Davis, John, J. Moses and the Gods of Egypt. Studies in Exodus. Second Edition. Baker Book House, Grand Rapids, Michigan. 1986

De Jong, Peter Y. Crisis in the Reformed Churches. Essays in commemoration of the great Synod of Dordt, 1618-1610. Peter Y. De Jong, editor. Published by the Reformed Fellowship, Inc. Grand Rapids, Michigan, 1968

Drews, Robert. The End of the Bronze Age. Changes in Warfare and the Catastrophe ca. 1200 B.C. Princeton University Press, Princeton, New Jersey. 1993

Flexner, Stuart, with Doris Flexner. The Pessimist's Guide to History. Avon Books, New York. 1992

Gardiner, Sir Alan, Egypt of the Pharaohs, Oxford University Press, 1964

Bibliography

Ginzberg, Louis. Legends of the Bible. Konecky & Konecky, Old Saybrook, Ct 1956. A shorter version of "The Legends of the Jews."

Ginzberg, Louis. The Legends of the Jews. Translated by Henrietta Szold. Seven Volumes. The John Hopkins University Press, Baltimore and London. 1948

Henry, Roger. Synchronized Chronology. Rethinking Middle East Antiquity. Algora Publishing, New York, 2001

Heredotus, The Histories. A new translation by Robin Waterfield. Oxford University Press, Oxford, New York. 1998

Homer, The Illiad. Translated by Samuel Butler. Barnes & Noble Books, New York. 1995

Josephus, Flavius, the works of. Translated by William Whiston, A.M. In four volumes. Baker Book House, Grand Rapids, Michigan. 1985

Josephus, Flavius. The life and Works of. Translated by William Whiston, A.M. Holt, Rinehart and Winston, New York. 1977

Lerner, Eric J. The Big Bang Never Happened. Vintage Books. A Division of Random House, In. New York. 1991

McDowell, Josh. Evidence that Demands a Verdict. Historical Evidence for the Christian Faith. Revised Edition. Campus Crusade for Christ International. Published by Here's Life Publishers, Inc. San Bernardino, Ca. 1979

McDowell, Josh. Prophecy Fact of Fiction? Daniel in the Critics Den. Campus Crusade for Christ International. Published by Here's Life Publishers, Inc. San Bernardino, Ca. 1981

Nicoll, W. Robertson. The Expositor's Bible. A complete exposition of the Bible, in six volumes, with index. Vol. II Samuel - Job. Baker Book House, Grand Rapids Michigan.

Owusu, Heike. Symbols of Egypt. Sterling Publishing Co. Inc, New York 1998

Oxford, The, History of Ancient Egypt, edited by Ian Shaw. Oxford University Press. 2000

Romer, John. People of the Nile. Everyday life in Ancient Egypt. Crown Publishers, Inc. New York.

Pliny, Natural History, with an English translation in ten volumes. Volume I. By H. Rackham, M.A. Harvard University Press, 1938.

Scott, Donald E. The Electric Sky, a Challenge to the Myths of Modern Astronomy. Mikimar Publishing, Portland, Oregon. 2006

Seindorf, George, and Keith C. Seele. When Egypt Ruled the East. Revised by Keith C. Seele. Phoenix Books. The University of Chicago Press, Chicago and London.

Seneca, in nine volumes. IX, tragedies II. With an English translation by Frank Justus Miller, Ph.D., LL.D. Thyestes. 1937.

Simpson, William Kelly. The Literature of Ancient Egypt, an anthology of stories, instructions and poetry. New Edition, edited by William Kelly Simpson, with translations by R.O. Faulkner, E.F. Wente, Jr., and W.K. Simpson. New Haven and London, Yale University Press. 1972

Smith, Ethan, View of the Hebrews. Poultney (VT) 1825 edition, reprinted by Utah Lighthouse Ministry, Salt Lake City, Utah.

Bibliography

Swift, Jonathan, Gulliver's Travels into Several Remote Nations of the World. Barnes & Nobles, 2002

Thiele. Edwin R. The Mysterious Numbers of the Hebrew Kings. New Revised Edition. Academie Books, Grand Rapids, Michigan. Zondervan Publishing House. 1983

Thornhill, Wallace. The Electric Universe. Slide presentation and notes, 1996

Thoth, A Catastrophic Newsletter. Available on the Web, www.kronia.com

Velikovsky, Immanuel. Worlds in Collision. Pocket Books, New York. 1950

Velikovsky, Immanuel. Earth in Upheaval. Pocket Books, New York. 1955

Velikovsky, Immanuel. Oedipus and Aknhnaton. Myth and History. Pocket Books, New York. 1960

Velikovsky, Immanuel. Ages in Chaos. Doubleday & company, Inc. Garden City, New York. 1952

Velikovsky, Immanuel. Peoples of the Sea. Doubleday & Company, Inc. Garden City, New York. 1977

Velikovsky, Immanuel. Ramses II and His Time. Doubleday & Company, Inc. Garden City, New York. 1978

Planets, Ages, and Empires

Bibliography

[1] Rashi The Torah: with Rashi's Commentary translated, annotated and elucidated. The Sapirstein Edition. P.119
[2] The Literature of Ancient Egypt, p.137, 138
[3] Clayton
[4] -
[5] -
[6] -
[7] -
[8] -
[9] -
[10] -
[11] -
[12] -
[13] -
[14] -
[15] -
[16] -
[17] -
[18] -
[19] -
[20] -
[21] -
[22] -
[23] -
[24] -
[25] Reprint naos
[26] -
[27] -
[28] -
[29] -
[30] -
[31] -
[32] -
[33] -
[34] -
[35] -
[36] -
[37] -
[38] -
[39] -
[40] -
[41] -
[42] -

⁴³ giants
⁴⁴ _
⁴⁵ _
¹ _
² _
³ _
⁴ _
⁵ Donald E.Scott, The Electric Sky, A Challenge to the Myths of Modern Astronony. P. 144, 145.
⁶ _
⁷ Kuiper
⁸ saturnalia
⁹ _
¹⁰ _
¹ _
² _
³ In "The Literature of Ancient Egypt," in a footnote to "The Victorious King," R.O.Faulkner identifies Punt as "applied to a region in or adjoining Syria; perhaps Transjordan is meant." (P.286)
⁴ _
⁵ _
⁶ _
⁷ _
⁸ _
⁹ keret
¹⁰ _
¹¹ _
¹² _
¹ _
² _
³ _
⁴ _
⁵ _
⁶ _
⁷ _
⁸ _
⁹ _
¹⁰ _
¹ _
² _
³ _
⁴ _
⁵ _
⁶ _

[33] Ibid p. 137
[34] Nisroch